THEORISING THE CONTEMPORARY
zombie

HORROR STUDIES

Series Editor
Xavier Aldana Reyes, Manchester Metropolitan University

Editorial Board
Stacey Abbott, Roehampton University
Linnie Blake, Manchester Metropolitan University
Harry M. Benshoff, University of North Texas
Fred Botting, Kingston University
Steven Bruhm, Western University
Steffen Hantke, Sogang University
Joan Hawkins, Indiana University
Alexandra Heller-Nicholas, Deakin University
Agnieszka Soltysik Monnet, University of Lausanne
Bernice M. Murphy, Trinity College Dublin
Johnny Walker, Northumbria University
Maisha Wester, Indiana University Bloomington

Preface

Horror Studies is the first book series exclusively dedicated to the study of the genre in its various manifestations – from fiction to cinema and television, magazines to comics, and extending to other forms of narrative texts such as video games and music. Horror Studies aims to raise the profile of Horror and to further its academic institutionalisation by providing a publishing home for cutting-edge research. As an exciting new venture within the established Cultural Studies and Literary Criticism programme, Horror Studies will expand the field in innovative and student-friendly ways.

THEORISING THE CONTEMPORARY

CONTEXTUAL PASTS, PRESENTS, AND FUTURES

EDITED BY SCOTT ERIC HAMILTON
AND CONOR HEFFERNAN

UNIVERSITY OF WALES PRESS
2022

© The Contributors, 2022

All rights reserved. No part of this book may be reproduced in any material form (including photocopying or storing it in any medium by electronic means and whether or not transiently or incidentally to some other use of this publication) without the written permission of the copyright owner except in accordance with the provisions of the Copyright, Designs and Patents Act. Applications for the copyright owner's written permission to reproduce any part of this publication should be addressed to the University of Wales Press, University Registry, King Edward VII Avenue, Cardiff, CF10 3NS.

www.uwp.co.uk

British Library Cataloguing-in-Publication Data

A catalogue record for this book is available from the British Library.

ISBN   978-1-78683-857-5
eISBN 978-1-78683-858-2

The rights of The Contributors to be identified as authors of this work have been asserted in accordance with sections 77 and 79 of the Copyright, Designs and Patents Act 1988.

Typeset by Chris Bell, cbdesign

Printed by CPI Antony Rowe, Melksham, United Kingdom

Contents

Abstract	vii
Author Biographies	ix
List of Figures	xiii

Introduction — 1
Scott Eric Hamilton and Conor Heffernan

Part One: Zombified Bodies — 17

1. Zombies, Deviance and the Right to Posthuman Life — 19
   Poppy Wilde

2. The Apocalypse Workout
   Health, Identity and Zombies — 39
   Conor Heffernan

3. Abject Bodies and Borders
   What Zombies and Porn Indicate about Sex,
   Stigma and Society — 59
   Caroline West

4. *Aloha 'Oe*
   Goodbye and Hello in *Train to Busan* (2016) — 79
   Harvey O'Brien

Part Two: Critical Environments — 101

5. The Stalking Dead
   Ireland's Ambiguous Revenants and the Case for
   a Folk-zombie Revival — 103
   Jack Fennell

6. M. R. Carey's *The Boy on the Bridge*
    Ethics and the Apocalypse   119
    Scott Eric Hamilton

7. **Zombie Colony**
    The Heteronomy of the Greek State and the Datura
    of Cultural Capital   139
    Konstantinos Kerasovitis

8. **Last Ones Left Alive**
    Zombies and Post-Celtic Tiger Ireland   159
    Deirdre Flynn

Part Three: Undead Cultures   177

9. **Beware the Zuvembies**
    Comics, Censorship and the Ubiquity of *Not-quite* Zombies   179
    Chera Kee

10. **Cinematic Voodoo and the Reanimation of Death**
    Jacques Tourneur's *I Walked with a Zombie*   197
    Peter J. Wright

11. **'Violence *is* Italian art'**
    Art and Adaptation in Lucio Fulci's 'Gates of Hell' Trilogy 213
    Miranda Corcoran

12. **Surviving the Shambling Signifieds**
    Zombies, Language and Chaos   231
    Andrew Ferguson

    Bibliography   247

    Index   273

Abstract

ZOMBIES HAVE BECOME an increasingly popular object of research in academic studies and, of course, in popular media. In the past decade zombies have been employed to explain mathematical equations, vortex phenomena in astrophysics, the need for improved laws, issues within higher education, and even the structure of human societies, to identify only a few examples. This collection expands on previous volumes and marries new topics with older approaches. Reflective of the diversity of Theorising Zombiism(s), the collection offers several new roads of enquiry related to the physical body, posthumanism, the environment and pornography among other topics. Likewise, more traditional areas of research, like zombies and the economy, the films of Lucio Fulci, politics and language are approached through the use of new theoretical frameworks and/or materials. Understanding and defining zombiism as a means of theorising and examining various issues of society within any given era by immersing those social issues within the destabilising context of apocalyptic crisis, this collection studies a series of different contexts and mediums.

Author Biographies

Miranda Corcoran is a lecturer in twenty-first-century literature at University College Cork. Her research interests include Cold War literature, genre fiction, popular fiction, sci-fi, horror and the gothic. She is currently writing a monograph on adolescence and witchcraft in American popular culture. She is also the co-editor (with Steve Gronert Ellerhoff) of *Exploring the Horror of Supernatural Fiction: Ray Bradbury's Elliott Family* (Routledge, 2020).

Jack Fennell is a writer, editor, translator and researcher whose academic publications include pieces on science fiction, utopian and dystopian literature, monsters, Irish literature and the legal philosophy of comic books. He is the author of *Irish Science Fiction* (Liverpool University Press, 2014), a contributing translator for *The Short Fiction of Flann O'Brien* (Dalkey Archive Press, 2013) and a former visiting fellow at the Moore Institute in NUI Galway.

Andrew Ferguson is a College Postdoctoral Fellow at the University of Virginia. He works at the intersection of media-textual studies, cultural theory and popular culture, which results in him doing things like willingly signing up to write an article that will require watching *The Star Wars Holiday Special* several times. Other ongoing projects include a study on editorial labour and style in science fiction, essays on born-digital horror and the writings of Dr Chuck Tingle, and a manuscript on glitches and narrative theory.

Dr Deirdre Flynn is a lecturer in twenty-first-century literature at Mary Immaculate College, Limerick. She has worked at University College Dublin, NUI Galway and University of Limerick. Her research interests include world literature, literary urban studies, postmodernism, Haruki Murakami, Irish studies, theatre and feminism. She has written, directed and acted for theatre, and worked as a journalist for over seven years. She is currently preparing a monograph on Haruki Murakami and has published two co-edited collections on Irish literature. From 2015 until 2017, she was the chair of Sibéal, the gender and feminist network.

Scott Eric Hamilton is a former research associate at the University College Dublin Humanities Institute. Hamilton has published in various journals on Samuel Beckett and other topics. He has co-organised a successful series of international conferences entitled 'Beckett and the "State" of Ireland' (2001–13), 'Palimpsests: V International Flann O'Brien Conference' (2019) and 'Theorizing Zombiism' (2019). He has co-edited a volume of essays from both the 'Theorizing Zombiism' conference and the 'Flann O'Brien' conference as well as guest edited a special issue of *The Parish Review: Journal of Flann O'Brien Studies*.

Conor Heffernan is a lecturer in the sociology of sport at the University of Ulster. He has published widely on the history of fitness and exercise in the nineteenth and twentieth century. In 2020, Conor published *The History of Physical Culture in Ireland* with Palgrave MacMillan.

Chera Kee is an associate professor of film and media studies in the Department of English at Wayne State University. Her essays on zombies have been published in the *Journal of Popular Film and Television* and the edited volume *Better Off Dead: The Evolution of the Zombie as Post-Human* (Fordham University Press, 2011).

Konstantinos Kerasovitis is a researcher with Wolverhampton University, working towards his PhD in the crux of labour, affect and critical theory.

Harvey O'Brien is currently head of film studies at University College Dublin. He is the author of numerous articles and book chapters relating to film, and is a frequent contributor to Irish radio on the subject. He has also authored *Action Movies: The Cinema of Striking Back* (Columbia University Press, 2012), *The Real Ireland: The Evolution of Ireland in*

Documentary Film (Manchester University Press, 2004) and co-edited *Keeping it Real: Irish Film and Television* (Wallflower, 2004).

Caroline West is a lecturer, writer, media commentator, sexpert and podcast host. She qualified with her doctoral degree from Dublin City University. Her research interests focuses on sex, feminism and the body. Aside from academia, Dr West is an active contributor to Irish media on sexual health.

Poppy Wilde is a lecturer in media and communication at Birmingham City University. Her research interests include posthumanism and posthuman subjectivity, digital cultures, game studies, embodiment, performance in online contexts and the lived experience in research methods. More recently her explorations have turned to posthuman conceptions of death, and zombification.

Peter J. Wright is a doctoral student at the University of Sydney. His research explores the interactions between zombies, media and symbolism.

List of Figures

Figure 3.1. Rubin's Charmed Circle.   61

Figure 4.1. *Train to Busan.* The song dies on Su-an's lips as only a camera lens, and not her absent father, bears witness.   81

Figure 4.2. *Train to Busan.* Su-an, seen through a sniper scope, emerging from a darkened train tunnel.   82

Figure 4.3. Here Seok-woo sleeps while Su-an has just seen a zombie attack on the platform at Seoul as the train departs.   91

Figure 4.4. The metaphor of the inward-facing eye and the incapacity to see the world outside is given a sympathetic dimension in Seok-woo's death. His last inward vision is the happy memory of the birth of his daughter.   92

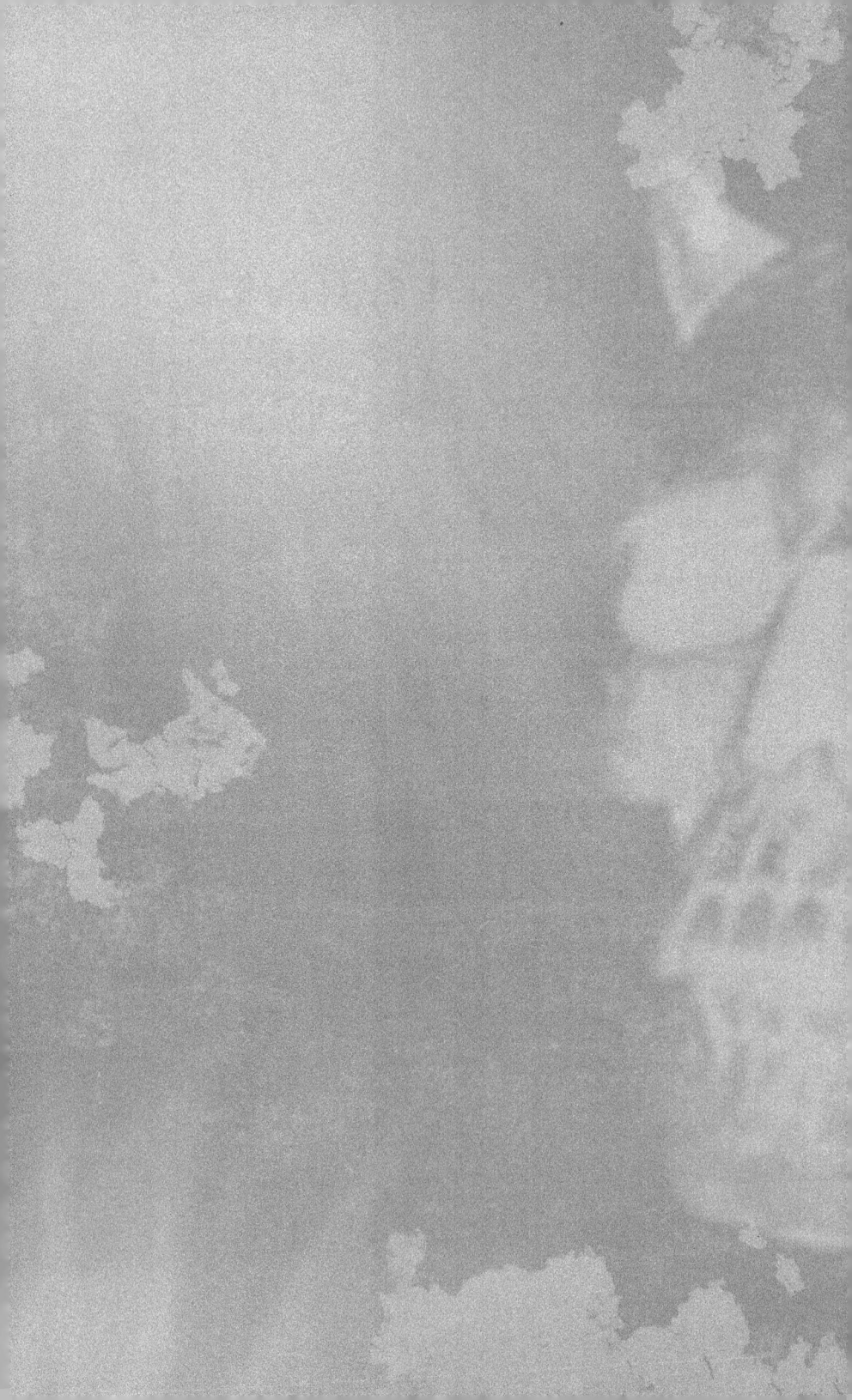

Introduction

Scott Eric Hamilton and Conor Heffernan

I. Zombie Studies

THE ONSET OF the millennium brought an outbreak of zombie scholarship. Especially since 2010, an exponential growth in academic work utilising the zombie as a critical figure has resulted in an interdisciplinary horde of valuable insight into the parameters of what potentially constitutes zombiism. While the term zombiism will be discussed later in the introduction, a brief definition is that the study of zombies in popular and scientific works offers a means of dissecting broader social anxieties and issues. A brief survey of academic work related to the zombie highlights some potentially unexpected results.[1] The zombie was introduced to Western culture around the beginning of the twentieth century through anthropological avenues such as Irish writer Lafcadio Hearn's series of travel articles on the West Indies for *Harper's New Monthly Magazine*, 1888–90 and W. B. Seabrook's 1929 *That Magic Island*, which inspired the 1932 film *White Zombie*.[2] These works enthralled the Western imagination and injected the zombie into its lasting role in popular culture. Despite an almost instant popularity, in the 1940s the zombie would be referenced only occasionally in academic articles such as 'Haitian Magic' (1940) by George Eaton Simpson in *Social*

Forces and 'Musical Instruments of Haiti' (1941) by Harold Courlander in *The Musical Quarterly*.[3] Other sparse references tend to equate something or someone to a zombie in newspapers or reviews of movies or books.[4] The increasing occurrence of passing comments on zombies in the public sphere indicates that the figure was commonplace in the social consciousness but had yet to inspire any substantial scholarly engagement. The 1950s were quite similar, other than more regular reviews of films in newspapers and sometimes media journals. However, in the 1960s this vacuum of zombie research began to diminish. Articles like 'Ro-Langs: The Tibetan Zombie', by Turrell Wylie (1964), and 'Profit Maximization: Economics' Zombie Concept', by Stephen Black (1968) indicate that the zombie was beginning to be considered more seriously, and, interestingly, by other disciplines than the humanities.[5] Likewise, the term 'zombie' began to appear more frequently in various journals.[6] In the 1970s the trend continued with a slight increase in the zombie being incorporated as a means of describing something difficult to eradicate in medical, engineering and economics journals.[7] The difference being that towards the later part of the decade psychology and philosophy journals started including articles incorporating the zombie as a critical metaphor for exploring issues of comprehending consciousness which lead to the p-zombie (philosophical zombie). For instance, Robert Kirk's 1974 'Sentience and Behaviour' and 1977 'Reply to Don Locke on Zombies and Materialism' comprised a series of philosophical considerations on 'the possibility of zombies'.[8] The p-zombie debate is still ongoing. The 1980s generated more studies, including full-length articles on films, mostly concerned with the 1940s, *White Zombie* and *I Walked with a Zombie* specifically, and more non-humanities journals dedicated to economics, toxicology and psychiatry, to name a few.[9] The 1990s followed suit and studies in postcolonialism, phenomenology, artificial intelligence, ecology and even sports law utilised the zombie as a critical metaphor for various issues that were challenging to resolve or eradicate.[10] Interestingly, the following decade, more than fifty years after the emergence of the zombie in Western culture, brought a noticeable increase in humanities-based work on the zombie figure.[11] In the 2000s the zombie attained a forceful presence as a critical metaphor across all disciplines, from biology to physics to business to infectious disease and, of course, the humanities.[12] The above is, of course, not an exhaustive account but provides a glimpse of the relatively slow development of something that resembles zombie studies.[13] Nonetheless, zombiism, like a zombie virus, has increased exponentially in usefulness for a substantial amount of everyday and academic purposes.

Scholarship to date relates mostly to the three commonly accepted developmental eras of the zombie in popular culture: the emergence of the zombie in Western culture (from Haitian and Caribbean folklore); the so-called Romero era (1968–2000), which established the walking-corpse zombie as the standard for popular culture; and, the post-Romero era (2000–present). Although Romero's zombies do regularly demonstrate signs of remedial thinking, the trend of zombies with cognitive function has grown in recent years. The zombie from Haitian folklore depicted in films presents and functions as human but has no internal agency. The recently reanimated zombie that breaks Barbara's car window in *Night of the Living Dead* to Big Daddy's problem-solving and leadership skills in *Land of the Dead*, are examples of the Romero era, and television series like *iZombie*, where the protagonist is a zombie that works in a morgue, and *Santa Clarita Diet*, where the protagonist Sheila Harmon (Drew Barrymore) is a conscious, functioning member of a suburban family, exemplify the post-Romero era. Even in such an abbreviated description the zombie is a figure that resists confining parameters.

The zombie of the 1930s to the 1950s is commonly aligned with issues of colonial and postcolonial studies. The Romero era of the 1960s to the 2000s primarily approached the zombie as representing the detrimental effects of capitalism and fetishistic consumption, philosophy and consciousness studies, modern forms of the gothic, and the horror genre in cultural studies. The post-Romero era has expanded the zombie as a critical metaphor for posthumanism, eco-horror, as well as becoming a figure that devours interdisciplinary boundaries. In this regard, the latest wave of zombies, those found in media produced after 2000 for instance, have proven useful for advancing new meanings and interpretations. This new iteration, from which this collection owes a considerable debt, has seen the undead used to critique climate change, to challenge gendered and racial hierarchies while simultaneously advancing messages about political inequalities. Such is the popularity of zombies that zombie media now includes a variety of archetypes from which creators can choose. Whereas in the past, zombies were traditionally typified by the slow lumbering figure with an insatiable lust for human flesh, recent media has showcased a vast remit of zombie frameworks ranging from the fast-moving, vicious zombies depicted in *Train to Busan*, and other Korean iterations such as the speculative fiction Netflix series *Kingdom* and the 2020 film *#Alive*, directed by Cho Ill-hyung. This zombie is complimented, not contradicted, by those works which have sought to humanise the undead, *Santa Clarita Diet* being an example.

The zombie is not a one-dimensional character. Consequently, the zombie serves a variety of purposes. This multidimensional aspect explains, in part, why the term zombie has come to be adapted, and appropriated, to serve a number of different contexts and academic fields. In economics, the term zombie company has become increasingly popular as a means of describing those firms in need of bailouts or that are unable to repay loans.[14] In mathematics, the zombie has become a useful term for modelling disease transmission and exponential growth in populations, a point that has become very relevant in the time of the Covid-19 pandemic.[15] For environmentalists, climate zombies is used to describe those theories about climate change which refuse 'to die'.[16] For some nutritionists, zombie diets have become an easy means of describing those diets which dampen individual cognitive ability or, written more sensationally, cause the loss of brain cells.[17] Related to academia itself, the term zombie has been applied to the seemingly inevitable decline of academic rigour and creativity in the face of increasingly neo-liberal learning models.[18] All of this is to emphasise that whatever the zombie is, or perhaps is not, it nevertheless becomes a point of increasing fascination in popular, and professional, societies.[19]

This fascination has, unsurprisingly, led to the zombie figure becoming an increasingly disruptive and critical metaphor. This aspect of the zombie was always built into the genre –especially with regard to race or otherness – but the sheer popularity of zombies in popular culture has increased its potency. Zombie narratives have become particularly adept at utilising the once, but no longer, human creature as a means of criticising humanity's often inadequate response to important challenges, such as climate change, the isolationist responses regarding the migration of foreign peoples and the seemingly never-ending wheel of Western consumerism and the troublesome gender tropes still found in societies, to offer only a few. Oftentimes, the zombie's inability to speak, and its resistance towards rationality or reason, has made it such a powerfully adaptive metaphor. The openness of representation from the zombie, its essence as a blank or empty vessel, generates its cultural power. This adaptive representational power is what the present collection addresses. Zombiism provides the means to examine other theoretical frameworks by disrupting the stability and coherence of the analytical function of a given theory in society through catastrophic destabilisation. The apocalyptic premise becomes a type of model simulation in which any weaknesses could allow for the devouring of the other aspects of a theory and/or scientific discipline or social system. As purported by the Theorizing Zombiism project, zombiism as a theoretical framework offers the means through which other theoretical models, schools of thought, ideological formations, and philosophical concepts and investigations can be confronted and tested.

The zombie, which originated in the realm of the humanities, has proliferated perhaps almost every academic discipline, as indicated above. This unique quality of the zombie demonstrates the valuable potential of zombiism. However, at present zombiism has only generated a misalliance of scholars under a common topic. A more coherent and unified field of zombie studies would undoubtedly yield a wealth of potential lines of interdisciplinary and interdisciplinary research hitherto unexplored.

II. Theorizing Zombiism: Conference & Context

Speaking at the inaugural Theorizing Zombiism conference at University College Dublin in the summer of 2019, Scott Kenemore, author of numerous zombie prose narratives, poignantly highlighted the importance of the zombie in offering 'a type of stress test for social issues'. In his own writing, most notably *Zombie-in-Chief: Eater of the Free World*, Kenemore used the prospect of a zombie apocalypse to examine America's increasingly conflicted political scene and the role of the press within the increasingly aggressive and turbulent relationship between the two. Similarly, Kenemore's fellow co-panellist at the conference, Sarah Davis-Goff, author of *Last Ones Left Alive* (2019), subsequently expanded on this point to discuss the various ways in which femininity and, in particular, adolescent femininity, could be evaluated through the medium of the zombie.[20] One of the first Irish authors to engage with the zombie medium, Davis-Goff's debut novel wove issues of ecological apocalypse, family, femininity and authority through the trials and tribulations of the protagonist Orpen, and her dog, Danger. Unaware of each other prior to the conference, that Kenemore and Davis-Goff came to such conclusions is perhaps not surprising. Differing in their writing styles, locations and interests, both authors nevertheless stressed the value of the zombie in unpacking much broader societal anxieties and aspirations across a range of issues. Whether discussing warped visions of adolescent femininity, the breakdown of successful government or the role of the fourth estate, the zombie became a tool of analysis rather than a literary ornament. In effect, the zombie offered a pathway for Kenemore and Davis-Goff's interests and critiques, as indeed it has for many other authors.

If zombies are to remain a lively academic field, which appears to be the case, it is imperative that scholars begin to create theories, think broadly and truly engage with the socio-cultural and political implications of the zombie or zombie apocalypse, which this volume in part attempts. Comparable works to the present collection includes *…But if a Zombie Apocalypse Did Occur*, *Zombies in the Academy* and *Better Off Dead: The Evolution of the Zombie as Post-human*. Such collections have contributed to a greater understanding of the zombie figure but have confined their interest to a single event (a hypothetical zombie apocalypse) or a single field (education studies). Where Sarah Lauro's edited collection, *Zombie Theory: A Reader* (2017), provides an assortment of insightful individual studies of the zombie as metaphor, this collection goes one step further and builds a broader zombie framework, or zombiism theory, for future work.[21]

Theory, which should be considered as an application-based endeavour, requires repeated re-evaluation and adaptation to remain a vital means of critical analysis and investigation. The theory outlined here is not intended to be a definitive understanding of zombies and the zombie apocalypse. Instead, the collection offers an invitation to its readers to engage, critique and ultimately advance uses of zombie frameworks. The first step to progressing the field of zombie studies is an exploration of what zombiism actually entails. Understanding and defining zombiism as a means of theorising and examining various issues of society within any given era by immersing those social issues within the destabilising context of apocalyptic crisis, this collection studies a series of different contexts and mediums. Put another way, 'zombiism' as a framework seeks to dissect the zombie metaphor in both popular and scientific works to understand how this metaphor is both a reflection of, and contributor to, broader social anxieties and issues. Rather than a mere literary trope, the zombie figure is treated as an object of utmost critical importance.

The roots or origins of this collection lie in the Zombie Studies Network's inaugural Theorizing Zombiism conference held at University College Dublin in late 2019. Open to PhD students, early career researchers, independent scholars and established academics, the conference was created in response to the growing academic interest in zombies and the need to create an international network of like-minded scholars. Welcoming individuals from around the world, and from a variety of different disciplines, the conference highlighted the fact that academic interest in the zombie is not confined to a single field or department. Instead, interest in the zombie approaches the ever elusive 'interdisciplinarity' often touted in university departments. The present collection provides a representation of the enthusiasm, support and excitement generated by the Theorizing Zombiism conference as well as acting as a first step towards greater engagement with zombiism.

From horror comics of the 1930s and 1940s to discussions of post-economic crash Greece, the scholars in the current collection have eagerly and, indeed richly, engaged with the aforementioned zombiism framework to help build and substantiate a theoretical framework applicable to issues of health, gender, politics, economics, literature and society itself. At present, an opportunity exists in the field of zombie studies to develop a framework with the adaptive potential to bridge gaps in a variety of disciplines situated within a given era. In addressing this point, the collection incorporates aspects of history, literature, film studies and linguistics among other disciplines, to provide a new interdisciplinary approach to zombie studies. It is hoped that this collection will not be viewed as an endpoint but rather as a platform for future studies on zombies and zombiism. Speaking to *Vanity Fair* in 2010, the doyen of zombie films, George A. Romero claimed that, 'My stories are about humans and how they react, or fail to react, or react stupidly. I'm pointing the finger at us, not at the zombies. I try to respect and sympathize with the zombies as much as possible.'[22] Much like Romero, the goal of zombiism is not to critique or attack the zombie figure but instead to use the zombie as a mechanism to examine both the detrimental and redemptive aspects of the experience of a shared humanity.

III. Structure

The chapters are divided into the related themes of 'Zombified Bodies', 'Critical Environments' and 'Undead Cultures'. The first theme of 'Zombified Bodies' investigates the social, physical, sexual and familial bodies in contention with restrictive social categorisations and expectations as embodied by the zombie figure. The second theme of 'Critical

Environments' juxtaposes cultural and ecological issues to explore the adaptability of the zombie as representative of human activity which is detrimental to themselves and the world. The third theme 'Undead Cultures' explores different media cultures of previous decades to demonstrate how revisiting the portrayal of the zombie in previous historical medias and contexts can contribute to expanding zombie studies.

As befits the broader implications of the zombie metaphor, the collection begins with Poppy Wilde's critique of the present popular culture fascination with zombies using a posthuman lens. Wilde depicts the zombie as a reaction against neo-liberal capitalism and mass consumption, which ultimately leads to a rejection of the modern notion of the liberal human subject. Done in this way, the zombie apocalypse represents a cultural imperative to resist and, if possible, break from contemporary society constraints, which values conformity above all else. Wilde's thought-provoking chapter, which stresses the 'right to a posthuman life', calls into doubt the notion of the 'good citizen' defined by existing neo-liberal structures and instead discusses alternative pathways offered by the zombie. As becomes clear throughout the collection, the idea of a zombie apocalypse, or a potential apocalypse, offers a challenging thought experiment for new ways of being in the twenty-first century.

Conor Heffernan's contribution discusses the zombie in health and fitness periodicals. Since the early 2000s, the health and fitness industry in the United States has repeatedly used the zombie threat to market a host of zombie-inspired exercise systems. Ranging from losing weight to building muscles, such systems have used the growth of zombie films, television shows and books to market new products to the public. Providing a close reading of these products, and their advertising, the chapter focuses on the meaning of the zombie within these writings. Although written humorously, such advertisements often point to a heightened importance of the zombie metaphor. The potential zombie apocalypse is used to critique modern Western lifestyles defined by comfort and a lack of physical activity. Preparing for a zombie attack thus provides a platform to critique twenty-first-century modernity and its impact on the body. Such systems provide a rallying call for a return to pre-civilised, and seemingly perfect forms of masculinity and femininity as defined by raw strength and athleticism. The zombie in such writings is simultaneously used to critique the ills of Western society and, also, acts as the solution or salvation.

Addressing the topic of gender, and in this case sexuality, is Caroline West's discussion of zombie pornography and adult paraphernalia. Where Heffernan's contribution deals with issues of normative masculinities and femininities, West turns our attention to female and male sexuality. West draws clear parallels between the zombie metaphor and the adult entertainment industry. The chapter depicts the zombie as a metaphor for unrepentant sexuality and a rejection of the sexual hierarchy. Highlighting the porn industry's embracing of necrophilia, West discusses the production of zombie sex toys and movies as well as the meanings behind the zombie porn films made by director and performer Joanna Angel. Beginning from the position that sexuality, and especially female sexuality, has long been viewed as monstrous in public society, West examines the corporeal language of zombies and pornography, thereby illustrating the discourses of fear emanating from both.

Also concerned with film, albeit with a much different genre, Harvey O'Brien's analyses Yong Sang-ho's 2016 film *Train to Busan* in terms of the struggle to remain human amidst a hostile inhuman world. In the film a 9-year-old girl, with a strong sense of empathy and kindness of spirit is confronted by the collapse of the existing society with all its failings, including those of her busy self-centred father who accompanies her on the fateful train from the north to the south of South Korea. Her vision of people is clearer than his, and of the blind infected who work their way through the train and its demographically diverse collection of stratified citizenry. Though the contours of this genre piece are familiar, the child's perspective makes the film entirely singular. In the end, rather than being a narrative of succession and salvation, it is posited that there is much about human society that made its failure inevitable, but that there is much in humanity that is worth preserving. O'Brien ties in elements of adventure films, death and art, and addresses questions of mobility and mobilities across national, social and gendered borders. In a fitting end to the collection, O'Brien stresses the importance of family and community in the human experience.

Working in the Irish context, Fennell begins with an interrogation of zombie characteristics in storytelling. Far from static, or indeed, monolithic, Fennell uncovers the numerous instances that the zombie character is re-imagined to suit local tastes and cultures. Fennell echoes Chera Kee's later contribution on the ever-malleable zombie figure. Fennell's examination of twentieth-century Irish horror literature cites Ireland as just one of many places where the distinction between corporeal and non-corporeal undead failed to take root. Like many other comparable figures from around the world, the Irish undead were depicted as both reanimated corpses *and* ghosts. Operating in this liminal space, the Irish zombie could hold grudges, walk through walls and, in some cases, teleport. Fennell's study expands our understanding of what a zombie is, or indeed, does.

Scott Eric Hamilton's contribution likewise highlights the many ways in which the zombie figure can be understood and deployed. Hamilton examines Mike Carey's *The Boy on the Bridge*, the companion novel to *The Girl with All the Gifts*, in terms of human and nonhuman ethics. Analysing the threat of the zombie apocalypse in *The Boy on the Bridge*, Hamilton uses zombie horde as an opportunity or, perhaps more fittingly, as an invitation to discuss and reflect on issues related to scientific inquiry and experimentation, species curation and human extinction. Where *The Girl with All the Gifts* confronts the contentious relationship between information and knowledge, *The Boy on the Bridge* utilises the fear and anxiety of the zombie to bring the ethics of extinction to bear when considering the means of ensuring survival. Exploring both works in tandem, Hamilton highlights Carey's ability to use the horror of being confronted with the reality of human extinction as an opportunity to evaluate the Anthropocene context and the ethics involved in the response to the potential crisis facing homo sapiens.

Konstantinos Kerasovitis explores the prospect, and indeed, the reality, of economic disaster or death. Utilising the autonomist theories of Greek and French philosopher, Cornelius Castoriadis, he persuasively argues for the necessity of viewing the modern Greek state as a type of 'zombie colony'. Beginning with a discussion of the parallels between colonial Haiti and the foundation of the Greek state, Kerasovitis interrogates the social, cultural and political similarities between the two states. Understanding the zombie condition as the removal of the drive to act and, in effect, the loss of subjectivity, Kerasovitis applies this zombie condition to the modern Greek state and its often-scrutinised economy. This chapter serves as an excellent reminder that the zombie condition is not confined to one person or group but can, in fact, encompass whole states.

Deirdre Flynn's contribution analyses Sarah Davis-Goff's debut novel *Last Ones Left Alive*. Davis-Goff situates her novel in a dystopian rural Ireland, specifically in islands off the western coast. Tracing the fortunes of a 12-year-old narrator named Orpen and her family,

Davis-Goff's protagonist anxiously travels across Ireland in search of a secret community named Phoenix City. Roaming through abandoned housing estates and once populated towns, Orpen's travels, Flynn argues, speaks to a Celtic Tiger Ireland destroyed by economic greed, poor planning and social isolation. Flynn's close reading of the novel cites Davis-Goff's challenge to the traditional zombie narrative. Flynn understands Davis-Goff's writing as an invitation to reimagine society in the wake of the collapse of patriarchal capitalism. Orpen's strength, determination and survival instincts speak to the growing role of women in new capitalist beginnings.

Chera Kee's chapter adopts a historical approach to dissect early zombie comic book depictions of variant zombie figures. Centred on horror comic books dated from the 1930s to the late 1970s, Kee's contribution to the field of zombiism is twofold. In the first instance Kee's chapter, entitled 'Beware the Zuvembies', highlights the way comic-book zombies have anticipated later shifts in how zombies have been portrayed in other media. In effect, the comic-book zombie acts as a ground zero for later depictions of the undead. Following this and leading into Kee's main argument, attention is given to Marvel Comics' zombie-inspired characters from the 1970s and 1980s. Written in direct relation to a comic-book censorship on zombies during these decades, the Marvel characters carefully and deliberately pushed the boundaries of what was, or was not, regarded as a zombie. Situating the 'zuvembies' in this way, Kee argues that from the beginning of their tenure in American comic books, zombies have existed as 'zuvembies', both embodying and challenging popular expectations of the undead. Such a history of comic-book zombies questions assumptions of zombie characteristics, thereby expanding current debates on film- and literature-centric scholarship of zombies.

Much of the present collection, for obvious reasons, focuses on the zombie as depicted through modern media. Peter Wright's investigates the very mediums through which audiences visually consume the zombie. Examining the now almost-forgotten VHS format, which first helped to bring zombie movies to a much wider audience, Wright dissects the process by which zombie films of the 1980s were designed specifically for the VHS format. Examining the relationship between zombie films and VHS images, Wright argues that the visual style and themes associated with the 1980s' zombie film cycle operated in direct correspondence to the degraded VHS image. Drawing on the zombie films of Italian director Lucio Fulci, who reappears later in the collection as part of Miranda Corcoran's chapter, Wright discusses how logic and narrative continuities collapse in relation to the emergence of the zombie and subsequent destruction of reality, but also the physical breakdown of the distorted and degraded VHS image.

Similar to Kee's examination of comic books and Wright's study of VHS tapes, Miranda Corcoran's chapter, entitled 'Violence is Italian Art', revisits Lucio Fulci's films as an object of historical enquiry. Comprised of *City of the Living Dead* (1980), *The Beyond* (1981) and *The House by the Cemetery* (1981), Fulci's trilogy was released in both the United States and Italy. In the United States, Fulci's films were renamed to capitalise on a growing interest in the films of George Romero, whose 1978 movie *Dawn of the Dead* captured the imagination of cinema goers. Situating Fulci's works simultaneously in their contemporaneous Italian and American cultures, Corcoran envisions such films as a commentary on American society and also as an insight into the Italian cultural context in which Fulci found himself. Corcoran's contribution, as becomes clear, highlights the multiplicity of meanings found within the zombie film, and indeed the zombie itself.

Andrew Ferguson's contribution to the collection calls into question the nature of the zombie itself. Other chapters within the contribution highlight the numerous ways in which the zombie has been used to critique societal trends, to express them and, in some cases, as a means of catharsis. Encompassing much of this work, Ferguson calls on a wide range of zombie literature and combines it with the theoretical work of Friedrich Kittler and N. Katharine Hayles to analyse the many meanings deployed using the zombie figure. Far from an easy task, Ferguson develops a model of the zombie as data degradation, as the ultimate victory of randomness over the chaotic patterning of information – and of literature and the Enlightenment project as already infected by zombiedom. The emergence of the zombie figure is not taken to be a coincidence of history, nor a banal topic, but rather as a pattern and result of the post-Enlightenment world. The zombie is seen then as a product and a producer of modern culture and learning.

The diversity of contributions in this collection exemplifies the variety of critical theorisations currently at play in the field of zombie studies. In their diversity, the chapters still point to a single truth, namely, that the zombie figure is not a fickle or tired trope but rather an explanatory mechanism for human existence. Returning to the previously defined zombiism, that is a means of theorising and examining various issues of society within any given era by immersing those social issues within the destabilising context of apocalyptic crisis, the collection now invites readers to critique, question and most of all engage with the zombie and the zombie apocalypse in a substantive way. As such, zombiism can remain an ever-adaptive living (and undead) theory that examines all that has plagued and will plague humanity and academia.

Notes

1. The search for this introduction consisted of entering the terms 'zombie' and 'zombiism' into the Google Scholar search engine. Of course a more thorough examination utilising several search engines would provide a more in-depth history of zombie scholarship.
2. Sarah J. Lauro, *The Transatlantic Zombie: Slavery, Rebellion, and Living Death* (New Jersey: Rutgers University Press, 2015), p. 213.
3. George Eaton, 'Haitian Magic', *Social Forces*, 19/1 (1940), 95–100; Harold Courlander, 'Musical Instruments of Haiti', *The Musical Quarterly*, 27/3 (1941), 371–83.
4. For example, Stanley Edgar Hyman quotes John Steinbeck saying, 'The War is Simply "a Zombie War of Sleep-walkers"', 'Some Notes on John Steinbeck', *The Antioch Review*, 2/2 (1942), 185–200, 198.
5. Turrell Wylie, 'Ro-Langs: The Tibetan Zombie', *The History of Religions*, 4/1 (1964), 69–80; Stephen Black, 'Profit Maximization: Economics' Zombie Concept', *South African Journal of Economics*, 3/7 (1968), 264–7.
6. Joseph Lyons, '"The Pawnbroker": A Study of the Flashback in Novel and Film', *Western Humanities Review*, 20/3 (1966), 243–8, is one example of many.
7. Even non-English-language journal titles were appearing, such as J. Legauldt, 'Zombie bacteria', *Recherche*, 4/38 (1972), 898–900.
8. Robert Kirk, 'Sentience and Behaviour', *Mind*, 83 (1974), 43–60, and 'Reply to Don Locke on Zombies and Materialism', *Mind*, 86/342 (1977), 262–4, 262.
9. Michael Boccia 'Versions (Con-, In-, and Per-) in Manuel Puig's and Hector Babenco's *Kiss of the Spider Woman*, Novel and Film', *Modern Fiction Studies*, 32/3 (1986), 417–26.
10. Andrew Tudor, 'Unruly Bodies, Unquiet Minds', *Body & Society*, 1/1 (1995) 25–41.
11. One of the most notable being Kyle William Bishop, *American Zombie Gothic: The Rise and Fall (and Rise) of the Walking Dead in Popular Culture* (Jefferson: McFarland, 2010).

12. Gregory A. Waller, *The Living and the Undead: Slaying Vampires, Exterminating Zombies* (Illinois: University of Illinois Press, 2010).
13. Some other influential works include Shawn McIntosh and Marc Leverette (eds), *Zombie Culture: Autopsies of the Living Dead* (Lanham: Scarecrow Press, 2008); Kyle William Bishop and Angela Tenga (eds), *The Written Dead: Essays on the Literary Zombie* (Jefferson: McFarland, 2017); Deborah Christie and Sarah Juliet Lauro (eds), *Better Off Dead: The Evolution of the Zombie as Post-human* (New York: Fordham University Press, 2011); Stephanie Boluk and Wylie Lenz (eds), *Generation zombie: Essays on the living dead in modern culture* (Jefferson: McFarland, 2011); Laura Hubner, Marcus Leaning and Paul Manning (eds), *The Zombie Renaissance in Popular Culture* (Basingstoke: Palgrave Macmillan, 2014).
14. Although a substantial amount of zombie economics scholarship is available, see John Quiggin, *Zombie Economics: How Dead Ideas Still Walk Among Us* (Princeton: Princeton University Press, 2010), as an overview of the topic.
15. See Robert F. Allen, Cassandra Jens and Theodore J. Wendt, 'When Zombies Attack, We Can Survive!', *Letters in Biomathematics*, 1/2 (2014), 173–80, and João Paulo A. de Mendonça, Leonardo M. V. Teixeira, Fernando Sato and Lohan R. N. Ferreira, 'Modeling a Hypothetical Zombie Outbreak Can Save Us from Real-World Monsters', *The Mathematical Intelligencer*, 41/3 (2019), 72–9, for two examples.
16. See Johannes Fehrle, '"Zombies Don't Recognize Borders": Capitalism, Ecology, and Mobility in the Zombie Outbreak Narrative', *Amerikastudien/ American Studies*, 61/4, Environmental Imaginaries on the Move: Nature and Mobility in Literature and Culture (2016), 527–44, for an example.
17. M. L. Wei, 'If More People Cut Out Gluten, the Zombies Would Wake Up: The Construction of Health-related Concerns by Gluten-free Food Consumers', *British Food Journal* (2021), 1–12.
18. See Andrew Whelan, Ruth Walker and Christopher Moore (eds), *Zombies in the Academy: Living Death in Higher Education* (Bristol: Intellect, 2013).
19. Much of this is explored in Bishop, *American Zombie Gothic*.
20. Scott Kenemore, *Zombie-in-Chief* (New York: Talos, 2017); Sarah Davis-Goff, *Last Ones Left Alive* (Dublin: Tinder Press, 2019).
21. Sarah Juliet Lauro (ed.), *Zombie Theory: A Reader* (Minneapolis: University of Minnesota Press, 2017).
22. Eric Spitznagel, 'George A. Romero: Who Says Zombies Eat Brains?', *Vanity Fair*, https://www.vanityfair.com/hollywood/2010/05/george-romero (accessed 12 January 2021).

PART ONE

ZOMBIFIED BODIES

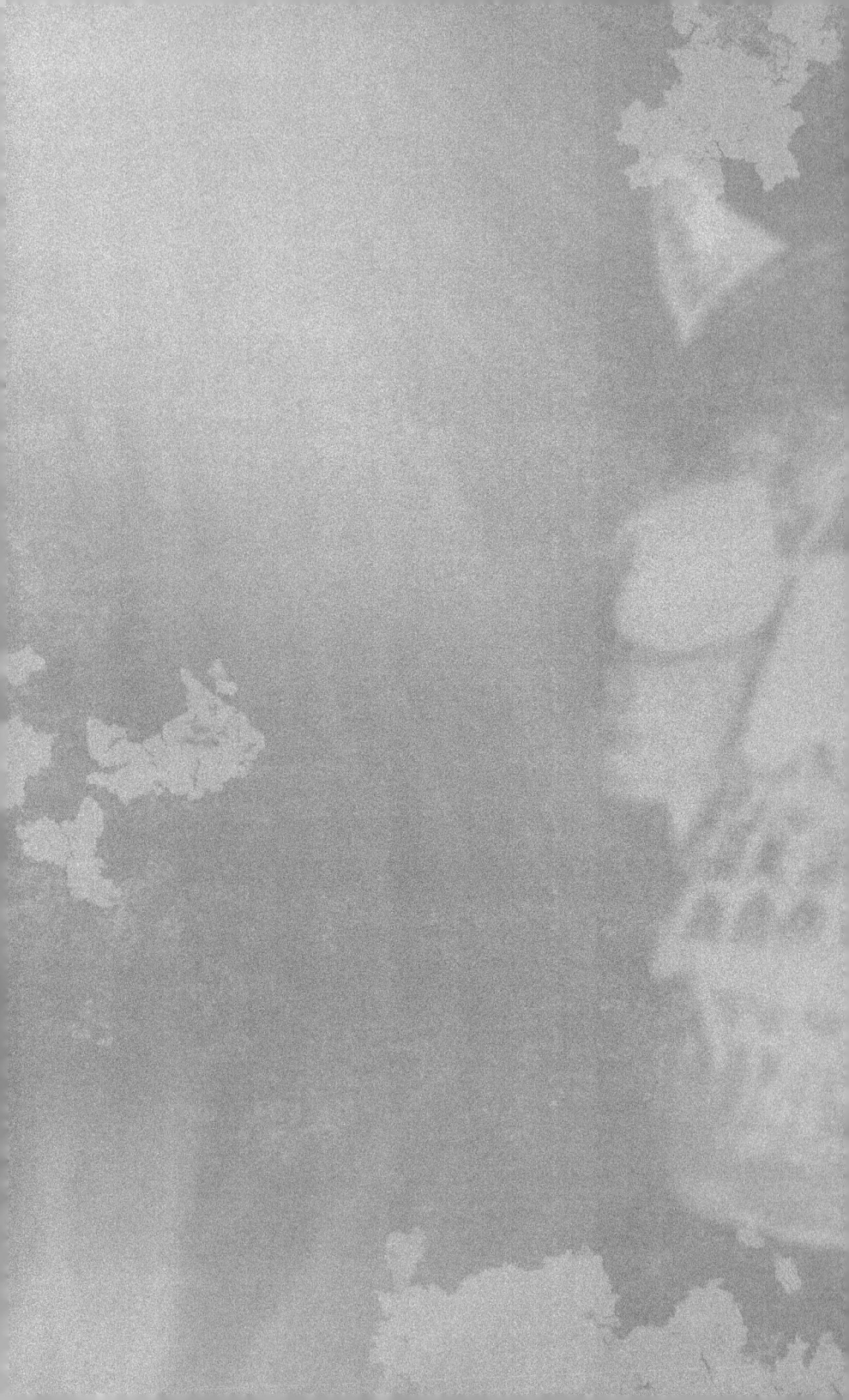

1

Zombies, Deviance and the Right to Posthuman Life

Poppy Wilde

ZOMBIES HAVE BECOME increasingly prolific in popular culture. Films from *Dawn of the Dead* to *Shaun of the Dead*, novels such as the Mira Grant *Newsflesh* series, zombie games including *Dying Light*, are all excellent examples of affective zombie mediations.[1] Some fantastic zombie podcasts, including *We're Alive*, and the audiobook of *After the Cure*, by Deirdre Gould, create wonderfully creepy atmospheres that should appeal to horror fans.[2] But why zombies? Societies and cultures are strangely overcome (or overrun) with morbid fascination. As Sarah Lauro asks, 'Whence does our cultural fascination with zombies come?'[3] The answer is both obvious and not obvious. Post-apocalyptic scenarios allow access to a world that is both similar-yet-strange. Audiences experience stories and journeys of survivors and victims and ask important self-reflexive questions – 'what would I do, how long would I survive, where would I go?', and this imaginative exploration allows the consideration of how humans would fare in this world, but not as it is presently known.

This chapter explores the cultural fascination with zombies through posthumanism. Through this critical perspective, the zombie apocalypse represents the cultural imperative to break with aspects of contemporary society that constrain people to conformity. Bound by the neo-liberal, capitalist expectations on society, there is a belief that everyone should always be producing, competing, innovating and consuming. The underlying expectation says that contributing members of society should embody 'the good citizen': active members of society, demonstrating personal responsibility and embodying the entrepreneurial self. However, against a backdrop of dystopian realities, a burgeoning scepticism exists within these societal expectations: the beginning of an understanding that the enterprising self and the good citizen are in fact capitalist traps, designed to keep people 'in check' and their behaviours managed. This realisation allows for wider understandings of society as a biased construction, with its own agendas and powers in place. By disrupting these normative tropes (which the zombie apocalypse forces), alternative possibilities emerge. Within the fascination with zombie narratives, then, there is evident a desire to escape the current capitalist, neo-liberal lifestyles, to deviate from the trend, and to therefore embody posthumanist values – rejecting the attributes ascribed by the liberal human subject. A zombie outbreak becomes almost romantically representative of a desire to 'return to our roots', to test one's mettle against nature, and to embrace humanity's most 'animalistic' sides.

Ultimately, in the zombie apocalypse scenario, the age-old 'stand-off' of human versus nature arises. Would contemporary Westernised humans be capable of killing monsters; foraging and hunting for food? How would they fare if removed from the daily comforts they know so well in the Western world?[4] Somehow this return to a world without contemporary luxuries is both intriguing and appealing. The argument posed in this chapter is twofold. First, the current fascination with zombies should be considered a possible rejection of the ultimately humanistic contemporary society. Zombies and zombie stories have often been considered metaphors for consumerism amongst other things, an argument made particular valid with the aforementioned *Dawn of the Dead*, set in a shopping mall.[5] Secondly, this chapter argues that the zombies are actually the ones who have been most successful in breaking free of the capitalist venture. From this perspective the zombie is not a virus, or a stand-in for the negatively 'othered' in society, but an exploration of alternative ways of living and life that might sit outside societal norms, but in ways that could be considered subversive and even progressive. This extends the current debates within the field of zombie studies, and allows access to the zombie figure as something, arguably, more revolutionary, rather than regressive.

In its most basic form, posthumanism can arise from the desire to critically investigate and redefine what exactly is meant by 'human' and what attributes it embodies. As such, the 'posthuman' signals 'the end of a certain conception of the human' – the liberal human subject, a rational and reasonable being.[6] From this perspective, the zombified breakdown of civilisation signals an enforced 'posthuman' turn. However, this chapter demonstrates the ways that humanism, neo-liberalism and capitalism are deeply entrenched social values that do not take long to rise from the dead themselves – even whilst surrounded by reanimated corpses.

Capitalism, neo-liberalism, humanism

The model of capitalism has changed through mechanical capital, to industrial, to the current informational age of capitalism. However, within all of these models the same basic tenets arise: produce, compete, innovate and consume. Whilst capitalism promotes the privatisation of property and wealth, it also promotes a continuous spiral of innovation and productivity. Neo-liberalism transfers these same values to the self. Rather than only businesses producing, competing, innovating and consuming, personal value becomes inextricably linked to the material goods owned by individuals. Once again value is measured in terms of achievement, through material wealth – the money in the bank, the affordable holidays, the houses owned (or that are strived for), the latest smartphone, consumer gadgets, cars and '[c]onsumption thus becomes a vehicle for authenticating the self and/as product in a cyclical process that, once constructed, is used to validate its own manifestations'.[7] However, the neo-liberal imperative is also evident through the ways in which individuals work on themselves, not just their possessions. The self is an enterprise – an entrepreneurial self – a project to be worked again. Nikolas Rose explains that, '[t]he enterprising self will make an enterprise of its life, seek to maximize its own human capital, project itself a future, and seek to shape itself in order to become that which it wishes to be'.[8] Self-worth is built through qualifications, and self-branding helps craft a careful image of success and intelligence. As Ilana Gershon states 'how one manages one's self is a consistent, reflexive engagement . . . Now that you are a business, there is no break from being a business.'[9]

Society has shifted from industrial capitalism to cognitive capitalism, 'which is founded on the accumulation of immaterial capital, the dissemination of knowledge and the driving role of the knowledge economy'.[10]

This move aims to capture value from things other than traditional forms of labour. Here, labour is about connectivity, responsiveness, autonomy, inventiveness. Citizens are motivated by the desire to know but also, crucially, to express their knowledge. Aesthetic labour becomes incorporated into daily routines to ensure the portrayal of the appropriate style as well as the right financial capital. An emphasis is placed on being presentable, making a statement, whether being 'in fashion' and well groomed or constructing an alternative statement or counter-commentary on aesthetic. Aesthetic labour is unavoidably linked to health and fitness, where 'the responsibility for "global health" falls eventually on the individual's shoulders in neoliberal logics of self-help'.[11] Social lives form the basis of social capital, wherein personal connections are resources to be mined for support, information and guidance. Social capital is not just forging social connections, but forming relationships with people from whom something valuable can be gleaned. Dong Liu, Sarah Ainsworth and Roy Baumesiter argue that this attitude means '[p]eople are therefore motivated to form, strengthen, and maintain connections with other people who can provide emotional support, information, and material help, and perhaps other benefits – and also motivated to sustain the other people's willingness to provide those benefits'.[12] As such, individuals are conditioned to consider their relationships and how others contribute to their lives, as well as how these connections are displayed, because personal capital (including social) needs to be showcased to the world.

This form of social conditioning creates a belief that one must keep accruing all of these different forms of capital; and yet, neo-liberalism operates on the basis that all of these forms of labour – from finance to cognitive to social – are believed to be within individual control. This conditioning is not based on an acknowledgement of the implications of the governing and surrounding societal structures, nor the many ways in which these impact on an ability to succeed. Instead, humans have traditionally been addressed and represented as a particular type,

> suffused with an individualized subjectivity, motivated by anxieties and aspirations concerning their self-fulfilment, committed to finding their true identities and maximizing their authentic expression in their life-styles. The images of freedom and autonomy that inspire our political thinking equally operate in terms of an image of each human being as the unified psychological focus of his or her biography, as the locus of legitimate rights and demands, as an actor seeking to 'enterprise' his or her life and self through acts of choice.[13]

This standardised 'norm', so often taken for granted, actually assumes a great deal – individuality, motivation, commitment, maximisation, freedom, autonomy, unification and control. Yet, this norm is highly presumptuous and works to serve those in power in a variety of ways. For example, this individual, who is self-responsible, is the epitome of the 'good citizen'. Citizenship itself is considered as, for example, 'a set of norms of what people think they should do as good citizens', or as Michael Schudson suggests 'the political expectations and aspirations people inherit and internalize'.[14] The good citizen therefore may be one who displays the 'desired modes of participation' (though, as Neta Kligler-Vilenchik notes, these modes are actually in flux, rather than fixed understandings).[15] This model is again altogether a subjectivity that is collectively defined and designed: someone who behaves correctly, gives back to society, is the archetype of the correct way to be, to behave and to strive. Moreover, the veneer of standardised citizenship silences differences in race, gender, sexuality, class, etc. The message here is that everyone is equal; differences are levelled. But this is not the case.

These ever-expanding forms of labour related to the self have been noted previously. In their work from over a decade ago, Rosalind Gill and Andy Pratt suggest that there has been a transformation in the consideration of workers' subjectivities that moves the world of work outside the confines of the workplace to instead encompass all aspects of life.[16] Gill and Pratt indicate that 'creative labour, network labour, cognitive labour, affective labour and immaterial labour' are examples that 'point to the significance of contemporary transformations, and signals – at the very least – that "something" is going on'.[17] This 'something' seems nothing less than the strengthening of the neo-liberal death grip, reducing human worth to the sum of its labour, and expanding those labour forms to encompass all aspects of life. Ultimately this makes the subject-as-citizen more manageable, predictable and controllable, as the monitoring of this citizenship is evident through neo-liberal governmentality; that is, rather than a central governing force being required to monitor everyone, citizens operate in a way wherein they each guide their own behaviours in line with a certain understanding of what is deemed 'appropriate'. Michel Foucault used the example of the panopticon – subjects are all looking at each other, monitoring each other's behaviour and measuring their own against that observed behaviour.[18] Subjects intrinsically embody and internalise the notion of some behaviours being 'correct' and 'desirable', while others are not. Citizens police themselves and others through comparison and critique. Once again, this places responsibility back on to the self – the central aim, and arguably the success, of neo-liberalism is precisely the targeting of fully autonomous citizens, charging individuals with their own responsibilities, and holding them accountable for their own actions.

Social media could be argued to exacerbate the pressure of neo-liberal governmentality, in a variety of ways. Not only does social capital extend to an online domain through a variety of platforms; social capital is also exemplified through accumulating 'likes' and friends and followers from further afield, and thus digital brands grows and digital capital amasses. Consequently, a constant imperative exists to update, check in, feedback, respond, upload and so forth, and thus the entrepreneurial self takes on another form, embarking upon self-commodification. Tobias Raun highlights the ways in which intimacy and authenticity are utilised and wielded online, again as resources to be mined, and thus further, affective layers of labour are integrated.[19] Through social media and internet access, the metaphorical panopticon also grows; individuals have more people to monitor (to measure themselves against), and more people by which to be monitored. Thus, the more individual content uploaded (that the self-commodifier *must* put out) the more there is to refine to withstand social scrutiny.

The neo-liberal implication that humans are each individually responsible for their achievements is internalised in such a way that the neo-liberal citizen believes that they are responsible for their own success and happiness: they 'strive(s) for personal fulfilment . . . to find meaning in existence by shaping its life through acts of choice'.[20] This reintroduces the figure that the liberal human subject embodies – one that is autonomous, responsible, self-determined and individually governed.[21] However, the rational subject of humanism does not acknowledge the much more porous, dispersed, intra-connected aspects of 'being' that influence daily existence. Individuals are constantly entwined with others – human and nonhuman – around them, and this recognition has led to a renewed understanding of how and what they are affected by and how they are moved; the fact that individual embodiment extends beyond the confines of skin shows that the supposed boundaries that separate 'us' from the rest of the world are flawed when taking into perspective 'our' distributed awareness and permeability.

Much of the basic premise of a human being individual, autonomous and fully in control of their own thoughts and actions has, in more recent years, come into question. This idea of the 'rational' being can be linked to the 'fiction of autonomous selfhood'.[22] As Lisa Blackman explains, '[t]his fiction is one that assumes that the human subject is ideally bounded, responsible for their actions, self-enclosed and able to develop or enact the capacity for change and transformation through their own agency', and as such has 'become part and parcel of how we are governed and managed as citizens and populations'.[23] The rational, autonomous being is therefore a particular construction designed to suit a particular style of governmentality; by making the subject accountable they are also made controllable. The liberal human subject has traditionally applied to a white, male, heterosexual, Western, fully abled, educated human (educated being key here, when considering who education has historically been denied to) where other parts of society have been excluded even the most basic rights. Liberal humanism operates within hierarchical understandings of what, or who matters, and deceives people into the belief that meritocracy is evident.

In this hellish merry-go-round of producing, buying, grooming, branding, and of being 'good', responsible, clean, authentic, and uploading, commenting, connecting, it is not surprising that people yearn for and fantasise about gore, monsters, the dissolution of fashion, shops, Netflix, Instagram, and the 'work, work, work' and 'money, money, money' necessary for the achievement of social capital. Steven Shaviro argues that:

> [t]he life-in-death of the zombie is a nearly perfect allegory for the inner logic of capitalism , whether this be taken in the sense of the exploitation of living labor by dead labor, the deathlike regimentation of factories and other social spaces, or the artificial, externally driven stimulation of consumers.[24]

There is an argument, therefore, that the consistent parade of capitalism makes zombies of us all: mindless, mass-driven, staggering in the footsteps of those who trod the same path before.

As if this zombification did not suffice, the early twenty-first-century political climate resembles a dystopian reality, where political leaders insist on building walls and suspending parliaments rather than promoting diversity, embracing different cultures and allowing open debate. Accordingly, the idea that we are living in equal and democratic societies is more heavily scrutinised and met with greater scepticism by the general public. As social hierarchies are more and more evident the divide between those who are able to achieve the higher status in society and those who are not also becomes more and more apparent: 'bearers of *social* risk are expected to continue to get by on their own. At all costs, though, they must keep shopping. Exploiting crisis conditions, we must remember, has been a hallmark of neoliberal governance.'[25] By noticing these conditions, 'the enterprising self' and 'the good citizen' are becoming understood as capitalist, neo-liberal traps, designed to keep people 'in check'. As such, when faced with this exhaustion and the dawning realisation that all this work is based on a foundational lie, a zombie outbreak becomes almost romantically representative of a desire to shirk the problematic, societal expectations of the contemporary age. The zombie apocalypse allows dreams and fantasies of overthrowing these humanist, capitalist and neo-liberal constructions to thrive. In these narratives, therefore, the fascination with the zombie apocalypse is an embodiment of a posthumanist way of living.

Posthuman perspectives

Posthumanism is not only about technology, as many interpretations may suggest. Rather, as Elaine Graham states, 'technologies call into question the ontological purity according to which Western society has defined what is normatively human', and this 'questioning' that the influx of technologies has provoked has spread throughout the interrogation of the ontology of the human in other areas, aside from digital augmentation.[26] As Rosi Braidotti states, 'the posthuman is not so much a dystopian vision of the future, but a defining trait of our historical context'.[27] Here then, 'talk about representations of the post/human is an occasion for acknowledging what has always been the case – that "human nature" is as much a piece of human artifice as all the other things human beings have invented'.[28] Accordingly, 'human nature' should be understood as culturally and historically contingent – the human subject as a 'rational' being privileged those in power – the educated, white, male.[29] Feminist posthumanism provides a critique of humanism: 'deconstruct[ing] humanism from within, tracing its internal tensions and conceptual discrepancies'.[30] The rejection of the 'liberal human subject' therefore stems from the acknowledgement that what actually counts as 'human' is already flawed considering that, historically, only a particular kind of human has had full access to rights. Thus, it is possible to start from a point of critique wherein the title of human is not so all-encompassing as one might expect. The liberal human subject is always based on a 'norm' that actually excludes most of the population of the world.

Posthumanism also challenges the binaries that are historically evident, such as self/other, male/female, culture/nature, mind/matter, human/machine/animal. These binaries have always created hierarchies, wherein one end of the spectrum is seen as the norm (self, male, culture, mind, human), and the opposite end as 'other'. Rejecting these binaries, then, ultimately leads to a rejection of hierarchies, by acknowledging the bias implicit within them. However, more than that, by understanding the ways in which meanings have been constructed through oppositions, this forces an acknowledgement of how much different subject positions are explicitly intra-dependent on the 'others' around them. Karen Barad utilises the concept of 'intra-action' rather than 'interaction'. Where interaction suggests two separate entities coming together, intra-action embodies a philosophy of emergence, where one position is entirely reliant and dependent on another for its specific process of becoming to arise.[31] The self as static, stable, responsible and individual begins to disintegrate by considering how each 'self' is entangled with 'other' entities, both human and nonhuman. Accordingly, 'the posthuman, however, is not just a critique of Humanism. It also takes on the even more complex challenge of anthropocentrism.'[32] As soon as the disruption of these binaries occurs, and the self is no longer static but occurs in mutual construction with a variety of 'others' and possibilities, the human as the most important, or dominant, species or even 'thing' becomes undermined. A posthumanist philosophy embodies a disruption of hierarchies in favour of a more rhizomatic understanding of relations, and a consideration of the self as distributed, wherein agency is dispersed.

Initially, in some ways, the way in which the zombie apocalypse is utilised by media producers and consumers 'works' in disrupting the humanistic model – often, within these narratives, there is a better understanding of self as entangled – reliant on others, environments, materials, technologies. Survivors can no longer consider themselves as entirely autonomous – their survival depends not just on themselves but the environments and tools at their disposal. Survivors are therefore in a less hierarchical relationship with the world around them. This post-hierarchical state also leads to a (potentially) more post-anthropocentric understanding of the world. Survivors are no longer 'top of the food chain' and cannot, should not, see the world as revolving around them anymore.

Moreover, there is a rebalance of the significance lent to embodiment. Liberal humanism privileged the mind (with the infamous words of Rene Descartes: 'I think therefore I am') and 'reason' over the body.

This privileging created a mind/body dualism that allowed anyone who was deemed to have less reason or more bodily concerns (women, people of colour, disabled people and the lower classes) to be effectively discarded from historical philosophy.[33] The zombie apocalypse brings bodies (leaky ones at that) and flesh back to the forefront. As David McNally explains, drawing on Bakhtin:

> contrary to the defined and enclosed heroic body of the bourgeois/aristocratic male, then, the grotesque body 'is unfinished, outgrows itself, transgresses its own limits. The stress is laid on those parts of the body that are open to the outside world' . . . with respect to the zombie genre . . . the cut, the sore, the dangling limb.[34]

McNally further suggests that zombies represent a 'grotesque corporeality' and are an example of 'hyperembodiment' moreover, leaving aside the mind and reason, '[z]ombies also reveal what bodies are capable of, and what they can endure'.[35]

Yet, society always returns to conformity – the 2.4 member family and the heroic father figure often emerges, for example in *World War Z*, *I am Legend*, even *Cargo*.[36] There is the celebration of enforced heterosexuality 'for survival', and as Shaka McGlotten and Steve Jones explain 'many zombie narratives reproduce or even celebrate norms tied to romance, gender, ability, and heterosexuality'.[37] The links between zombie narratives and contemporary 'keep fit' regimes are also rife, with *Zombieland* stressing the importance of cardio, whilst Conor Heffernan has demonstrated the utilisation of the zombie as a threat/motivation in fitness magazines.[38] This focus on fitness assumes and accepts that, in the zombie apocalypse, the physically disabled will be some of the first to die. Alternatively, in certain narratives their disability is exploited as inspiration porn, or as another trope that is utilised to demonstrate what the human can 'overcome'. The desire to kill or overcome the zombie becomes indicative of the desire to defeat death itself – the ultimate goal in asserting that the human is agentic, and in control.

Throughout these narratives, as the male hero saves the day, heterosexuality signifies 'hope', ableism is lauded and disability utilised, this is where the posthumanist dream crumbles. How is it possible to imagine society outside what is known? Hierarchies, belonging, measuring worth, individualistic attitudes always emerge. Imaginations fail. And, of course, humanistic, anthropocentric ways of thinking resurface. Distinctions between self and other continue to occur, perhaps not as much through environment, but through zombie-as-other. In these scenarios, then, is it in fact the zombies who have truly escaped, and succeeded? Is becoming a zombie, then, becoming posthuman? As Sarah Lauro and Karen Embry suggest, 'the zombie, [is] a consciousless being that is a swarm organism, and the only imaginable specter that could really be posthuman'.[39] This swarm becomes almost a vision of an alternative society, wherein networked affect (often seen as operating through, for example, mob mentality) is evident and embraced as, despite zombies being out for their own survival, they operate as a conjoined body (for example, the iconic swarm scene in *World War Z*, where zombies pile upon one another to build a ramp over a walled city –behaviour echoed in the White Walkers in *Game of Thrones*, who lay themselves across a burning border, for the others behind them to cross).[40]

Zombie as posthuman

There is reasoning behind the argument of zombies (and the zombie apocalypse) embodying posthumanist theory from a variety of perspectives. As McGlotten and Jones state,

> [t]he levelling of social difference, and of society itself, is paradoxically facilitated by the zombie's lack of subjective agency . . . the zombie's revolution is not only social: it also represents day zero for human identity, and the imbricated experiences of individuality and interdependence on which sociality is founded.

Zombies embody a collapse of all previous understandings of 'human identity' thereby allowing a whole new reconsideration of those taken-for-granted norms — thus enabling at least one parameter of posthumanism. Due to the ways '[z]ombies are freed of any obligations, other than to their own hunger', they are accordingly freed of the expectations, and hierarchies apparent within liberal humanism, whilst simultaneously pointed to its lie: 'zombies are evacuated of self, but they also reveal that for the living, autonomous will is empty'.[42] George A. Romero famously said that in the event of a zombie apocalypse his strategy would be to go out and get bitten quickly.[43]

The zombie is 'othered' in the same way that those who fell outside of the scope of the liberal human subject: people of colour, women, disabled people, the working classes and members of the LGBTQIA+ have all been feared, scorned, excluded and have elicited disgust.[44] Furthermore, in the Haitian legend the zombie is seen as that which lacks the rational and reasonable mental behaviour 'the body is resurrected and retained: only consciousness is permanently lost'.[45] They are conceived as '"dead men working", unthinking body-machines, lacking identity, memory and consciousness – possessing only the physical capacity for labour' whilst still being left with their reanimated body.[46] The zombie is othered because of this – again linking back to women, POC, disabled people and all of those historically denied an education, and who are seen to be more 'bodily' beings than 'brain beings' (Hannabach also states that 'in popular culture zombies and people with disabilities are constructed in problematically similar ways'[47]).

For the most part, the zombie is the one that manages to live in a truly posthuman state regarding the rejection of humanism, and so perhaps they are where hope should lie. They symbolise a 'rupture in the fabric of the normal', and seem to embody the posthumanist requirement for a reconsideration of taken-for-granted norms.[48] Lauro and Embry state that the zombie is a 'threat to stable subject and object positions'.[49] Margrit Shildrick argues that the dominant Western view of subjectivity is 'the concept of a free and rational sovereign individual, aware of himself as a self, and claiming some kind of authority, whether sanctioned transcendentally or materially, over those "others" who are disqualified'.[50] This is precisely what posthumanism, too, troubles, in order to move away from an anthropocentric worldview and acknowledge the ways in which 'objects' explicitly impact subjectivities and make other ways of being possible. These are important alignments that can be made between posthumanism and the zombie category. McGlotten and Jones indicate that '[a]s monsters that straddle the gulf between life and death, zombies disturb established ontological and epistemological categories, as well as hegemonic norms', and it is this opening up of these binary categories that allows alternative conceptions of being to enter the philosophical debate.[51] Avoiding binary oppositions, 'the zombie is uncontrollable ambiguity', and, as such, embodies the breaking of boundaries and binaries necessarily for a posthumanist reimagining.[52] This ambiguity is evident through the boundaries and binaries that the zombie eradicates, such as male/female: Patricia MacCormack states with regards to certain films that 'their zombie state ablates gender, which thus ablates definable sexuality through object choice'.[53] The sanctity of selfhood is further disrupted through the zombie as it is constructed in and as an assemblage – the individual is lost in favour of the masses, 'the zombie horde is a swarm where no trace of the individual remains'.[54] Lauro and Embry argue that the zombie is a figure that 'crashes borders' and this includes the border between life and death, which has long been a subject of fear and loathing in itself.[55] From this perspective the Westernised 'taboo' of death is also evidence of engrained, humanistic value structures, and, as per Braidotti '[w]e need to re-think death, the ultimate subtraction, as another phase in a generative process', if people/anyone are to fully engage with posthumanist alternatives.[56]

The all-too-human(ist)-zombie

However, even in *The Girl with All the Gifts*, an example of the 'zombie' as inheritor of the world, humanistic tendencies pervade in the final scene, where the sole, human survivor teaches the new generation of 'Biters', schooling them from within the safety of her hermeneutically sealed chamber.[57] Likewise, although Sheila Hammond in *Santa Clarita Diet* embraces and enjoys her zombie-embodiment in ways that might refute a humanistic hierarchy, again in other ways she plays into normative, neo-liberal tropes. Lorna Jowett notes that Sheila has 'i-zombie responsibilities' of selfhood: her job, her position as wife and mother, and her requirements to keep up appearances and not let her neighbours become aware of her zombie-ness.[58] This aligns specifically with the issues of neo-liberal governmentality and indicates the ways in which these forms of surveillance determine specific 'desired' behaviours. Moreover, in the novel *Warm Bodies* this humanisation of the zombie is taken even further, through the complete reversion of the zombie.[59] Sasha Cocarla explains that even though 'R', the main zombie protagonist, 'is a literal monster himself (and thereby queered in relation to the human norm), he clings to the dominant notion of normalcy and the neoliberal mantra of achievement ("if you work hard enough, you will be successful"), implying that he has more in common with living humans than he does with the Boneys', and so internalised ideals of meritocratic neo-liberalism are evident from his own aspiration.[60] Denied the normal exit route of work (death) the zombie has potentially no choice but to accept a meritocratic hope for his future. Cocarla explains that R also has 'desire for neoliberal values, including romance and heteronormative desire', which become the driving aspect of the narrative (and further link to aspects of social capital as described above).[61] Whilst Cocarla's reading of the *Warm Bodies* novel suggests that 'neoliberal success is tentative', in the 2013 film adaptation the neo-liberal success seems complete, as the complexities of the prose narrative are skimmed over, and a Hollywood-esque 'happy ending' is desired.[62] Elsewhere, the reinstitution of the hierarchy of mind over matter is seen in, for example, *Day of the Dead: Bloodline*, when the cure is derived specifically from a zombie who still retains some mental capacity, whose brain is still alive.[63] Therefore, mind over matter, brain over body, has not died as a binary, and zombies are graded by their mental capacities rather than physical ones. This therefore extends the debate that zombies are a metaphor for humanity's contemporary mindless consumption to argue that even zombies are also victims of humanistic systems; they are not merely metaphor for contemporary human practice (which is, in itself a highly anthropocentric way of utilising the zombie-other purely as a contemporary referent for the category of human). Even in death the interminable production chain cannot be escaped.

From this perspective, whilst zombies in some ways embody posthumanist stances, humanism, neo-liberalism and capitalism are deeply entrenched values, and their structures do not take long to rise from the dead themselves – even whilst surrounded by, or embodied through, reanimated corpses. These values seem too ingrained to escape, even when undead. What does the attack upon the posthuman zombie then signify, but an attack on the very threat that fascinates and, potentially, appeals? There is a *dual* fascination: first, a captivation of the crash that the zombie apocalypse can give. McNally expands by suggesting that 'the attraction of such displays, and of much of the horror genre generally, resides, of course, in its capacity to gratify as much as to frighten'.[64] Viewers derive a deep pleasure from images of fantastic beings wreaking havoc upon polite citizens of well-ordered society. Yet, secondly, audiences are then intent upon the attack on those who embody that crash. This echoes Lauro and Embry's ascertain that the zombie both 'terrifies and tantalizes'.[65] Ultimately (presumed) gratification seemingly comes, in the end, from seeing humanity 'triumph', whether through the survivors or through the zombie-turned-human reclaiming its place in society. Donna Haraway once wrote of 'the promises of monsters', the possibility exists that humanistic society has thwarted even that. Not even zombies can save us now.[66]

Notes

1. *Dawn of the Dead*, dir. George A. Romero, Laurel Group Inc. (1978); *Shaun of the Dead*, dir. Edgar Wright, WT2 (2004); Mira Grant, *Newsflesh* (London: Orbit, 2010–12); *Dying Light*, Techland, Warner, Bros. Interactive Entertainment (2015).
2. *We're Alive*, Wayland Productions (2009–14); Deirdre Gould, *After the Cure*, narrated by Miles Taber (Audible, 2016).
3. Sarah Lauro (ed.), *Zombie Theory: A Reader* (Minneapolis: University of Minneapolis Press, 2017), p. 7.
4. This chapter examines the Western world and contemporary Western media portrayals of the zombie outbreak. The zombie figure has a long and international history, which several of the other contributors of this book explore in fascinating detail.
5. Romero, *Dawn of the Dead*.
6. N. Katherine Hayles, *How We Became Posthuman* (Chicago: University of Chicago Press, 1999), p. 286.
7. Stéphanie Genz, 'My Job is Me', *Feminist Media Studies*,15/4 (2015), 548.
8. Nikolas Rose, *Inventing our Selves: Psychology, Power, and Personhood* (Cambridge: Cambridge University Press, 1998), p. 154.
9. Ilana Gershon, '"I'm not a businessman, I'm a business, man": Typing the neoliberal self into a branded existence', *Hau: Journal of Ethnographic Theory*, 6/3 (2016), 234, 243.
10. Yann Moulier Boutang, *Cognitive Capitalism* (London: Polity Press, 2011), p. 50.
11. Katariina Kyrölä, *The Weight of Images: Affect, Body Image and Fat in the Media* (London: Routledge, 2014), p. 47.
12. Dong Liu, Sarah Ainsworth and Roy Baumeister, 'A meta-analysis of social networking online and social capital', *Review of General Psychology*, 20/4 (2016), 370.
13. Rose, *Inventing our Selves*, p. 170.
14. Russell Dalton, 'Citizenship Norms and the Expansion of Political Participation', *Political Studies*, 56 (2008), 78; Michael Schudson, T*he Good Citizen: A History of American Civic Life* (Cambridge, MA: Harvard University Press, 1998), p. 6.
15. Neta Kligler-Vilenchik, 'Alternative citizenship models: Contextualizing new media and the new "good citizen"', *New Media & Society*, 19/11 (2017), 1887–903.
16. Rosalind Gill and Andy Pratt, 'In the Social Factory? Immaterial Labour, Precariousness and Cultural Work', *Theory, Culture & Society*, 25/7–8 (2008), 1–30.

17. Gill and Pratt, 'In the Social Factory?', 3.
18. Michel Foucault, *Discipline and Punish* (New York: Penguin, 1991).
19. Tobias Raun, 'Capitalizing Intimacy: New Subcultural Forms of Microcelebrity Strategies and Affective Labour on YouTube', *Convergence: The International Journal of Research into New Media Technologies*, 24/1 (2018), 99–113.
20. Rose, *Inventing our Selves*, p. 151.
21. See Tzvetan Todorov, *Imperfect Garden: The Legacy of Humanism* (Princeton: Princeton University Press, 2002), p. 33.
22. Lisa Blackman, '"Loving The Alien": A Post–Post-Human Manifesto', *Subjectivity*, 10/1 (2017), 23.
23. Blackman, 'Loving The Alien', 23; Lisa Blackman, *The Body* (Albany: Berg, 2008), p. 113.
24. Steven Shaviro, 'Contagious Allegories: George Romero', in Sarah Juliet Lauro (ed.), *Zombie Theory: A Reader* (Minneapolis: University of Minneapolis Press, 2017), pp. 7–8.
25. Jamie Peck, 'Zombie Neoliberalism and the Ambidextrous State', *Theoretical Criminology*, 14/1 (2010), 109.
26. Elaine Graham, *Representations of the Posthuman* (Manchester: Manchester University Press, 2002), p. 5.
27. Rosi Braidotti, *Posthuman Knowledge* (London: Polity Press, 2019), pp. 1–2.
28. Graham, *Representations of the Posthuman*, p. 37.
29. See also Kurt Danziger, *Naming the Mind: How Psychology Found Its Language* (London: Sage, 1997), p. 40; Rose, *Inventing our Selves*, p. 9.
30. David Roden, *Posthuman Life* (London: Routledge, 2015), p. 9.
31. Karen Barad, *Meeting the Universe Halfway: Quantum Physics and the Entanglement of Matter and Meaning* (Durham: Duke University Press, 2007).
32. Braidotti, *Posthuman Knowledge*, p. 8.
33. Rene Descartes, *Discourse on the Method* [1637] (Peterborough: Cosimo Classics, 1924), p. 31.
34. David McNally, 'Ugly Beauty: Monstrous Dreams of Utopia', in Sarah Juliet Lauro (ed.), *Zombie Theory: A Reader* (Minneapolis: University of Minneapolis Press, 2017), p. 125.
35. McNally, 'Ugly Beauty', p. 128; Shaka McGlotten and Steve Jones (eds), *Zombies and Sexuality: Essays on Desire and the Living Dead* (Jefferson: McFarland, 2014), p. 3.
36. Rain Shuen Chan, 'The Family Trouble in Post-Millennial Zombie Cinema: The Father-Hero in *I Am Legend* (2007) and *World War Z* (2013)', *Theorizing Zombiism Conference*, University College Dublin (2019); *World War Z*, dir. Marc Forster, Skydance Productions, 2013; *I am Legend*, dir. Francis

Lawrence, Village Roadshow Pictures, 2007; *Cargo*, dir. Ben Howling and Yolanda Ramke, Umbrella Entertainment, 2017.
37. McGlotten and Jones (eds), *Zombies and Sexuality*, p. 6; Cathy Hannabach, 'Queering and Cripping the End of the World: Disability, Sex, and Race in *The Walking Dead*', in Shaka McGlotten and Steve Jones (eds), *Zombies and Sexuality: Essays on Desire and the Living Dead* (Jefferson: McFarland, 2014), pp. 106–22.
38. *Zombieland*, dir. Ruben Fleischer, Columbia Pictures, USA, 2009; Conor Heffernan, 'The Apocalypse Workout: Health, Identity and Zombies', *Theorizing Zombiism Conference*, University College Dublin (2019).
39. Sarah Juliet Lauro and Karen Embry, 'A Zombie Manifesto: The Nonhuman Condition in the Era of Advanced Capitalism', *boundary 2*, 35/1 (2008), 88.
40. *World War Z*; *Game of Thrones*, dir. David Benioff and Daniel Brett Weiss, HBO, 2011–19.
41. McGlotten and Jones (eds), *Zombies and Sexuality*, p. 6.
42. McGlotten and Jones (eds), *Zombies and Sexuality*, pp. 6–7.
43. Lauro and Embry, 'A Zombie Manifesto', 88.
44. Amy Bride highlights the ways zombies are seen as 'less than human'. Amy Bride, 'Mindless Consumers: Zombies, Subprime Borrowers, and the 2008 Financial Crash', *Theorizing Zombiism Conference*, University College Dublin (2019).
45. Lauro and Embry, 'A Zombie Manifesto', 89.
46. McNally, 'Ugly Beauty', p. 124.
47. Hannabach, 'Queering and Cripping the End of the World', p. 106.
48. McNally, 'Ugly Beauty', p. 124.
49. Lauro and Embry, 'A Zombie Manifesto', 88.
50. Margrit Shildrick, *Leaky Bodies and Boundaries: Feminism, Postmodernism and (Bio)ethics* (London: Routledge, 1997), p. 147.
51. McGlotten and Jones (eds), *Zombies and Sexuality*, p. 6.
52. Lars Bang Larsen, 'Zombies of Immaterial Labor: The Modern Monster and the Death of Death', in Sarah Juliet Lauro (ed.), *Zombie Theory: A Reader* (Minneapolis: University of Minneapolis Press, 2017), p. 157.
53. Patricia MacCormack, 'Zombies without Organs: Gender, Flesh and Fissure', in Shawn McIntosh and Marc Leverette (eds), *Zombie Culture: Autopsies of the Living Dead* (Lanham: The Scarecrow Press, 2008), p. 97.
54. Lauro and Embry, 'A Zombie Manifesto', 89.
55. Lauro and Embry, 'A Zombie Manifesto', 91.
56. Braidotti, *The Posthuman*, p. 121.
57. *The Girl with All the Gifts*, dir. Colm McCarty, BFI, London, 2016.

58. *Santa Clarita Diet*, dir. Victor Fresco, Kapital Entertainment, Netflix, USA, 2017–19; Lorna Jowett, '"I got a new kill poncho": *Santa Clarita Diet* and the Pleasures of Zombie Embodiment', *Theorizing Zombiism Conference*, University College Dublin (2019).
59. Isaac Marion, *Warm Bodies* (New York: Atria Books, 2010).
60. Sasha Cocarla, 'A Love Worth Un-Undying For: Neoliberalism and Queered Sexuality in Warm Bodies', in Shaka McGlotten and Steve Jones (eds), *Zombies and Sexuality: Essays on Desire and the Living Dead* (Jefferson: McFarland, 2014), pp. 61–2.
61. Cocarla, 'A Love Worth Un-Undying For', p. 62.
62. *Warm Bodies*, dir. Jonathan Levine, Mandeville Films, 2013; Cocarla, 'A Love Worth Un-Undying For', p. 62.
63. *Day of the Dead: Bloodline*, dir. Hector Hernandez, Saban Capital Group, 2018.
64. McNally, 'Ugly Beauty', pp. 124–5.
65. Lauro and Embry, 'A Zombie Manifesto', 88.
66. Donna Haraway, *The Haraway Reader* (London: Routledge, 2003), p. 63.

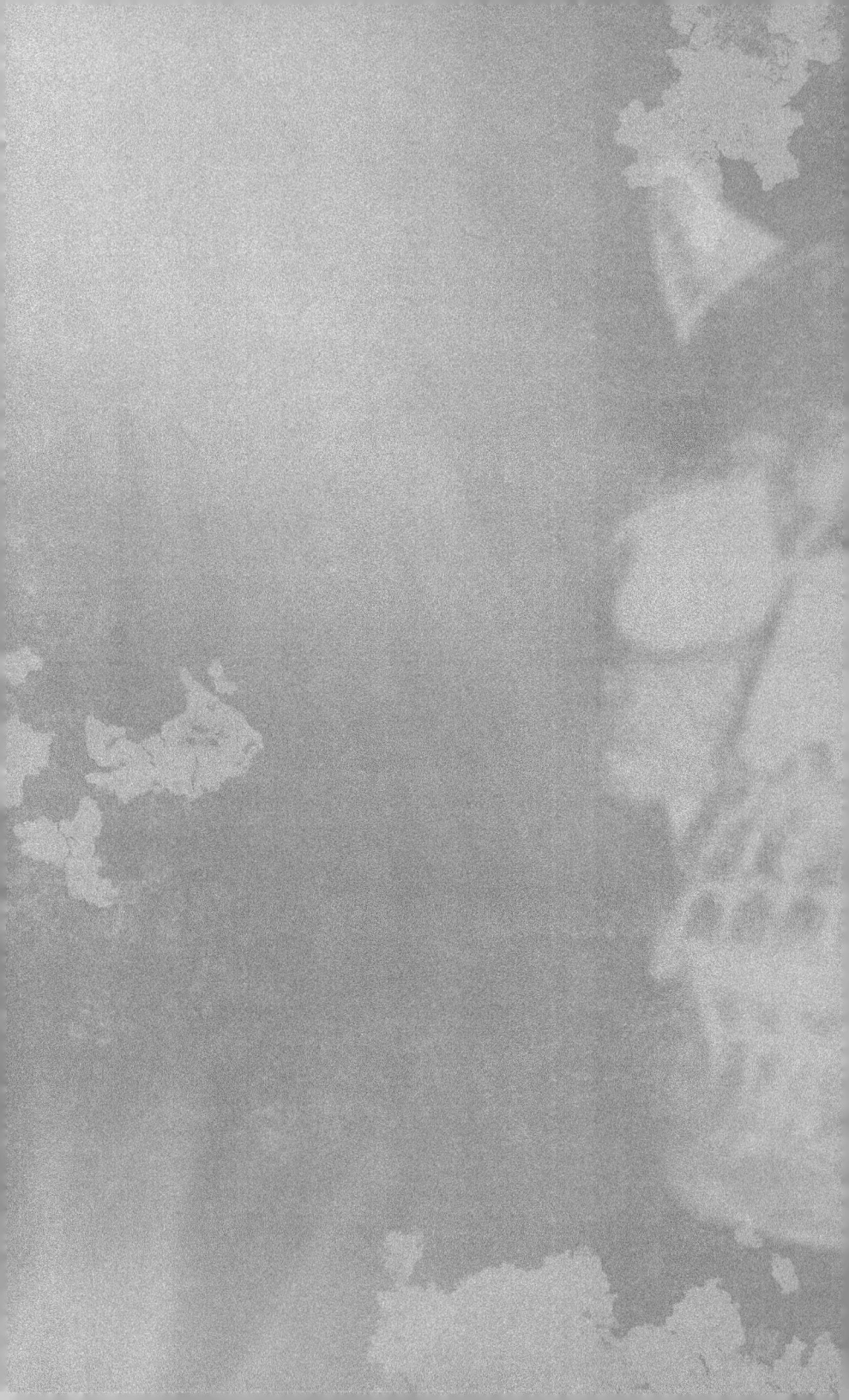

2

The Apocalypse Workout

Health, Identity and Zombies

Conor Heffernan

> 'Welcome to Zombieland . . . Rule #1 Cardio.
> Zombies live a very active lifestyle, so should you'[1]

SET IN A DYSTOPIAN America under siege by zombies, Ruben Fleischer's *Zombieland* is driven by the protagonist's rules for survival. Appearing throughout the movie, the experientially derived lessons supposedly saved the protagonist, named Columbus, on several occasions. Importantly for Columbus, and the present chapter, rule #1 is dedicated to physical fitness. Far from trivial, the message that strong and fast physiques are desirable, if not necessary, in zombie encounters has begun to infect societal thinking. Less than a year after *Zombieland*'s premiere, *Wired.com* featured an article inspired by the film on how to 'get fit enough to fight the undead'.[2] Soon after, bodybuilding and general fitness platforms, like *Muscle and Fitness*, *T-Nation* and *Men's Health*, produced articles dedicated to zombie defying workouts.[3] In a convergence between health and popular culture, zombies have become health icons or, at least, health motivators. The validity of the latter statement can be found in a smartphone app, *Zombies, Run!*, predicated on the idea that zombies help people run faster.

Zombie movies, articles and television shows all contribute to discourses applied to zombie inspired health advice. As such, the zombie has become a mechanism for critiquing modern comforts as well as a motivator for athletic and strong bodies. In making this argument, a brief outline is given to the emergence of the 'zombie threat' as a popular device in health and fitness communities. Subsequently, zombie workouts are examined; first, with reference to modernity and, secondly, with reference to the physical body. Ultimately, this chapter argues that zombies have been used in the fitness industry as motivating forces to combat the potential zombiism of contemporary life which has supposedly left individuals bereft of health, vigour or excitement.

Zombies in health and fitness

The zombie was not initially a specimen of fitness. In George Romero's iconic 1968 movie *Night of the Living Dead* the zombies are slow moving because, 'they're dead, they're all messed up'.[5] In such an environment, wherein the zombie hunter never tires but never poses an immediate physical threat, survival is predicated on tactical knowledge, cooperation and luck.[6] Aside from the obvious importance to the genre, Romero's film popularised the image of slow-moving zombies. Dan O'Bannon's *Return of the Living Dead* (1985) may have been one of the first films to introduce faster-moving and physical zombies; however, not until the early 2000s did the hyper athletic and strong zombies emerge. The slow-paced zombies associated with Romero evolved. For instance, Zack Snyder's remaking of *Dawn of the Dead* (2004) opened with a scene of a small child bursting through a wooden door in search of human flesh. From there, the film's protagonists faced ever-increasing numbers of strong, aggressive and fast zombies. Synder's depiction of 'athletic zombies' are mirrored in films like *28 Days Later* (2002), *Resident Evil* (2002) and *House of the Dead* (2003).[7] Zombies, echoing a broader western concern with external threats, have become increasingly menacing in their danger as embodied by their physical attributes.[8]

That audiences appear to respond favourably to fast-paced and strong zombies has not gone unnoticed by screenwriters and authors. In response, films are far more likely to stress the importance of physicality and health among the human survivors. Fleischer's *Zombieland* featured several survival tips for surviving a zombie apocalypse, many of which related to the ability to outrun or outfight the undead – 'Limber up'.[9] Francis Lawrence's 2007 *I Am Legend*, adapted from Richard Matheson's novel, includes a short montage in which the scientist Robert Neville, played by Will Smith, exercises in his home using a combination of calisthenics and 'cardio'. Given the fast-moving and powerful zombies in these movies, and others like *State of Emergency* (2011) or *World War Z* (2013), Hollywood movies have taken the term 'fighting' zombies in a literal sense. In these movies, unathletic bodies are often the first to be targeted. Authors, too, now focus on health in their zombie works. Light-hearted zombie novels, like Michael O'Hearn's *Zombies vs. Mummies* or Teejay LeCapois's *Vampire's Guide to The Zombie Apocalypse*, have devoted space to evaluating a zombie's physical strengths and the physicality needed to overcome them.[10] Regarding the human side of the zombie disaster, Max Brook's 2003 *The Zombie Survival Guide* indicates that the human body, 'if cared for and trained properly, is the greatest weapon on earth'.[11] Furthermore, Colson Whitehead's *Zone One*, features a lieutenant whose authority is implicitly exhibited by his noticeably large bicep muscles.[12] As the athletic body has grown in social importance, so too has the zombie genre been 'infected' with anxieties surrounding a muscular body often taken to present safety during a zombie threat.[13]

Such interest is mirrored by broader societal discourses which have tended to link the increasing comfort of Western society with ill-health, boredom or obesity. In this context, the athletic or muscular body is often presented as a form of salvation. For this reason, the zombie trope is regularly used by fitness personalities to sell workout programmes, books, nutrition manuals or to simply attract more interest. Aside from *Linnea Quigley's Horror Workout*, a low-budget zombie movie produced in 1990, zombie inspired workouts date from the mid-2000s.[14] Encouraged by a new turn in zombie film-making whereby fast, strong and aggressive zombies hunted humans, message boards and fitness websites began marketing zombie-proof workouts. A key development in this regard was the expansion of the Internet. Rebecca Black previously highlighted the importance of Internet access in the growth of fan fiction in general.[15] Zombie workouts are a continuation of this trend. Whereas previously the term zombie was applied in a derogatory sense in fitness articles, often with reference to a mindless activity, fitness coaches began to use it as a motivator and as a means of critiquing the modern body.[16] None went so far as to recommend the 'all-brain diet' advocated by a 'zombie nutritionist' in *The Onion*, a satirical US website, but a definitive trend emerged.[17]

By 2010, a plethora of zombie apocalypse-themed workouts were published by popular websites like *Wired.com* and more specialised sites such as *Men's Fitness*.[18] In both instances zombies became a light-hearted way of stressing the importance of holistic training programmes. Some, including popular fitness personality Roger Lawson, sold their own personalised zombie apocalypse workout, but the majority of workouts were produced solely for public consumption.[19] Recently, fitness entrepreneurs have begun to monetise interest in zombies through the production of fitness apps for smart phones, like *Zombies, Run!*, or zombie obstacle course races held in several European and American cities.[20] The diversity of zombie-inspired fitness programmes distinguishes them from other factions in the fitness industry. Where Leslie Heywood discusses a tendency among fitness coaches to distinguish themselves from one another, and in doing so create marketable differences, zombie fitness programmes are characterised by their uniformity.[21] Some stress aerobic forms of fitness, as evidenced by *Zombies, Run!* or Tallahassee's (the key protagonist of *Zombieland*) promotion of cardio. Others promote weight training or rudimentary forms of parkour. Differentiated in their systems, they share one belief: zombies disrupt the banal safety of modern life. Comforts and conformity crumble before the zombie horde. Like the characters in Synder's *Dawn of the Dead*, one needs to escape from the shopping mall, an emblem of modernity, and return to one's survival instincts. For health and wellness writers, a return of this instinct means a return to the strong body. For this reason alone, *Zombie Experiences UK*, a live-action horror course, has stressed the need for fitness when confronted with fictitious zombie hordes.[22]

Several themes emerge in typical zombie workout plans. In responding to the new, fast-paced, zombie threat presented in movies and novels, popular fitness writers have placed a great deal of importance on the ability to move quickly. Hence, some form of running or agility training is encouraged. Once a suitable level of fitness has been achieved, attention is dedicated to 'functional' strength training, which in the case of a zombie apocalypse, means the ability to hurl objects, climb over walls and carry heavy objects for prolonged periods of time. Finally, writers stress the need for all-round endurance. Zombie workouts mirror the fad functional training programmes studied by Susan Beckham and Michael Harper, which tend to emphasise a holistic, somewhat atavistic, form of fitness deemed necessary when faced with fast, strong and aggressive zombies.[23] Zombie workout regimens build a body ready for every hardship and every eventuality. Zombies have been used to critique a form of modernity said to be defined by a sedentary and sanitised lifestyle. Seeking to combat these problems and therein live a full life, zombies are used to motivate individuals to take charge of their health in the pursuit of the ideal body.

Zombie fitness and reversing modernity

For the protagonists' in *Zombieland* survival is predicated on their ability to reject social norms and devise and adhere to their own rules. The characters are forced to reject certain comforts and behaviours which, although useful in a modern civilised society, prove ineffectual against zombie attacks. The zombies reveal the limits to a westernised standard of living defined by inactivity and consumption. Critiques of modern comfort is not unique to *Zombieland*. Fans and scholars of *Game of Thrones*, the HBO series based on G. R. R. Martin's novel series, view the 'white walkers', a zombie-like horde, as a metaphor for climate change, migrant crisis and other political problems unsolved by neo-liberal politics.[24]

A common trope among fitness entrepreneurs is that modernity has weakened individual discipline, physique and athleticism. This message has long held considerable societal gravitas. In Britain, the claim that modern luxuries weakened society is given full expression in Edward Gibbon's several volume work, *The History of the Decline and Fall of the Roman Empire*, published in the late eighteenth century.[25] In the early twentieth century, Britain and North America health reformers decried the scourges of modernity, said to have deprived citizens of unbounding physical energy.[26] Concerns intensified during the 1930s when Fascist regimes like Germany and Italy attempted to use state-endorsed fitness programmes to strengthen citizens while simultaneously indoctrinating them into the new political world view.[27] The Fascist obsession with health is featured in several zombie films dealing with Nazi Germany from Jean Rollin's *Zombie Lake* (1981) to J. J. Abrams's film, *Overlord* (2018). The jogging 'boom' of the 1960s was similarly a rejection of modern comforts in the form of unhealthy foods and sedentary lifestyles.[28] In short, at least a century-long discourse has ensued on the supposed damaging effects of modernity on the human body. More recently, a series of government reports, at both the national and supranational level, have cited modern comforts, increased sitting times and food abundances with the unhealthy standard of living found in middle- to high-income countries.[29] The long-standing fear of modernity, and supposed attendant ills, has intensified with the rise of obesity, cancer and mental-health problems in many of these countries.

In zombie fitness books, articles and videos promoted online, modern comforts are also cited as an enemy of health. In an advertisement for his 'Zombie Survival Guide', John Romaniello, owner of *Roman Fitness*

Systems, specifically stresses the disconnect between modern life and the toughness required to survive disaster:

> I'd like you to have read this when you're safe and cozy in your house, enjoying the life's little luxuries, like TV and Internet. I'd like to think that this information is reaching you in a time when those things exist; a time when tablets and phones and computers are prevalent, and the power to give them life is always available at an outlet. Perhaps you still live in a time when there are schools to go to and post offices with lines to wait in[30]

The safety defined by modern living, as epitomised by one's cosy home or 'little luxuries', is dismissed by Romaniello as he implores individuals to consider his zombie fitness plan. Romaniello is unique in being one of the first online fitness coaches to sell a zombie workout plan. He was followed by countless others who railed against the comforts of modern technologies or the conformity of popular consumption. Those for whom modernity had failed, like the original zombies.

Explaining the motivation behind *Zombies, Run!* – a popular smartphone app designed in the early 2010s – Naomi Alderman told readers of *Medium* that the app was designed as a fun, inexpensive and welcoming place for individuals to improve their health without judgement.[31] Shunning the typical, and oftentimes verbose, culture promulgated by mainstream health figures, Alderman wished to create an app that could be used by everyone, including herself. Identifying as 'fat', Alderman felt irrelevant in an online fitness community defined by lean, muscular physiques. Her physique was itself a product of modernity, albeit in this case its ills as understood by overwork, high calorie foods and poor healthcare.[32] Alderman saw running as a means of escaping a 'tedious' office job and as a pathway towards a better relationship with her body. The message of Alderman's article, aside from the fact that zombies can provide excellent motivation for runners, was that an unexamined life in modern America often left one unfulfilled, and unprepared. Zombies, strangely given their destructive nature, offered a pathway for greater self-expression as found in the body.[33] Zombies were at once the threat and the solution.

Zombies are a means of escaping modernity for many in the fitness community. Stemming from the same motivation as Alderman, a number of zombie-inspired obstacle courses have emerged in Europe and the United States over the past decade and a half.[34] Similar to the 'tough mudder' and spartan obstacle courses studied by Matthew Lamb and Cory Hillman, zombie obstacle courses comprise 5–10 km outdoor runs where the object is to complete the race and overcome a series of challenges, in this case evading zombie actors.[35] Speaking to the *New York Times*, one participant claimed, 'I think in this day and age, everything's so serious . . . You have to worry about your jobs and your mortgage. This was a time for us to not worry, to go get made up and be stupid and just have a good laugh.'[36] Zombies are also a way of escaping from a life centred on work. Sarah Juliet Lauro and Karen Embry have highlighted their symbolic importance in critiquing human behaviours.[37] In the case of zombie-inspired races, the zombie comes to be seen as fun and creative in a world where these aspects of existence are often perceived to be lacking. Commenting on the race to the *New York Times*, Lauro describes them as a release valve for relieving anxiety brought about by modern living.[38] This same anxiety is evident in Adam Dachis's article for *LifeHacker* in which the zombie apocalypse creates a light-hearted exercise programme seeking to combat the seriousness of office life, which has deprived individuals of real enjoyment.[39]

Others take a much more functional approach when it comes to zombie attacks. In doing so, they provide a more damning indictment of modernity, namely that individuals are grossly unprepared for disasters. The very same zombie races, seen by some as whimsical, were adopted by the US Center for Disease (CDC) Control in 2012 to publicise disaster preparedness.[40] As part of the campaign, a 5 km fun run was scheduled in North Carolina, whose promoters claimed that the ability to survive a zombie attack would prepare participants for man-made or natural disasters.[41] Such was the campaign's success that the US Department of Defense trialled its own zombie challenges soon after.[42] Non-government bodies have also used this approach. In an article for *End of Three Fitness*, entitled 'Are You Fit Enough to Survive a Zombie Apocalypse', Jerred Moon critiques the sedentary lifestyle exhibited by many in modernised countries.[43] Surmising the basic requirements needed to escape a horde of zombies, Moon cites the need to jump fences, climb stairs, carry friends and crawl.

Moon indicates that many individuals fail to match the requirements needed to survive a zombie attack. Popular and modern forms of training divorce individuals from the basic requirements needed to survive. Concluding his report, Moon states that large swathes of the population would be decimated by a zombie horde, not because of the zombies' ferocity but because of a 'lack of functional fitness'.[44] This is a particularly common claim in fitness literature. Where Alderman sees zombies as a playful motivator to engage in a fitness community that so often shunned people of size, Moon uses them to disparage living systems in high-income countries that have left individuals physically unprepared for conflict or disaster.

Depictions of modernity, as damaging to individual expression, also extend to current health practices. Moon, for one, uses the possibility of a zombie apocalypse to criticise forms of physical activity deemed grossly inefficient in the real world. Moreover, Heywood highlights the rise of 'functional training' in Western societies.[45] Contrasted with established practices, such as bodybuilding or powerlifting, functional training is often represented as a holistic development of the body distinguishable from those interested solely in muscle or strength building. The rise of functional training has accompanied a fierce assessment of supposed 'outdated' training methods.[46] Writing for *Testosterone Nation* in 2015, Christian Thibaudeau and Chris Shugart, both bodybuilding coaches, present a workout for those interested in being 'prepared for anything' and building 'a zombie fighting body'.[47] Much like Moon, building this body necessitated a departure from traditional bodybuilding programmes, those routinely promoted by the website, towards functional forms of training. Crossfit, founded by Greg Glassman and Lauren Jenai in the late 1990s, promotes functional exercise in contrast to traditional training systems.[48] Unsurprisingly, Crossfit has its own zombie-inspired workouts and exercises for members.[49] These exercises are presented as functional, unlike the mainstream, 'modern' approaches found in other gymnasiums whose inhabitants are occasionally depicted as mindless zombies in Crossfit videos.

The 'zombie proof' body on screen

A point that distinguishes the horror genre more generally from other Hollywood films is often the physiques of the protagonists involved. Since the early 1980s, action movies have tended to privilege muscular male and female bodies, whereas zombie films appear far more egalitarian in comparison, welcoming individuals of all shapes and sizes.[50] In zombie movies, as in other horror movies, those possessing substantial sporting abilities, or 'jocks', are often the first individuals captured, killed or converted into zombies.[51] This point was evidenced in Fred Dekker's 1986 *Night of the Creeps* in which the jocks were quickly converted into a zombie horde.[52]

Heather Addison and Nick Jones both cite a near century-long promotion of lean and muscular bodies in Hollywood films.[53] Initiated by a wider societal interest in muscular bodies for men and specified body shapes for women, several films specifically highlight the importance of physical fitness for survival. Robert Neville's workout in *I Am Legend* is one example. Equally important was the tongue-in-cheek opening of *Zombieland*, in which the protagonist Tallahassee stated that 'when the virus struck, the first ones to go, for the obvious reasons, were the fatties'.[54] The *Resident Evil* franchise, which began in 2002, was in part predicated on the superhuman strength and agility displayed by the protagonist Alice. Not that the muscular and strong physique found in the *Terminator*, *Rocky* or *Avengers* franchises has become ubiquitous in the zombie genre – the protagonists of Edgar Wright's 2004 film *Shaun of the Dead* being one counterexample – but rather, athletic physiques have become increasingly popular.[55]

The recent privileging of athletic bodies in films has been echoed in popular fitness outlets, which utilise zombies to privilege certain bodies over others. R. W. Connell's theory of hegemonic masculinity, 'the most honored way of being a man', has been greatly problematised in recent years as scholars have pointed to communities of masculinity, the situational importance of gender and the multiplicity of gender tropes in existence for men and women.[56] Despite these concerns, fitness writings promote idealistic body images and their attendant characteristics for both men and women.[57]

For men, a relationship is presented between their masculinity and physical body. In contrast to generic fitness articles, whereby motivation for obtaining an athletic build is usually coached in vanity or some form of self-actualisation, zombie fitness articles are characterised by the hyperbole contained therein. *HybridAthlete*, arguing for the need for athletic bodies, plainly indicates that 'if you are overweight or out of shape you are going to be an easy target for a zombie'.[58] Tongue-in-cheek articles on *NerdFitness* reiterate this claim: 'zombies love out of shape people'.[59] Furthermore, the anonymous author maintains that, 'They're easier to chase down, have more flesh to eat, and put up far less of a fight. Compare that with a highly intelligent nerd in peak physical condition . . . won't go down without a fight.'[60] The message here is relatively straightforward: those in peak physical condition survive, and those in abject physical condition perish. Whereas *HybridAthlete* and *NerdFitness* are relatively vague on the kind of body needed to survive a zombie attack, Pete McCall, a popular fitness writer, praises physiques capable of running quickly and with an immense amount of strength.[61] This message is echoed by a *T-Nation* article, which advertises a workout to build strength and endurance for men facing a zombie attack.[62] Notably, *T-Nation*'s advice is accompanied by images of several muscular men posing in a variety of settings. The privileging of the muscular male body, through both images and text, ends with the assertion that 'this program will also make you strong, lean, capable and fast. And that's cool too.'[63] Zombies provide fitness writers with a motivating force to combat the potential zombiism of contemporary life that leaves individuals bereft of real health or fulfilment.

A military masculinity resides in many of these writings. Like the highly restrictive, and oftentimes sacrificial, masculinities fostered in European militaries during the twentieth century, many zombie articles implore readers to build up their bodies for the sake of others.[64] In his *YouTube* zombie workout video, Jeff Cavaliere details eight exercises needed to survive a zombie attack.[65] The reasoning behind many of the movements is based on the need to fight or carry fallen comrades and protect one's family.[66] Bennet Goldstein, in his *Telegraph Herald* article, 'I've been Fitbit by a zombie', explains his initial interest in Cavaliere's workouts. It highlights the masculine discourses underpinning Cavaliere's video and its, at times, corrosive effects: 'My friends can't understand why I like Jeff. Normally, machismo turns me off, but it's exactly what I want in a fitness coach. Please yell at me. Make it like boot camp, but harder. Truth be told, I might be overdoing it.'[67] The muscular male physique, so often valorised in Western media, is viewed as advantageous in zombie invasions. Unlike the average male body, often said to be weakened by modern comforts within these fitness articles, the muscular body has the strength and agility presumably needed to emerge from a zombie apocalypse unscathed.

For women, an equally normative body is linked to the zombie invasion. The most obvious example is, of course, presented in the *Resident Evil* film franchise. Throughout the series (2002–16), Alice, the protagonist, survives based primarily upon her physical prowess acquired from the T-Virus, the very thing which created the zombies. Once more the zombie acts as the threat and the solution. The ability to move quickly and defeat others, both living and undead, in combat, privileges a specified form of strength and endurance for women. Similarly, *Terminator 2* (1991), was praised by many as a feminist film owing to the visible biceps and training montage of protagonist Sarah Connor, played by Linda Hamilton.[68] Leslie Heywood credited *Terminator* with encouraging a wave of interested women to take to the gymnasium in the hope of creating a Terminator-defeating body.[69] Similar montages are later found in *Terminator: Dark Fate* (2019) and *Halloween* (2018); the same is arguably true for Alice, whose zombie-defeating ability has promoted a series of *Resident Evil*-inspired workouts.[70] Alice is not alone in this matter either: more recently workout routines for other *Resident Evil* characters, like the Claire Redfield character, have begun to emerge online.

Beyond *Resident Evil*, arguably the most popular zombie franchise featuring several strong female characters, the desire to recreate zombie-fighting female bodies remains. In 2014, the *MailOnline* highlighted a story which had gained remarkable traction online. Wishing to emulate Danai Gurira's physique in the AMC popular series *The Walking Dead*, Siobhan Maccow lost roughly six stone in weight. Imagining zombies chasing her in the gym for motivation, she states, 'Danai Gurira plays the character brilliantly – she has such a good body, and is so strong. I wanted to be just like her.'[72] Hence, bodies shown on screen matter greatly. As too does the context. Like the male-centred discourses examined above, Ms Maccow, the *MailOnline* article's focus, comments on the need to be fit enough to survive the zombie apocalypse. Like the articles aimed at men, zombies are presented as a motivator for women. Likewise, women capable of defeating or surviving zombie attacks are routinely assumed to have enviable physiques.

Social media and blogs are also important in this regard for women. For instance, Erike Nicole Kendall's highly popular website, *A Black Girl's Guide to Weight Loss*, includes the article 'How to Survive a Zombie Invasion'.[73] Echoing many of the discourses discussed previously, Kendall stresses the ability to run, jump, fight and carry; when the zombie attack arrives, she wants to 'be able to run consistently for a mile straight without needing to take breaks along the way'.[74] As is typically the case, Kendall's fitness article juxtaposes the fictitious zombie threat with the desire to develop a certain kind of body. Though done humorously, she nevertheless implores women to train so that they can protect their own lives or those of their loved ones when faced with danger.

Weight training and dedication are part of this regimen. Where male fitness articles promote a specific kind of male body, fitness articles for women prove vaguer on this point. Aside from one article on *Fit Bottomed Girls*, female exercise programmes generally emphasise strength and speed without the mention of specific body parts.[75] Despite this vagueness, these writings, like their more mainstream counterparts, stress the importance of slenderness for women. Unlike men, women are not encouraged to build up large amounts of muscle, but rather to ensure that they build strength. Less attention is placed on visible muscularity, but rather with an implicit ability to use strength when necessary is promoted. Heywood argues that during the 1990s female muscularity, taken to its extreme form in female bodybuilding, is often a subversive process, which destabilises traditional standards for male and female bodies.[76] The 'overweight' body is perceived as undesirable or unhelpful – as demonstrated in Ms Maccow's zombie-inspired transformation. In films like *Resident Evil* or *Dawn of the Dead*, the obese zombie is often presented as monstrous. Likewise, female muscularity is downplayed. Even *Resident Evil* workouts promote slender, as opposed to muscular, bodies.[77] Female fitness articles have privileged a female body that, although implicitly or potentially powerful, is defined primarily by its slenderness.

While tempting to view such discourses as totalising or dehumanising – a form of zombiism – recent work on physical culture highlights the manner in which physical exercise can be transformative.[78] Despite stressing the often religious-infused ethos underpinning the disciplinary regimes of many fitness programmes, Michelle Mary Lelwica discusses how physical exercise, and bodily transformation, can help individuals develop a new sense of selfhood.[79] Loïc Wacquant's ethnographic account of boxing in inner-city Chicago highlights how physical exercise opens a dialogue with one's own body.[80] Furthering this line of enquiry, Broderick Chow, in his study on weightlifting, cites a form of personal salvation, liberation and expression through the routinised forms of exercise discussed above.[81] Where the gender tropes within these articles are often seen as dehumanising, the zombie-inspired workout may also be transformative. Zombies, despite their fictitious danger, may also mean real salvation for some.

Conclusion

In 2017, Chris Longridge expressed dismay with the rise of zombie movies, books and other products in popular culture: Had the time not come, he wondered, for zombies to die off?[82] The continued popularity of the genre suggests that zombies will remain *living* undead figures in popular media for the foreseeable future. This sustained presence necessitates a greater engagement by scholars with the symbolic and material importance of the zombie. Zombies, by nature, are rarely depicted engaging in health and fitness practices but this has not stopped a stream of videos, articles and books on the importance of human strength and endurance during a zombie attack.

The physicality, and indeed the growing physicality, of the zombie, has prompted a flurry of zombie workouts in recent years. Consequently, workouts specifically designed to survive a zombie apocalypse often critique a Western lifestyle defined by its debilitating comfort; these comforts of modernity have been criticised for enfeebling individuals. Tackling these perceived ills, zombies have reinforced traditional tropes regarding muscular male bodies and slender female ones. For a cohort often defined by its incessant desire for brains, zombies have much to provide about the healthy, or unhealthy, body.

Notes

1. Melissa Campbell, 'Survival Rules of Zombieland: Finals Edition', *The Odyssey* (2016), https://www.theodysseyonline.com/survival-rules-of-zombieland-finals-edition (accessed 11 May 2019).
2. Christina Couch, 'Zombie Workout: Get Fit Enough to Fit the Undead', *Wired.com* (2010), https://www.wired.com/2010/05/st-zombie-workout/ (accessed 29 April 2019).
3. Andy McDermott, 'The Zombie Apocalypse Survival Workout', *Muscle and Fitness* (2015), https://www.muscleandfitness.com/workouts/workout-routines/zombie-apocalypse-survival-workout (accessed 15 April 2019); Christian Thibaudeau and Chris Shugart, 'The Zombie Apocalypse Workout: Train to be Prepared for Anything', *T-Nation* (2015), https://www.t-nation.com/workouts/zombie-apocalypse-workout (accessed 29 April 2019); Tom Banham, 'How to Survive the Apocalypse', *Men's Health* (2016), https://www.menshealth.com/uk/adventure/a749837/how-to-survive-the-apocalypse/ (accessed 22 May 2019).
4. Naomi Alderman, 'There's No Morality in Exercise: I'm a Fat Person and Made a Successful Fitness App', *Medium* (2015), https://medium.com/matter/i-really-love-my-fat-body-eca64ca3ec78 (accessed 11 April 2019).
5. David Fear, 'Zombie Apocalypse Now: "Night of the Living Dead" at 50', *Rolling Stone* (2018), https://www.rollingstone.com/movies/movie-features/night-of-the-living-dead-50-anniversary-730207/ (accessed 18 May 2019).
6. Rikk Mulligan, 'Zombie Apocalypse: Plague and the End of the World in Popular Culture', in Karolyn Kinane and Michael A. Ryan (eds), *End of Days:*

Essays on the Apocalypse from Antiquity to Modernity (Jefferson: McFarland, 2009), pp. 349–68.
7. Michael Newbury, 'Fast Zombie/Slow Zombie: Food Writing, Horror Movies, and Agribusiness Apocalypse', *American Literary History*, 24/1 (2012), 87–114.
8. Peter Dendle, 'The Zombie as Barometer of Cultural Anxiety', in Niall Scott (ed.), *Monsters and the Monstrous: Myths and Metaphors of Enduring Evil* (Amsterdam: Brill Rodopi, 2007), pp. 545–57.
9. Campbell, 'Survival Rules of Zombieland'.
10. Michael O'Hearn, *Zombies vs. Mummies: Clash of the Living Dead* (Mankato: Capstone Press, 2011); Teejay LeCapois, *Vampire's Guide to the Zombie Apocalypse* (North Carolina: Lulu, 2019).
11. Max Brooks, *The Zombie Survival Guide: Complete Protection from the Living Dead* (New York: Broadway Books, 2003), p. 30.
12. Colson Whitehead, *Zone One* (New York: Anchor, 2012), p. 241.
13. Shelly McKenzie, *Getting Physical: The Rise of Fitness Culture in America* (Kansas: University Press of Kansas, 2013).
14. *Linnea Quigley's Horror Workout*, dir. Kenneth J. Hall, Fright Film Factory (1990).
15. Rebecca W. Black, 'Access and Affiliation: The Literacy and Composition Practices of English-Language Learners in an Online Fanfiction Community', *Journal of Adolescent & Adult Literacy*, 49/2 (2005), 118–28.
16. Christian Thibaudeau, 'Refined Physique Transformation: What if I Had to Do It All Over Again', *T-Nation* (2007), https://www.t-nation.com/workouts/refined-physique-transformation (accessed 23 May 2019).
17. 'Zombie Nutritionist Recommends All-Brain Diet', *The Onion* (2002), https://www.theonion.com/zombie-nutritionist-recommends-all-brain-diet-1819566596 (accessed 2 May 2019).
18. See n. 3.
19. Roger Lawson, 'The Zombie Apocalypse: Friends Don't Let Friends Get Eaten', *Rog Law Fitness* (2012), http://roglawfitness.com/zombie-apocalypse-survival-workout/ (accessed 2 April 2019).
20. Alderman, 'There's No Morality in Exercise'; Courtney Ryan, 'At Zombie Races, It's Survival of the Undeadest', *The New York Times* (2013), https://www.nytimes.com/2013/08/01/fashion/at-zombie-races-its-survival-of-the-undeadest.html (accessed 23 May 2019).
21. Leslie Heywood, 'We're in This Together: Neoliberalism and the Disruption of the Coach/Athlete Hierarchy in CrossFit', *Sports Coaching Review*, 5/1 (2016), 116–29.

22. 'FAQ', *Zombie Experiences UK* (2019), *http://zombieexperiences.co.uk/frequently-asked-questions/* (7 June 2019).
23. Susan G. Beckham and Michael Harper, 'Functional Training: Fad or Here to Stay?', *ACSM's Health & Fitness Journal*, 14/6 (2010), 24–30.
24. Wolfgang Muno, 'Winter Is Coming? *Game of Thrones* and Realist Thinking', in Ulrich Hamenstädt (ed.), T*he Interplay between Political Theory and Movies* (Cham: Springer, 2019), pp. 135–49.
25. Norman Vance, 'Decadence from Belfast to Byzantium', *New Literary History*, 35/4 (2004), 563–72.
26. Charlotte Macdonald, *Strong, Beautiful and Modern: National Fitness in Britain, New Zealand, Australia and Canada, 1935–1960* (Vancouver: UBC Press, 2013), p. 27.
27. Joan Tumblety, 'Rethinking the Fascist Aesthetic: Mass Gymnastics, Political Spectacle and the Stadium in 1930s France', *European History Quarterly*, 43/4 (2013), 707–30.
28. William J. Stone, 'Physical Activity and Health: Becoming Mainstream', *Complementary Health Practice Review*, 9/2 (2004), 118–28.
29. Stephen Corbett et al., 'The Transition to Modernity and Chronic Disease: Mismatch and Natural Selection', *Nature Reviews Genetics*, 19 (2018), 419–30.
30. John Romaniello, 'The End is About to Begin' (2012), *http://romanfitnesssystems.com/articles/zombie-apocalypse/* (accessed 2 May 2019).
31. Alderman, 'There's No Morality in Exercise'.
32. Alderman, 'There's No Morality in Exercise'.
33. See Jon Stratton, 'Zombie Trouble: Zombie Texts, Bare Life and Displaced People', *European Journal of Cultural Studies*, 14/3 (2011), 265–81.
34. Ryan, 'At Zombie Races, It's Survival of the Undeadest'.
35. Matthew D. Lamb and Cory Hillman, 'Whiners Go Home: Tough Mudder, Conspicuous Consumption, and the Rhetorical Proof of Fitness', *Communication & Sport*, 3/1 (2015), 81–99.
36. Ryan, 'At Zombie Races, It's Survival of the Undeadest'.
37. Sarah Juliet Lauro and Karen Embry, 'A Zombie Manifesto: The Nonhuman Condition in the Era of Advanced Capitalism', *boundary 2*, 35/1 (2008), 85–108.
38. Ryan, 'At Zombie Races, It's Survival of the Undeadest'.
39. Adam Dachis, 'Zombies, Run! Turns Your Exercise Routine into a Game of Survival', *LifeHacker* (2012), *https://lifehacker.com/zombies-run-turns-your-exercise-routine-into-a-game-o-5892625* (accessed 15 April 2019).
40. Ali S. Khan, 'Run For Your Lives', *CDC.com* (2012), *https://blogs.cdc.gov/public healthmatters/2012/03/run-for-your-lives/* (accessed 13 May 2019).

41. 'Zombie Escape at Panic Point 5k Run to Attract 1,850 Participants', *NCHeadlines* (2012), *https://www.ncheadlines.com/releases/zombie-escape-at-panic-point-5k-mud-run-to-attract-1850-participants* (accessed 15 April 2019).
42. Jamie Crawford, 'Pentagon Document Lays Out Battle Plan Against Zombies', *CNN* (2014), *https://www.cnn.com/2014/05/16/politics/pentagon-zombie-apocalypse/* (accessed 12 May 2019).
43. Jerred Moon, 'Are You Fit Enough to Survive a Zombie Apocalypse?', *End of Three Fitness* (2012), *http://www.endofthreefitness.com/are-you-fit-enough-to-survive-a-zombie-apocalypse/* (accessed 11 May 2019).
44. Moon, 'Are You Fit Enough to Survive a Zombie Apocalypse?'.
45. Heywood, 'We're in This Together'.
46. Heywood, 'We're in This Together'.
47. Thibaudeau and Shugart, 'The Zombie Apocalypse Workout'.
48. Marcelle C. Dawson, 'CrossFit: Fitness Cult or Reinventive Institution?', *International Review for the Sociology of Sport*, 52/3 (2017), 361–79.
49. 'The Zombie WODS', *ZombieWODS.com* (2019), *http://thezombiewods.com* (accessed 25 May 2019).
50. Yvonne Tasker, *Spectacular Bodies: Gender, Genre and the Action Cinema* (Abingdon: Routledge, 2012).
51. Bryan McCullick et al., 'Butches, Bullies and Buffoons: Images of Physical Education Teachers in the Movies', *Sport, Education and Society*, 8/1 (2003), 3–16.
52. Tasker, *Spectacular Bodies*, pp. 109–31.
53. Heather Addison, *Hollywood and the Rise of Physical Culture* (Abingdon: Routledge, 2003); Nick Jones, *Hollywood Action Films and Spatial Theory* (Abingdon: Routledge, 2015), pp. 6–7.
54. Campbell, 'Survival Rules of Zombieland'.
55. Tasker, *Spectacular Bodies*.
56. Robert W. Connell and James W. Messerschmidt, 'Hegemonic Masculinity: Rethinking the Concept', *Gender & Society*, 19/6 (2005), 829–59; Demetrakis Z. Demetriou, 'Connell's Concept of Hegemonic Masculinity: A Critique', *Theory and Society*, 30/3 (2001), 337–61.
57. Shari L. Dworkin and Faye Linda Wachs, *Body Panic: Gender, Health, and the Selling of Fitness* (New York: New York University Press, 2009).
58. HybridAthlete, 'Fitness for the Zombie Apocalypse', *HybridAthlete.com (2017)*, *https://thehybridathlete.com/zombies-eat-fat-people/* (accessed 17 May 2019).
59. NerdFitness, 'How to Survive a Zombie Apocalypse', *NerdFitness* (2011), *https://www.nerdfitness.com/blog/how-to-survive-a-zombie-apocalypse/* (accessed 2 May 2019).

60. *NerdFitness*, 'How to Survive a Zombie Apocalypse'.
61. Pete McCall, 'How Can I Physically Prepare for a Zombie Apocalypse', *Ace Fitness* (2012), https://www.acefitness.org/education-and-resources/lifestyle/blog/2940/how-can-i-physically-prepare-for-a-zombie-apocalypse (accessed 15 April 2019).
62. Thibaudeau and Shugart, 'The Zombie Apocalypse Workout'.
63. Thibaudeau and Shugart, 'The Zombie Apocalypse Workout'.
64. Robert A. Nye, 'Western Masculinities in War and Peace', *The American Historical Review*, 112/2 (2007), 417–38.
65. Jeff Cavaliere, '8 Best Exercises for the Zombie Apocalypse (Be Ready!)', *YouTube.com* (2016), https://www.youtube.com/watch?v=1i3bU5zV8sI (accessed 14 May 2019).
66. Cavaliere, '8 Best Exercises for the Zombie Apocalypse (Be Ready!)'.
67. Bennet Goldstein, 'I've been Fitbit by a Zombie', *Telegraph Herald* (2018), http://www.telegraphherald.com/news/features/article_17b4dc65-94b6-51b0-a768-c5e56c79e990.html (accessed 2 April 2019).
68. Jeffrey A. Brown, 'Gender and the Action Heroine: Hardbodies and the Point of No Return', *Cinema Journal* (1996), 52–71.
69. Leslie Heywood, *Bodymakers: A Cultural Anatomy of Women's Body Building* (New Brunswick: Rutgers University Press, 1998), p. 49.
70. 'Milla Jovovich Workout Routine and Diet Plan: Train like Leeloo, Alice, The Blood Queen and Artemis', SuperheroJacked.com (2019), http://superherojacked.com/2019/04/11/milla-jovovich-workout/ (accessed 14 April 2019).
71. 'Claire Redfield Workout Routine: Train like the Resident Evil TerraSave Member', *SuperheroJacked.com* (2019), http://superherojacked.com/2019/04/02/claire-redfield-workout/ (accessed 12 May 2019).
72. Katy Winter, 'Obese Mother Lost Nearly SEVEN STONE after She Became a Fan of TV Show *The Walking Dead* and Wanted to be Fit Enough to Survive a Zombie Apocalypse', *MailOnline* (2014), https://www.dailymail.co.uk/femail/article-2821666/Obese-mother-lost-nearly-SEVEN-STONE-fan-TV-Walking-Dead-wanted-fit-survive-zombie-apocalypse.html (accessed 11 April 2019).
73. Erike Nicole Kendall, 'How to Survive a Zombie Invasion', *A Black Girl's Guide to Weight Loss* (2011), https://blackgirlsguidetoweightloss.com/exercise-101/how-to-survive-a-zombie-invasion/ (accessed 12 May 2019).
74. Kendall, 'How to Survive a Zombie Invasion'.
75. Erin Whitehead, 'Workout I Did: The Zombie Apocalypse Workout', *Fit Bottomed Girls* (2014), https://fitbottomedgirls.com/author/erin-whitehead/ (accessed 5 May 2019).
76. Heywood, *Bodymakers*.

77. See nn. 71 and 72.
78. Pirkko Markula, 'The Technologies of the Self: Sport, Feminism, and Foucault', *Sociology of Sport Journal*, 20/2 (2003), 87–107.
79. Michelle Mary Lelwica, *Shameful Bodies: Religion and the Culture of Physical Improvement* (New York: Bloomsbury Publishing, 2017).
80. Loïc Wacquant, *Body & Soul* (Oxford: Oxford University Press, 2004).
81. Broderick D. V. Chow, 'A Professional Body: Remembering, Repeating and Working out Masculinities in fin-de-siècle Physical Culture', *Performance Research*, 20/5 (2015), 30–41.
82. Chris Longridge, 'Why Zombies Have Taken Over Pop Culture', *DigitalSpy* (2017), *https://www.digitalspy.com/tv/a827385/why-zombies-have-taken-over-pop-culture/* (accessed 26 May 2019).

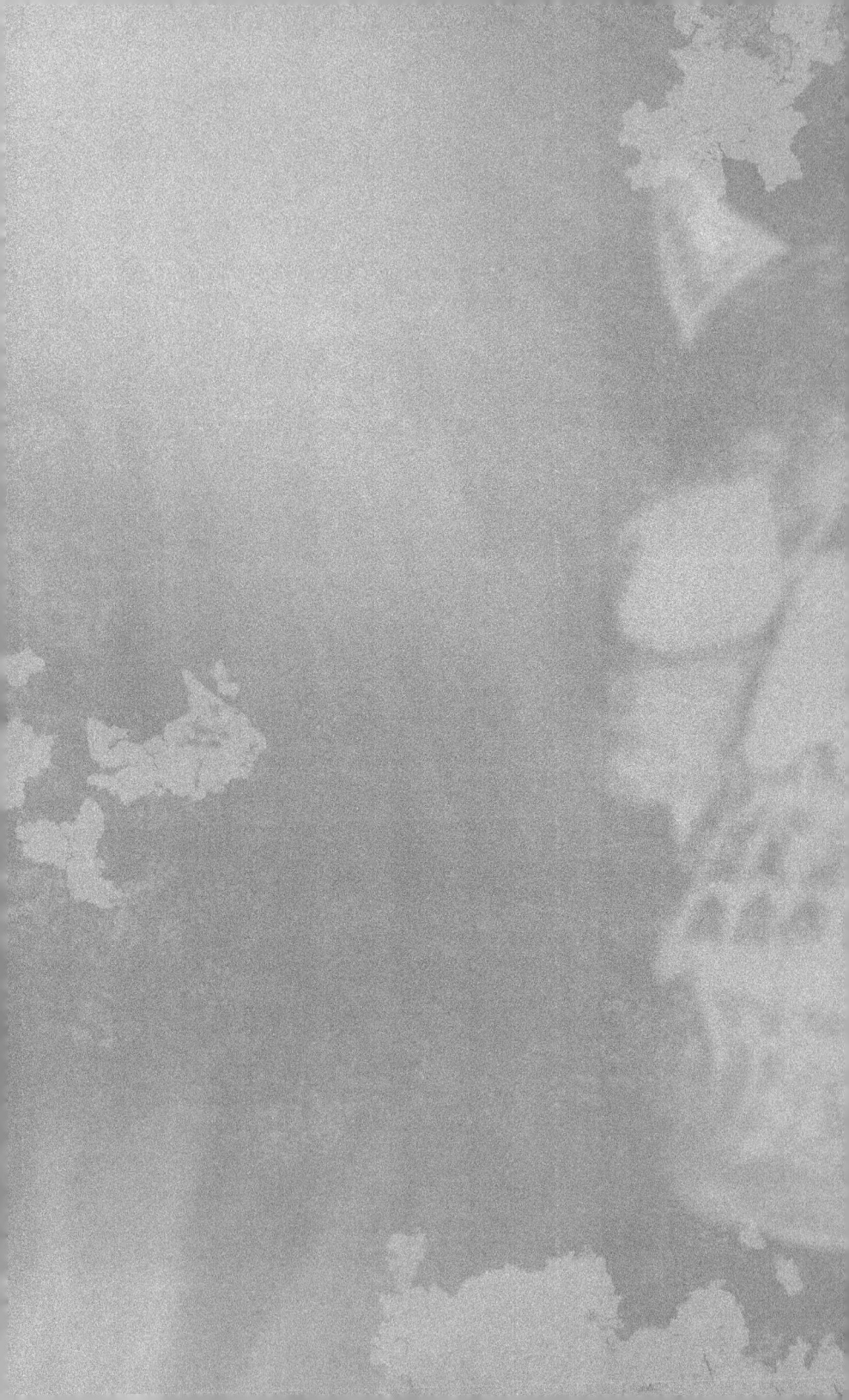

3

Abject Bodies and Borders

What Zombies and Porn Indicate about Sex, Stigma and Society

Caroline West

ZOMBIISM, IN THIS CHAPTER, addresses the impact of the zombie on borders, and both porn and zombies function as borders in the battle to maintain socially accepted expressions of sex and sexuality. Framing the abject body as erotic, zombie porn offers a space to critique social norms and the pornified body's place in society, narratives of disgust, necrophilia and gendered iterations of the monstrous. The transgressive corporeality of zombies is also embodied by the porn performer, and this chapter examines how fear is weaponised to maintain the futile illusion of a non-porous boundary between 'good' sex and 'bad' sex. While the zombie apocalypse is generally depicted as sexless in mainstream films, zombie porn unrepentantly portrays excessive, contaminating sex. This chapter thus argues that zombie porn and the zombie mouth and vagina function as liminal spaces that have the potential to contaminate societies.

The zombie porn genre features titles such as *Porn of the Dead* (2006), *Night of the Giving Head* (2008), *Otto; or Up with Dead People* (2008) and *L.A. Zombie* (2010). The latter two are written as socio-political commentary on gay communities by American director Bruce LaBruce. The former two function as direct parodies of the original film on which they are based. The undisputed queen of zombie porn is Joanna Angel, whose *oeuvre* of zombie films include *Evil Head* (2012) and *The Walking Head* (2013).

All the above examples have varying degrees of commitment to storylines and make-up, with some expending minimal production effort and others featuring prosthetics and full body make-up and an attempt at following the plot of the original film that they are parodying. *Evil Head* parodies the 1981 cult classic *The Evil Dead* (written and directed by Sam Raimi). But while zombie porn films are a niche within the mainstream porn industry and do not seem to have found mainstream success, Laura Helen Marks suggests that they provide an opportunity to explore the division between socially acceptable sex and sex that is framed as disgusting, offensive, or potentially corrupts viewers.[1] The sexualised zombie body, as personified by actors like Angel, challenges the borders between safe sex and dangerous sex, and cinematic concoctions of abjection, sex and fantasy combine to challenge societal norms.

Borders

Porn has historically operated mutually with stigma and fear from, particularly, the fields of medicine and sexology in the nineteenth and twentieth centuries.[2] Those who engaged in both consuming and working in porn were pathologised and subjected to stigmatisation. In *Thinking Sex*, Gayle Rubin calls for a radical theory of sex and outlines how stigma arises from societal hierarchies of what is considered 'good sex' and 'bad sex', and she utilises the concept of a 'charmed circle' (fig.1) to illustrate this distinction.[3]

In the centre of the circle, Rubin places sex that is married, heterosexual, monogamous and occurs for free in the private sphere, with no toys or accessories. These acts are acceptable sexual activities. The outer circle is designated as the outer limits, where certain sexualities and sex acts are deemed to be deviant, and something to be avoided by 'respectable' members of society. These activities consist of being promiscuous, BDSM, public sex acts, using toys, selling sex for money or making/consuming pornography. In this category of 'bad, abnormal, unnatural, damned sexuality', stigma is applied to participants, and they are excluded from 'blessed sexuality' and respectability as 'bad' sexual acts are viewed as utterly repulsive and devoid of all emotional nuance.[4]

Figure 1. Rubin's Charmed Circle.

Rubin argues that those engaging in acts relegated to the outer limits were viewed as 'socially inferior, or symptomatic of psychological impairment', and far outside the realm of respectability.[5] The line between these two categories of 'good' and 'bad' is enforced by society, lest one may fall prey to the deviance flourishing in the outer limits. This sexual value system perpetuates fear – what Rubin terms a 'domino theory of sexual peril' – and thus a strict line must protect the good people engaged in the correct acts.[6] Rubin suggests that: 'The line appears to stand between sexual order and chaos. It expresses the fear that if anything is permitted to cross this erotic demilitarised zone, the barrier against scary sex will crumble and *something unspeakable* will skitter across.'[7]

This fear of the unspeakable is also a fear of the power attributed to the outer limits and how easily this unspeakable *thing* can corrupt the 'good' people. This line is also the partition between pleasure and disgust, and a universalistic approach versus a particularist, nuanced reading of sexual behaviour. The fear of alleged deviancy has historically co-existed with porn in various guises. Zombie porn, considered in this context of unspeakable fear, is firmly in the furthest reaches of the outer limits, a place where even those who view or perform in mainstream porn themselves might disavow or view with disgust. The pornified zombie embodies this unspeakable *thing*. While Rubin argues that the fear around sex creates 'demons and boogiemen', zombie porn relishes literal boogieman status, transforming disgust into desire.[8]

The transformation of disgust into desire is apparent in *Evil Head*. Parodying the horror film *Evil Dead*, the male protagonist Ash fights to protect himself from three female zombies. He kills them, buries them and marks their graves with a cross; however, as they re-emerge and shamble towards him, he continues to fight back until his clothes are removed and Linda begins performing fellatio. At this point Ash gives into pleasure, abandoning his recent feelings of terror in favour of desire. Ash has sex with all three zombies in an outdoor setting while the zombies also interact sexually with each other, breaking several rules of what acceptable sex is purported to be. Ash is no longer a helpless victim, but an active agent in depravity. The depiction of zombies here expands zombiism to explore the concept of sexual borders within society.

The hierarchy of porn assumes another dimension when considering zombie porn, which firmly relishes its deviant status with no nods to glamour or pretence at desire to be considered high class erotica. Zombie porn delights in its taboo status. Peter Wagner highlights how taboo is an essential element of porn, stating that the definition of porn should be 'the written or visual presentation in realistic form of any genital or sexual behaviour with a deliberate violation of existing and widely accepted moral and social taboos'.[9] Zombie porn is a taboo within a taboo which may add an extra frisson to the experience. Zombie porn contests the borders regulating pleasure, sex and death in a way that mainstream porn often avoids. Death is overtly depicted in *Evil Head* as Linda is decapitated and buried, an element of on-screen violence that even aggressive pornography dares not depict.

Due to its abject nature, zombie porn redraws the boundaries between human and nonhuman, but also agitates the boundaries of pleasure and sex.[10] The foursome scene in *Evil Head* encapsulates the refusal to stay within the boundaries of what is socially acceptable desire and what are socially acceptable desirable bodies. David McNally argues that zombies celebrate the grotesque realism of the body and reject the anticorporeal approach from mainstream society to the body and rigid beauty standards.[11] However, the body of the female performer may conform to standardised Western beauty norms, but in zombie porn they are depicted as dead and decaying bodies and framed as a source of arousal. Zombie porn, then, allows for transgressive sex appeal to become explicit which functions as a place to critique accepted norms of sex and beauty in mainstream society.

Gender

Gender plays a distinct role when considering monsters and sex. Barbara Creed explains that throughout history women have been viewed as monstrous. They have been viewed as both corrupt and corruptors, as women's 'monstrosity constitutes a moral deviation which leads to monstrous deeds'.[12] Margaret Shildrick claims that '[m]onsters . . . [l]ike women . . . refuse to stay in place: they change shape, they combine elements which should remain separate'.[13]

The transformative nature of the monster also highlights the evasive and perpetually transformative nature of the porn industry. Transgressive adaptability in zombie porn combines sex, blood, horror, death and decay, defying the social dictation that these should remain separate. Distinct parallels exist between the leaky body of the woman and the leaky body of the zombie. Both leaky bodies are combined in zombie porn to produce the monstrous pornified body with the potential to contaminate others both physically and mentally.

The female zombie further represents this dual fear of becoming monstrous and creating monsters through a disruption of the womb or contamination. The womb and vagina as a source of fear has been reflected in Freud's work on the fear of castration and portrayed as such in Hollywood films such as *Teeth* (2007), which addresses the myth of vagina dentata and the woman as castrator. In *Evil Head*, the male performer Ash must cut his hand off with a chainsaw after he tries to finger a zombie's vagina and his hand becomes possessed. The lure of the zombie vagina proves too powerful for men in zombie films, who, even after dismemberment, continue to have sex. This type of dismemberment is also seen in *Porn of the Dead*, where a female zombie bites off a penis and a finger, and finally disembowels a man after sex. The risk of this occurring does not appear to have been considered by the male protagonist; instead, he is reduced to thinking only about satisfying his desire to explore this monstrous vagina.

Kyle Christensen examines the lure of the zombie mouth and the lure of castration, positing that this allure might be a repetitive compulsion.[14] He suggests that zombie sex toys also reveal this compulsion for castration; or, at the very least, the compulsion to explore this imagined risk of trauma. Fellatio can often be violent in mainstream pornography, but in zombie porn there is a reversal of the potentiality of violence. Christensen emphasises the importance of 'zombie orality' depicted in horror films, and oral violence is very much present in films such as *Porn of the Dead*.[15]

The mouth is a liminal space and traditionally treated with violence in mainstream porn, but in zombie porn the potential for violence is returned to the female zombie as she takes the fleshy human penis in her dangerous mouth. A receptacle in mainstream porn, the mouth in zombie porn becomes a space of danger and desire. Christensen outlines how this violent-erotic dichotomy materialises in zombie sex toys such as the Fleshlight toy. Christensen's 'monstrous orality' serves as a useful point to analyse how the mouth is a source of violence and violation in both porn and zombie porn. While vampires in porn also engage in violent-erotic orality, the zombie makes this violence and potential castration more overt and saturates the interaction with sexual body fluids.

Christensen's examines how the zombie Fleshlight toy removes the visibility of the ejaculation, and indeed the penis itself, suggesting that 'figurative castration' is made invisible by the toy. Regarding fellatio in zombie porn, figurative castration is prominent in *Porn of the Dead*. Each time the penis disappears inside the zombie's mouth the potential result is its permanent disappearance, and yet the erotic drive overrides the death drive.

Monstrous female desire was infamously demonstrated in the porn film *The World's Biggest Gang Bang* (1999) starring Annabel Chong, who had sex with 251 men. Chong had participated in the film to demonstrate powerful female sexuality, and states, 'We're not wilting violets, we're not victims, for Christ's sake. Female sexuality is as aggressive as male sexuality. I wanted to take on the role of the stud. The more [partners], the better.'[16] Like the insatiable zombie looking for brains, Chong's quest to have sex with more and more partners was greeted with shock, disgust and rejection from both society and the mainstream porn industry who judged her for unsafe sexual practices. Chong became the abject, rejected by peers, colleagues and society who disavowed her as they would the zombie, protecting their social order from her transgressive corporeality. Chong's face mid-sex was also depicted as monstrous, contorted with either pain or pleasure, a reminder of the pornified zombie face also contorted in death and desire.

Gender also plays a part in regard to men, monsters and borders. Creed argues that:

> The male monster 'disturbs identity, system, order'. It does not 'respect borders, positions, rules'. He embraces meaninglessness and self-annihilation. There is no concomitant desire for a return

to normality or re-affirmation of the symbolic on the part of the monster. He is the point where meaning collapses. This gives rise to a sense of meaningless horror, sometimes registered by the cry not of the victim but of the monster himself... the male monster embodies the 'limit of interpretation'.[17]

The undead zombie forces death on the living but the sexualised zombie also forces death upon socially sanctioned sex, romance and gentle sex. In *Evil Head*, Linda is insatiable in her quest for sex with Ash, her monstrous desire being literal and figurative in her zombie state. With zombie porn, death consumes the living, but it also consumes and transforms sex into an act that does not have a place in the established social order. Without sex, a complete picture of social norms and transgressions cannot be achieved.

The pornified zombie becomes uncanny when engaging in more familiar porn acts. Linda was Ash's girlfriend when alive; the sex they have when she is a zombie is somewhat familiar to their previous sex life but made strange through her zombification. The zombie retains a human-esque appearance, albeit with missing parts or open wounds; this uncanny confrontation with this human-like creature 'evokes fear, unease, disquiet and gloom'.[18] Sex mixed with horror becomes even more abject. Zombie porn disrupts depictions of formulaic sex: the sexual scripts seen in mainstream porn are also present but rendered monstrously uncanny.

Abjection

Both the zombie and the porn performer, in breach of socially sanctioned sexual norms, are expelled as outcasts. Marginalisation is necessary to maintain borders, society and meaning as according to Creed, 'the constitution of acceptable forms of subjectivity and sociality demands the expulsion of those things defined as improper and unclean. Whatever is expelled is constituted as an abject, that which "disturbs identity, system, order".[19] What disgusts one person has appeal for another. Sex, then, is as unruly as the zombie. Subjectivity is challenged by sexual borders that cannot contain these horrors.

Julia Kristeva argues that those who seek to solidify their identity by creating an impenetrable border between themselves and the abject are doomed to fail:

A crucial aspect of the abject is, however, that it can never be fully removed or set apart from the subject of society; the abject both threatens and beckons. The abject constitutes the other side of seemingly stable subjectivity, 'beseeches, worries, and fascinates desire'.[20]

This mix of horror and desire challenges the meanings safely attached to sex, and zombie sex creates a hinterland of new meaning to explore. A proverbial pandora's box is offered by zombie porn which may be too abject for some to apprehend; others may be aroused by the fact that zombie porn allows for meaning to become more malleable and fluid. Ash, for example, attempts to fight his desire for the zombies but quickly gives in to this new form of sex.

Kristeva asserts that the abject is neither subject nor object, and this uncertainty is unsettling for those who assert that sexuality is stable. This breakdown of subjectivity is where zombie porn flourishes. Porn takes what a person has learnt about sex from their parents, society, sex education, mainstream media, and twists it into graphic spectacle. However, zombie porn makes this spectacle even more grotesque, refusing to shy away from the animal nature of the body and its clear statement that decay and death await everyone. Zombie porn is a reminder of mortality, in a way that mainstream porn does not address. The draw of mainstream porn is the suggestion that sex is endless, available at every opportunity, and every orifice is a source of pleasure. In zombie porn those same orifices are used to kill both humans and zombies but also as a reminder to the viewer of the inevitability of decay, the rotting body that awaits after death. However, death in zombie porn does not mean the end of sex as it continues to exist, unsettling attempts at a closure of the sexual life and the body's lifecycle. Those orifices are also a point of no return: after sex with a zombie in *Porn of the Dead*, an orderly is killed and disembowelled post-coitus, and another man has his penis bitten off after oral sex with a zombie. The lure of death, or at the very least castration, proves to be tied closely to desire and offers a space for the viewer to safely explore these abject concepts from the safety of the screen.

Necrophilia

While kink and fetish are in the outer limits in Rubin's charmed circle theory, societal changes have meant that books and films such as *50 Shades of Grey* have changed the status of fetish as an automatic pariah sexuality.

However, some paraphilias, such as paedophilia, remain banished to the outer limits. Alongside paedophilia, necrophilia is unlikely to improve its standing in society soon.

In mainstream zombie films the zombie is utterly devoid of sexuality, such is the taboo of necrophilia. However, porn rejoices in taboo. Consequently, the necrophile completely disrupts the border between acceptable sex and socially unaccepted sex.

Erich Fromm defines necrophilia as:

> Necrophilia in the characterological sense can be described as the passionate attraction to all that is dead, decayed, putrid, sickly; it is the passion to transform that which is alive into something unalive; to destroy for the sake of destruction; the exclusive interest in all that is purely mechanical. It is the passion to tear apart living structures.[21]

This passion allows the border between 'good'/'bad' sex to be disintegrated further with zombie porn. Fromm's theory of necrophilia posits that as human society becomes more mechanised, it turns away from life towards death. As individual lives are increasingly mediated through technology, unsurprisingly the porn that is readily available also turns towards death. Zombie porn flirts with the death instinct to disassemble the porous border between eros, life and stable sexuality, and instead offers a place to disband taboo and explore sex and desire without the pressure to decide to act on desires such as necrophilia.

As porn allows viewers to explore beyond socially accepted sexual activity, necrophilia allows its practitioners to explore the body beyond the concrete nature of death. Supervert argues that the necrophile does not preach the immortality of the soul but does deny the finality of death.[22] For the necrophile, the decomposing body is thus not something to recoil from in horror, but an entity to explore and position as a sexual object just as a living body may be for non-necrophiles. Usually, the corpse is stripped of desire and is an object that survival instincts result in avoidance for fear of contamination. However, in zombie porn this avoidance is absent. For example, even when Ash's contaminated infected hand must be removed, he still does not recoil from the zombie and potentially further contamination. Kristeva postulates that the corpse is the ultimate form of abjection, the 'most sickening of wastes . . . a border that has encroached upon everything'.[23] In zombie porn, the corpse is devoid of the self, the 'I', a former living structure that once was acceptable but is now monstrous and ready to sexually corrupt others.

For anti-porn writer Joe Parker, the porn viewer, the consumer of the sex industry, is the abject object, and compares them to necrophilies:

> Necrophiles . . . take pleasure in filth, degradation, and destruction. They are the users of the sick, the old, the psychotic, the brain damaged, the 'tracked' and tattooed casualties of the sex industry who are in the end stages of their lives. For necrophiles, broken bodies and broken minds are a turn on. They glory in their superiority over ruined human beings and feel entitled to express their contempt in every way.[24]

Here, the porn viewer is the zombie, an unfeeling, unempathetic creature using living bodies as fodder for their needs. Parker has firmly placed the women in porn as victims that are 'broken', 'ruined', 'casualties' or mentally ill. This sweeping statement has the converse effect of dehumanising performers and placing them exclusively in 'victim' status, stripping any agency or differing individual experience from a singular 'truth' about the porn industry.

This theme of monsters and victims is repeated in the claims of anti-porn campaigners. Revelling in shock value, zombie porn might have more in common with anti-porn campaigns than previously thought. For those who oppose porn, zombie porn is an example of extreme content. Porn viewers for these theorists are framed as passive zombies themselves. Male porn performers are theorised to be empty, emotionless bodies who use female performers as tools to satisfy their urges. Gail Dines describes them as 'depicted as soulless, unfeeling, amoral life-support systems for erect penises', who do not make noise or communicate except for grunts when orgasming.[25]

Male viewers are considered innocents at risk of being tainted by porn: 'porn is actually being encoded into a boy's sexual identity so that an authentic sexuality . . . is replaced by a generic porn sexuality limited in creativity and lacking any sense of live, respect, or connection to another human being'.[26] This language also resembles the decaying zombie ready to corrupt and consume any innocents in its path. The destruction of the body is reflected in the emotive language used to describe the bodies in porn: 'boys are catapulted into a never-ending universe of ravaged anuses, distended vaginas, and semen-smeared faces'.[27] This statement portrays the female body in porn as broken and abject, a passive thing to use by the dominant performer: the zombified male performer uses the female performer for his own, and the audiences', needs. Jensen also draws parallels with zombies when he proclaims that porn is 'what the end of the world looks like'.[28]

The idea that sex and the female body is forever at risk of imminent invasion is reflected in the language surrounding porn. When former Irish Taoiseach Enda Kenny encouraged Ireland to have a national conversation on porn in 2016, he invoked this same fear: '[O]lder generations . . . just can't reach into those spheres where young minds are in some cases being tainted and corrupted by an avalanche of this kind of material.'[29] This consuming deadly 'avalanche' evokes the fear of the sexualised zombie, an innocent victim will be 'corrupted' by the boundary breakers of porn and this risk is imminent and enormous.

Clarissa Smith and Feona Attwood also challenge this positioning of male sexuality as being easily corruptible.[30] The fear of the male viewer being turned into a mindless consumer of flesh denies any agency on the part of the viewer and frames porn as a powerful entity that, like the zombie, taints everyone it encounters. This panic around the zombification of society through porn is not new, and the use of the ever-present danger label is a tool to attempt to reign in this fear. Smith and Attwood state that these

> panics about sex draw on narratives of danger, disease, and depravity to which 'we' are all susceptible and rely on the repetition of 'evocative sexual language and imagery' that urges 'us' to be vigilant at all times, both as members of communities and as individuals.[31]

This fear that sex – and porn – is lurking, ever ready to corrupt is a reminder of why people fear zombies. Gumpert argues that zombie fantasy distracts 'from a terrifying truth: we are all, potentially, zombies'.[32] Zombiism theorises about outbreaks in terms of viral outbreak, but also theorises an outbreak of 'bad' sex that will infect others as a phenomenon that unsettles sexual borders as well as geo-political borders. The pornified zombie weaponises the fear existing around sex. Rubin claims that this fear is omnipresent and that '[o]ur sexual system contains a vast vague pool of nameless horror'.[33] This nameless horror includes humanity's own mortality and inevitable rotting flesh.

George Romero's *Dawn of the Dead* (2004) epitomises the zombie as a narrative tool to critique consumerism. The sexualised zombie in porn also centres consumption, albeit through genitals instead of commercial goods. Capitalism in *Dawn of the Dead* is viewed differently from the narcissism of the porn zombie who only seeks to satisfy a sexual urge while the porn industry seeks to satisfy a financial urge. Uncontrollable and narcissistic sex has the potential to wreak as much havoc on society as a traditional zombie outbreak; however, this fear can also be virulent as sexual differences are dismantled in 'good' society.

Regarding gender in connection to necrophilia, female necrophilia is often not conceptualised in the same way that female porn viewers are often not conceptualised. Both Freud and Fromm assert that women could not be necrophiles, and, for a long time, studies on porn viewers excluded women. Corradino argues that this exclusion of women is due to men being viewed as active and women as passive in society, suggesting that 'female necrophilia not only transgresses the tabooing boundary between life and death, but it may also be considered a sexual deviancy from the normative gender role dialectics'.[34] The female performer occupies a space of dual transgression as she plays a human who has sex with a zombie and is both perceived as a necrophile and a stigmatised person for acting in porn, while the female performer who plays the zombie occupies three states of transgression: as a creature of horror, as an active subject and as a porn performer. The defilement of the body is the abject and within zombie porn defilement is an explicit selling point.

Disgust

Those who transgress these borders are subject to socio-moral disgust from those concerned about interpersonal contamination.[35] Disgust is a tool that maintains borders and both zombies and porn performers have been subject to both socio-moral disgust and physical disgust. Martha Nussbaum posits that disgust is a powerful weapon 'that helps maintain the sanctity of social order'.[36] She outlines how humans need another

> group of humans to bound [themselves] against, who will come to exemplify the boundary line between the truly human and the basely animal. If those quasi-animals stand between us and our own animality, then we are one step further away from being animal and mortal ourselves[37]

The pornified zombie troubles these boundaries, being both monstrous and humanesque. The porn performer is subject to this disgust as an entity that flouts social and sexual norms.

The relationship between an individual and society is described by Peter Berger and Thomas Luckmann as a 'dialectical' relationship that 'once crystalised, it is maintained, modified, or even reshaped by social relations'.[38] Subsequently, the identity of the performer can be impacted by society. The dominant episteme on porn can shape how society perceives the assumed identity of the performer and encapsulate them in a stigmatised identity that they then have to choose to accept or to fight against. The performer can be objectified through being subsumed into this collective identity of what a performer 'is', rather than being viewed as an individual with agency. To navigate the effects of stigma, the affected person can engage in identity work.[39] Identity work consists of the affected person adopting tactics to manage their self-identity and minimise impact on their self-esteem. Identity work in pornography can take several forms, from making a clear distinction between the performer's personality and their work persona, and disassociating themselves from performers who are deemed to be drug users or less than professional. Since zombie porn remains a niche category in the overall porn industry, performers may refuse to make this kind of content to separate themselves from the 'bad' kind of porn and the 'bad' kind of performer.

Blake Ashforth and Glen Kreiner argue that some jobs are seen as 'dirty' work, and pornography can be included in this classification.[40] The stigma attached to this so-called 'dirty work' can be threefold: physical, social or moral taints. Porn can be potentially tainted by all three categories. As the physical side in porn includes the use of the body and the incumbent risks with this (body fluids, injury and exposure of genitalia), porn performers experience all three forms of taints. The secretion of body fluids apparently makes stigma stickier, with the stigmata of this particular dirty work being saliva, semen and STIs. Zombie porn has the addition of blood, gore and open wounds, and thus faces increased stigma and feelings of disgust. Miller argues that disgust is about 'leakage and escape through skin, about permeation and penetration and with body fluids as part of the iconography of porn. Disgust is thus 'graphically displayed on the canvas of the body soaking.'[41] Zombiism constructs a binary between the intact, innocent body, and the decaying, infected zombie body; but zombie porn disrupts this binary by locating copulation and desire between these two entities.

The zombie itself cannot be rehabilitated as it cannot experience regret or empathy, and Ruthven claims that there is 'no room for sympathising with them, or falling in love with them. They must be slain or you risk becoming one of them.'[42] This projective disgust is a way to keep the border intact, and to keep both zombies and sex workers in the outer limits as a way of preserving the 'good' self. Miller outlines how disgust is 'fundamentally about protecting and maintaining the self', and while physical disgust protects us from disease, socio-moral disgust protects the sense of self and of having a 'normal' sexuality.

This rigidity is difficult for some people to bear. Miller suggests that disgust stems from 'our need to feel sound, the desire to believe we are good inside also is important (though less so, being a desire and not an absolute need). The desire for goodness likely derives from the need for soundness.'[43] However, that boundary may not always be solid, which provokes anxiety. Zombie porn exploits that anxiety and forces examination of the gaps in the border. The non-sexual zombie might dismantle physical barriers to get to its victim, but the pornified zombie manipulates and disrupts sexual categorical barriers. According to Shaka McGlotten and Sarah Vangundy zombies queer the process of reproduction and kinship while offering a space to critique society and capitalism.[44] They suggest that the zombie offers a space to reclaim what is considered to be perverse, and what is outside the boundaries of heteronormative sexuality. This liberatory stance offers potential, but still overlaps with anxiety around borders and identity.

Miller argues that the anxiety around stable readings of sexuality might actually be soothing in the long term:

> Hair-trigger disgust will protect the self from contamination but wizen it to physical and psychological skin and bones by allowing nothing in. An absence of disgust will degrade the self and end our access to resources reserved for the 'good' or so we fear. These are the challenges of intimacy and boundary.[45]

This fear can lead individuals to project their fears around sex in general and sex that they find disgusting. Examining the compulsive relationship between fear, sex and stigma, Carol Queen argues that this relationship is sexualised, and identifies, as erotophobia, a fear of sex reproduced over generations and linked to shame and disgust.[46] As much as a thin line separates love and hate, a precarious line appears to distinguish between sexual disgust and sexual arousal.

Saliva

The zombie mouth is not only a risk for castration, but it is a potential source of contamination through saliva. While saliva and spit are also part of the iconography of porn, spitting can be perceived to be a particularly violent act in society. Spit is a body fluid linked to disgust and disease. William Ian Miller argues that disgust is also linked to danger, stating that 'disgust must be accompanied by ideas of a particular kind of danger, the danger inherent in pollution and contamination, the danger of defilement'.[47] This follows with Rubin's claim that the line dividing 'good' sex and 'bad' sex protects us from danger and the fear that if the boundary is not maintained, danger will breach the boundary. Martha Nussbaum suggests that disgust is part of a denial of humanity, part of a politics of humanity.[48] Disgust is also linked to anxiety, that the disgust associated with the 'dirty' body will contaminate those on the good side of sex.

Daniel Kelly posits that disgust is also a response to the breaking of traditional social norms, and sex that is considered deviant is also perceived to be a 'disgust elicitor'.[49] The pornified zombie mouth is a disgust elicitor that can contribute to an outbreak of violence, disease and socially unacceptable sex.

Conclusion

Despite the transgressive nature of copulation between zombies and humans, the content of zombie porn conforms to the typical iconography of pornography.[50] Mainstream porn can be formulaic in the sexual acts depicted, with activity usually progressing from fellatio, vaginal penetration, anal penetration and an external cum shot. Zombie porn has overall not strayed greatly from this formula. Steve Jones identifies this adherence to conformity in his analysis of *Porn of the Dead* (2006), outlining that 'despite the deviance insinuated through overtones of necrophilia, the film still functions according to a hetero-sexed binary and appears to maintain, rather than challenge, normative ideologies'.[51] Jones suggests that sex is not actually radically transgressive in *Porn of the Dead*, because there is no zombie-zombie sex and no homosexuality which means that the mainstream porn formula is maintained. He wonders if zombies really exist in porn to change the social order of socially accepted sex, perhaps true zombie sex would be more radical instead of adhering to gender roles and formulas already established in mainstream porn.

Zombie porn does also contain allegories of sexual deviancy being punished and many of the humans lose bodies parts or are disembowelled after sex, and many of the zombies are killed post-coitus. While zombie porn offers a temporary dissolution of the borders governing sex and the body, the consequences of deviancy still function as a warning to stay within the charmed circle of sex – or risk death. Zombiism often tests borders that do not encompass the sexual self, and this gap misses an exploration of the amalgamation of desire and disgust.

Overall, zombie porn offers the means to explore the pressure to keep sexual boundaries intact, and the perhaps misguided attempts to maintain an impermeable border. Jeffrey Weeks argues that the 'erotic is inevitably, and probably eternally, caught in the web of value debates, trapped in the domain of moral agonising, ethical debate, personal choice and collective decisions'.[52] The porn industry capitalises on this fear of lack of sexual certainty, and zombie porn makes this fear explicit, challenging the very nature of what is positioned as acceptable sex. Just as the zombie exists in a state of perpetual horror, sex exists in a state of flux which can cause horror to some. The abject invokes fear but is also a source of discovery for how society approaches sex and its depictions of sex. Perhaps zombie porn, then, contains some truths that should be heard alongside the groans and moans.

Notes

1. Laura Helen Marks, 'I Eat Brains . . . or Dick": Sexual Subjectivity and the Hierarchy of the Undead in Hardcore Film', in Shaka McGlotten and Steve Jones (eds), *Zombies and Sexuality: Essays on Desire and the Living Dead* (Jefferson: McFarland, 2014), pp. 159–79.
2. Walter Kendrick, *The Secret Museum: Pornography in Modern Culture* (Berkeley: University of California Press, 1987); Jefferey Weeks, *Invented Moralities: Sexual Values in an Age of Uncertainty* (New York: Columbia University Press, 1991).
3. Gayle Rubin, *Deviations: A Gayle Rubin Reader* (Durham: Duke University Press, 2011), p. 152.
4. Rubin, *Deviations*, p. 151.
5. Rubin, *Deviations*, p. 31.
6. Rubin, *Deviations*, p. 151.

7. Rubin, *Deviations*, p. 151. Emphasis added.
8. Rubin, *Deviations*, p. 110.
9. Quoted in Sarah Toulalan, 'Pornography, Procreation and Pleasure in Early Modern England', in Bradford K. Mudge (ed.), *The Cambridge Companion to Erotic Literature* (Cambridge: Cambridge University Press, 2017), p. 108.
10. Barbara Creed, *The Monstrous-Feminine: Film, Feminism, Psychoanalysis* (London: Routledge, 2012), p. 14.
11. David McNally, 'Ugly Beauty: Monstrous Dreams of Utopia', in Sarah Juliet Lauro (ed.), *Zombie Theory: A Reader* (Minneapolis: University of Minnesota Press, 2017), pp. 124–36.
12. Barbara Creed, *Phallic Panic: Film, Horror and the Primal Uncanny* (Victoria: Melbourne University Publishing, 2005), p. x.
13. Quoted in Steve Jones, 'Porn of the Dead Necrophilia, Feminism, and Gendering the Undead', in Cory Rushton and Christopher Moreman (eds), *Zombies Are Us: Essays on the Humanity of the Walking Dead* (Jefferson: McFarland, 2011), pp. 40–60.
14. Kyle Christensen, 'The Reparative Bite of the Zombie Mouth', *The Velvet Light Trap*, 85 (2020), 4–15.
15. Christensen, 'The Reparative Bite of the Zombie Mouth', 9
16. *Sex: The Annabel Chong Story*, dir. Gough Lewis (1999).
17. Creed, *Phallic Panic*, p. xviii.
18. Creed, *Phallic Panic*, p. 1.
19. Julia Kristeva, *Powers of Horror: An Essay on Abjection* (New York: Columbia University Press, 1982), p. 4.
20. Creed, *The Monstrous-Feminine*, pp. 1–10.
21. Erich Fromm, *The Anatomy of Human Destructiveness* (London: Random House, 1973), p. 441.
22. Supervert, *Necrophilia Variations* (New York: Supervert 32C Inc., 2005), p. 185.
23. Kristeva, *Powers of Horror*, pp. 3–4.
24. Joe Parker, 'How Prostitution Works', in Christine Stark and Rebecca Whisnant (eds), *Not For Sale* (Melbourne: Spinifex, 2004), p. 4.
25. Gail Dines, *Pornland: How Porn Has Hijacked Our Sexuality* (Boston: Beacon Press, 2010), p. xxiv.
26. Dines, *Pornland*, p. xi.
27. Dines, *Pornland*, p. xvii.
28. Robert Jensen, 'Pornography is What the End of the World Looks Like', in Karen Boyle (ed.), *Everyday Pornography* (New York: Routledge, 2010), p. 105.

29. Caroline West, 'Hashtags and Hand Wringings: Conversations on Porn in Ireland', *Porn Studies*, 6/2 (2018), 258–61.
30. Clarissa Smith and Feona Attwood, 'Emotional Truths and Thrilling Slide Shows: the Resurgence of Antiporn Feminism', in Tristan Taormino, Constance Penley, Celine Parrenas Shimizu and Mireille Miller-Young (eds), *The Feminist Porn Book: The Politics of Producing Pleasure* (New York: CUNY Press, 2013), p. 53.
31. Smith and Attwood, 'Emotional Truths and Thrilling Slide Shows', p. 45.
32. Matthew Gumpert, 'The Hollow Men: Towards a Zombie Semiotics', *The Journal of Popular Culture*, 53/2 (2020), 303.
33. Rubin, *Deviations*, p. 110.
34. Anna Chiara Corradino, 'Performing Necrophilia', *Whatever. A Transdisciplinary Journal of Queer Theories and Studies*, 3 (2020), 373–400.
35. Paul Rozin et al., 'Individual differences in disgust sensitivity: Comparisons and evaluations of paper-and-pencil versus behavioral measures', *Journal of Research in Personality*, 33/3 (1999), 330–51.
36. Martha Nussbaum, *Hiding from Humanity: Disgust, Shame, and the Law* (New Jersey: Princeton University Press, 2009), p. 107.
37. Nussbaum, *Hiding from Humanity*, p. 107.
38. Peter L. Berger and Thomas Luckmann, *The Social Construction of Reality: A Treatise in the Sociology of Knowledge* (London: Penguin, 1991), p. 194.
39. Anthony Giddens, *Beyond Left and Right: The Future of Radical Politics* (London: Polity Press, 1994), p. 7.
40. Blake E. Ashforth and Glen E. Kreiner, '"How Can You Do It?" Dirty Work and the Challenge of Constructing a Positive Identity', *Academy of Management Review*, 24/3 (1999), 413–34.
41. Susan Miller, *Disgust: The Gatekeeper Emotion* (New York: Routledge, 2013), p. 17.
42. Andrea Ruthven, 'Pride and Prejudice and Post-Feminist Zombies', in Maria Alonso Alonso, Jeannette Bello Mota, Alba de Béjar Muíños, and Laura Torrado Mariñas (eds), *Weaving New Perspectives Together: Some Reflections on Literary Studies* (Newcastle upon Tyne: Cambridge Scholars Publishing, 2012), p. 159.
43. Miller, *Disgust*, p. 16.
44. Shaka McGlotten and Sarah Vangundy, 'Zombie Porn 1.0: Or, Some Queer Things Zombie Sex Can Teach Us', *Qui Parle: Critical Humanities and Social Sciences*, 21/2 (2013), 101–25.
45. Miller, *Disgust*, p. 16.
46. Carol Queen, *Real Live Nude Girl: Chronicles of Sex-Positive Culture* (New Jersey: Cleis Press, 2002), p. x.

47. William Ian Miller, *The Anatomy of Disgust* (Cambridge, MA: Harvard University Press, 1997), p. 8.
48. Nussbaum, *Hiding from Humanity*, p. 107.
49. Daniel Kelly, *Yuck! The Nature and Moral Significance of Disgust* (Cambridge, MA: The MIT Press, 2011), p. 31.
50. Linda Williams, *Hardcore: Power, Pleasure, and the 'Frenzy of the Visible'* (Berkeley: University of California Press, 1989), p. 128.
51. Jones, 'Porn of the Dead Necrophilia', pp. 40–60.
52. Jeffrey Weeks, *Invented Moralities: Sexual Values in an Age of Uncertainty* (New York: Columbia University Press, 2013), p. 46.

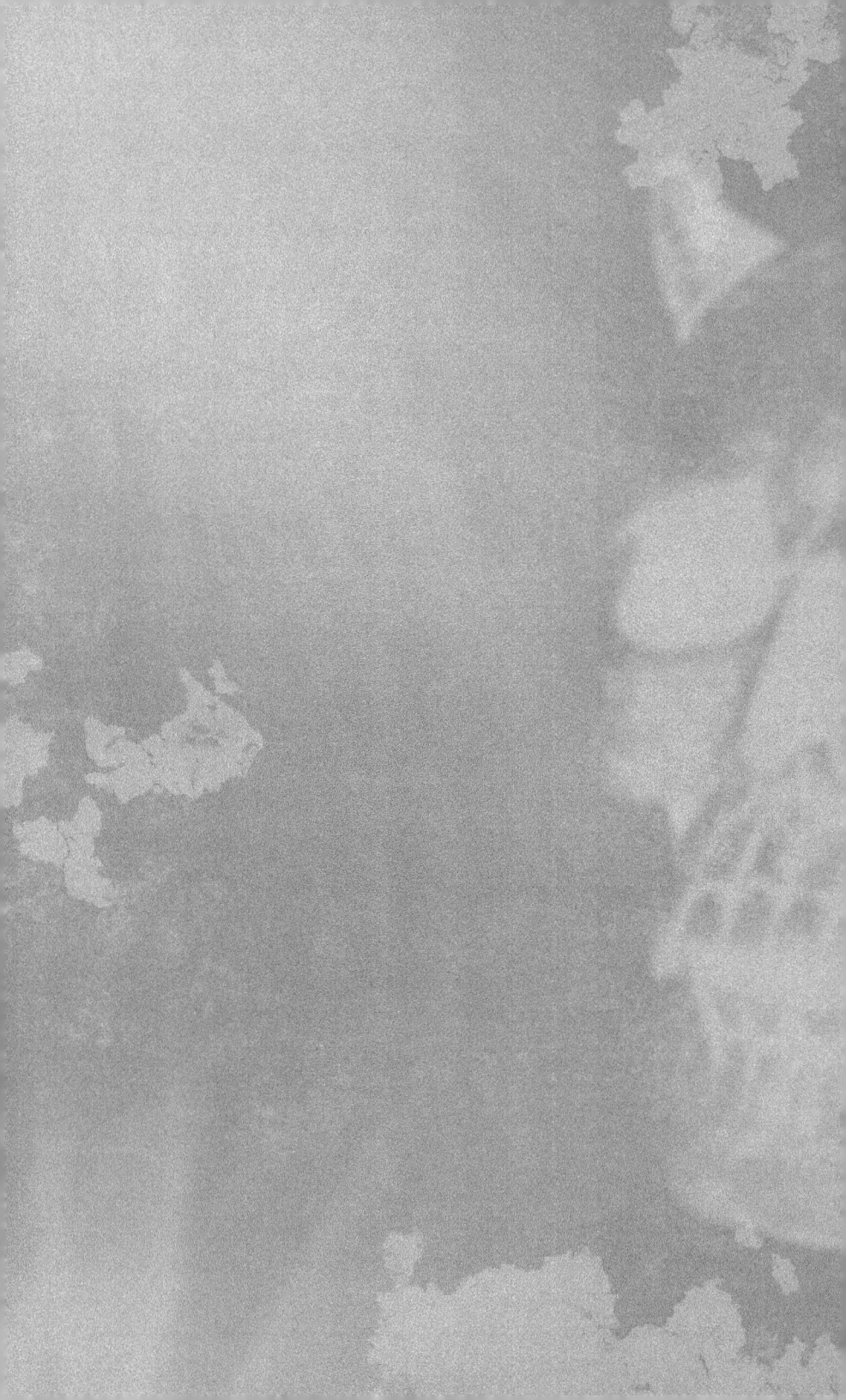

4

Aloha 'Oe

Goodbye and Hello in *Train to Busan* (2016)

Harvey O'Brien

THE SONG *ALOHA 'OE* is sung twice in the film *Train to Busan/ Pusanhaeng*, Yeon Sang-ho's 2016 breakout horror adventure.[1] The singer is Su-an (Kim Su-an), a 10-year-old girl taking the KTX bullet train from Seoul to Busan accompanied by her increasingly estranged father, Seok-woo (Gong Ji-chul). Each time Su-an sings, the camera meets her gaze. First, she stares angrily into her grandmother's video camera in a recording made at a school recital which her father has failed to attend. The video captures her embarrassment and disappointment, and the song falters on her lips (fig. 4.1). Seok-woo is too busy working as a fund manager ('an expert at leaving people behind', as another character comments) to be present in her life. When he views the videotape, Su-an looks into the lens and directly at him, but also, effectively, directly at the audience. Her regard is one of resentful accusation at the deficiencies of a world that is about to end. Initially, the train to Busan seems to inadvertently allow father and daughter to avoid a zombie outbreak which has just begun, but just as the departing train doors close, a young woman slips on board, bleeding from a bite, repeatedly apologising. She becomes patient zero, and the plague spreads. The second time Su-an sings the same song and looks towards the camera and again at the audience, she stares with growing composure and resolution. As she and pregnant passenger Sung-kyung (Jung Yu-mi), the last survivors of the journey, emerge from a dark railway tunnel to the sanctuary of Busan, the sound of her singing affirms her humanity and prevents a sniper from mistaking them for zombies (fig. 4.2). As Su-an walks towards salvation, she leaves behind a world literally and figuratively on the rails. Her father is now dead, having stepped off the train in his last human moments before 'turning', and her song is both a farewell to him and a hello to the world that awaits her in Busan.

The song constitutes a recurring motif and serves a metaphoric function that makes it worth discussing briefly before we begin.[2] *Aloha 'Oe* was composed by the last Hawaiian queen, Lili'uokalani in 1878, ten years prior to the annexation of her kingdom by the United States.[3] The tune, famously recorded by Elvis Presley in 1961, persists as a leitmotif for romantic escape, but is actually a song of parting and loss inspired by the sight of a separating couple. The word *aloha* is an auto-antonym meaning both hello and goodbye. In Polynesian culture, the term is synonymous with the promotion of social harmony.[4] The contranym of the word itself is apropos of *Train to Busan*, which views the zombie apocalypse as both goodbye and hello. In contrast to the reading of the zombie film as inherently nihilistic and posthuman, *Train* offers a delineation of pro-social and anti-social human qualities through careful plotting of both selfish and selfless acts witnessed by a child who literally and figuratively embodies the future for a humanity re-defined by recognising its shortcomings. The train passes through the fall of civilisation, and on the journey establishes the threads of a new society that might emerge from the familial and socio-political purgation inherent in zombie apocalypse narratives: one defined by kindness and empathy. The film's resolution suggests better ways for humans to interact than predation and consumption and that there *is* a future if humans do so.

The zombiism in *Train* is not an evolutionary mutation or other ascendence of an alternative species as in *The Girl with All the Gifts* (2016) where the plant-based Hungry/Human hybrids inherit the earth, their core values ultimately more flora than fauna,[5] or *Land of the Dead* (2005) where the semi-sentient undead are the repressed underclass who may have as much right to the world as living humans. In *Train*, the infected are a threat similar to that in *World War Z* (2013): a largely undifferentiated mass whose lives are over and, in their post-mortem state, signify the blindness of a society en route to destruction.[6]

Figure 4.1. *Train to Busan*. The song dies on Su-an's lips as only a camera lens, and not her absent father, bears witness.

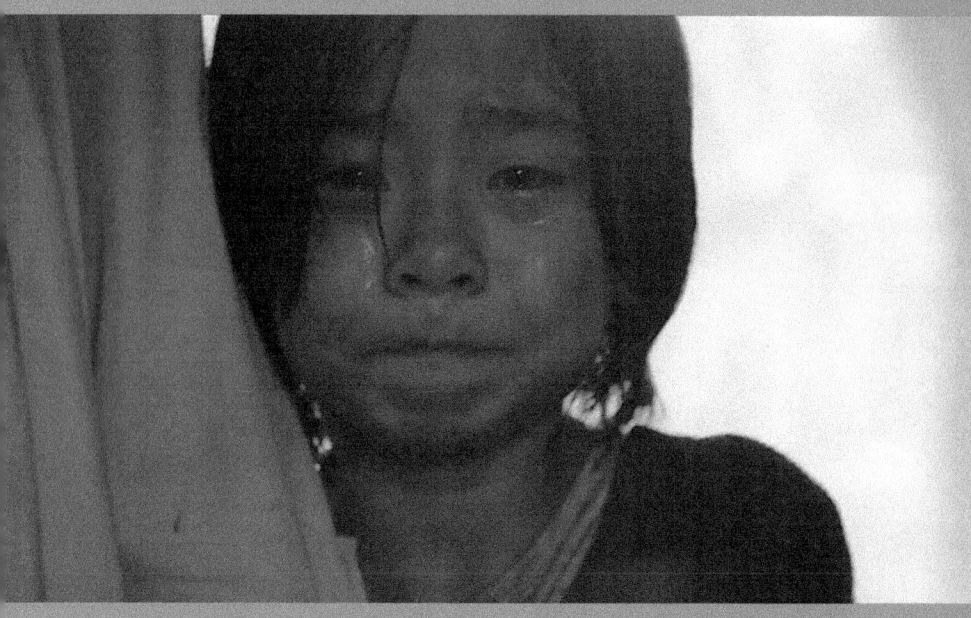

Figure 4.2. *Train to Busan*. Su-an, seen through a sniper scope, emerging from a darkened train tunnel.

The outbreak is linked to unethical economic speculation and environmentally destructive science. The divisions and failures of society are allegorised by the passengers on the train, including an affable everyman and his pregnant wife, a homeless man whose muttering about 'all dead' may refer to escaping the outbreak or identify him as a war veteran, dutiful railway employees facing an unprecedented workplace emergency, two elderly sisters with opposing views of past and future, a young baseball player[7] and his would-be cheerleader girlfriend, and a ruthless corporate executive who tries to leverage chaos to protect himself to the detriment of others. As the characters who survive say goodbye to the old world and those who represent it, they say hello to a new one. The poster advertising for the film invited viewers to 'get on board'. To where? To somewhere new.

Korea's history as a persistently invaded, colonised and divided nation (which itself may add a layer to the use of a Hawaiian song in the film) has led to the evolution of a cinema that struggled with the means and measures of self and national expression. There was nonetheless a distinctive Korean cinema throughout the twentieth century summarised by Hyangjin Lee as proceeding through phases corresponding with prevailing political conditions: Japanese occupation, national division, autocratic anticommunism and democratisation.[8] In all phases, tensions between the systems and means of production and the desire of individual artists to examine or comment upon the social world make the reading of Korean film inherently bound up with a dialectic between state and citizen. Keith Wagner claims that Korea's 'particularly unique and unforgiving' adherence to neo-liberalism largely champions pro-capitalist, patrimonial values, and much of Korean cinema presents a conservative representation of traditional family melodrama that obligingly propagandises the status quo.[9]

In an influential study of new Korean cinema, Darcy Paquet describes the distinct stages in the emergence of the contemporary, confident and largely genre-based popular Korean cinema that Wagner terms 'glocalised', meaning that Korean cinema speaks clearly both within and outside Korea.[10] Paquet distinguishes between the socially conscious proletarian-leaning (but not particularly popular) Korean New Wave of the 1980s and 1990s following the assassination of President Park Chung-Hee (1979), the collapse of military dictatorship and the new Korean cinema of the 'Hallyu' era in which Korean culture became trendy throughout Asia, driven by music, gaming and fashion, even while the country was in the throes of an economic crisis involving IMF intervention (1997–8).[11]

The Hallyu has led to the term 'Hallyuwood' being used to describe some more recent outward-looking film productions, including *Train*.[12]

K-horror, or Korean horror cinema, was part of the wave, primarily focused on genre films and usually associated with extreme violence. Hye Jean Chung notes this association has been promoted internationally but argues that Korean cinema is no more or less violent than other national cinemas. She does note, however, that the representation of violence in Korean cinema can 'shed light on the culturally specific mechanisms of power' where 'vulnerable bodies that are at risk of being brutalised, mutilated, dismembered, and segmented – literally and figuratively – according to the calculating logic of global capital'.[13]

Donato Totaro argues that even in films accused of misogyny and sexism, such as Ki-duk Kim's notorious 2000 psychosexual K-horror hit *The Isle*, political meaning can be carried. Examining the sadomasochistic, co-dependent and self-destructive dimensions of an intense relationship allows the 'highly metaphoric' qualities of horror to facilitate the examination of contemporary and historical Korean social reality.[14] Jinsoo An contends that K-horror films characteristically address the impact of colonial trauma through displacement. According to An, Korean drama often contains the historical through narratives which frame the past within a mode of retrospection rather than reflection.[15] In horror, the motif of the return of the repressed, with all its historical and postcolonial force, disrupts the compartmentalisation of historical trauma and visits the legacy of the past on the immediate present. This eruption is associated with violent retribution through spectral agency typical of classic ghost stories, frequently melded with the typical Korean melodramatic form of the 'fallen woman' story. In such narratives, the female ghost is given agency to act against repression, denial or disavowal in an act of ontological dissonance which 'compels us to perceive and understand the meanings of historical violence and justice'.[16]

Lee further amplifies analysis of the conflation of female victimhood with national suffering (which is a common national cinema trope[17]):

> Compared with [these] male protagonists, nearly all female characters are depicted as defenceless victims of forces beyond their control. The ordeals they undergo figuratively stand for the plight of the entire country. Aside from poverty and insanity, prostitution and rape serve as particularly acute metaphors for the country's traumatic experiences of humiliation and helplessness.[18]

Lee notes that the narrative of family and nationhood is common in North and South Korean cinema, and that in North Korean cinema the burden of leadership falls on father figures whereas in the South the male-female romantic coupling is usually more in focus. *Train* presents a failed patrimony and broken couple as the starting point. The film is not a story of 'deadbeat dad made good', or of heteronormative reconciliation, but of the endurance of a 10-year-old girl whose steady gaze and clear voice are the hope for the future of humanity, even in the face of present apocalypse.

The film mobilises gender positions in significant ways. Though female characters undergo suffering and trauma and remain largely passive as figures of narrative agency compared to the males, females explicitly and particularly outlive the patrimonial order (and even contribute to its extinction). In a key scene, the three male heroic protagonists, Seok-woo, the affable everyman Sang-hwa (Ma Dong-seok), and the high school baseball player Yong-guk (Choi Woo-sik) share a bonding moment in a public toilet. As they plan to face the infected in a high-risk frontal assault that will be the film's signature action sequence and which they may not survive, Sang-hwa suggests a man's lot in life is sacrifice. All three of these men will, in fact die, though not immediately. Seok-woo survives until near the end; Sang-hwa will sustain a bite during the coming battle, but voluntarily holds back the horde while the others escape;[19] Yong-guk dies later because he will not leave Jin-hee (Ahn So-hee) behind after she is bitten. These deaths problematise the concept of agency and influence and signify the end of multiple forms of masculinity associated with the neo-liberal order.

Train has been examined primarily as a critique of neo-liberalism.[20] Johannes Fehrle observes that classic zombie narratives often inherently but 'unwittingly' include anti-capitalist themes resonating from the colonial labour exploitation roots of the genre.[21] He explains, however, that more contemporary iterations following the 'outbreak' model can be seen as more closely linked with images of population movement, border crossings and biopolitical motifs around infection, contamination and ecological disaster. Similarly, Sherryl Vint, referencing Slavoj Žižek's overarching proclamation, states that when living in end times it is easier to imagine catastrophe than change.[22] Vint notes 'The metaphor of the body politic shifts from taking as its referent the body of the sovereign to the aggregate body of the population whose "health" is now the object of good governance', and examines how individual and social death become intertwined metaphorically when imagining the biopolitics of infection and consumption in zombie narratives.[23]

In a Korean context, Chung highlights the concept of mobility and the corollary motif of immobility where through various acts of institutional and personal violence, bodies are consistently violated, or destroyed in the midst of movement, which ceases. Although her focus is Korean crime films about organ and body trafficking, she does mention the ways zombie epidemics follow the same logic of apocalyptic capitalism on a slightly divergent generic path. She draws correlations between these and the logics of transnational migrations in light of capitalist exploitation, claiming that 'depictions of dismembered bodies and bloodshed in Korean films are symptomatic of the growing pains (or "globalising pains") of nation-states and national subjects put under the strains of globalisation'.[24] These logics of mobility also apply in *Train*, where the journey from northern to southern Korea by train serves as, at least, a partially metaphoric space in which a microcosmic cross-section of characters and types represent varying social and economic strata, most of which are erased and in this show the ever-watchful Su-an what mistakes lead to erasure.

As a conceptual space, trains have always offered ideal microcosmic settings for tales of catastrophe; as Ian Christie indicates, trains are even part of one of cinema's founding myths (audiences in fear of the train arriving at the station).[24] Train journeys also provide intrinsic narrative structure, providing an origin, destination and stops for thickening plots, and, in the case of low-budget films, a relatively contained space in which to stage the action. There are extensive writings about the broader relationship between trains, cinema and society, including observations on the interconnections between representations of and the logistics of empire and the paradox of offering social and geographical mobility on a vehicle which preserved the class structure.[26] An observes similar configurations analysing the ideology of the Japanese occupation of Korea where:

> The empire as space offers the promise of opportunity and potential, so the Korean people are no longer constricted either by ethnic difference or by geographical marginality. Instead, they are on board perpetually moving vessels, traversing along the lines and arteries of empire.[27]

This allegory also appears in Bong Joon-ho's *Snowpiercer* (2013, South Korea/Czech) based on the French *bande dessinée* later adapted for television (2020). The paradoxes of mobility and immobility (represented by the fateful train journey crossing the country) and questions of authority, hierarchy and systematic socio-political dysfunction are all features of *Train* which deploys the zombie as avatar of empire.

Wagner indicates that the zombie film is a comparatively recent addition to the K-horror roster, dating only from *The Guard Post* (Kong Su-chang, South Korea, 2008), but sees *Train* as critically engaged with the problematic of neo-liberal disaster management in contemporary South Korea, an abdication of social responsibility he links with crises in public underfunding and privatisation of services. Wagner observes that journalistic critiques of South Korea's post-dictatorship governments have referred to their mindless incorporation of elements of the *ancien régime* as being 'zombie-like', a usage of the term that, like 'zombie bank', connects genre to political metaphor.[28] Similar themes are examined by Christian Long who considers infrastructure after the zombie apocalypse where 'zombie management' is as much about reconceptualising and repurposing civilisation to maintain it.[29] In spite of elements of commentary, apocalyptic/disaster narratives usually present a measure of continuity of the status quo, often through redemptive patrimonial self-sacrifice.[30] Primary agency is inevitably given to the socially integrated male whose actions ensure continuity of the existing order, with or without his actual presence. As Linnie Blake claims: 'the family is clearly a means of inculcating the child with a sense of self that is firmly embedded in the political necessity of the present while allowing for the transmission of property along dynastic lines'.[31]

However, very little property remains by the end of *Train*. The route from Seoul has incorporated stops at Daegu and Daejon stations which, in classic train narrative style, have intensified the plot as civilisation collapses step by step. Media broadcasts show the early stages of unrest and outbreak occurring behind the train in Seoul, then scattered information obtained by phone calls and messages fill in the scant detail as communications fade. At Daejon the promise of military rescue falters when passengers find the outpost has been overrun. The passengers are attacked and overwhelmed by the zombified soldiers in a transparent and resonant metaphor for the failure of the military to protect society and, indeed, actively contribute to its destruction. At Daegu, the scale of disaster is visible in the derailed, zombie-filled trains around the abandoned junction as the train driver (Jeong Soek-yong) secures a fresh locomotive to carry the few survivors on the final stage. Yon-suk then uses him, and Jin-hee, as human shields to facilitate his own escape, an apt image of the self-serving neo-liberal manager whose petty dictatorship collapses as the number of survivors dwindles.

Seok-woo is implicated in this apocalypse. He learns by speaking to his assistant on the phone that the outbreak is linked to corrupt practices within his own suite of companies where there have been irregularities around environmental safety.[32] Therefore, in *Train*, the martyrdom of the father does not preserve the family nor perpetuate the father's values. Though Jaecheol Kim sees the trajectory of the film as still being coterminous with 'the process of recovering lost fatherhood', this is a narrative of interruption, not continuity.[33] It is the father that will have to forego the legacy of patrimonial values. Su-an's kinder, more evidently 'human', outlook is based on more collective and empathetic social values. To paraphrase Lauro and Embry, the trigger is pulled not only on the ego, but on the consciousness and social roles and positions which define patrimonial succession.[34] Seok-woo belongs to a world his daughter will never share. The father's journey is one of alignment with his daughter, then death.

Steven Kirsh examines, somewhat playfully, the theme of parenting through the zombie apocalypse and concludes with a section analysing post-apocalyptic resilience and the moment of moving past the horror. Kirsh theorises with reference to literature on post-war trauma and survivors of violent trauma, but always with the assumption that something of the old system does survive and that a parent continues to be a parent.[35] In *Train*, Seok-woo's shaky parenting is associated with the failures of a neo-liberal South Korea lacking empathy. The family is 'valued' but not a lived reality. Su-an is caught between her separated mother and father. Her time with her father is spent as much with his mother, her grandmother, as with him. The train to Busan is a journey from father to mother on Su-an's birthday because she does not want to share the day with him. Su-an is compassionate by instinct and inclination, but resentful and angry at what she sees as Seok-woo's selfishness. 'You only care about yourself', she says, 'that's why Mommy left'. His parenting has been dutiful, but distant, and ineffective. His birthday gift to her is the same console he got her for Children's Day.[36] He tries to give her life lessons by indicating that he does everything for her, but he criticises her for not finishing what she started, namely her performance of *Aloha 'Oe* at the pageant, which he watches on video. This begs the question is he fathering a child for which he provides no parenting?

The film has a strong sense of generational diversity, reflected in the cross-section of characters on the train, including elders, adults, young adults, children (well, one: Su-an) and even a foetus called 'Sleepy', to which Sang-wha points proudly in Sung-kyung's pregnant belly, saying 'I made that'.[37] Su-an nonetheless witnesses the failure and collapse of the status quo and all of its hierarchies. As adults around her enact the drama of self-erasure in a theatre of violence she consistently acts humanely towards others and contradicts her father's exhortations of self-interested continuity. In an early scene she offers her seat to In-gil (Ye Soo-jung), one of the two elderly sisters travelling together. Seok-woo takes Su-an aside afterwards and tries to explain that in such situations, namely survival, it is okay to not be kind. Su-an retorts that 'granny used to have weak knees', reminding him of his own mother, whom he has just lost. Later, it is Su-an that persuades her father to open the connecting door and allow Yon-suk and Sung-kyung into the carriage as they flee from the horde.

Centred by Su-an, her perspective, behaviour and status as a moral anchor, the film has a surprisingly humanist heart. *Train* emphasises kindness, empathy and social co-operation over competition and individualism; it embraces the inevitability of change as something positive, not by completely erasing or replacing humanity with another species. In Vint's terms, Su-an is removed from the subjectivities of neo-liberal capitalism and returned to the service of humanity.[38] By taking the good in humans forward, *Train* embraces the more consciously positive values embodied in Su-an. In essence, she is the film's true protagonist and her perspective the real subject.

Sight is an important motif in *Train*. Throughout the film themes and events unfold through Su-an's eyes – not entirely from a narrative and focal point of view – but in terms of how the audience is expected to evaluate what they see. The infected are characterised by having all-white eyes[39] and are completely blind in low light (fig. 4.3). Much of the suspense revolves around attempts to avoid detection, to operate out of sight of the horde and what it represents. Social, political and personal blindness abounds in the adult world,[40] but Su-an is always watching, always attentive. When the train is leaving the platform at Seoul, Seok-woo is dozing in his seat, eyes closed, but Su-an catches sight of a zombie hurling itself upon the platform guard and falling out of sight so rapidly that it defies a clear view. She turns in alarm to her father, but the patriarch has seen nothing (fig. 4.4). The film is often shot from close to her eye level and keeps her in the centre of the frame (often staring directly at the camera). She is the structuring anchor from a cinematic point of view. *Train* privileges the perspective of a child seeing one world change into another. The audience is invited to share her view, not his. At the conclusion of the film, the camera again meets Su-an's eyeline as she looks directly at the audience, towards the new world.

A substantial body of theory exists about seeing and looking in film, mainly informed by psychoanalytic and semiotic analysis.[41] In sum, to observe the system of 'looks' or 'gazes' by which audiences view what they see on screen imbues sight with meaning which usually corresponds with a hegemonic (white male) point of view. The 'gaze' is structured around a set of inscriptive practices whereby the viewer is 'sutured' into the image in the classic formulation of shot-reverse-shot.

On a metaphoric level the gaze outward and inward informs *Train*'s moral argument that the future lies in an outlook away from patrimonial continuity and towards female inheritance. It is also a gaze away from the self and towards the other. The blind, inward gaze of the (hegemonic) horde reflects an atrophied perspective, the are literally dead. This is true even for Seok-woo, who 'turns' before he dies. In one of the film's many gestures of kindness towards its characters, his last memories are of the birth of Su-an, framed against an impossibly white backdrop to reflect the purity of the memory of a life full of potential, and, of course, is an echo of the uncanny mirror of the whitening eyes. His last gaze is therefore figuratively within, as he voluntarily falls to his death from the rear of the locomotive, leaving Su-an and Sung-kyung. This is not quite redemption, but his death enables the world to continue without him. His death is cause for hope, not nihilism. However, this hope is based on Su-an's helping him to realise his best self in being selfless, rather than in her adherence to the ruleset he sought to teach her by telling her how to behave and missing out on her life. Su-an's palpable (feminised) suffering and grief for the loss of her father (however flawed) are not permanent, they are part of an ennobling of his love. He was unable to express that love, being overly absorbed with being a dutiful patriarch, but, eventually, he acted on it.

It is not difficult to read this configuration of family patrimony in terms of broader discourse around citizen and state in contemporary South Korea, and indeed this is precisely how Wagner and Kim read the film. Following his thread of analysis around neo-liberal disaster management, Wagner concludes, 'its critique of neo-liberal man-made disasters, global health discourses, and class stratification, however ancillary these subtexts may be on first viewing, is an incarnation of the global issues we all face now'.[42] *Train* revolves around themes of responsibility to self and others; fault, blame and apology (both personal and social); inclusion and exclusion (encompassing motifs of class, gender, age); and control (which comes with explicit political reference in the form of a TV broadcast over

Figure 4.3. Here Seok-woo sleeps while Su-an has just seen a zombie attack on the platform at Seoul as the train departs.

Figure 4.4. The metaphor of the inward-facing eye and the incapacity to see the world outside is given a sympathetic dimension in Seok-woo's death. His last inward vision is the happy memory of the birth of his daughter.

zombie attack footage where the announcer says 'we must stay calm and trust the government' as the city burns, but mainly plays out on a micro level as control of self and other – the loss of control, of course, signified by succumbing to the infection), which have broader relevance pertaining to social order. The distrust of patrimonial government and the failure of control are important elements in play, and in seeing the failure of the old world on all of these levels the audience is invited to consider that the end might be a good thing. They say goodbye to the old and hello to the new and possibly better.

Unlike in many disaster films where death is ordered by moral failure and survival a matter of repentance, there is a measurably global (should that be 'glocal'?) locus of blame in *Train*. Though the chemical plant in Seok-woo's funding package is the source of the contamination, the matter of personal incrimination is deflected, appropriately, to the systemic. Seok-woo's assistant, Analyst Kim, cries down the phone to him at one point when he realises the truth and asks, 'is this my fault?' Clearly an attribution of blame on a personal scale is inappropriate, and equally neither could Seok-woo be held accountable on an individual basis even as his 'manager'. Neither man caused the outbreak, but suspicious activity by one of their suite of companies went unchecked. As Wagner notes, this questions the degree to which hierarchical structures ultimately dissipate responsibility to the point where no one person is to blame, and the emphasis in response to disaster shifts to rhetorics of tragedy.

Though there are selfish and stupid characters, the film is even kind enough to understand that underneath every petty dictator is a scared little boy. As the infection takes Yon-suk, the film's most overtly villainous character, he becomes a pitiable figure. He reverts to child-like language, appealing to Seok-woo to take him home to his mother. Then he 'turns' and attacks. Kim indicates that the key difference between Seok-woo and Yon-suk is repentance.[43] Both men are corporate executives, and both represent the operations of unrestrained and unthinking exploitation. Seok-woo demonstrates callousness in his behaviour towards others and is called on this not just by Su-an, but by Sang-hwa, who is paradigmatic of the working man even if his economic status is not made explicit. Sang-hwa is the one who denounces Seok-woo as a 'bloodsucker' and voices a righteous proletarian disgust, although he, like Su-an, will come to see the good in him and work with him to rescue stranded survivors by crashing his way through the horde alongside him and Yong-guk in the film's most spectacular scene. But where Yon-suk seeks to blame, demonise and divide, sacrificing others to save himself, Seok-woo (aligning with Su-an's empathetic outlook) gradually moves from selfish to selfless and from blaming others to accepting his own shortcomings, making him 'recognise the alienation in his own work' according to Kim.[44] As Kim indicates, this is a classic melodramatic trajectory, with confrontation between two patrimonial figures representing opposing values, but both are ultimately erased as heroism and villainy are themselves binary oppositions from the world without empathy inhabited by the living dead.

Throughout *Train*, adherence to rule systems does not guarantee a positive outcome. This is seen in the erasure of the baseball team by the zombie soldiers (being team players does not help), and in Yong-guk's death in the unconsummated high-school romance that might have played out with Jin-hee (love does not conquer all). Throughout the film, the death throes of the old world are laced with a sense of inevitability, almost relief, as cliché after cliché fails. In an early scene, a female train attendant is gently advised by her co-worker to adjust her scarf to the 'right' position. A 'moment' passes between them. Minutes later she is the first victim of patient zero and then she infects the same co-worker involved in the would-be 'meet-cute'. There is no 'plot armour' in following the rules. Even the decent, dutiful train driver gets literally thrown to the zombies by the fleeing Yon-suk, and the homeless man who has clearly endured a lifetime of repeated traumas, but acts courageously in helping other survivors to escape, gets no reward. He too is a relic and a symptom of the deficiencies of the old order and is as equally devoured by it. No one wins. But no one is to blame either per se. *Train* depicts a catastrophic system failure and total erasure of the hegemonic order, or rather depicts that hegemony as exactly what it is – the zombie state of blind adherence to consumption and predation in which all are essentially victims.

How patient zero came to be infected is never revealed, and in the end it does not matter.[45] Her regret and apology, like analyst Kim's crying, invokes sympathy, but means nothing in terms of resolution or catharsis, because the infection is endemic and the world of law, order, government, rationality and hierarchy is gone. The final collapse (on the train) comes through the agency of an elderly woman who has seen enough of history to know when it is time to let it end. Early in the film, In-gil (Ye Soo-jung) and Jong-gil (Park Myung-Sin) watch the riot footage on TV and Jong-gil comments that in the old days dissidents would be sorted out by re-education; a reference to the notorious internment of political dissidents in military detention centres by the Chun regime in the 1980s. In-gil is appalled and hushes her. Jong-gil is frustrated by In-gil's inherent positivity and gentleness, seeing it as a weakness – reflecting the unyielding and non-empathetic viewpoint of the old world. It is In-gil to whom Su-an gives up her seat, an exchange of virtues from which Jong-gil and Seok-woo are excluded by a selfish outlook. Ultimately both of them will voluntarily join the horde. When In-gil becomes infected, she appears in un-death more like a lost and passive soul than the frenzied horde around her, perhaps reminiscent of one of An Jinsoo's female ghosts. This compels Jong-gil, in An's words 'to perceive and understand the meaning of historical violence and justice'.[46] She sees her undead sister and looks back and forth between the living and the dead in the carriage where Yon-suk is bullying the surviving passengers, having ejected Seok-woo and the others from the train. She realises that her intransigent misanthropy is ultimately the same as his selfishness and knows this way of life is not worth preserving. She literally opens the door to extinction.

Kim's analysis concludes by observing that although *Train* is dystopian, zombie narratives in general offer 'exploration of potential state polities in the apocalyptic world', some of which are utopian 'in which social continuity and the survival of the next generation is possible'.[47] More so than many apocalyptic narratives, *Train* ends with hope, and not a nihilistic 'let's see what happens when we run out of helicopter fuel'[48] type of hope, but a sense that in Su-an's witness to the apocalypse, she has much to say farewell to, but also has asserted how to make things better by retaining her values of empathy, attentiveness and kindness to others. This encapsulates the aloha spirit of love and fellowship, and *Aloha 'Oe*'s note of bittersweet parting is a reminder that every goodbye can also be a hello. *Train to Busan* is bracketed by two renderings of that same song by the same character with a different inflection. Though Su-an is crying as she sings in the final scene, she begins to compose herself, suggesting determination and facing forward. Her father and his world are gone; and failure, blame and apology are all in the past, but there is an open path to a new future where she knows a man can change his outlook. There is a visible path forward towards humanity from humanity, and if not a utopia exactly, Busan represents possibility for Su-an's way of seeing the world. Hope exists beyond the barricade, and hope is embodied in that final image of a person understood to be human because she has a voice.[49]

Notes

1. *Train to Busan/Busanhaeng*, dir. Yeon Sang-ho, Next Entertainment World, South Korea (2016).
2. Edward Comentale examines the role of song in zombie films with particular focus on the disruptive otherness of counter-rhythms and harmonies of ethnic music: 'Zombie Race', in Sarah Juliet Lauro (ed.), *Zombie Theory: A Reader* (Minneapolis: University of Minnesota Press, 2017), pp. 189–211.
3. Then Princess Lydia Kamakaeha, daughter of King Kalakaua. The song was translated as 'Farewell to Thee' in 1923.
4. There are many ways to interpret the word *aloha*, but it could be appropriately translated conceptually as 'safe journey', 'peace be with you' or variants.
5. Poppy Wilde, 'Zombies, Deviance, and the Right to Posthuman Life', *Theorizing Zombiism Conference*, University College Dublin (2019).
6. The animated prequel *Seoul Station*, dir. Yeon Sang-ho, South Korea (2017) is even more overtly political. *The Girl with All the Gifts*, dir. Colm McCarty, BFI, London (2016); *Land of the Dead*, dir. George A. Romero, Universal Pictures, USA (2005); *World War Z*, dir. Marc Forster, Skydance Productions (2013).
7. As an American sport with an unavoidable historical legacy linked to international intervention during the civil war, the presence of the baseball team can also be seen as a reference to the assimilation of elements of the (quasi) colonial past.
8. Hyangjin Lee, *Contemporary Korean Cinema: Culture, Identity, and Politics* (Manchester: Manchester University Press, 2013), pp. 1–22.
9. Keith Wagner, '*Train to Busan* (2016): Glocalisation, Korean Zombies, and a Man-Made Neoliberal Disaster', in Sangjoon Lee (ed.), *Rediscovering Korean Cinema* (Ann Arbor: University of Michigan Press, 2019), p. 516.
10. Darcy Paquet, *New Korean Cinema: Breaking the Waves* (London: Wallflower Press, 2009), pp. 39–49; 'glocalised' being a term borrowed from Roland Robertson, sourced from Wagner, 'Glocalisation', p. 515.
11. Paquet, *New Korean Cinema*, pp. 39–49.
12. See Sangjoon Lee (ed.), *Rediscovering Korean Cinema* (Ann Arbor: University of Michigan Press, 2019).
13. Hye Jean Chung, 'An Economy of Bodily Violence: Fragmented Bodies and Porous Borders in Korean Cinema', *Journal of Popular Film and Television*, 47/1 (2019), 31, 30.
14. Donald Totaro, '*Seom/The Isle*', in Justin Bowyer (ed.), *The Cinema of Japan and Korea* (London: Wallflower Press, 2004), p. 21.

15. Jinsoo An, *Parameters of Disavowal: Colonial Representation in South Korean Cinema* (Berkeley: University of California Press, 2018), p. 7.
16. An, *Parameters of Disavowal*, p. 123.
17. Analysis of Woman as Nation is a well-worn path in film and cultural studies which will not be pursued here.
18. Lee (ed.), *Rediscovering Korean Cinema*, p. 138.
19. Reversing the earlier scene where Seok-woo closed the door on Sang-hwa and Sung-kyung, trapping them with the horde, prompting Su-an's intervention.
20. At the time of writing the film was recent, but specific focus is found in Jaecheol Kim, 'Biocalyptic imaginations in Japanese and Korean films: undead nation-states in *I Am a Hero* and *Train to Busan*', *Inter-Asia Cultural Studies*, 20/3 (2019), 437–51 and Wagner, '*Train to Busan* (2016)'. An image from the film adorns the cover of Lee (ed.), *Rediscovering Korean Cinema*.
21. Johannes Fehrle, '"Zombies Don't Recognise Borders": Capitalism, Ecology, and Mobility in the Zombie Outbreak Narrative', *Amerikastudien/American Studies*, 61/4 (2016), 531.
22. See Sherryl Vint, 'Abject Posthumanism: Neoliberalism, Biopolitics, Zombies', in Sarah Juliet Lauro (ed.), *Zombie Theory: A Reader* (Minneapolis: University of Minnesota Press, 2017), pp. 171–81.
23. Vint, 'Abject Posthumanism', p. 173.
24. Chung, 'An Economy of Bodily Violence', 32.
25. Ian Christie, *The Last Machine* (London: BBC Education, 1995), p. 12.
26. Rebecca Harrison, 'Inside the Cinema Train: Britain, Empire, and Modernity in the Twentieth Century', *Film History*, 26/4 (2014), 33.
27. An, *Parameters of Disavowal*, p. 7.
28. Wagner, 'Glocalisation', p. 518.
29. Christian B. Long, 'Infrastructure after the Zombie Apocalypse', *Journal of Asia-Pacific Pop Culture*, 1/26 (2016), 181–203.
30. Seen, of course, in *War of the Worlds*, dir. Steven Spielberg, Paramount, US (2005), which traces its lineage through an even more patrimonial 1953 version back to the literally Victorian novel by H. G. Wells.
31. Linnie Blake, *The Wounds of Nations: Horror Cinema, Historical Trauma and National Identity* (Manchester: Manchester University Press, 2008), p. 58.
32. *Train* opens with a farmer passing through a biohazard emergency checkpoint and accidentally running over a deer which resurrects after he drives away.
33. Kim, 'Biocalyptic Imaginations', p. 447.
34. Sarah Juliet Lauro and Karen Embry, 'A Zombie Manifesto: The Nonhuman Condition in the Era of Advanced Capitalism', *boundary 2*, 35/1 (2008), 407.

35. Steven J. Kirsh, *Parenting in the Zombie Apocalypse* (Jefferson: McFarland, 2019).
36. An annual celebration held on 5 May, where families take time off work to appreciate their children.
37. Kim, 'Biocalyptic Imaginations', p. 447.
38. Vint cites theorist Giorgio Agamben in constructing her observation on this point, 'Abject Posthumanism', p. 178.
39. Which may itself be a metaphor if that phrase is given a racial inflection, though that may be a reading too far.
40. Seen also in *Seoul Station* where characters operate at the margins while the military shut down 'important' areas.
41. Fuller analysis can be found in introductory textbooks like Bordwell, Thompson and Smith (McGrawHill, 2020) or Monahan (2019).
42. Wagner, 'Glocalisation', p. 530.
43. Kim, 'Biocalyptic Imaginations', p. 447.
44. Kim, 'Biocalyptic Imaginations', p.447.
45. Though Kim suggests that she may be the runaway prostitute from *Seoul Station* who kills her pimp at that film's climax, 'Biocalyptic Imaginations', p. 447.
46. An, *Parameters of Disavowal*, p. 123.
47. Kim, 'Biocalyptic Imaginations', p. 448. Similarly, *#Alive*, dir. Il Cho, South Korea (2020) emphasises that survival is more than just endurance of trauma (again zombie-related trauma in that case), but embracing life and the possibilities of living.
48. As in *Dawn of the Dead*, dir. George A. Romero, US (1979).
49. Postscriptum: this chapter was written prior to the release of *Bando/Peninsula*, dir. Yeon Sang-ho, South Korea (2020).

PART TWO

CRITICAL ENVIRONMENTS

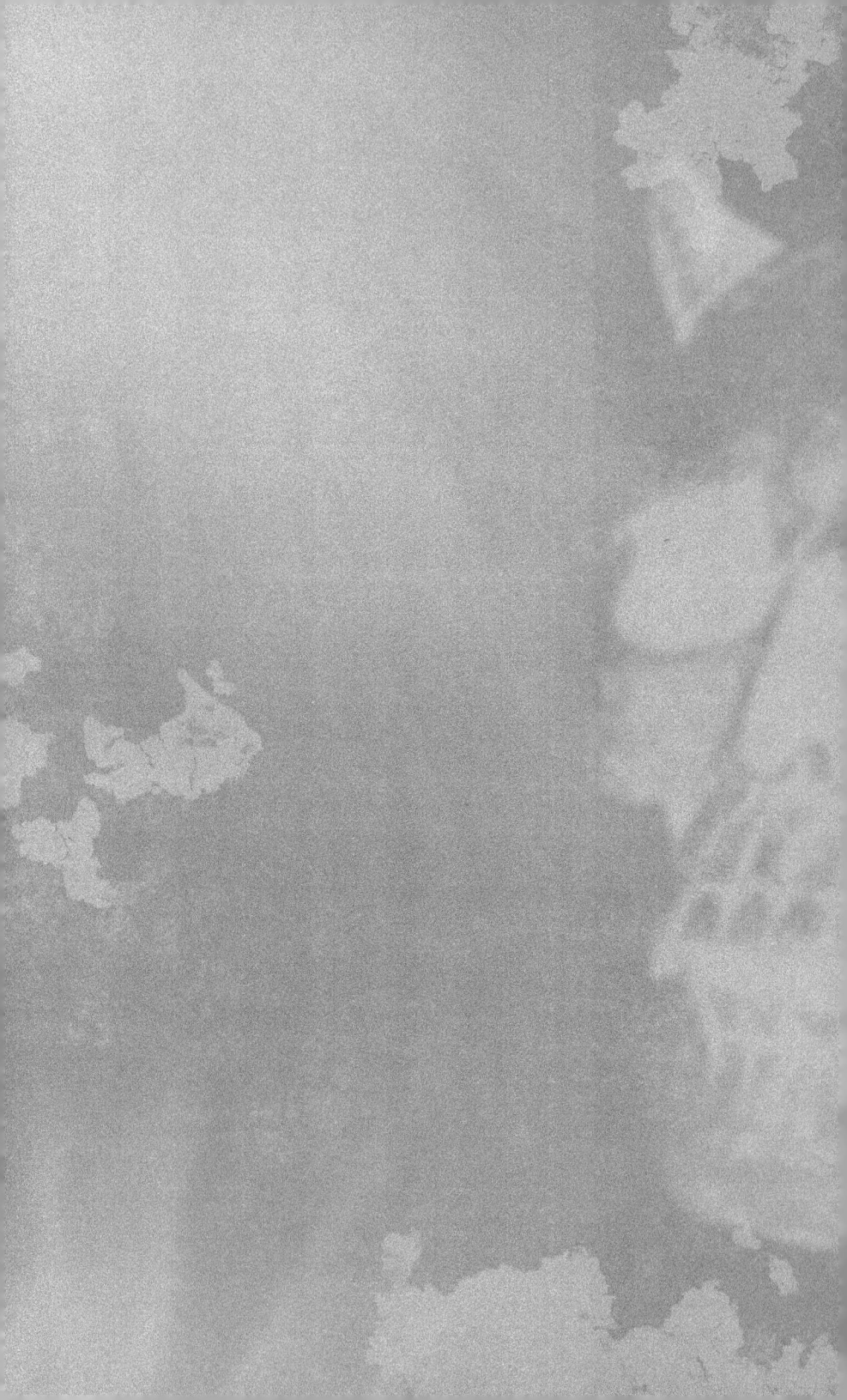

5

The Stalking Dead

Ireland's Ambiguous Revenants and the Case for a Folk-zombie Revival

Jack Fennell

ORIGINALLY PUBLISHED as a chapter of *Jack Hinton, the Guardsman* (1843), 'The Mountain Pass' by Charles Lever has subsequently been included in sundry anthologies as a stand-alone short story. The book follows the narrator and a priest around the Irish countryside, when they hear of a fatal assault. The priest rushes to the victim's hovel to administer the last rites, and before long the perpetrators of the attack arrive. Obviously, they are worried that their victim might identify them, and that the priest will go to the police with this information. However, this does not happen, and the priest swears the narrator to secrecy for as long as all the other witnesses are still alive. The reason for this secrecy is that while the victim did identify his attackers, he was in fact already dead when he did so:

> the priest stopped suddenly, and fell upon his knees, while, with a low, faint sigh, he who seemed dead lifted his eyes and looked around him; his hands grasped the sides of the bed, and, with a strength that seemed supernatural, he raised himself to the sitting posture. His lips were parted and moved, but without a sound, and his filmy eyes turned slowly in their sockets from one object

to another, till at length they fell upon the little crucifix that had dropped from the priest's hand upon the bed. In an instant the corpse-like features seemed inspired with life – a gleam of brightness shot from his eyes – the head nodded forward a couple of times, and I thought I heard a discordant, broken sound issue from the open mouth, and, a moment after, the head dropped upon the chest, and the hands relaxed, and he fell back with a crash, never to move more.[1]

The story obviously has plenty of antecedents in folklore, where murder victims regularly return from the grave in one form or another to reveal the identities of their murderers, and the accusation from beyond the grave is a well-worn archetypal ghost story. A year after the original publication of the above story, the detective in Edgar Allen Poe's 'Thou Art the Man!' (1844) forced a confession from a murderer by staging a similar resurrection through the use of ventriloquism. The uncanniness of the corpse is dramatised by presenting the continuation of a human personality inside it, and this uncanny dread is augmented by giving that lingering personality a legitimate reason to pursue the living.

The distinction between ghosts and corporeal revenants, China Miéville argues, is a product of Victorian propriety, and he points out that in contrast to the physically robust ghosts of yore, 'As Victorian ghosts grew more ostentatiously moralistic, they decorporealised.'[2] This casting-off of the flesh thus coincides with increased industrialisation, bureaucracy and the medicalisation of difference during the latter half of the nineteenth century. The key element of 'The Mountain Pass' is the vow of secrecy: even though he has a moral obligation to relay the incriminating information to the police, the priest is well aware that the story cannot be repeated, because it cannot be accounted for under established legal and scientific norms. Meanwhile, the murderers' concern that their dead victim might still identify them indicates that this is, to their minds at least, not only a possibility but a common occurrence. The story is thus temporally situated at the historical moment where ghost and zombie decohered from one another and evolved along separate lines. However, this decoherence was not as total as might be supposed, and the blurred line between these categories suggests that future evolutions of the zombie will be 'folkloric' in tenor.

False formulae

When one considers zombies in popular culture through history, it becomes clear that, like most other monsters, they change and are utilised according to the needs of the zeitgeist.

Colonial narratives persist in zombie stories, with any number of tales in which the lord of an anachronistic, opulent estate or 'big house' profits from the labour of reanimated slaves; these zombies typically free themselves of the master's control, and often turn on him violently, in endings that are undoubtedly representative of abolition and slave revolts.[3] This archetypal story was a deviation from established folklore. Referring to William Buchler Seabrook's account of zombie labour in *The Magic Island* (1929), occultist Montague Summers agreed without question that it is possible to raise a body from the dead, but he drew the line at reanimated servants toiling in the fields, on the grounds that this kind of reanimation is both extremely dangerous and very short-lived.[4] Summers is lagging behind here, not just in terms of how many zombies can be 'safely' resurrected at a given time, but also in his implicit expectation of where the reader's sympathies lie in this situation. As Stacey Abbott argues, zombies are not 'an idealised fantasy of death like the vampire, in which we are reborn', but rather, they 'embody the corporeality of our mortality and as a result sympathy and horror are intermingled'.[5] It is difficult to conceive of a scenario in which a slave-driving reanimator could plausibly be posited as foolhardy rather than evil.

The importance of magic declined significantly in Western culture over the course of the twentieth century, and many horror tropes adapted to exploit the niche of scientific positivism. Zombie narratives moved away from associations with voodoo (and thus with foreignness) and towards representations of consumer culture, thus shifting the emphasis from cultural to viral contagion.[6] For the moment, the concept of a zombie virus clearly serves the needs of globalised culture, with regional variations adapting the outbreak 'template' to local geography, infrastructure and circumstances. Famously, a 2009 scientific paper modelled a zombie outbreak as an actual epidemic, with slow-moving, reanimated, flesh-craving zombies as the disease's vector and saliva as the infecting agent.[7] The model showed that, in true horror-movie fashion, a zombie uprising could be contained if humans respond immediately and with unrelenting force; however, if the timeframe of the outbreak is extended, the inevitable result is human annihilation, regardless of the tactics employed. 'Thus,' the authors conclude, 'if zombies arrive, we must act quickly and decisively to eradicate them before they eradicate us.'[8] This paper, while largely tongue-in-cheek, is instructive in the way that the authors – obviously fans of zombie media – model the outbreak patterns of their favourite films, rather than an actual disease. This is an expression of a culturally informed desire to strengthen the shared premise of modern zombie media: the fans' enjoyment of the viral-zombie concept is enhanced by making it seem more real.[9] Furthermore, this reinforcement underlines the current dominance of US cinematic convention in defining what a zombie is, with Kyle William Bishop going so far as to argue that 'The term *zombie* has specific references and connotations, representing a species of monster unique to modern American culture, and its haphazard application to other creatures, cultures and narratives belies either a lazy taxonomy or a strategic marketing ploy.'[10]

Alongside the reconfiguration of zombiism as an infection, the twentieth century also saw the zombie's 'mindlessness' transform into an epistemological 'emptiness'. As summarised by Güven Güzeldere, the 'phenomenal zombie' of philosophical thought-experiments comes in three major categories: behaviourally, functionally and physically identical (to human beings). Each of these three categories can be cross-referenced against three kinds of possibility (natural, logical and metaphysical), to produce a total of nine types of 'p-zombie'. The common denominator between all these hypothetical creatures, the quality that makes them all 'zombies', is that although they appear to be human on the outside, no cognitive activity is occurring within: they are mere shells, little more than embodied algorithms that respond to external stimuli in such a way as to simulate sentience and sapience.[11] As a 'blank slate', the zombie serves as a useful figure through which to crystallise philosophical conundrums that might otherwise be very difficult to articulate, and this has also ensured its continued use as a metaphor in political analysis and rhetoric.

As noted above, however, these qualities are not innate to the figure of the zombie but, rather, they are historically determined: the zombie is whatever humanity needs it to be in a given historical moment – as Bishop indicates, present-day zombies emerged from a cultural ecosystem delineated by globalisation, post-9/11 Western politics and the 'War on Terror', and present-day zombie narratives have also been stylistically influenced by video games.[12] Many of the aforementioned characteristics, held to be central to zombie lore, are actually quite recent inventions. Even George A. Romero's original *Dead* films, considered to be codifying texts for the 'standard' modern zombie, omit or ignore many of them. In *Night of the Living Dead* (1968), a brief mention is made of a space probe returning from Venus and contaminating Earth's atmosphere, but this rationalisation is dropped in the sequels, and a general rule is established that is explicitly stated in the later film *Land of the Dead* (2005) – that every human is fated to resurrect as a zombie, and being bitten by one merely ensures that the transformation will happen faster. In the documentary *Birth of the Living Dead* (2012), Romero states that as he imagined it, the catalyst was an ontological one – 'God changed the rules'.[13]

Furthermore, Romero's zombies are consistently shown to be problem-solving animals: the first zombie seen in the series uses a rock to smash a car window; the undead hordes of *Dawn of the Dead* (1978) congregate around places that meant a lot to them in life, suggesting the continuation of some kind of rudimentary personality at least; and in *Day of the Dead* (1985), a zombified former soldier named Bub salutes a higher-ranking officer, and demonstrates a working knowledge of firearms. *Land of the Dead* takes this to its logical conclusion in the character of Big Daddy, a more-or-less conscious zombie who becomes a community leader for the undead. Meanwhile, intelligent (or quasi-intelligent) zombies occur with such frequency in films inspired by Romero's work that the view of the prototypical zombie as a mindless, cannibalistic automaton does not seem to be justified by the evidence. Even in works that parody Romero's films, such as *Return of the Living Dead* (1985) and *Shaun of the Dead* (2004), there is a sense that fans-turned-film-makers are lampooning conventions that were not actually central to the source material. Most zombies, it turns out, are not like this at all: despite appearances, they are not mere automata, which means that the qualitative difference between zombies and humans must lie somewhere else.

Stacey Abbott underlines the fact that individualised zombies regularly appear in Western media, with conscious zombies appearing in comics back in the early 1970s and making repeat appearances in film ever since; the emergence of conscious zombies is, in fact, co-incident with the emergence of sympathetic vampires, but it was not until 'the post-millennial zombie renaissance' that the 'I-zombie' acquired significant momentum. Though many fans might regard the trend as 'illogical',[14] zombies narrating their own stories are becoming increasingly common.[15] This suggests that mindless 'walkers' might ultimately turn out to be a short-lived deviation from a folkloric norm, and that older folk-derived materials might hint at the shape of zombies to come.

May you die in Ireland

Ireland was just one of many places where the distinction between corporeal and non-corporeal undead failed to take root: the Irish undead were both reanimated corpses *and* ghosts – either simultaneously or switching back and forth as the mood took them. Corporeal enough to commit horrendous violence, they were nonetheless able to disappear, to move soundlessly, and to gain access to secure places. In Lever's 'The Mountain Pass', the dead man could have told his tale as a spirit, but he went to the trouble of reanimating his old body. In some stories, the ambiguity between physical and non-physical undead is heightened, and a revenant may even enlist others' aid in getting what it wants. Most importantly, they always have a grievance, and most of them have a disturbing need for retribution. As Sarah Juliet Lauro indicates, the zombie story is an inversion of the haunted house story: the house is not 'a container of strange, evil forces but the fortress that must be defended from outside threats'.[16] Thus, zombie narratives are much more reminiscent of 'traditional' gothics than other monster-centred tales, and it makes sense that a zombie should be able to 'haunt' as well as a ghost can.[17]

In Ireland, the Folklore Commission's Schools' Scheme contains copious examples of corporeal undead who behave like ghosts and display many ghostly attributes. One of the closest examples to a 'standard' zombie story comes from Castlecomer, County Kilkenny, which tells of a man who dies in a hospital and is then placed in the 'dead house' at midnight by the nuns who administer the place. After putting the corpse inside, laying him out on a slab and locking the door, they hear a knock from within, and run off in terror. The following morning, they find the dead man lying on the floor 'and blood coming from his face'.[18] Stories like this, in which the revenant is foiled by a locked door, are decidedly in the minority; in most of the Schools' tales, gathered by schoolchildren between 1937 and 1939, the distinction between fleshly and spiritual undead is not strictly observed. Not only can dead bodies come back to life, but they often come back more powerful than they were before.

In a story from Oberstown, County Louth, one of the contestants in a boxing match dies before the fight can take place but comes back from the dead to insist that the bout go ahead. Before the fight begins, the undead boxer stipulates that if the living fighter loses, he too will die. The living man goes to the parish priest, who advises him to bring a bottle of holy water with him; if he senses that he is about to lose, he is to grab the holy water and make use of it. The match goes ahead, and the dead man seems to have the upper hand until the living man picks up the holy water. The dead man is defeated, but the living man dies in his sleep that night, presumably from exhaustion.[19] There is nothing overtly Satanic about the dead pugilist in this story, but from an orthodox Catholic standpoint, this objection is mere hair-splitting – reanimated corpses have no place in the natural order ordained by God, which makes them functionally no different from an unclean spirit. This suggests that in religiously inflected folklore, all undead beings might partake of the same 'wrongness', and their shared contravention of divine law might account for the absence of firm distinctions between them. This story is also notably similar to Joseph Sheridan Le Fanu's Chapelizod ghost story, 'The Village Bully'. In Le Fanu's version, the living man is the titular villain, having caused the death of a local hero who stood up to him, and the reader's sympathies lie with the revenant.[20]

Interpersonal conflict is at the centre of another story, from Foghill in County Mayo. Here, we are introduced to two men who are constantly fighting, with one of them continually getting the upper hand over the other. The less-skilled fighter swears that if he should die, he will return from the grave to wreak his revenge. Sure enough, he dies, and appears to his old enemy just as the latter is preparing to go to the wake. The dead man announces his intention to kill his nemesis, and in self-defence, the living man grabs a fork and stabs the dead man with it. The dead man disappears, and the living man, thinking he has been the target of a prank, continues to the wake and announces that the other man is not really dead at all. However, the corpse is laid out in the house, in the traditional manner, and when the living man tears open the dead man's shirt, the marks of the fork can clearly be seen in his flesh.[21] The deceased in this story is very active, combining a mastery of bilocation with the ability to appear and disappear at will, and his corporeality is attested to not just by the post-mortem wounds, but also by the evident fact that he can still feel pain. The ambiguous corporeality of these undead figures persisted in Irish fiction throughout the twentieth century.

In 'The Homing Bone' (1924) by Feardorcha Ó Conaill, writing as 'Conall Cearnach', a professor visiting Dublin for a medical conference happens to pass by a cemetery where recent works have disturbed some of the graves. The professor sees a long femur amid a pile of bones that the workmen have set aside, and seeing the potential for 'an interesting and instructive paper', he steals it.[22] Following two nights of bad dreams involving the vengeful Norse skeleton and its compatriots, the professor awakes to hear the bone rattle inside the bag where he has stashed it, and it starts to glow so brightly that he can almost see its outline. After the spectral lightshow comes to an end, the professor hears 'a dull, thudding sound, as of someone walking in the room with a wooden leg or crutch'; the unseen intruder then pushes open the bedroom door and leaves the lodging house by the front door.[23] There are two somewhat comical conclusions to be drawn from the ending – either the skeleton has simply given up on convincing the professor to do the right thing, and fetched the femur on its own, or (as implied by the title) the bone itself has sprung to life and hopped out of the place by itself. In either case, the revenant in question is ultimately quite a pathetic figure, despite its terrifying appearance.

In Mary Lavin's 'The Green Grave and the Black Grave' (1940), a father and son recover the body of a drowned man from the sea around one of Ireland's western islands, and as they row their boat to shore, they discuss how they are going to break the news to his wife; when they reach her cottage, however, they find it empty. A neighbour tells them that the young woman, who came from the mainland and thus was not used to the cruelties of island life, lived in dread of her beloved's body being lost forever to 'the green grave' of the deep ocean instead of lying beside her in the 'black grave' of a cemetery. Consequently, she never allowed him to go out to sea by himself – both of them have drowned, and the fishermen have unwittingly interfered with the couple's resolution to remain together in death. When they return to where they left the body, they see that it is missing, and the final line tells us that while other drowned men are bound in the depths by rocks and seaweed, this man 'would be held fast in the white sea arms of his one-year wife, who came from the inlands where women have no knowledge of the sea and have only a knowledge of love'.[24] It is not stated whether those loving arms are substantial, spiritual or a mixture of both. Lavin's 'The Dead Soldier' (1943) recalls W. W. Jacobs's classic 1902 story 'The Monkey's Paw', with a heartbroken mother praying to see her son for one last time on All Souls' Eve, several months after his death in combat and burial in a far-away country. When she hears slow footsteps in the yard and it appears that her prayer has been answered, she is suddenly filled with horror and begs her son to leave again. The following morning, the visitor is revealed to have been a concerned neighbour who noticed the fire burning late, and the bereaved woman, though embarrassed, has had an epiphany: 'It isn't that the dead can't come back, but that we don't have the strength to face them. We don't want them to come back! That's the truth.'²⁵ In the end, however, it is suggested that the dead soldier did return after all, but in a subtler form, as evidenced by the discovery that his photograph has been burned out of its frame.²⁶

The above revenants are 'ghostly' in their motivations. They have come back from the dead to address a specific grievance, and once this is done, they 'die' again. In Cearnach's tale, apparently there is no upper time-limit for this kind of resurrection, since the dead man has already decomposed away to a skeleton, and in the Lavin stories, the dead only trespass in the world of the living when provoked. As in a great many ghost stories, death is represented as a kind of sleep, or a state of inactivity that can at any point be interrupted. Once this happens, the awakened dead are not inclined to observe social niceties. This is one of the defining aspects of Máirtín Ó Cadhain's classic *Cré na Cille* (1949), translated by Alan Titley as *The Dirty Dust* (2015) and by Liam Mac Con Iomaire and Tim Robinson as *Graveyard Clay* (2016).²⁷ In this novel, the corpses buried in a small Connemara cemetery retain their consciousness after death, and they talk, gossip, bicker and curse each other as they lie in their graves. They have nothing to do but argue and complain, and all eternity to do so. The only variation in their undead existence is the occasional arrival of new bodies, who are immediately pestered for news about the outside world. The corpses' chatter is remarkable for its vulgarity and cruelty, particularly towards the new arrivals, who are implied to be frightened and confused by their new state of being.

What these ambiguous undead seem to have in common is a tendency towards brutal honesty, a traditional concept alluded to in Ó Cadhain's work as *slí an fhírinne*, meaning 'the way/path of truth'. While on one level this idea may be an exaggeration of the bluntness and tactlessness stereotypically linked to senescence, it also calls to mind the truism that, in death, all are equal – hence, there is no need for the dead to deceive themselves or anyone else.

Human-minus and its limitations

Currently, zombies are for the most part conceived of as humans *minus* something essential, most often summarised as individuality. Abbott argues they are 'humanity stripped of identity and controlled by primal hungers, namely the need to feed'. This is part of what makes them monstrous – they are uncanny, the familiar rendered unfamiliar, Othered to the extent that their destruction becomes necessary.[28] The parameters of the mathematical zombie outbreak model mentioned earlier reflect the centrality of the human-minus conception to present-day zombie media, as well as the narrative rigidity that comes with it. The only scenario in which any humans survive at all is a zombie-free equilibrium: quarantine measures always fail in the long run, and the only tactic that guarantees human survival is 'impulsive eradication' – that is, repeating attacks of increasing force, with cool-down time in between to gather resources.[29]

There are obvious limits to the capabilities of human-minus zombies, however. Since they can only pose a serious threat in vast numbers, these zombies inevitably fade into the background of the stories in which they appear. Their lack of character means that, collectively, they amount to a lumbering environmental hazard in the backdrop to political morality tales, in which small bands of human survivors attempt to establish new webs of social relations. Typically, zombie apocalypse stories focus on the dissolution of democracy and the breakdown of civil society (literally, or in microcosm), and the rise of demagoguery, authoritarianism and violence; for the most part, the zombies are not really 'present' until the siege walls are overrun in the final act. There is a limited number of ways in which this kind of story can be told, and variation within this pattern is usually limited to setting rather than characterisation or plot. This, I argue, is the direct cause of the growing number of 'I-zombie' texts, to use Abbott's term – the present historical moment needs something more than an undead monster which is simply an incomplete human, and zombies are adapting once again to fulfil this need.

Ireland's zombie film output is interesting in this context because, as is the case with other kinds of genre fiction, until quite recently the zombie-outbreak concept was played for laughs in Irish media. Conor McMahon's *Dead Meat* (2004) invokes the BSE crises of the 1990s with a mutant strain of mad cow disease as its zombifying catalyst.[31] *Boy Eats Girl* (2005), written by Derek Landy and directed by Stephen Bradley, parodies teenage romantic comedies in a zombie-infested Irish setting.[32] The animated short film *Dead Murphy* (2006) by Stephen McCollum, free from the budgetary constraints and moral scrutiny of large-scale live action films, makes gleeful use of vulgarity to tell the story of a thug's ill-fated attempt to rob the eponymous zombie.[33] In each of these examples, the comic treatment of the premise allows the story to stray outside the inflexible parameters of the 'standard' zombie plot. The undead terrorising the Leitrim countryside in *Dead Meat* display several subtle bovine characteristics that set them apart from other cinematic zombies: they disregard humans if they are already eating, with the disinterest of grazing cattle, and at one point they surround a car on a narrow country road, but quickly lose interest and move on, much like a herd moving from one field to another. In one scene, they are shown sleeping upright in an open field, a trait often erroneously attributed to cattle in popular culture. The film is also book-ended with images of culls – of infected cattle at the beginning, and human survivors at the end. The main character of *Boy Eats Girl*, meanwhile, is a teenage boy who accidentally hangs himself, and is resurrected by his mother using a 'voodoo' spell book. Thereafter the story follows the pattern of a viral outbreak, with zombiism transmitted by biting. The character of Dead Murphy, meanwhile, became so through a curse laid on him by his own mother (as he strangled her to death in a drunken rage), and his vengeance upon the 'Man From Strabane' is motivated mainly by frustration at the robber's failure to kill him; in an additional fairy-tale flourish, the background detail is provided by a talking crow.

As in the parodies and pastiches of Romero's films mentioned previously, many of these particular zombies are self-aware. The protagonist of *Boy Eats Girl* retains his consciousness and personality, though he is the only zombie in the film to do so, and he experiences unpleasant urges to bite his peers. Dead Murphy is foul-mouthed and foul-tempered, though always true to his word. The zombies of *Dead Meat* are in most respects very close to Romero's undead, and in a couple of instances are seen using farming implements as weapons. These parodies, however, dovetail very neatly into a pre-existing tradition of reanimated corpses with wills, personalities and desires beyond simply consuming human flesh, and because of this pre-existing tradition, Irish texts are starting to appear in which zombie subjectivity is once again treated seriously, rather than comically or ironically. David Freyne's film *The Cured* (2017), set in Ireland in the aftermath of a zombie outbreak that was contained and halted by medical science, follows a number of former zombies who now find themselves under suspicion from the rest of society.[34] One key element of the Cured's subjectivity is that they retain detailed memories of everything they did as zombies. Another is that being cured has robbed them of something they shared while they were infected – a telepathic link that bound them into pack-like groups and gave them a sense of intimacy that is missing from their human lives. Sarah Davis-Goff's novel *Last Ones Left Alive* (2019) features fast-moving, shrieking creatures called 'skrake' (from the Irish *scréach*, meaning 'scream'), which are functionally zombies in all the necessary respects, but retain enough of their prior personalities to try to manipulate their loved ones, cajoling them to come within striking distance.[35] While skrake are implied to have little control over their emotions or impulses, the attempt to draw their prey near with sweet tones and piteous pleas for help adds guile and deliberate cruelty to a monster that is usually held to lack those qualities.

Conclusion

The point of this survey is not to argue for Irish zombie media as a unique case. As was discussed, Ireland was just one of many places where conceptions of the ghost and the reanimated corpse did not fully diverge from one another in the late nineteenth century. Nor is the aim to defend the taxonomic sins criticised by Bishop – namely, (mis)labelling all kinds of folkloric undead as 'zombies', and deliberately blurring the definitions to exploit zombies' present wave of popularity.[36] What this sampling of the Irish undead suggests, rather, is that cultures that do not rigidly adhere to the corporeal/non-corporeal distinction may have an advantage when it comes to shaping the next stage of zombie evolution. I argue that the mindless, shuffling 'walker' zombie, a human-minus figure paradoxically excluded from the texts that it defines, is reaching the end of its usefulness: just as sorcery was eclipsed by science (first 'radiation', then virology), and the lone zombie was surpassed by immense hordes, the human-minus zombie is being rapidly superseded by fully conscious zombies. It seems likely that this is a matter of necessity, though it may also be a response to environmental concerns: audiences may finally be running out of sympathy for creatures that mindlessly consume and destroy the world around them. Restoring consciousness to the zombie is merely a first step, though.

The fact of death itself is perhaps not sufficient to distinguish a thinking zombie from a necrotic human; the difference might be further marked with 'undead' behaviours such as the frankness of the *slí an fhírinne*, a disregard for social niceties, or even manipulation and cunning. We may see a new wave of zombies with vendettas 'haunting' the ones who wronged them in life, driven to avenge injustices real and perceived. Additionally, if zombies can be presented as telepathic, what other kinds of quasi-scientific powers might they be endowed with? There will probably not be a wholesale return to tales of occultists raising bodies from the dead, but we might very well see zombies with the full range of spectral abilities attributed to them in folklore, provided those abilities can be satisfactorily rationalised in scientific terms for the sensibilities of present-day readers and audiences. A new breed of zombie is imminent, and while they will still be dead, they will not necessarily be all 'messed up'.

Notes

1. Charles Lever, 'The Mountain Pass', in *Weird Tales: Irish* [1843] (Edinburgh: William Paterson, 1886), pp. 144–5.
2. China Miéville, 'M. R. James and the Quantum Vampire: Weird; Hauntological; Versus and/or and and/or or?', Collapse: *Journal of Philosophical Research and Development*, IV (2008), 119.
3. Sarah Juliet Lauro, 'Ron Honthaner's *House on Skull Mountain*: Zombie Gothic', in Simon Bacon (ed.), *The Gothic: A Reader* (Oxford: Peter Lang, 2018), pp. 71–2.
4. Montague Summers, *Witchcraft and Black Magic* [1946] (London: Arrow Books Ltd, 1974), pp. 238–9.
5. Stacey Abbott, *Undead Apocalypse: Vampires and Zombies in the 21st Century* (Edinburgh: Edinburgh University Press, 2016), p. 162.
6. Lauro, 'Zombie Gothic', pp. 69–70.
7. Philip Munz, Ioan Hudea, Joe Imad and Robert J. Smith, 'When Zombies Attack! Mathematical Modelling of an Outbreak of Zombie Infection', in Jean Michel Tchuenche and Christinah Chiyaka (eds), *Infectious Disease Modelling Research Progress* (Hauppauge, NY: Nova Science Publishers, Inc., 2009), p. 134.
8. Munz et al., 'When Zombies Attack!', p. 146.
9. Of course, this kind of 'enhancement' is not limited to zombie fandom: clear analogues can be seen in the 'Sherlockian Game', whereby Arthur Conan Doyle devotees derive biographical data for Sherlock Holmes from references in the written canon, and in *Star Trek* fans' observations of the franchise's apparent predictions of technological change. A folkloric equivalent can perhaps be identified in the phenomenon of ostension, or 'legend-tripping'.
10. Kyle William Bishop, *How Zombies Conquered Popular Culture* (Jefferson: McFarland, 2015), pp. 149–50.
11. Güven Güzeldere, 'Zombies', in Lynn Nadel et al. (eds), *Encyclopedia of Cognitive Science*, vol. 4 (New York: John Wiley & Sons, 2006), pp. 593–5.
12. Bishop, *How Zombies Conquered Popular Culture*, p. 24.

13. *Birth of the Living Dead*, dir. Rob Kuhns, Glass Eye Pix/Predestinate Productions, New York (2012).
14. Bishop, *How Zombies Conquered Popular Culture*, p. 13.
15. Abbott, *Undead Apocalypse*, pp. 162–3.
16. Lauro, 'Zombie Gothic', p. 69.
17. Lauro, 'Zombie Gothic', p. 70.
18. Irish Folklore Commission, *Schools' Folklore Scheme*, 864 (1937–9), 138–9.
19. *Schools' Folklore Scheme*, vol. 44, pp. 668, 383.
20. Sheridan Le Fanu, *Ghost Stories of Chapelizod* (Dublin: Good Press, 2020).
21. *Schools' Folklore Scheme*, pp. 141, 213.
22. Frederick O' Connell (as 'Conall Cearnach'), 'The Homing Bone', in David Marcus (ed.), *The Poolbeg Book of Irish Ghost Stories* [1924] (Dublin: Poolbeg Press Ltd, 1993), p. 16.
23. O'Connell, 'The Homing Bone', p. 21.
24. Mary Lavin, 'The Green Grave and the Black Grave', in Peter Haining (ed.), *Great Irish Stories of the Supernatural* (New York: Pan Books, 1993), p. 378.
25. Mary Lavin, 'The Dead Soldier', in David Marcus (ed.), *The Poolbeg Book of Irish Ghost Stories* (Dublin: Poolbeg, 1993), p. 77.
26. Lavin, 'The Dead Soldier', pp. 78–9.
27. Máirtín Ó Cadhain, *The Dirty Dust/Cré na Cille* (New Haven: Yale University Press, 2015); Máirtín Ó Cadhain, *Graveyard Clay*, trans. Liam Mac Con Iomaire and Tim Robison (New Haven: Yale University Press, 2016).
28. Abbott, *Undead Apocalypse*, pp. 161–2.
29. Munz et al., 'When Zombies Attack!', pp. 135–7, 140–3, 144–6. Munz et al. also include a scenario where the model allows for treatment – effectively a cure for death in general, since it transforms zombies back into humans regardless of how they died. Even with this unorthodox concession, human die-back is colossal, and humanity survives the apocalypse with a drastically reduced population (pp. 143–4).
30. Abbott, *Undead Apocalypse*, pp. 161–2.
31. *Dead Meat*, dir. Conor McMahon, Three Way Productions, Ireland (2004).
32. *Boy Eats Girl*, dir. Stephen Bradley, Element Films, Vancouver (2005).
33. Dead Murphy, dir. Stephen McCollum, Raw Nerve Productions, Beverely Hills (2006).
34. *The Cured*, dir. David Freyne, Tilted Pictures/Bac Films/Savage Productions, Ireland (2017).
35. Sarah Davis-Goff, *Last Ones Left Alive* (London: Tinder Press, 2019), pp. 192–9.
36. Bishop, *How Zombies Conquered Popular Culture*, pp. 20, 150.

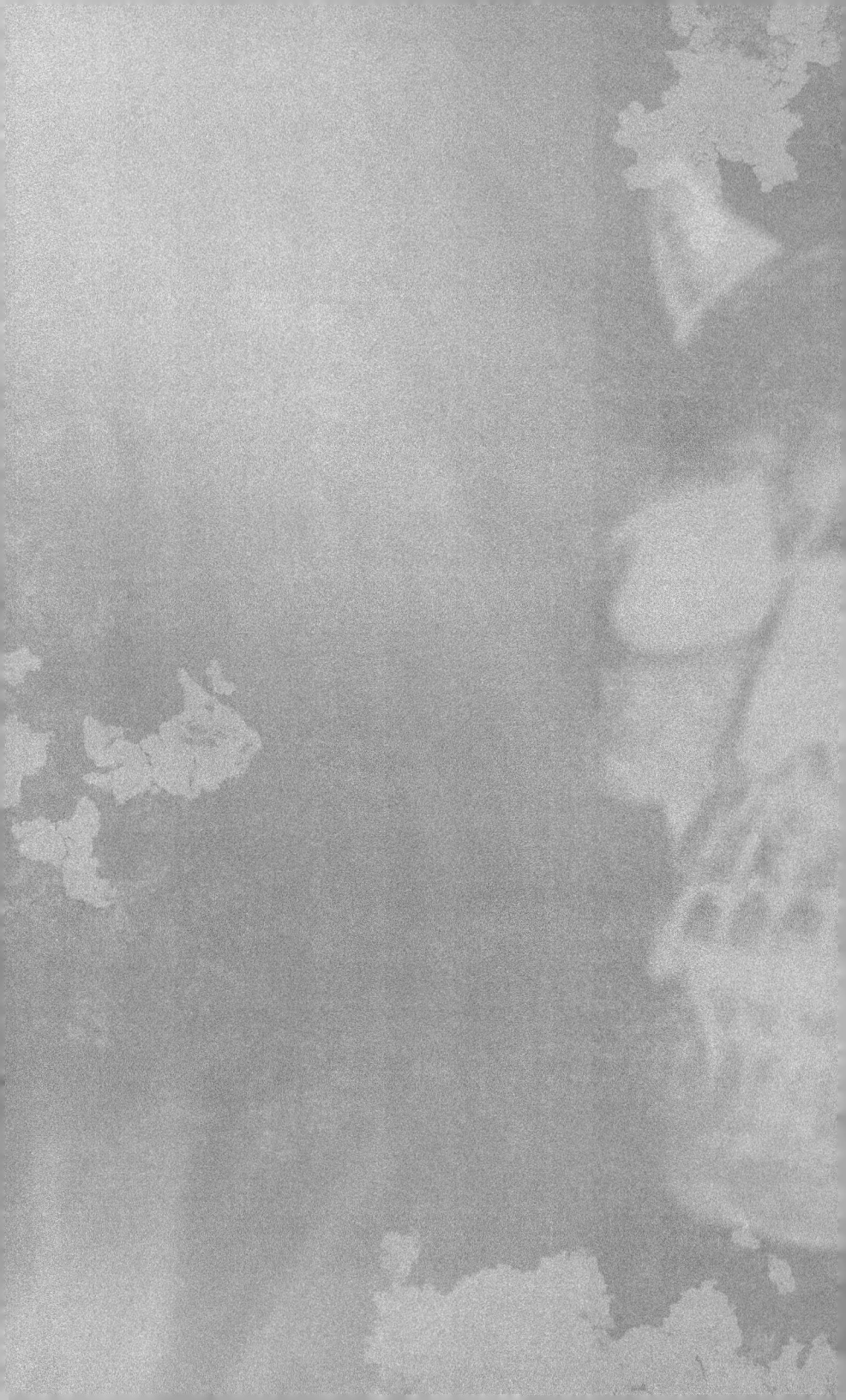

6

M. R. Carey's *The Boy on the Bridge*
Ethics and the Apocalypse

Scott Eric Hamilton

'A Human Being is a very hard thing to be'[1]

THE BURDEN OF EXISTENCE is never so apparent as during a zombie apocalypse. M. R. Carey's *The Boy on the Bridge* confronts the elitist mentality of humans as a species and designations of value placed on both human and nonhuman existence within an apocalyptic setting. Subsequently, the novel achieves the fictional capitulation of species elitism by adapting the real-world scientifically verified behaviour of *Ophiocordyceps unilateralis*, or zombie-ant fungus, into the catalyst for the apocalypse. Although unclear exactly which sources Carey consulted, the accuracy of the functioning of the *cordyceps* fungus indicates a familiarity with the science behind the zombie ant phenomenon. Colonel Carlisle, commander of the military science team searching for a cure, indicates explicitly that the 'hungry plague' causes the loss of elitism through nostalgia of dominance:

> When humankind was in the ascendant, when we ruled the world and the whole of creation bowed down to us ... where people were poor and miserable and governments were parasitic ... But when the plague struck, that all changed. It changed forever.[2]

The result is a human species increasingly unable to survive an ecosystem not conducive to maintaining that survival in a context where they are not 'in the ascendant'. In this regard, Carey's zombie novels resonate with the threats of the Anthropocene to planetary biodiversity, threats which, in part, are the result of human elitism and the consequential devaluing of the nonhuman.

Sarah Juliet Lauro and Karen Embry posit that zombiism 'calls for the destruction of the reigning [social] model'.[3] Zombiism is the catastrophic negation of self, but also the necessary onslaught on the canonical theories that threaten to become authoritarian critiques of ideology that threaten to subsume any authentic individual self. Stefan Herbrechter and Ivan Callus claim, 'theory can only reinvent itself as worthwhile . . . through its own critical self-evaluation'.[4] Zombiism, then, is indicative of what theory purports to achieve, ensuring its own evolution through the process of self-evaluation through the act of self-deconstruction. The ability to self-deconstruct would enable any theoretical framework to avoid succumbing to any reigning model of thought by confronting or dismantling reigning models of power. Therefore, this chapter argues that zombiism, as a theory of crisis, dismantles power structures that inform elitist discourses of extinction.

Moreover, as related to the elitism behind the anthropocentric effects on biodiversity, a subsequent argument will be made for zombiism as theory of extinction revelation. Through such revelations, a world-against-humans can become a world-including-humans contingent on sustaining biodiversity instead of exploiting resources to the point of catastrophe. Thus, the zombie apocalypse of Carey's *The Boy on the Bridge* revokes the elitism of the human species to examine the ethics of extinction whilst emphasising the need to acknowledge the intrinsic value in the nonhuman even if that value is beyond human comprehension.

M. R. Carey, tradition . . . and zombies

The zombie figure has experienced its own evolution, from its origins in Haitian folklore to the Romero era to its current position in popular culture.[5] To provide context for *The Boy on the Bridge* (2017), Carey's first zombie novel *The Girl with All the Gifts* (2014) contributes to this evolution by basing its zombie-like menace on verified science embodied in a sentient and seditious threat to human survival.[6] The opening of *Girl* introduces the second generation of infected, called 'hungries', as children being studied in a military facility. The first wave of infection rendered its victims closer to the traditional mindless zombie; however, the second generation, for reasons unknown to the humans, has evolved, obtaining a degree of consciousness. One of the central narrative conflicts is the tension between the head military scientist, Dr Caldwell, and protagonist Melanie, a second-generation hungry who is a subject in the military facility. Dr Caldwell, perhaps unnecessarily, dissects countless hungry children in an insatiable drive for data with the hopes of finding a cure. In contrast, Melanie, through her education – primarily the humanities – understands that data (accumulated information) does not equal knowledge. Both *Girl* and *Boy* reflect on, among other issues, the ethical dichotomy between information and knowledge; data and significance; survival and extinction.[7] These dichotomies lead to information substituted for knowledge, resulting in Caldwell's unethical actions; a warning for all academic pursuits that may, without critical self-reflection, supplement data for knowledge.

Boy, with a split narrative timeframe occurring before and after *Girl*, engages more explicitly with the ethics of human action in reaction to possible extinction. *Boy* inverts the subject of conservation and de-extinction debates of nonhuman species to the potential preservation and extinction of the human species. Daniel Knickerbocker argues that in rejecting 'human exceptionalism in favor of a view of humanity as just one of many species', the 'zombie . . . attempts to wrest humanity from its dominion over the planet'.[8] As such, the zombie forces humanity to acknowledge the detriment of its own elitism by making it confront its own extinction as a crisis of its own making. Peter Singer states in general terms that 'Ethics deals with values'.[9] The zombie apocalypse, then, challenges the value of survival by hypothesising the crisis of human extinction. To examine the loss of domination, existing scholarship on species de-extinction and conservation – both scientific and philosophical – provides the foundation for the ethical consideration involved in the potentiality of human extinction in Carey's zombie apocalypse.[10] Audra Mitchell suggests that hypothesising human extinction 'creates important opportunities for ethical reflection and political critique', arguing that humanity 'as a subject of extinction engenders a productive dynamic of abjection in which humans must confront the possibilities of becoming-otherwise'.[11] The confrontation of the zombie as abject other is apt for exploring the ethics involved with 'becoming-otherwise' if humans cease to be the elite species on Earth.

The hubris of humanity, often criticised within de-extinction, extinction and posthuman debates, is considered here as evidence of species elitism. Even in what is being called the nonhuman turn, the focus of scholarly investigation is founded on identifying the nonhuman in terms of value as related to human notion of utility. As such, humanity often views the nonhuman world through a paradigm of species elitism.

An elitist mentality is evident in the inability of individuals comprehending their own death and their relationship to the world they inhabit. Eugene Thacker, *In the Dust of this Planet*, posits three ways to think about the planet, 'world-for-us', 'world-in-itself' and 'world-without-us'.[12] The problematic 'world-for-us' (elitist) mentality produces a world-for-only-us outlook that fosters destructive exploitation of resources.[13] However, the 'world-without-us' poses the paradoxical problem of comprehending a world completely void of comprehension. Thacker indicates that 'Horror is about the paradoxical thought of the unthinkable.'[14] A world-without-us invokes the horrific unthinkable. Consequently, a fourth category may be more appropriate for the purpose of exploring the ethics of extinction: examining a 'world-against-us', like that of Carey's novels, offers speculative ethical investigations for establishing a more biologically inclusive 'world-including-humans'.

Apocalypse narratives draw from similar fascinations with the world-against-us that deflect confrontations with the horror of a world-without-humans. However, the narrator in *Boy* indicates that the central character Stephen 'Greaves finds the prospect of his own non-existence fascinating and dizzying'.[15] This 'dizzying' fascination performs and confronts the paradox of comprehending, or theorizing, the lack of comprehension. Therefore, humans being unable to comprehend the absence of their own existence (contributing to the sense of elitism) equates to theorising a world without theory.

The ethics of extinction ... and zombies

The philosophical considerations of de-extinction are appropriate for exploring zombiism, and *Boy* explicitly. Shlomo Cohen claims that 'de-extinction may create some "unnatural" transgenetic organisms; and, *worst of all*, de-extinction attempts to *revive the dead*'.[16] The language Cohen uses, 'worst of all . . . to revive the dead', reflects a common undertone of condemnation found in de-extinction scholarship. This resurrection-of-the-dead taxonomy indeed carries connotations of the threat of the undead. As such, mirroring a common trope of the zombie genre, the process of de-extinction, as posed by commentators, is comparable to raising the dead, or creating 'zombies'.[17]

Advancements in DNA modification and cloning techniques has initiated ethical concerns regarding the possibility of resurrecting extinct species. More specifically, these concerns centre around species that have become extinct on account of human activity. Although more extensive than can be addressed here, two interrelated concepts drive the philosophical consideration of de-extinction and conservation, an obligation for justice and acknowledgement of intrinsic value. The argument for justice contends that humans have an obligation to revive or conserve species which have become extinct, or are threatened to become extinct, because of the Anthropocene.

Roland Sandler explains that 'motivation behind . . . de-extinction is that humanity has done something terribly wrong in causing so many animals to go extinct. Therefore, we have a responsibility to make up for it in some way.'[18] Here, the moral contention results from justifying an obligation for survival, or conservation, of the self to right a wrong ultimately self-inflicted. *Boy* confronts such notions and demonstrates the damage inflicted on species and environment by showcasing the damage humans inflict on themselves: the devaluing of others is the devaluing of the self. For example, Dr Samrina Khan holds contempt for Colonel Carlisle as 'the man who burned half of Hertfordshire, who rained more napalm down on the home counties than America rained on Vietnam without causing the hungries to even miss a meal'.[19] Any positive ethics of survival loses any potential moral value if granted to oneself, especially if justifying deplorable acts of violence in the name of survival. The obligation for survival, in the novel at least, is directly proportionate to the degree of value acknowledged. Cohen presents the following philosophical insight: 'What is the content of the obligation toward species? The answer is easy, since only one thing is in species' interest: their continued propagation to the future. Hence, we have a moral obligation not to render species extinct.'[20] However, this raises a complex question, if *Homo sapiens* are endangered do they have the obligation to preserve themselves if that obligation serves unethical self-interest, that is, survival that results in the disproportionate damage to biodiversity? Consequently, no simple answer can determine the degree of obligation a species may have in relation to both themselves and other species, especially when value is often granted or denied subjectively.

The premise of acknowledged value holds that the nonhuman has intrinsic value regardless of human interaction. This premise could be strengthened to include the possibility that intrinsic value exists in the nonhuman beyond human comprehension. Stephen struggles with this paradoxical comprehension of meaning with the hungry children: 'The children shift in his mind, semiotically adrift. They are hungries, but not hungries.'[21] The 'scarred girl', who leads the tribe of child hungries, affords him the opportunity to progress from seeing the nonhuman children as representing a lack of meaning to accepting the possibility that they represent a multitude of meanings: 'She might be nobody, devoid of meaning or value. But it doesn't feel like that. If anything, it feels the opposite. She is supercharged with potential meanings, none of which can be subtracted until he knows her better.'[22] Stephen may not know exactly what the children are, being 'semiotically adrift' in his mind, but he accepts that they are 'supercharged with potential meanings' precisely because they are not easily categorised. He does not anthropomorphise these nonhuman beings and thus they retain their own intrinsic value.

The problem with some of the de-extinction arguments, and related counterarguments, is that the premise, inadvertently in most cases, is often the limited analysing of the nonhuman through various designation of human economic value. The economic cost and labour effort of de-extinction or conservation is regularly weighed in contrast to the viability of realising any moral obligation. For example, Cohen lists one of the primary 'Factors associated with negative utility' as being economic in scope: 'Unwise expenditure. De-extinction may prove a bad investment, as the chances that resurrected species will not last are realistic.'[23] Commentary on de-extinction or conservation that examines the cost of effort usually lacks consideration of general cruelty towards that species being subjected to a potentially second extinction.

Arguments for cost benefit tend to link value of life to the profit of exhibition and scientific development – specifically biomedical and pharmaceutical production. Although few concerned with the issues of extinction and conservation would reject that in principle all endangered nonhuman species are worth preserving if at all possible; nonetheless, commentators on conservation debates are preoccupied with funding such endeavours being contingent on 'selling' such projects as economically viable, if not profitable.[24] Hence, the regular reference to what conservation or de-extinction may offer in terms of scientific and biomedical advances. The dependency of medicine is regularly emphasised in *Boy* which contributes to confronting the possibility of unethical biomedical production.[25] For instance, when hungry children are a possible source for a cure, the following is Khan's reaction: 'What would be monstrous would be pulping their brains and spines to make medicine.'[26] Therefore, any value of species-being is negated in favour of use-value, which is to be thought of as monstrous in this context.

The argument for the resurrection of extinct species, although well intentioned, exemplifies the elitism inherent in conservation and de-extinction as it relates to little more than Marxist-like use-value. Resurrected species offer returns on investment with exhibit and research value. Although valid in certain regards, other concerns seem to avoid consideration. Although notions of obligation do not exist in the nonhuman natural world, as far as can be discerned, humans nonetheless have an obligation to conserve, or resurrect, species to promote a high degree of planetary biodiversity regardless of investment returns. However, *Boy* presents a context where humanity, on the precipice of annihilation, engages in a type of pre-emptive de-extinction for which cost is a driving concern. Similarly, the act of, arbitrarily, determining one species to be more valuable than others to be revived is a form of elitism. In the apocalypse, the drive for survival, in many ways, is the attempt to conserve human elitism despite all of its failings. Zombiism, however, deflates human elitism, forcing the re-conceptualisation of how humanity will proceed as one species equal to others, dependent on sustaining biodiversity.

The ethics of knowledge ... and zombies

Boy, like all effective literature, attempts to force humanity to place itself in the context of the Other. Greg Garrett claims that the 'Zombie Apocalypse offers a laboratory for observing human emotions and experience ... The story of the Zombie Apocalypse [asks] questions about what it means to be human.'[27] Accordingly, zombiism provides the grounds to examine ethical dilemmas around what being nonhuman means, as much as what being human means. *Boy* decentralises human elitism by emphasising the benefit of gaining knowledge of the value of the nonhuman other, even if knowledge of that nonhuman other is elusive.

Stephen's genius and trauma is the cause of his anti-socialism and otherness; referred to mockingly as 'the Robot' by some of the crew he is almost posthuman, or perhaps transhuman. Stephen does not subscribe to human elitism, and as a result is antithetical to Caldwell and the mentality of the Beacon military facility. In this regard, Stephen is the human equivalent of Melanie from *Girl*. His uniqueness is not necessarily his savant-like intellect but, like Melanie, the proportionate sense of moral values. The narrative establishes Stephen as occupying a liminal space progressing towards a posthuman state, a potential world-without-humans. Khan assumes a moral responsibility for Stephen having found him during the migration of survivors to Beacon, which she describes as 'a column of about eight hundred desperate people shepherded – harassed, it sometimes seems – by soldiers in urban camouflage colours'.[28] During the dehumanising pilgrimage the column crosses a bridge on which a scene of carnage had recently unfolded. In the middle of the bridge is where Khan finds Stephen as 'a small boy – maybe five or six years old – lying between two adults. Their bodies are bowed outwards, shielding him from attack on either side. They are like a pair of brackets around him, cordoning him off from the world.'[29] More than just corpses, the bodies of his dead parents create a parenthetical bracket around him, testament to the sacrifice they made to preserve the potential future Stephen as a child represents.

However, their sacrificial bodies, which 'bear so many wounds – bite marks, incisions and lacerations, in the man's case a gunshot wound to the head – that it is impossible to piece together how they died', reflect the trauma responsible for his unreconcilable parenthetical positioning isolated between both hungries and humans.[30] This liminal space provides Stephen his unique perspective:

> In the whole of Beacon, there is nobody who has a fuller understanding of what the human race is up against. But it seems to Khan that part of Stephen is still lying on the damp asphalt of a Surrey street. In Parenthesis. Waiting for an all-clear that will never come.[31]

Stephen's liminality signifies his capability of producing knowledge that bridges the ontological gap between both species.

The traumatic experience of being overpowered by the force of extinction facilitates Stephen's ability to produce knowledge and not just generate information according to preordained concepts. Stephen, not institutionalised by predominant modes of thinking, 'was only twelve when he synthesised the e-blocker gel . . . he was the first to suggest *Ophiocordyceps unilateralis* as the fungus responsible for the hungry plague'.[32] Stephen's intelligence allows him to begin the search for a potential cure. However, his lack of life experience disallows any initial consideration of the ramifications that knowledge may carry, the slaughter of countless hungries in the pursuit of profitable science.

Nonetheless, the horrors Stephen witnessed fosters a moral viewpoint emphasising the value of life, both human and nonhuman: 'He . . . has dissected dozens of cadavers with no qualms at all, but the thought of cutting into a living body, human or animal or hungry, is nauseating. Impossible. Like telling a lie or initiating touch, it is simply not in his behavioural repertoire.'[33] The brackets of his dead parents shielding him from the dangers of the world results in the avoidance of human touch. Positioned between the world of the hungries and the world of humans, he understands the destruction of all life is 'nauseating' and tragic.

As events unfold, Stephen develops a treatment for the symptoms of infection. The primary motivation becomes the personal need to save the life of Khan's unborn after being bitten. She, as the narrative testifies, after finding him on the bridge acted as guardian and mentor to foster his intellectual potential:

> Rina . . . took him out of school for weeks at a time to teach him herself, in her canvas-walled lab – to teach him science mostly, but other things too. She reasoned that [...] he would have a taste for science fiction and fantasy in general [...] He learned the pleasure of stories which is like no other pleasure.[34]

The intellectual engagement with both the sciences and humanities in *Girl* and *Boy* is suggested as a prerequisite for a moral perspective. Stephen's morals seem to accept that all life has value, and facilitates a perspective that, along with other species, to adapt Claire Colebrook's claim that, '"humanity" is never simply data . . . but an excess potentiality that remains unactualized'.[35] Any 'excess of potentiality', for Stephen, resides in all living organisms, which is perhaps the most effective acknowledgement of the intrinsic value of the nonhuman. Stephen is more objectively moral because of the acceptance of potential value beyond his own comprehension.

Evidence abound of human proclivity to exploit the nonhuman for its own benefit. This is not to argue that nonhuman resources should never be used for human benefit – but this benefit should not be excessive in indulging in this utility to the point of exploitation and degradation of life. However, Stephen's intellectual and moral balance forces him into an ethical dilemma. Stephen knows that his discovery of a potential cure will undoubtedly result in humans seeing only the use-value of the second-generation children in terms of their survival. In other words, elitism occurs in 'treating living beings as if they are mere genomic pieces or building blocks', to adopt Sandler's words. Not knowing if she understands, Stephen explains to 'the scarred girl', when he relinquishes Khan's infected newborn:

> You have to [take him] . . . Otherwise, when they ask me, I'll tell them. That there's a cure. How to make it. Men with weapons will come after you – many, many more than are here now. They'll take you and turn you into medicine. Kill you all, just so they can have a few more years of life themselves. They won't even feel sorry about it.[37]

Stephen's warning exemplifies what Colebrook regards as the human propensity towards exploitation: 'that humanity is and must be parasitic: it lives *only* in its robbing and destruction of a life that is not its own . . . whereby we have consumed and ingested blindly'.[38] The body politic reverberates in Stephen's internal earlier testimony:

> *If I bring this home . . . We'll scour the whole country, from one end to the other . . . And when that isn't enough – not nearly enough – we'll start a breading [sic] programme. Capture female hungries alive and impregnate them. Take the babies, and* . . . *Mulch them down. Liquidise and synthesise and mass produce. Build massive battery farms full of insentient brood mares. Fill them and empty them again and again.*[39]

Expendable bodies do not carry the moral obligation of regret if a sacrifice for profit is required.[40] Profit in this sense does not always equate to economic profit, although monetary gain is often a factor: the sacrifice of the body politic is usually a profit for maintaining or establishing power, that is, a state of elitism. The 'robbing and destruction of a life', to invoke Colebrook, is something Stephen knows accompanies the consistent human disregard for intrinsic value, such as Colonel Carlisle for example. Lieutenant McQueen, second in command, however, is more like Stephen than Carlisle in his outlook on killing: 'You shouldn't kill a man without being aware of the possibilities, the futures, you're are snuffing out . . . Killing a child is like killing a vast multitude.'[41] Stephen understands that any dead body, similar to the bodies of his parents, represents a sacrifice, and although sometimes unavoidable, he, like McQueen tends to make better moral decisions by accepting the implications any death carries. Consequently, the ethical dilemma for Stephen is whether to share his knowledge of a cure resulting in the detrimental exploitation of a new sentient species, or allow the potential extinction of *Homo sapiens*, of which he is a part, to ensure the hungries have a chance to propagate their own future:

> Stephen has made up his mind, he's with . . . the scarred girl's tribe. He can't be one of them but he has chosen his allegiance . . . though he's on their side he is the plague, the pathogen that could destroy them. The knowledge in his mind has to be safely disposed of.[42]

He concludes that the most ethical option is to sacrifice himself, eradicating the knowledge necessary for survival and allowing an already exhausted species to become extinct.

Colebrook suggests that with 'the destruction of man . . . [t]here would no longer be a privileged center of knowing'.[43] Stephen's development of a cure would perpetuate humans as the 'privileged center of knowing' even if only temporarily. His solution is to ensure that his cure is never discovered. In this regard, Carey's two zombie novels stage the crisis of the Anthropocene as the result of the devaluing of the nonhuman, and the lack of knowledge regarding the potential devastation resulting from that devaluation.

Post-elitism, conservation . . . and zombies

The epilogue of *The Boy on the Bridge* finds a small group of human survivors, including some of the crew, 'twenty years later' in dwindling health and running low on supplies in the remote area of Cairngorm, in the Scottish mountains.[44] On account of the altitude of Cairngorm not being conducive to the cordyceps pathogen, as revealed in the narrative, the mountain range acts as a type of preserve. Decades after the battle at Beacon and Stephen's death, the survivors are approached by, a now adult, Melanie, from *Girl*. She explains that 'The world is poison to you now. Apart from this one place, apparently . . . It's been plain for a long time that the plateau is an island in an invisible toxic ocean.'[45] She tells McQueen that her group had been 'watching you from a distance, as discreetly as we could. Building up a picture . . . Probably your colony has two years or maybe three left. Maybe not so long.'[46] The allusion to human-generated toxic pollution aside, Melanie and the '*next* people', as she called them in *Girl*, engage in a type of bio-conservation which establishes Cairngorm as a type of preserve. The altitude, as explained, is not conducive to the pathogen's life cycle which had spared them, from when Melanie released the airborne version of the pathogen near the end of *Girl*: she justified her actions in ethical terms:

> If you keep shooting [the hungries] and cutting them into pieces and throwing them into pits, nobody will be left to make a new world . . . This way is better. Everybody turns into a hungry all at once, and that means they'll die, which is really sad. But the children will grow up, and they won't be the old kind of people but they won't be hungries either . . . They'll be the *next* people. The ones who make everything okay again.[47]

The burden of redemption is thrust upon future generations – 'The ones who make everything okay again' – and perhaps only a more evolved version of humanity, 'they won't be the old kind of people but they won't be hungries either'.[48]

However, because she did not actually eradicate the entire human race, Melanie's actions regarding those in Cairngorm suggest a moral obligation to preserve the endangered species. In this context the humans have become what conservation biology has deemed 'living dead species', which, as Genese Sodikoff explains, 'refers to species populations that have become . . . doomed to die out' but yet continue to survive.[49] Both novels suggest that the activities of humans are not only detrimental to the vitality of biodiversity but also to evolutionary development. Therefore, any threat to biodiversity may also be a threat to evolution itself. Evolution is a constant, albeit slow, process and given a long-enough timeline a new species could evolve out of humanity. Consequently, assuming that any one species is the pinnacle achievement of evolution would, indeed, be hubristic. Therefore, any moral obligation to biodiversity, then, is the moral obligation to the possibility of what evolution has yet to realise.

In Carey's post-elitist world, humans, almost undeniably, threaten biodiversity and Melanie, like Stephen, realises that the ethical act is to allow their extinction rather than risk their destructive survival. However, since the majority of the species was eradicated, and cease being a threat to biodiversity, Melanie and the '*next* people' engage in bio-conservation to maintain the addition to diversity even humans can provide, and curate a type of living archive. Related to conservation, Thaddeaus Miller notes that,

> within this context of the crisis of biodiversity loss ... PAs [protected areas] are defended as beachheads on the global war against extinction. Such martial language, in fact, is commonplace in the literature and on the conservation 'front lines' ... the dominant PA approach ... 'fortress conservation' in which people-free parks and reserves are viewed as nature's last line of defence against development and eventual biological destruction[50]

Cairngorm, then, is 'fortress conservation' park in reverse, where biological containment becomes 'nature's [best] line of defence' against the 'biological destruction' of the Anthropocene.[51] Cairngorm becomes a protected area, similar to those defined by biological conservationists. Stephen's self-sacrifice and Melanie's desire to learn from the humans in exchange for conservation, indeed, positions humans as no longer the elite species or centre of knowledge. The degree of hope offered at the end of the novel is that the new nonhuman centre of knowing might be more ethical in the management of natural resources. The confines of Cairngorm[52] are allegorical of the juxtaposition between the finite and confined human existence on Earth against the infinite and, presently, unquantifiable nonhuman universe. And yet the single planet that houses human life is thought of, by humans, as contingent on the continued existence of that singular species, *Homo sapiens*, expressed in the cliche 'the end of the world'. That is, if the Anthropocene ends in catastrophe for humans, as predicted by numerous scholars, it will not be 'the end of the world' apocalypse but an Anthropocalypse.[53] That is, an event which renders the human redundant as the dominant influence on the planet, even if that event is as common as evolution.

Potentially, the Anthropocene could negatively affect evolution in general, including that of humans. François Sarrazin and Jane Lecomte highlight that 'anthropogenic extinctions ... may greatly constrain ... evolutionary trajectories'.[54] However, evolution is not necessarily exclusive to physiology: the mentality of society can evolve to exclude such a high level of destructive elitism. In other words, elitism should not be exclusive to one species but inclusive of all species contributing to the unique biosphere of Earth. Consequently, the entire Earth could be understood as a type of PA, or preserve, for all species that inhabit the planet. Until proven otherwise, every species on Earth has intrinsic value because they are unique to the universe.

Miller contends that 'biodiversity conservationists frequently hold that protected areas (PAs) – traditionally understood as those areas with minimal human presence and history of alteration – are the best, if not the only means to adequately protect all elements of biodiversity (i.e., genes, populations, and landscapes)'.[55] Comparably, Cairngorm acts as a type of preserve for the endangered human species. However, PAs as a means of preservation and/or de-extinction raise issues regarding the degree of cruelty that accompanies a species being forced to exist in an environment that is not conducive to its survival. John Cairns argues that '[w]ithout the habitat in which the species thrived, it almost certainly would be not self-maintaining and, worse yet, without its natural habitat, it would be a caricature of the living creature that once existed'.[56] The apocalypse narrative invokes the fear reaction to the idea of humanity existing only in zoos, becoming a caricature of the once 'ascendant' species. The unsettling reaction to human zoos, or PAs, makes *Boy* effective in presenting humans as a 'living dead species' to invoke anxiety, and revelations, about the anthropocentric threat to human existence. Denial of that threat could result in humans becoming a caricature of what they once were capable of becoming.

Colebrook argues that post-apocalyptic narratives offer a 'new mode of the question of life [that] has come to dominate cultural production: not, "Why are humans subjected to the brutal force of existence?" but: given human brutality and life-destructiveness, by what right will humans continue to survive?'[57] The zombie genre, indeed, encapsulates the 'brutality and life-destructiveness' pervasive in modern society and industry. As an extension of Colebrook's argument, zombiism is a theorisation of the inherent, self-imposed, brutality of human existence. Within the apocalyptic context, facing extinction forces a re-evaluation of the meaningful and noble aspects of humane existence which may be of benefit to itself as well as to nonhuman development.

Carey's inversion of the humane-centred conservation and extinction context denies humans the perspective of elitism to emphasise that conservation in itself is the most ethical approach to ensuring biodiversity. That is, ensuring the existence of a biodiverse planet is directly related to ensuring the existence of humanity. Any decision that potentially counters conservation activity is unethical. Zombiism, then, offers the opportunity to examine the consequences of the unethical activity of humans manifested in the body of the undead Other, potentially inflicting apocalyptic horror on a species that may well deserve its fate of de-elitism. The colony PA in Cairngorm is indicative of all survivors of the zombie apocalypse as a 'living dead species'. As such the colonists exemplify aspects of the post-human-elitism which has capitulated the centre of knowledge, the 'next people' propose a world-including-humans.

The de-extinction of theory . . . and zombiism

Theory finds itself in an apocalypse-like academic landscape, or as Kurt Spellmeyer claims, 'Theory . . . has outlived its own "death".'[58] Perhaps as an advantage of operating as a living dead theory, zombiism assimilates and challenges other theories by subjecting them to a state of crisis demonstrating that Theory lives beyond its own assumed demise because it functions more as a diverse network than semblance of theoretical paradigms. The zombie has become a de-centred critical metaphor incorporated into almost every academic discipline.[59] Zombiism is an academic anomaly and theory in similar ways: 'Anomalies explode old theories and engender new ones. They are dangerous and glorious.'[60] Colebrook argues that, 'Theory follows from being exposed to a world that is not ourselves' and therefore 'theory . . . can be considered rigorously only with something like an extinction hypothesis'.[61] Moreover, Christopher Peterson asserts:

> the scandal of theory lies in the failure to decenter the human. The real scandal, however, is that we keep trying. We can no longer presume our privilege and exceptional status above all other beings, animate or inanimate, sentient or insentient. Nevertheless, our phantasmatic humanness engenders an aporetic relationship between us and nonhumans.[62]

Peterson, here, speaks to the negative effects of human elitism pervasive in theorising the nonhuman separate from the human. The zombiism in Carey's *Boy*, then, as 'extinction hypothesis' pervades that 'dangerous and glorious' aporia between human and nonhuman where decentring of the human is achieved and the 'privilege and exceptional status' of dominion over the nonhuman is negated.

The zombie apocalypse works towards achieving the promises offered by Theory by examining the moral cost of uncritically perpetuating the pretence of global dominance. Zombiism, then, provides the ability to analyse potential 'fallenness of a particular historical situation and the powers confronted there' before enduring any apocalyptic revelations.[63] It offers a means of investigating existence through revelations about the ethics of extinction and, perhaps more importantly, the moral obligation to the survival of all species. Perhaps learning to be a little less human (by expelling elitism) would afford the possibility of becoming the *next* people instead of ignoring the potential crisis of extinction by remaining a mindless zombie.

Notes

1. M. R. Carey, *The Boy on the Bridge* (London: Orbit, 2017), p. 326.
2. Carey, *Boy on the Bridge*, p. 84.
3. Sarah Juliet Lauro and Karen Embry, 'A Zombie Manifesto: The Nonhuman Condition in the Era of Advanced Capitalism', *boundary 2*, 35/1 (2008), 85–108.
4. Stefan Herbrechter and Ivan Callus, 'Introduction: Post-Theory?', in Stefan Herbrechter and Ivan Callus (eds), *Post-Theory, Culture, Criticism* (Amsterdam: Rodopi, 2004), p. 9.
5. This evolution has been well chronicled and will not be revisited here. See Roger Luckhurst, *Zombie: A Cultural History* (London: Reaktion Books, 2018).
6. *Boy* hereafter, unless otherwise indicated; M. R. Carey, *The Girl with All the Gifts* (London: Orbit, 2014). *Girl* hereafter, unless otherwise indicated.
7. See Scott Eric Hamilton, '*The Girl with All the Gifts*: Eco-Zombiism, Critical Lucidity, and the Anthropocalypse', *LIT: Literature, Interpretation, Theory*, 32/4 (2021), 285–304.
8. Daniel Knickerbocker, 'Why Zombies Matter: The Undead as Critical Posthumanist', *bohemica litteraria*, 18 (2015), 68.
9. Peter Singer, 'Introduction', in Peter Singer (ed.), *A Companion to Ethics* (London: Blackwell, 1993), p. v.
10. The wider complexities of these debates will not be addressed here. Nonetheless, Carey's zombie novels offer an inroad to many of the issues examined in conservation and de-extinction research regarding potential consequences of the Anthropocene.
11. Audra Mitchell, 'Beyond Biodiversity and Species: Problematizing Extinction', *Theory, Culture & Society*, 33/5 (2015), 36.
12. Eugene Thacker, *In the Dust of this Planet: Horror of Philosophy Volume 1* (Winchester: Zero Books, 2011), pp. 4–9.
13. Peter Godfrey-Smith suggests cephalopods are 'the closest we will come to meeting an intelligent alien': *Other Minds: The Octopus and the Evolution of*

Intelligent Life (London: William Collins, 2016), p. 9. Although elsewhere advocating against octopus farming (see n. 30 below), Godfrey-Smith's designation of 'intelligent alien' presupposes that intelligence, and consciousness, is exclusive to the human species, exemplifying the deeply engrained elitism within the human perception of other species.
14. Thacker, *In the Dust of This Planet*, p. 9.
15. Carey, *Boy*, p. 113.
16. Shlomo Cohen, 'The Ethics of De-Extinction', *Nanoethics*, 8 (2014), 173. Emphasis added.
17. The term 'zombie species' has been utilised in biology conservation scholarship.
18. Roland Sandler, 'The Ethics of Reviving Long Extinct Species', *Conservation Biology*, 28/2 (2013), 355.
19. Carey, *Boy*, p. 43.
20. Cohen, 'The Ethics of De-Extinction', 172.
21. Carey, *Boy*, p. 116.
22. Carey, *Boy*, p. 118.
23. Cohen, 'The Ethics of De-Extinction', 174.
24. The government of Scotland, for example, has dedicated considerable funding to rewilding. See Sophus O. S. E. zu Erdgasen et al., 'Ecosystem Service Responses to Rewilding: First-Order Estimates from 27 Years of Rewilding in the Scottish Highlands', *International Journal of Biodiversity Science, Ecosystem, Services & Management*, 14/1 (2018), 165–78. The Scottish Government plan for biodiversity can be found here, *https://www.gov.scot/policies/biodiversity/scottish-biodiversity-strategy/* (accessed 21 September 2019).
25. The dependency on medication in the novel suggests the biomedical industry generates its own clientele.
26. Carey, *Boy*, p. 367.
27. Greg Garrett, *Living with the Living Dead: The Wisdom of the Zombie Apocalypse* (Oxford: Oxford University Press, 2017), p. 9.
28. Carey, *Boy*, p. 104. Another theme of the novel is that of the apocalypse as the plight of the refugee, which is one example of the diversity of issues the zombie genre can accommodate.
29. Carey, *Boy*, p. 104.
30. Carey, *Boy*, p. 104.
31. Carey, *Boy*, p. 105.
32. Carey, *Boy*, p. 105. In both novels, the 'e-blocker gel', specially designed by Stephen, masks the smell of human pheromones to which hungries are attuned as predators.

33. Carey, *Boy*, p. 107.
34. Carey, *Boy*, pp. 73–5.
35. Claire Colebrook, *Death of the PostHuman: Essays on Extinction Vol. 1* (Ann Arbor: Open Humanities Press, 2014), p. 169.
36. Sandler, 'The Ethics of Reviving Long Extinct Species', 359.
37. Carey, *Boy*, pp. 434–5.
38. Colebrook, *Death of the PostHuman*, p. 178.
39. Carey, Boy, p. 366.
40. Jennifer Jacquet et al., 'The Case Against Octopus Farming', *Issues in Science and Technology*, 35/2 (2019), 37–44, explore this issue.
41. Carey, *Boy*, p. 132.
42. Carey, *Boy*, p. 436.
43. Colebrook, *Death of the PostHuman*, pp. 173–4.
44. Carey, *Boy*, p. 445.
45. Carey, *Boy*, pp. 451–2.
46. Carey, *Boy*, p. 453.
47. Carey, *Girl*, p. 456.
48. Carey, *Girl*, p. 456.
49. Genese Marie Sodikoff, 'The Time of Living Dead Species: Extinction Debt and Futurity in Madagascar', in Paik PY and M. Wiesner-Hanks (eds), *Debt: Ethics, the Environment and the Economy* (Bloomington: Indiana University Press, 2013), p. 141.
50. Thaddeus R. Miller et al., 'The New Conservation Debate: The View from Practical Ethics', *Biological Conservation*, 144 (2011), 949.
51. Miller et al., 'The New Conservation Debate', 949.
52. Cairngorm is a Gaelic formation of 'gorm', meaning 'blue', and 'cairn', a megalithic tomb in which the dead were interned, possibly as a gateway to the afterlife.
53. Hamilton, '*Girl with All the Gifts*'.
54. François Sarrazin and Jane Lecomte, 'Evolution in the Anthropocene', *Science*, 351/6276 (2016), 922.
55. Miller et al., 'The New Conservation Debate', 949.
56. John Cairns, 'Reparations for Environmental Degradation and Species Extinction: A Moral and Ethical Imperative for Human Society', *ESEP* (2003), 27.
57. Colebrook, *Death of the PostHuman*, p. 188.
58. Kurt Spellmeyer, 'After Theory: From Textuality to Attunement with the World', *College English*, 58/8 (1996), 894.
59. The zombie figure is a critical metaphor in numerous disciplines, including biology (zombie species, zombie ant), law (zombie legislation), politics

(zombie policies and politicians), linguistics (zombie pronouns) and even astrophysics (zombie vortex).
60. Carey, *Boy*, p. 64.
61. Claire Colebrook, 'Extinction Theory', in Jane Elliott and Derek Attridge (eds), *Theory After Theory* (London: Routledge, 2011), pp. 63, 64.
62. Christopher Peterson, *Monkey Trouble: The Scandal of Posthumanism* (New York: Fordham University Press, 2018), p. 23.
63. Judith Kovacs and Christopher Rowland, *Revelation: The Apocalypse of Jesus Christ* (Oxford: Blackwell Publishing, 2004), p. 2.

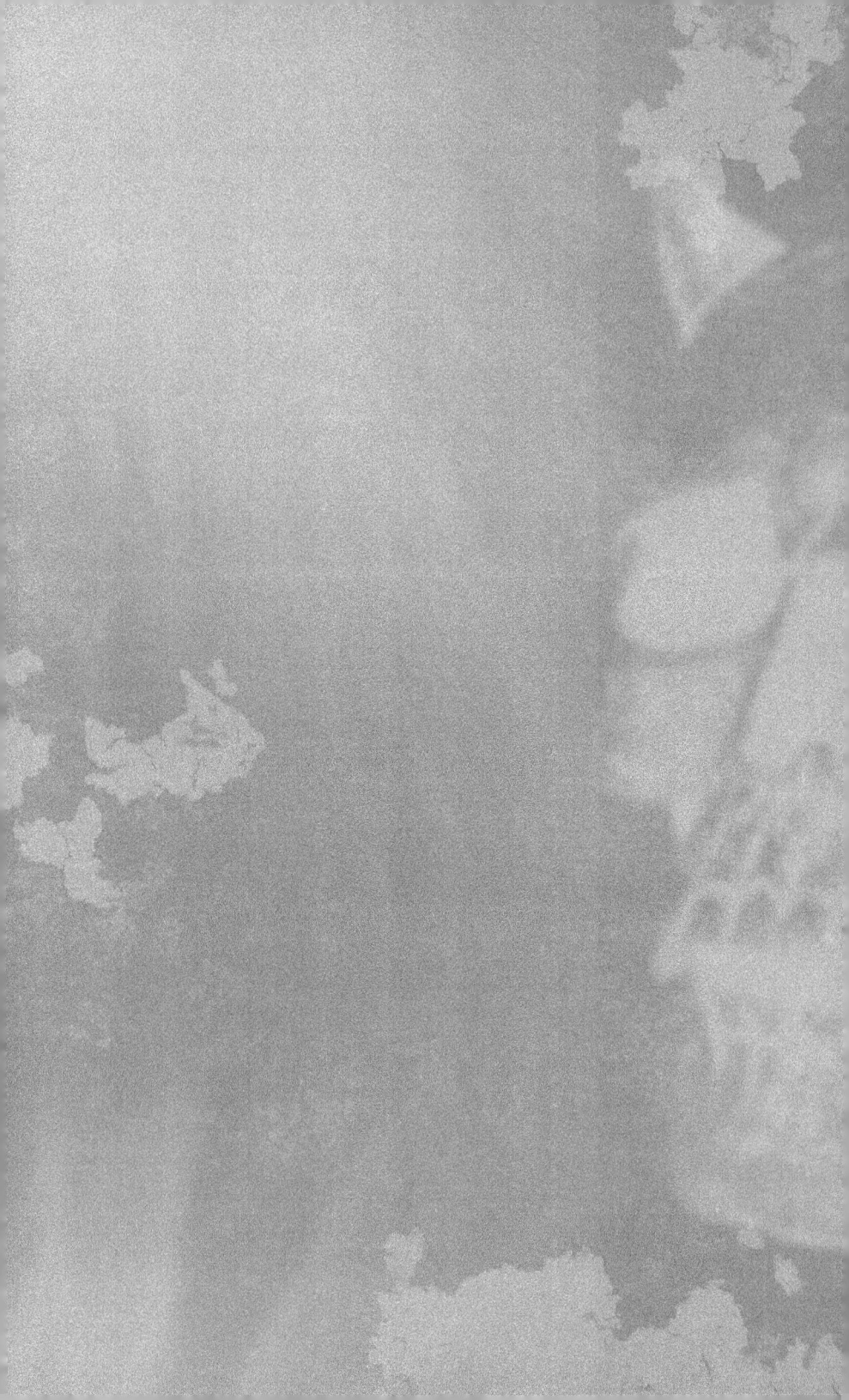

7

Zombie Colony
The Heteronomy of the Greek State and the Datura of Cultural Capital

Konstantinos Kerasovitis

GREECE HAS BEEN theorised by Michael Herzfeld as a crypto-colony, exhibiting the defining characteristic of a considerable reliance on claims to a historical civilisational superiority, coupled with an irrelevant cultural/theoretical output in the present. According to Herzfeld, crypto-colonialism is:

> articulated in the iconic guise of aggressively national culture fashioned to suit foreign models. Such countries were and are living paradoxes: they are nominally independent, but that independence comes at the price of a, sometimes humiliating, form of effective dependence.[1]

This chapter updates Greece's crypto-colonial designation, by arguing for the use of the term zombie colony. A term more efficiently describing this non-standard colony condition of the country, elucidating the causal nexus behind the irrelevance of its immaterial production.

The argument follows a dual pairwise comparison structure: Haiti and the zombie to Greece and the Acropolis. The chapter will establish a parallel between colonial Haiti and the modern Greek state, in their respective cornerstones of identity as products for tourist consumption. The ensuing analysis positions the Athenian Acropolis as a tool, instrumental in the conversion of lived identity into stagnant product and draws a picture-perfect analogy to the labour narrative inherent in the Haitian zombie. An analogy understood via the theoretical substrate of Cornelius Castoriadis's ontology, examining creativity under the distinct poles of autonomy/heteronomy. The chapter argues that an autonomist understanding of the foundational characteristics of the Greek state through the zombie figure informs the designation of Greece as a zombie colony in cultural production terms.

Haiti: voodoo as identity

Haiti, a former colony whose indigenous Taino population was exterminated by disease or by force as early as 1492, following its first contact with Europe, was re-populated with African slave labour. The slaves arrived in Haiti amidst a cultural void, a complete dissolution of every social structure. The new slave had not only to learn how to work the sugarcane plantations but also to relearn all social conventions. The acceptable ways to work, eat, dress or even fall in love were dictated through a process known as 'seasoning'.[2] If seasoning represents the way the new subject was re-cast to the master's demands, made palatable to the Western taste, voodoo became the way Haitians themselves counterbalanced this cultural dissolution. Voodoo paved the 'way back to a rudimentary form of collective life', by filling the social void and offering a common cultural backdrop.[3] As such Haitian identity is vested with a 'socialized ambivalence', owing to the tensions between the subject as forged by the European masters, and the self-definition afforded through voodoo.[4] Christianity, the dominant religion of the colonisers, was adopted openly, signalling the assimilation into the ways of humanity proper, but the Haitian's own indigenous ancestral beliefs were practised covertly: voodoo thus anchored Haitian self-determination. Even as the country moved into self-rule and slowly detached itself from colonial status, voodoo remained the ambivalent echo of a sharp divide between the masses and the local elite that succeeded the colonisers.

For the elite, Haitian reality and voodoo are considered less, lacking, primitive and backwards. For example, Dantès Bellegarde (1877–1966), one of Haiti's most prominent thinkers and political players, urged the country towards the disavowal of its actual history and identity: 'I remind my compatriots who may not know it, that peoples with the reputation of being uncivilized or simply retarded are placed under mandate or trusteeship of more civilized nations.'[5]

The regime of Dumarsais Estimé (1946–50), saw the state promoting a sanitised version of voodoo 'as performance', aimed at the Western tourists.[6] This performative version, deprived of any dangerous elements, became the focal point of former Haitian president Michel Martelly's 2011 efforts at rebranding the country.[7] This harmless attraction is the only thing the West will positively acknowledge, otherwise considering the country as a 'failed state' inhabited by 'others' to the rest of humanity.[8] The West draws from a fragmented view of Haitian history, also evident in the way Western legal discourse largely renders voodoo practises invisible by not granting them religious status.[9]

Zombie ritual

The contribution of anthropologist Wade Davis largely informs the understanding of the zombie.[10] In voodoo theology, zombification hinges on the removal of one of the five interlinked elements that are the make-up of the human.[11] The *ti bon ange*, or 'the aura of the individual', is where willpower, personality and character reside. The person is left a *zombi corps cadaver*, functioning flesh with the full potentiality of action but without the drivers of will, memory or emotion. The zombie is seen as the ownership of the Bokor (witch doctor), blindly executing orders in a state of complete domination.[12]

Folklorist Zora Neale Hurston, after two visits to Haiti (1937–8), considers the zombie as an actual reality for Haitians, not so much a supernatural state but rather a pharmacologically induced one. The administration of a hallucinogenic mixture, based on the plant Datura, cripples parts of the brain that govern speech and willpower, resulting in a person that 'can move and act but cannot formulate thought'.[13] Zombification is human reductionism: 'to reduce a person to a body, to reduce behaviour to basic motor functions, and to reduce social utility to raw labour'.[14] The zombie embodies the post-slave subjectivity, a subjectivity that has not developed naturally but occurs with the loss of personality and character. The zombie personifies the lack of free will, the lack of agency on the formation of desire.[15]

Métraux describes the zombie as a condition of reanimated life, displaced from society and fated to work as 'a beast of burden which his master exploits without mercy'.[16] Davis views zombification as a tripartite working in unison. The Bokor, who performs the rite, effectively becoming the master of the zombie, the social structure that allows for the Bokor, and the victim who is put in this condition by falling out of the protection of the social structure.[17] Exploitation and separation from community life bring the zombie close to the Marxist conception of the wage labourer.[18] Severed from human nature by their own labour, which confronts them as unnatural: 'posited as the worker's non-objectivity, as the objectivity of a subjectivity antithetical to the worker, as property of a will alien to him'.[19]

Celluloid zombie: a labour narrative

The zombie came to the attention of a wider public through William Seabrook's 1929 travelogue *The Magic Island*.[20] The first-ever cinematic appearance was in *White Zombie* (1932), starring Bela Lugosi: the narrative unfolds firmly within the colonial plantation and in terms of subjugated labour. When zombie master Legendre is asked about his workers the reply comes: 'They work faithfully, they are not worried about long hours . . . You could make good use of men like mine in your plantations.'[21] The cinematic zombie has always closely followed the evolution of labour. *White Zombie* portrays the de-skilled Fordist/Taylorist worker of the 1930s. To carry the load and motor the pulley are the tasks of zombie labour. The scientific division of labour that 'would replace workers' discretion over daily tasks' becomes to the labourer what the Bokor is to the zombie.[22]

During the 1970s through the 1990s, zombie portrayal has been largely based on George A. Romero's genre-defining *Night of the Living Dead* and its sequels.[23] In Romero's version, there is no human Bokor in control, rather zombification occurs due to some external environmental factor. The zombie is now defined primarily as driven by pure desire for consumption. Zombies do not procreate: consumption and reproduction merge in the carnal bite as the means of re-production.[24] The resulting product is more of the same, more zombies.

More recent depictions grant the zombie with rudimentary traces of individualism and enhanced mobility (for example, *28 Days Later*, *Resident Evil IV*, etc.), mirroring the semi-autonomous labourer, the faux independence of precarious self-employment. Zombification is even positioned as an empowering condition, as in *Zombie Strippers*, signalling independence and better work performance as super strippers.[25]

If one removes the gore from the cinematic zombie and views it as a commentary on the world of work, the observation voiced in Romero's *Dawn of the Dead* – 'they are us' – rings true.[26] Fear hinges on what is common between the zombie horde and human society. A society 'lacking in broader spiritual or communal purpose, left to the impulses of its unchecked power and its desires for consumption'.[27] The post-Fordist worker as zombie embodies 'the new slave, the capitalist worker, but also the consumer, trapped within the ideological construct that assures the survival of the system'.[28] Zombies who 'have no real purpose or telos in their existence beyond simply existing' mirror the ontological void of contemporary society: a society of infinitely unquenched desires channelled towards continuous void consumption.[29] In short like in Haiti where fear 'is not of zombies, but rather of becoming a zombie', society in fearing the zombie fears becoming a neoliberal working subject.[30]

The Greek republic

When regarding Greece, the Greek state should not be conflated with the people. As Thomas W. Gallant suggests, Greek history should be considered as a history of a people and not of a state, noting the existence of the 1950s perceptual chasm – reminiscent of the one encountered in Haiti – on what constituted Greekness between the ruling elites and rural populations.[31]

The 1821 revolt against Ottoman rule historically marks the first time that Greeks saw themselves organised as a sovereign state. The assassination of the first governor, and the enthronement of Bavarian King Otto by decree of the 1830 London Protocol, introduced a turbulent period, marked by a series of successive revolts, coups and border fluidity.[32] The 1974 fall of the military government, which came to power in the 1967 *coup d'état*, marks the beginning of a period of stability and the contemporary Greek republic.[33]

The central concept underlying the establishment of an independent Greek state did not reside entirely with the Greeks themselves. A pivotal figure who popularised an independent Greece to the rest of Europe is that of Lord George Gordon Byron. Byron's preoccupation was not with the liberation of the actual Greeks but with the liberation of the romantic ideal he had formed of Greece as the Hellas of the philosophers, and not that of the Ottoman subjects: 'I must do all that I can for the ancients.'[34] His notes and correspondence are filled with complaints towards the nature of the revolution. Byron states that he is tired of paying for troops unwilling to fight.[35] In the semi-autobiographical *Childe Harold's Pilgrimage* (1812), Byron deems the Greece he witnessed a 'sad relic of departed worth!'[36] Byron struggled towards the reinstitution of that relic in the form it had in his imagination, a literary fabrication.

The two fundamental texts on the Orient, Alain Grosrichard's *The Sultan's Court* and Edward W. Said's *Orientalism*, provide insight into the way Byron's Greece is concurrent with the overall Western narrative of the Orient.[37] A peculiar narrative emerges that is pure fiction as a description of the actual Orient, but also is, at the same time, the very kernel underlying the West in itself. The Orient is the backdrop on which Western social reality gets projected: it is perceived not as it really is, but as it would be if it was functioning as the West.[38]

An understanding of the context under which Byron wrote of Greece is crucial. Byron sought to establish himself as true nobility. Consequently, his travels, the *Grand Tour* as it was then called, afforded him a first-person *correct* account of Greece. Byron strived to be perceived as 'a source of indisputable knowledge'.[39] Travelling for the eighteenth-century British aristocracy was pivotal for the establishment of a place amongst the elite. As Barrell notes, the aristocracy, unburdened by lack of resources or the need to work, was expected to develop a full understanding of the world so that it would be fit for rule. This understanding bore heavily on aesthetics. The *correct* taste was the 'means of legitimating political authority'.[40]

That very notion of good taste, coupled with the growing popularity of the idea that fifth-century BC Greek art was its definition, placed the foundation of European culture with ancient Greece. A move that vested Europe with deciding power over 'what was, or what was not, acceptable as Greek culture in the modern age', effectively equating Greece to the European conception of its classical past.[41] The Greeks 'succumbed, perhaps in part for tactical reasons, to an alien, Western point of view', leading them to consider everything that was created after classical times, either socially or culturally, as polluting.[42] This brought about a disruption of their historical post-five BC thread, as parts of Alexander's empire, Roman, Byzantine or Ottoman subjects. Local elites urged the people to redefine themselves: 'no more as Greek-Orthodox "Romeoi" [Romans], but as "Hellenes"'.[43] This redefinition is the root of the 'Otherness in the self' modern Greek experience, and what accounts for their ambivalent position towards a Europe that they simultaneously view as the apex of their culture, yet also one in which they are other from.[44]

The common path trodden by both colonial Haiti and Greece is the incompatibility in the perception of identity, between state/elites and population. The defining divergence between the two countries lies in their identity cornerstones occupying different sides on the spectrum of desirability and reality. The Haitian cornerstone of voodoo, being what is experienced by the people as concrete reality, is considered backwards. Haitians need to be made into Westerners. A negative narrative that is not easy to internalise as it clashes with everyday experience. With Greek identity this is reversed: the cornerstone of the state has been a fiction from the start, but a positive one. The notion of peak achievement is perpetuated as a present condition and forms the sacrosanct of existence in the Greek state. The Greeks need only be Greek, but a Greekness as defined by Westerners.

Acropolis/necropolis

The tool that mirrors the very logic behind the foundation of the state, employed to legitimise the Greek identity narrative, has been the instrumentalisation of antiquity. An undertaking nowhere more exemplified than in the Athenian Acropolis. The positive tones are repeated in the Western perceptions of the Acropolis. A perfect structure symbolising thought in material form, cognition taming nature.[45] The West has, until recently, never considered the Acropolis as a material place, but rather consigned it to the plane of the imaginary, to the spectral. Telling is Sigmund Freud's 1904 reaction to the actual site recorded in a 1936 letter: 'So all this really does exist, just as we learnt at school!'[46] Freud likens the experience to having seen the Loch Ness monster, commenting on how his mind fails to register what he sees as reality: 'What I see here is not real.'[47] Freud calls his reaction de-realisation: to know that something is tangibly real but to subconsciously reject its existence.

Contrary to its relegation to the imaginary by the West, the Acropolis has always been a functional part of the city: a very material place with a lineage that closely followed the history of the land.[48] In Roman and medieval times, the pagan temple was converted to a Christian church, and later to a mosque. The Acropolis in its actuality has had a fluid identity shaped by the people, and most of all it was part of the wider commons of the city. A place one freely wandered into, a lived place. Acclaimed dancer Isadora Duncan conveys this openness in her 1927 autobiography: 'I could not sleep, and at dawn I went alone to the Acropolis. I entered the theater of Dionysus and I danced. I felt that this was the last time. So I climbed the Propylaea, and standing, I contemplated the Parthenon.'[49] The Acropolis as a material place in the commons is exposed to the free interpretation of the public; its identity re-invented according to use. The fixed Western imaginary conception of the Acropolis considers material reality as tainted, when in disagreement with the idealised perceived past.

Argyro Loukaki gives a sharp historical account of the efforts to bring the material Acropolis up to par with Western imaginary, evident in the 1881 landscaping interventions, carried out by the American School of Classical Studies.[50] The US needed a cultural anchor in Europe, yet the gothic cathedral was pregnant with unwanted notions of royalty. This made the Acropolis serve as the prototype of many emblematic government buildings.[51] The tidy gardens and paved walkways of those buildings found disparity with the goat trails and the barren rock of the actual Acropolis. Intense landscaping brought Western interpretation and Greek reality together. A well-meaning endeavour, but one which provided a result that, as to paraphrase Loukaki, was neat but not Greek.

The New Acropolis Museum epitomises the glorification of antiquity at the expense of continuity. 'In the year 2004, Athens will become . . . ancient', wrote the local newspapers, heralding the arrival of the museum.[52] The creation of architect Bernard Tschumi – a modern glass and metal structure aesthetically isolated from the landscape – imposed on the early nineteenth-century art deco buildings that formerly stood in its place, the same fate as the one reserved for indigenous Haitians: total and utter obliteration.[53]

The actual Acropolis now largely consists of patched up structural elements populated by replicas, a 'simulacrum of a ruin'.[54] The state-sanctioned repair-store-replace with replica triptych cumulated in the bulk of the original antiquities now residing in the museum.[55] This move incurred a switch in values, significance and function of the discourse surrounding the Acropolis.[56] The exhibits are now stripped of cultural context. Taxonomy reigns supreme, turning the displays from agents that had acted on the community that produced them into matter.[57] Affectivity is deliberately erased, a terracotta vase against a sacred offering, technique over context.

Annette Svaneklink Jakobsen sees the museum as offering a pre-conditioned experience, a Deleuzian *signaletic material*.[58] A term that Deleuze adopted from cinema to describe the reconfiguring of the whole through the different combination of its parts: 'a condition, anterior by right to what it conditions'.[59] A perfect application of the famous 1964 observation 'the medium is the message', as the actual site has been assimilated in the medium (the museum).[60]

The tourist gaze

Just as voodoo underwent a re-interpretation as a tourist spectacle, the Acropolis fell under a similar dialectic of sanitisation and care as early as the 1930s.[61] Antiquity, now a potential tourist attraction, was phased out of active life and restructured as a theme park. TheAcropolis, now dislodged from the commons, becomes an articulation of Pierre Bourdieu's cultural capital in material form.[62] The statues emerge as marble labourers, directly geared towards the production of economic capital. The care and safety of the museum are best viewed under the now prevalent neo-liberal concept of mindfulness: a way to gain insight on 'the way things are', by assuming an uncritical intensiveness of mind, a non-evaluative attitude. Mindfulness is conducive to a worldview that examines existence strictly in its present state, as not having a past or a future.[63]

Henri Lefebvre maintains that turning a city into an attraction removes it from concrete existence, making it conform to the conception of the spectacle to be consumed: 'As social text, this historic city no longer has a coherent set of prescriptions, of use of time linked to symbols and to a style . . . [the city] is no longer lived and is no longer understood practically.'[64] Beriatos and Gospodini add that resident and tourist come to occupy the same space, nodding towards the figure of the *flâneur* as read by Walter Benjamin.[65] The resident is not an active agent, but a passive stroller through a city that is 'no longer native ground': they are affected by the city but unable to affect the city.[66]

In a 1975 *New York Times* interview, the then minister of culture feels 'a horrible sense of responsibility . . . [towards] dealing with something unique in the world'.[67] The Acropolis, locally known as 'the sacred rock', is Athens's *genius loci* – the spirit of a place. This very rootedness is what is lost in the museum.[68] The sense of responsibility the state has adopted indicates the transformation of the Acropolis from *genius loci* to *mundus loci* – the spirit of the world. Greece, just like Haiti, must conform to Western standards.

The dialectic of 'correct' taste is pervasive, demanding a cleansed version of Greek history, free from 'impurities' and fit for consumption. The same taste Haitian slaves were seasoned to, as to satisfy the appetites of the Western masters. The zombie, an agent of procreation through consumption, embodies the act of turning the unwanted material mortality that constitutes reality into undead life in the plane of the imaginary. As the safe version of voodoo was offered for tourist consumption, a similar fate loomed for Greek identity. It was removed from material reality and fixed towards the desired version imagined by the West. To exist in the tangibly real means to be open to mortality, change, a relentless forward motion. To exist in the plane of ideas points to transcendence, a place outside the social. Transcendence is not directly malleable, as it is never approachable. The zombie can only enact the masters will, but not shape it. The zombie in its purest form, a mouth with a contagious bite, can be ascribed to the Acropolis, in its dual existence as both medium and message, with the same contagious function. The identity narrative becomes transcendent in the museum's bowels, the social cannot affect the exhibits, they are undead, and they now not represent, but reconfigure the social, as contagious biting zombie mouths.

Autonomy

The above can be contextualised through the ontology of Cornelius Castoriadis which hinges on the concept of autonomy, offering the theoretical substrate for examining Greece, original cultural productivity and zombies. For Castoriadis, the state is not to be confused with society.[69] The state brings itself into being with the institution of power-holding apparatus, separating it from a society on which power is exercised. There is alignment here with autonomist Antonio Negri, whose empire needs to impose itself not by actual force, but by appearing as legitimate-righteous.[70] Similarly for Castoriadis the affective function of state apparatus lies largely with the subjects internalising this false righteousness. Power is not direct but rests with signification, in the creation of 'imaginary belief in . . . imaginary legitimacy'.[71]

This is exactly the function of the Acropolis museum. A state apparatus poised to maintain the illusion of autonomy under a heteronomous regime. To impart a false subjectivity that subjects adopt as their own, by sustaining the illusion of a temporally displaced 5 BC, into the present.

The subject under heteronomy is 'a type of being that is kept on a leash and maintained in the illusion of its individuality and of its liberty by mechanisms which have become independent of all social control'.[72]

Autonomy, according to Castoriadis, is the interplay between fully powerful individuals and the fully fragile social environment that they occupy. Autonomy pivots on the always open, always questioning, but doing so in full knowledge of what one questions. Action occurs under an obscured knowledge of reality. It is never a lack of force that impedes the autonomous individual to institute a certain change, to create a new reality. Change is a fully informed choice, its realisation always within the power of an individual fully aware of what is desired, why it is desired and the limits of this knowledge in itself:

> What is a free, or autonomous society? It is a society that gives itself, effectively and reflexively, its own laws, while knowing that it is doing so. Who is a free, autonomous individual . . . ? It is an individual that recognizes in these laws and in this power his own laws and his own power.[73]

The reversal of this relation signals heteronomy – the stronger other as lawgiver, the colony condition. Obliteration of historical reference is a plunge into fiction and vests one with 'an indifference with respect to what is and to what one can do with it'.[74]

Original creation

In the *infans* stage, according to Castoriadis, existence resides in an a-social closed proto-universe, a complete monad, a nonhuman state of pure psyche. In that pre-individual mode of being there is no desire as there is no need, thus there is no creation: 'At the originary level . . . there cannot be any "missing object" and any "desire", for "desire" is always fulfilled – "realized" before it is able to be articulated as "desire".'[75] Humanity is ascribed by the realisation of individuality, an individuality 'socially fabricated or created in correspondence with the society's institutions'.[76] The endless reconfiguring that individuals (when allowed), impose on their society is but a struggle for a return to the completeness of the originary monad. The social imaginary, which for Castoriadis is where change is first instituted, is nothing more than the collective function 'of replacing, patching together, covering over what is necessarily a gaping hole, a split, a lack in the subject's being'.[77]

In considering creation as production aimed towards negating the lack inherent in the human condition, the question of the originality of the produce arises. First and foremost, the words produce and create are crude approximations, pointing to a repetition of what already exists. The completely new lies in the wider spontaneous function that Castoriadis deems active constitution:

> what is essential to creation is not 'discovery' but constituting the new: art does not discover, it constitutes; and the relation between what it constitutes and the 'real' . . . is not a relation of verification. And on the social plane . . . the emergence of new institutions and of new ways of living is not a 'discovery' either but an active constitution.[78]

Subsequently, consider the newly constituted thing, as the twofold summoning of the *eidos* and the *ousia*, the kind and its essence, working in unison. As Castoriadis clarifies, to simply give form to something does not signify original creation.[79] If one were to draw a flower, one has merely reproduced the flower kind: repetition. If the flower drawn is for the beloved, it is infused with some essence, it is a particular flower, it has an identity. Still, that identity cannot be original if conceived under a heteronomous social environment. The flower could only be a form vested with an iteration of the essence the social environment allows someone to feel towards the beloved.

In heteronomous societies, the very notion of the subject always contains subjugation. The limits imposed by the stronger other, lie beyond questioning. The social environment is fixed and unyielding. The social imaginary does not atrophy, but it never becomes *radical* because it keeps reproducing iterations of the same essence as it cannot conceive outside the given closure of meaning.[80]

For Castoriadis, the individual and the societal are two poles working together, and this synergy only leads to original creation, when a fully powerful individual operates in a completely malleable environment. The fluidity of the social environment is what allows for the individual to express the new meaning, the new essence constituted by the social imaginary. Castoriadis grouped his ontology under the term magmatic: magma, always in a state of flow, proceeding unimpeded, a signifier for the way the individual can manipulate the social, forming it into new shapes only to melt them away.[81] Thus the flower can only be original through the *ex nihilo* invention of its essence, its being-a-flower. In simple words, what is necessary is for the social environment to be autonomous, open to malleability, as to allow for the constitution of an original essence. A new way to love the beloved, a never-before felt essence embodied in the form. A completely new flower represents a completely new feeling.

To be an individual, an 'I', a self-reflexive subject, is deeply rooted in the Western worldview. Yet this 'I', as argued by C. S. Lewis in 1940, always defines itself in relation to the other within some context that they both occupy: 'a neutral something, neither you nor I, which we can both manipulate so as to make signs to each other'.[82] What the zombie narrative read through Castoriadis suggests is that the context in which subjects coexist – the social environment, when defined by heteronomy – is no longer neutral, but functions as Bokor. Creation, geared towards and limited by what is dictated by the Bokor, is predestined to repetition.

Zombie colony

Herzfeld's designation of Greece as a crypto-colony pivots on three focal points: a heteronomous-defined national culture, economic dependence and a lack of cultural/theoretical output in the present. Considering that production is increasingly moving onto the immaterial, the cognitive and, as evidenced above, creation under Castoriadis does not so much rely on economics, but on politics, a matter of autonomous subjectivity: therefore, the term zombie colony presents a more relevant descriptor for the Greek state.

The Greek state has come into being as a society instituted based on heteronomy, a realisation of Byron's narrative. Not a matter of self-institution but a matter of entering an already pre-given subjectivity as part of 'a Eurocentric world that defines itself in circular fashion by evoking a classical Greece that it has itself constructed'.[83]

The rite of zombification, the removal of the *ti bon ange*, of memory and desire, is performed on those outside society, those not in the lived commons. The removal of antiquity from the *vita activa*, and through the institutional cleansing of the museum, renders it unable to challenge the imported identity narrative. Identity is no longer malleable by the social. The museum severs memory, it becomes the bite that turns, and the Datura that keeps, the victim in a zombie state.

The zombie carries the trope of exclusion in its core, exemplified in the way the perceived backwardness of Haitian identity, post-five BC Greek lineage, or the citizen as an active agent, are considered as elements to be removed. Just as the zombie is less than human, and this reductionism confines it to repetition, so is the Greek identity made less by the removal of the elements that seem, or even actually are, unattractive. Kevin Alexander Boon's term 'cultural zombie' describes this loss of self-identity through a culturally induced zombification process.[84] For modern Greeks, reflection on the full spectrum of subjectivity becomes impossible.

The autonomous conception of original creation presupposes the existence of a void, of a lack of meaning. Humans are creatures of reality; they shape reality in accordance with the society in which they are brought into being. Should that reality be already fully and unyieldingly determined, no space exists to create the original new. This is the difference between the instituted and the instituting capacity of what Castoriadis called the radical imaginary. In a Greece whose glorified past occupies not memory but the present, there is no lack of meaning, no void, no gap. The social imaginary has reached completeness and has stopped radical institution. What is there to question when the peak of achievement is perceived as reached? Reached not in the past but perpetually, in the now. Desire has been satiated. There is no need for questioning or re-imagining, only the need to safeguard what is perceived as reality from corruption.

The three conditions of zombification are all present in the Greek state: the Bokor is the romantic notion of Greek identity that has no consideration of a post-five BC existence (consistent with the movie narrative of the Bokor not being a person but something in the environment). The society having internalised that notion allows for the decontextualisation of its antiquity and its consignment to the care of the museum. And finally, the Greek radical imaginary, on which original cultural production hinges, sated by the consumption of the stagnant state narrative of superiority becomes zombified, reduced to producing more of the same.

To conclude, if examined through the theoretical parameters of Castoriadis, the Greek state emerges as a zombie colony in cultural production terms. A state that has culturally consumed its 'citizens' through a narrative of historical reductionism and a temporal displacement of a glorified cherrypicked past to the present. An act that when internalised by Greeks reduces them to cultural zombies; cultural agents of repetition but not original institution. The Greek state appears as a zombie colony, colonised by its own perceived greatness of self.

Notes

1. Michael Herzfeld, 'The Absent Presence: Discourses of Crypto-Colonialism', *South Atlantic Quarterly*, 101/4 (2002), 900.
2. Sidney Mintz and Michel-Rolph Trouillot, 'The Social History of Haitian Vodou', in Donald J. Cosentino (ed.), *Sacred Arts of Haitian Vodou* (California: University of California Museum, 1995), p. 126.
3. Alfred Métraux, *Voodoo*, trans. Hugo Charteris, 2nd edn (London: Sphere Books, 1974), p. 39.
4. Melville Jean Herskovits, *Life in a Haitian Valley* (Princeton: Markus Wiener Publishers, 2007), p. 299.
5. Bellegarde, cited in Celucien L. Joseph, 'The Problem and Impossibility of Vodou Religion in the Writings of Dantès Bellegarde', *The Journal of Pan African Studies*, 6/8 (2014), 214.
6. Mintz and Trouillot, 'The Social History of Haitian Vodou', p. 143.
7. Colum Lynch, 'Rebranding Haiti: The Voodoo Tours', *Foreign Policy* (26 September 2011), *https://foreignpolicy.com/2011/09/26/rebranding-haiti-the-voodoo-tours/* (accessed 15 May 2018).
8. Amy E. Potter, 'Voodoo, Zombies, and Mermaids: U.S. Newspaper Coverage of Haiti', *Geographical Review*, 99/2 (2010), 224.
9. Kamari Maxine Clarke, 'Beyond Genealogies: Expertise and Religious Knowledge in Legal Cases Involving African Diasporic Publics', *Transforming Anthropology*, 25/2 (2017), 130.
10. Wade Davis, 'The Ethnobiology of the Haitian Zombi', *Journal of Ethnopharmacology*, 9/1 (1983), 85–104; Wade Davis, *The Serpent and the Rainbow* (New York: Simon & Schuster, 1985); Wade Davis, *Passage of Darkness: The Ethnobiology of the Haitian Zombie* (Chapel Hill: University of North Carolina Press, 1988).
11. Davis, 'The Ethnobiology of the Haitian Zombi', 98–9.
12. George Eaton Simpson, 'The Belief System of Haitian Vodun', *American Anthropologist*, 47/1 (1945), 52.
13. Zora Neale Hurston, cited in Mary E. Lyons, *Sorrow's Kitchen: The Life and Folklore of Zora Neale Hurston* (New York: Simon & Schuster 1993), p. 89.
14. Peter Dendle, 'The Zombie as Barometer of Cultural Anxiety', in Niall Scott (ed.), *Monsters and the Monstrous: Myths and Metaphors of Enduring Evil* (Amsterdam: Rodopi, 2007), p. 48.
15. Kette Thomas, 'Haitian Zombie, Myth, and Modern Identity', *Comparative Literature and Culture*, 12/2 (2010), 9.
16. Métraux, *Voodoo*, p. 166.

17. Davis, *Passage of Darkness*, p. 9.
18. Karl Marx, *Early Writings*, trans. Rodney Livingstone and Gregor Benton [1975] (New York: Penguin Books, 1992), pp. 418–19.
19. Karl Marx, *Grundrisse: Foundations of the Critique of Political Economy (Rough Draft)*, trans. Martin Nicolaus, 23rd edn [1973] (New York: Penguin Books, 1993), p. 512.
20. William Seabrook, *The Magic Island* (Mineola: Courier Dover Publications, 2016).
21. *White Zombie*, dir. Tod Browning, United Artists Corporation, USA (1932), 15:09.
22. Martha Crowley et al., 'Neo-Taylorism at Work: Occupational Change in the Post-Fordist Era', *Social Problems*, 57/3 (2010), 423.
23. *Night of the Living Dead*, dir. George A. Romero, Continental Distributing, USA (1968).
24. Simon Orpana, 'Spooks of Biopower: The Uncanny Carnivalesque of Zombie Walks', *TOPIA: Canadian Journal of Cultural Studies*, 25 (2011), 153.
25. *Zombie Strippers*, dir. Jay Lee, Sony Pictures Entertainment, USA (2008).
26. Stephen Harper, 'Zombies, Malls, and the Consumerism Debate: George Romero's *Dawn of the Dead*', *Americana: The Journal of American Popular Culture*, 1/2 (2002), http://www.americanpopularculture.com/journal/articles/fall_2002/harper.htm (accessed 5October 2017).
27. Dendle, 'The Zombie as Barometer of Cultural Anxiety', p. 54.
28. Sarah Juliet Lauro and Karen Embry, 'A Zombie Manifesto: The Nonhuman Condition in the Era of Advanced Capitalism', *boundary 2*, 35/1 (2008), 99.
29. Kyle William Bishop, 'The Idle Proletariat: Dawn of the Dead, Consumer Ideology, and the Loss of Productive Labor', *The Journal of Popular Culture*, 43/2 (2010), 242; Tara Brabazon, 'Don't Fear the Reaper? The Zombie University and Eating Braaaains', *KOME*, 4/2 (2016), 4.
30. Davis, *Passage of Darkness*, p. 9.
31. Thomas W. Gallant, *Modern Greece: From the War of Independence to the Present*, 2nd edn (London: Bloomsbury Academic, 2016).
32. Charalambos K. Papastathis, 'The Hellenic Republic and the Prevailing Religion', *BYU Law Review*, 4 (1996), 815–52.
33. Socrates Petmezas, 'History of Modern Greece', in *About Greece* (Athens: Hellenic Ministry of Press and Mass Media-Secretariat General of Information, 2001), pp. 17–43.
34. George Gordon Byron, *The Works of Lord Byron; in Verse and Prose. Including hisLetters, Journals, etc. with a Sketch of his Life*, ed. Fitz Greene Halleck (New York: George Dearborn, 1836), p. 218, from the letters section.

35. Byron, *The Works of Lord Byron*, p. 227, from the letters section.
36. Byron, *The Works of Lord Byron*, p. 16.
37. Alain Grosrichard, *The Sultan's Court: European Fantasies of the East* [1979] (London: Verso, 1998); Edward W. Said, *Orientalism* [1978] (London: Penguin Books, 2003).
38. Mladen Dolar, in Grosrichard, *The Sultan's Court*, p. xiv.
39. Padmini Ray Murray, 'Gender, Nation and Embodiment in Byron's Poetry' (unpublished PhD thesis, University of Edinburgh, 2008), 87.
40. John Barrell, 'The Public Prospect and the Private View', in John Barrell (ed.), *The Birth of Pandora: And the Division of Knowledge* (London: Palgrave Macmillan, 1992), p. 41.
41. Michael Herzfeld, *Anthropology through the Looking-Glass: Critical Ethnography in the Margins of Europe* (Cambridge: Cambridge University Press, 1987), p. 28.
42. Richard A. McNeal, 'Archaeology and the Destruction of the Later Athenian Acropolis', *Antiquity*, 65/246 (1991), 50.
43. Petmezas, 'History of Modern Greece', p. 19.
44. Herzfeld, *Anthropology through the Looking-Glass*, p. 15.
45. Panayotis Tournikiotis (ed.), *The Parthenon and its Impact in Modern Times* (Athens: Melissa, 1996), p. 202; Le Corbusier, *Towards a New Architecture* (New York: DoverPublications, 1986), pp. 202–23.
46. Sigmund Freud, 'A Disturbance of Memory on the Acropolis', in *The Complete Psychological Works of Sigmund Freud*, trans. James Strachey, vol. XXII (London: Hogarth Press, 1964), p. 241.
47. Freud, 'A Disturbance of Memory on the Acropolis', p. 244.
48. McNeal, 'Archaeology and the Destruction of the Later Athenian Acropolis', 50.
49. Isadora Duncan, *My Life* [1927] (New York: Liveright Publishing, 2013), p. 114.
50. Argyro Loukaki, 'Whose Genius Loci? Contrasting Interpretations of the "Sacred Rock of the Athenian Acropolis"', *Annals of the Association of American Geographers*, 87/2 (1997), 306–29.
51. Lambert Schneider, 'A Journey through Times and Cultures? Ancient Greek Forms in American Nineteenth-Century Architecture: An Archaeological View', *Economic History Working Papers*, 28/08 (London School of Economics and Political Science Department of Economic History, April 2008).
52. Dimitris Philippides, 'The Phantom of Classicism in Greek Architecture', *A SingularAntiquity – 3rd Supplement* (Athens: Benaki Museum, 2008), p. 375.
53. Jarrett A. Lobell, 'A New Home for the Treasures of the Acropolis', *Archaeology* (2009), 35.

54. Dimitris Plantzos, 'Behold the Raking Geison: The New Acropolis Museum and itsContext-Free Archaeologies', *Antiquity*, 85/328 (2011), 613.
55. Fani Mallouhou Tufano, 'Ē Anastúlōsē tōn Mnēmeíōn tēs Akrópolēs: 1975–2000 [Restoration of the Acropolis Monuments: 1975–2000]', Athens (Greek Ministry of Culture, 1999), *https://www.culture.gr/DocLib/appendix8-gr.pdf* (accessed 10 May 2021).
56. Mari Lending, 'Negotiating Absence: Bernard Tschumi's New Acropolis Museum in Athens', *The Journal of Architecture*, 23/5 (2018), 797.
57. Plantzos, 'Behold the Raking Geison', 621.
58. Annette Svaneklink Jakobsen, 'Experience In-between Architecture and Context: The New Acropolis Museum, Athens', *Journal of Aesthetics & Culture*, 4/1 (2012), *https://doi.org/10.3402/jac.v4i0.18158* (accessed 21 May 2019).
59. Gilles Deleuze, *Cinema 2: The Time-Image*, trans. Hugh Tomlinson and Robert Galeta, 5th printing [1989] (Minneapolis: University of Minnesota Press, 1997), p. 29.
60. Marshall McLuhan, *Understanding Media: The Extensions of Man* (Cambridge, MA: The MIT Press, 1994), p. 7.
61. Emilia Athanassiou et al., 'The Modern Gaze of Foreign Architects Travelling to Interwar Greece: Urban Planning, Archaeology, Aegean Culture, and Tourism', *Heritage*, 2/2 (2019), 1117–35.
62. Pierre Bourdieu, 'The Forms of Capital', in Nicole Woolsey Biggart (ed.), *Readings in Economic Sociology* (Malden: Blackwell, 2002), pp. 280–91.
63. Jon Kabat-Zinn, 'Mindfulness-based Interventions in Context: Past, Present, and Future', *Clinical Psychology: Science and Practice*, 10/2 (2006), 144–56.
64. Henri Lefebvre, *Writings on Cities*, ed. Eleonore Kofman and Elizabeth Lebas (New York: Blackwell Publishers, 1996), p. 148.
65. Elias Beriatos and Aspa Gospodini, '"Glocalising" Urban Landscapes: Athens and the 2004 Olympics', *Cities*, 21/3 (2004), 187–202.
66. Walter Benjamin, *The Arcades Project* [1999] (Cambridge, MA: Harvard University Press, 2002), p. 347.
67. Steven V. Roberts, 'Greece Striving to Protect Acropolis from Pollution and Tourists', *The New York Times* (19 February 1975), 6.
68. Loukaki, 'Whose Genius Loci?', p. 306.
69. Cornelius Castoriadis, 'Power, Politics, Autonomy', in Axel Honneth et al. (eds), *Cultural-political Interventions in the Unfinished Project of Enlightenment* (Cambridge, MA: The MIT Press, 1992), p. 281.
70. Michael Hardt and Antonio Negri, *Empire* (Cambridge, MA: Harvard University Press, 2000), p. 15.
71. Castoriadis, 'Power, Politics, Autonomy', 280.

72. Cornelius Castoriadis, 'Anthropology, Philosophy, Politics', *Thesis Eleven*, 49/1 (1997), 115.
73. Castoriadis, cited in Viviana Asara, Emanuele Profumi and Giorgos Kallis, 'Degrowth, Democracy and Autonomy', *Environmental Values*, 22/2 (2013), 227.
74. Cornelius Castoriadis, *The Imaginary Institution of Society*, trans. Kathleen Blarney (London: Polity Press, 1987), p. 112.
75. Castoriadis, *The Imaginary Institution of Society*, p. 291.
76. Castoriadis, 'Anthropology, Philosophy, Politics', 106.
77. Castoriadis, *The Imaginary Institution of Society*, p. 228.
78. Castoriadis, *The Imaginary Institution of Society*, p. 133.
79. Castoriadis, *The Imaginary Institution of Society*, pp. 197–8.
80. Cornelius Castoriadis, 'Democracy as Procedure and Democracy as Regime', *Constellations*, 4/1 (1997), 4.
81. A state antithetical to the complete fixedness of the zombie on the master's will.
82. C. S. Lewis, *The Problem of Pain* (New York: HarperCollins, 2009), p. 22.
83. Herzfeld, 'The Absent Presence', 916.
84. Kevin Alexander Boon, 'Ontological Anxiety Made Flesh: The Zombie in Literature, Film and Culture', in Niall Scott (ed.), *Monsters and the Monstrous: Myths and Metaphors of Enduring Evil* (Amsterdam: Rodopi, 2007), p. 40.

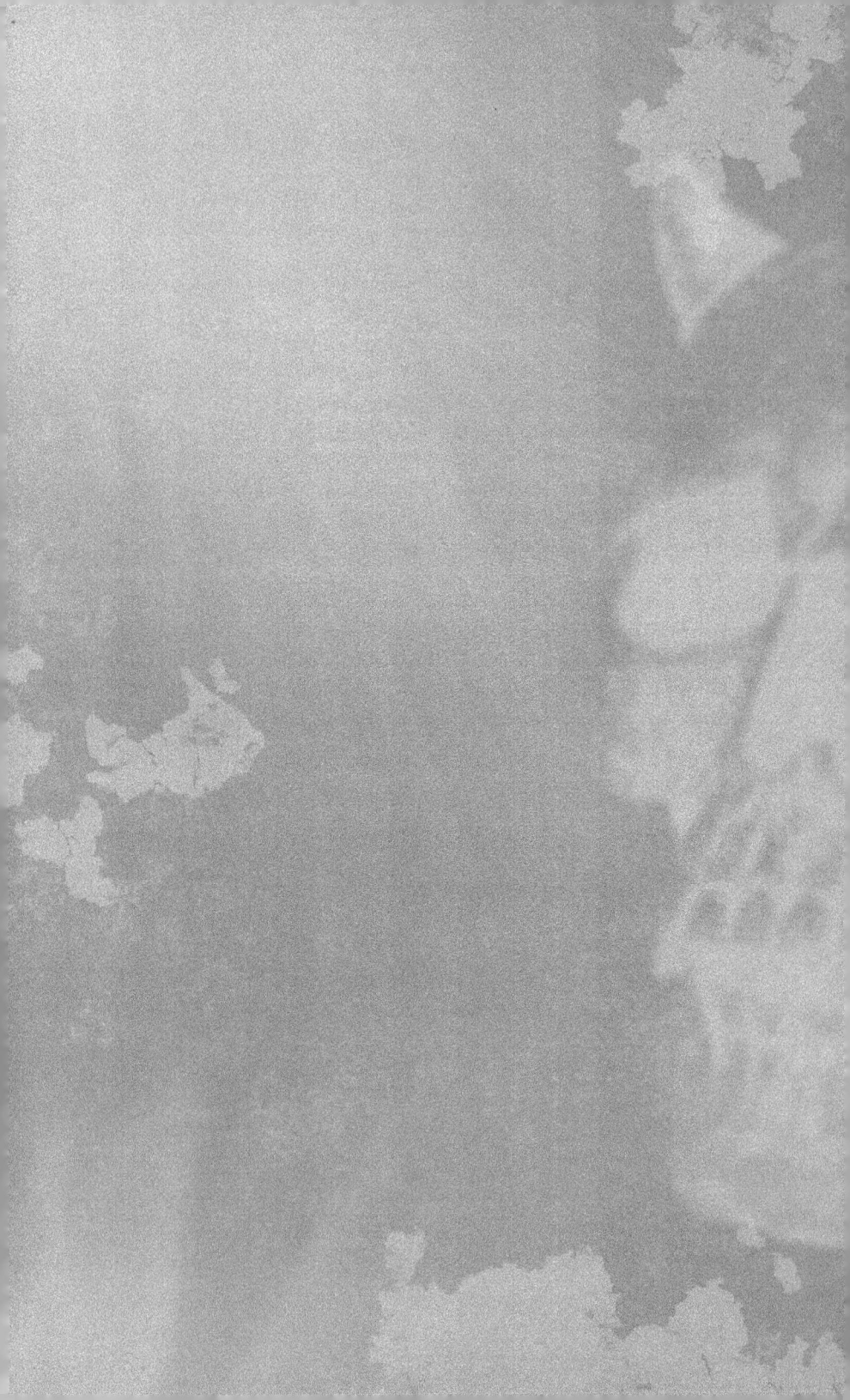

8

Last Ones Left Alive
Zombies and Post-Celtic Tiger Ireland

Deirdre Flynn

SET IN THE NEAR FUTURE, Sarah Davis-Goff's 2019 debut novel *Last Ones Left Alive* imagines Ireland after a zombie apocalypse. Told through the eyes of a teenage narrator, with flashbacks to her upbringing, the young adult novel offers no specifics about the 'emergency' that created this dystopian future. Like the protagonist Orpen, the reader is left to piece together the evidence in this speculative imagining. The Ireland Davis-Goff describes reels from an event that has created a new matriarchal society, which places the blame for the disaster with men. This is an Ireland coming to terms with a monumental and unexpected change. Although Davis-Goff does not mention the cause of the apocalypse, the echoes of Ireland's banking collapse and economic crash of 2008 are obvious. *Last Ones Left Alive* follows a similar thread to other post-crash novels, like Louise O'Neill's *Asking for it* or Eimear McBride's *A Girl is a Half-Formed Thing*, placing the girl at the centre of a new Ireland, trying to negotiate this change. Zombies, called 'skrakes', roam the abandoned towns and landscape of a country devasted by this unspoken disaster. Davis-Goff derived the name 'skrake' from the anglicisation 'of the Irish word for "screech" which is "scréach"'.[1] Like remnants of pre-crash Ireland, the skrakes, the abandoned towns and buildings that they inhabit, are reminders of a previous Ireland and the capitalist society that defined the time. They haunt the landscape and threaten the new emerging society. This chapter examines how Davis-Goff changes the traditional zombie narrative, by offering a new opportunity for society in the wake of the collapse of patriarchal capitalism. Orpen's narrative also offers a fresh perspective on the collapse of Celtic Tiger Ireland. Through the female-centred apocalyptic zombie genre, *Last Ones Left Alive* creates a speculative societal change.

The novel's narrator, Orpen, was raised on an island off the west of Ireland by her same-sex parents. Her mother Mairead and Mairead's partner Maeve brought Orpen to this isolated location to escape a new community called Phoenix City, founded after the apocalypse at a location in or near Dublin. The name suggests Phoenix Park, one of the largest urban parks in Europe, located in Dublin. However, this is never confirmed fully in the novel. Orpen's knowledge of Ireland and what happened is very sparse. She pieces together information from her parents and old newspapers she finds on the island. Maeve and Mairead wanted to shield Orpen from the dangers of the new Ireland, while also preparing her to survive in this new reality. Everyday Orpen is taught to hunt and fight, and her parents test her survival skills. Not long after her twelfth birthday, her mother is bitten by a skrake on a scouting trip to the mainland. Brought back to the island by Maeve, Orpen watches her mother die. Two years later, her and Maeve travel to the mainland to test Orpen's skills. When Maeve is bitten, Orpen starts a journey to Phoenix City with Maeve ill in a wheelbarrow, and the tritely named dog, Danger. Along the way she encounters a number of quick-moving skrakes and loses both Maeve and Danger. When she arrives near the entrance to Phoenix City, Orpen is stopped from entering by a man, his pregnant companion and a young girl. This is the first time Orpen has met any other humans, and in particular, this is her first encounter with a man. The group have escaped from the city and are being pursued by a female team on horses from the urban encampment. The novel ends with Orpen directing what becomes her group to the secret island and leaving with the women for Phoenix City. Davis-Goff leaves the novel open for sequels, and prequels, with lots of questions remaining for the reader. In an article in the *Irish Times*, Davis-Goff explains that she has 'created the kind of Irish feminist post-apocalyptic novel I wanted to see in the world. And maybe it'll even help start some conversations about the dystopia that so many women in Ireland find themselves living.'[2] *Last Ones Left Alive* uses speculative young adult fiction to investigate gender inequality in Ireland, and re-imagines how an apocalyptic crash could threaten the dominance of a zombie-like patriarchal neo-liberal capitalist regime.

The Celtic Tiger and collapse

From 1994 to 2008 Ireland was one of the fastest-growing economies, and most international countries, in the world. Described as the second richest country in the world, Ireland's GDP 'outstripped those of its Eurozone neighbours such as Germany, France and the UK'.[3] The AT Kearney Foreign Policy Globalisation Index had Ireland and Singapore competing for top place for the first few years of the twenty-first century. However, the unsustainable reliance on the Irish property market meant that economic collapse was inevitable. The Irish could no longer re-mortgage and re-build in a finite market, without cannibalising the country further. The level of debt in the country increased exponentially. The loans that the market depended on buckled under the pressure. Economic downturn was followed by what Gerry Smyth calls a 'serious assault' on national identity: 'it turned out that Ireland's great economic miracle was built upon very, very shaky foundations indeed; and once those foundations began to shake, they brought the whole edifice of the Irish economic miracle crashing to the ground in record time'.[4] The Celtic Tiger brought unprecedented levels of inward migration, wealth and consumerism. Spending and consumption were at an all-time high during this period. Kristine Larsen's description of the zombie is reminiscent of the Irish consumer during the Celtic Tiger, as well as Davis-Goff's skrakes: 'a mindless, marauding hoard driven by the single-minded primeval urge to feed'.[5]

Suddenly in 2008 the banks collapsed, lending ceased and questions had to be asked about what had initiated this crash. Ireland was propelled into austerity and the International Monetary Fund (IMF) arrived to assist the government in getting the national debt in order. Gerry Smyth identified this as 'the return of the real with a vengeance' as the reality of the 'momentous, ignominious fall' hit home: 'The levels of corruption, ignorance, incompetence and sheer stupidity that precipitated economic disaster shocked everyone.'[6] The growth however was plagued by inequality, and during the Celtic Tiger the disparity between rich and poor grew. The austerity that followed served to exasperate these issues, as Peadar Kirby explains:

> Ireland's 'miracle' resulted from prioritising economic growth over social development, and that the benefits were reaped mostly by an elite. The failure of the Celtic Tiger to foster an endogenous dynamic of innovation, the growing social polarisation that has accompanied

it and the reconfiguration of the Irish state in a decisive manner so that it attends to the needs of corporate capital over those of its own citizens, have all served to camouflage rather than resolve Ireland's long-standing development problems.[7]

The crash highlighted the failure of neo-liberal capitalism, and the austerity agenda that followed continued to support the same hegemonic system. Then Labour Party leader Pat Rabbitte criticised the then government in a debate in the Dáil Éireann (Irish parliament) for permitting 'the banks to cannibalise the State'.[8] This perceived powerlessness in the face of neo-liberal policy is echoed by Davis-Goff's *The Irish Times* article. She describes living in Ireland as equivalent to living 'in a dystopia . . . When we shout about it the only other people who can hear, apparently, are other people who are equally powerless to do anything about it.'[9]

Zombie economics

The zombie-like cannibalism of the collapse was also matched by the excessive consumption of the preceding Tiger period. In the period from 1991 to 2006 '762,631 housing units were completed in Ireland, peaking with 93,419 units being built in 2006 alone'.[10] For a country of just over 5 million people 'even allowing for replacing obsolescent stock, clearly more units were being built than there were households being formed'.[11] Price inflation matched the extent of building, with an average of 429 per cent increase in the price of a home in Dublin between 1991 and 2007.[12] Carmen Leah Kuhling claims that the housing bubble and subsequent collapse in Ireland demonstrates 'how Irish consumerism during the Celtic Tiger took on the mindless, voracious appetites of the zombie'.[13] Once the ability to purchase was removed, something else had to fill the void. Combined with the identity crisis that the collapse caused, the zombie has become the defining feature that can:

> capture the massive void Ireland now faces in terms of collective self-identity as the Celtic Tiger, the previous signifiers of collective identity and self-understanding. Nationalism, Catholicism and now Neoliberalism have been all proven to be deeply problematic, and no new collective signifiers of self-identity have emerged in their wake.[14]

The zombie is the ideal representation of this massive void, the crumbling collapse, the neo-liberal policy that led to the self-cannibalism of the Irish property market, the excessive consumption. In Davis-Goff's novel, the skrakes roam the landscape hunting and gorging on those left behind. The skrakes will do anything to continue the conspicuous consumption of the Tiger era, including devouring its own people.

Ghost estates

One of the biggest reminders of the Tiger and the collapse were the many 'ghost estates' left across Ireland. The phrase coined by David McWilliams in 2006, two years before the crash, perfectly captures these abandoned housing developments, often unfinished, or partially inhabited. They are often located in remote or rural areas across Ireland. Many of these ghostly liminal spaces still remain scattered across the country to this day. According to a 2018 *Irish Examiner* report, approximately 250 sites still await completion, approximately 10,000 units, 90 per cent fewer than the peak in 2009.[15] These, often isolated, housing developments were created when the economy collapsed. The oversupply and inflated market meant that they were over-valued and over-mortgaged, and credit-based builders no longer had the money to finish them; in turn, buyers could no longer get mortgages to purchase them. Abandoned estates became monuments to the failure of the Tiger economy, a ghostly presence haunting the landscape. David McWilliams describes:

> All over Ireland, 'ghost estates' are enveloping many of our towns. Driving back from the West, these spooky ghost estates emerged out of the mist announcing places like Tarmonbarry, Frenchpark and Edgeworthstown . . . In the years ahead, these ghost villages, like our famine villages, may stand testament to a great tragedy which, although predicted by concerned observers, was never fully appreciated until the morning the crops failed[16]

These ghost estates have been the subject of much artistic and academic work. Photographer Anthony Haughey's haunting project 'Settlement', for example, captures these spectral interact with the Irish landscape as reminders of the crash.[17] Haughey, reflecting on the environmental cost to the landscape of these abandoned homes, discusses how 'slowly, nature is starting to reclaim the exposed surface' and 'weeds and ash saplings have begun to take root in the gaps' of pavements and entrances.[18] His description of 'lichens and moss' covering 'the surfaces of untrafficked roads, and creeping vegetation is beginning to invade broken doorways and windows of unfinished and vandalized houses' is similar to the ghostly Irish landscape in *Last Ones Left Alive*.[19] He shares the same emotion as Orpen as he photographs these haunting homes.

The *Irish Independent*'s description of encountering a ghost estate in 2010 is also comparable to Orpen's interaction with the abandoned towns on the mainland. They wrote that: 'nothing prepares you for seeing them up close, for the echo of your footstep on the gravel, for the sight of a toilet abandoned in a hall, or a wing-backed three-piece suit in a derelict sitting room'.[20] As Orpen traverses Ireland she passes through towns where the 'quiet is unearthly', the road is 'cracked' with vegetation creeping through the tar, the shops are closed and empty.[21] The landscape reclaims the ghost estates and towns left behind by the historically evocative term 'the emergency'.[22] Even her own home on the island of Slanbeg is described by her as 'a ghost-house in a ghost-estate and a ghost country'.[23] The houses scattered around the island have been abandoned, 'everything covered in dust and dirt' with windows and doors missing, and the ghosts of previous inhabitants remaining. The bridge that once connected the island to the mainland has been 'chopped in half by something so big, something disastrous' with cars facing the island remaining on the ruined bridge.[24] The liminal presence of the dead haunts these uninhabited homes, and when her mother dies, she can no longer live in an unhomely home, haunted by the past. Maeve's skrake bite propels her across the country towards Phoenix City. Orpen's journey is the opposite of her parents escape from the city to Slanbeg; she now must return to the urban site of consumptive patriarchal power.

Environmental damage

The landscape in the novel highlights the environmental damage of this unlimited development. As a result of the 'emergency' nature is allowed to reclaim the built scars and Orpen sees '[l]ittle towns are nearly consumed back into earth with trees and vines delicately dismantling the stone works of the buildings'.[25] What Oona Frawley would call a 'pastoral turn', Ireland is allowed to return to 'a wild uncontaminated landscape and habitat'.[26] Brereton explains that these 'environmental tensions' are typical across Irish horror: 'suggesting that there is a lot to lose in accepting ongoing demands to transform and modernise the landscape, which over the centuries has been alternatively ravaged by British colonisation and subsequently through more insidious forms of global capitalism'.[27] Writing particularly about Irish cinema, Brereton claims that the horror-zombie storyline is also 'striving to re-imagine a future that supports sustainable' environmental concerns.[28] As Drezner explains the zombie is 'unique in genre literature in emphasizing the breakdown of modern society in the wake of an external threat'.[29] In *Last Ones Left Alive* this threat is internal, but it is also environmental.

The family at the centre of this story live off the land. Maeve, Muireann and Orpen grow their own food. The approved books include *Culpepper's Herbal and Complete Gardener*. The trio hunt, trap, fish, find water, keep seeds, ferment vegetables and keep chickens. Their kitchen is filled with traditional medicine and remedies. Muireann carries a herb pouch like a medicine bag, and they live their lives to be as sustainable as possible, leaving as little trace as possible: 'Failing to prepare is preparing to fail, is what Maeve says about that.'[30] Throughout are hints of environmental damage that may have led to the emergency:

> Mam told me, though, how the oven would work in the olden days, with a gas that was piped in all the way to the island, under the roiling sea. Seems like a lot of trouble when you can just go on and make a fire. Maeve says, No Matter, sure aren't we all paying for it now. She says it in the voice that means I needn't bother to ask more questions.[31]

Davis-Goff's novel follows the trajectory of Irish zombie narratives that 'actively call attention to the growth of environmental risk and food security'.[32] What Brereton calls the 'creative imaginary of horror' allows the space to speculate how the depletion of natural resources, like natural gas in this case, highlights 'the long-term seriousness of climate change'.[33] The mismanagement of natural resources means we will, as Maeve says, all pay for this negligence. The proliferation of zombie narratives highlights the environmental excess of Celtic Tiger development on the landscape. Emma Radley argues that these apocalyptic tropes reflect the 'crisis in/of the representable in the wake of the more general transformation in the landscape of Irish subjectivity post-Celtic Tiger'. [34]

An Irish zombie

The similarity of the landscape echoes the ghost estates of the defunct Celtic Tiger, their uncanny presence a 'testament' to some 'great tragedy', as McWilliams describes them.[35] However, the Irish landscapes in *Last Ones Left Alive* are inhabited by another liminal presence, the undead zombies. By using the name skrake, Davis-Goff creates a zombie specific to the Irish situation. This Irish zombie is generated by the temporality and the location; an Ireland coming to terms with the sudden end of a period of unprecedented wealth and greed. As Jeffery Jerome Cohen posits, the monster is born at a 'metaphoric crossroads' and becomes the 'embodiment of a certain cultural moment': 'The monster's body quite literally incorporates fear, desire, anxiety, and fantasy (ataractic or incendiary), giving them life and an uncanny independence.'[36] The skrake which was created 'by accident' aligns more with George A. Romero's zombie vision. The initial setting of an isolated house in rural Ireland is more reminiscent of the capitalism of *Night of the Living Dead* than the colonialism of *White Zombie*. Maeve and Muireann choose a rural farmhouse, that has 'boards on the windows' to camouflage the life contained inside.[37] The tension here is with the structures of power that are also manifested in the landscape. Davis-Goff moves the action from the farmhouse to the topography of post-apocalypse Ireland.

Skrakes are found clinging to the remains of capitalism, haunting the tall buildings and the towns, making the journey to create a new society all the more dangerous for Orpen. Just as in contemporary Ireland, Davis-Goff declares that 'We are, in fact, surrounded by monsters.'[38] In *Last Ones Left Alive* the monsters, the cannibalistic Irish zombies, along with the abandoned ghost estates and ghost towns, are all that remains of the old Ireland. Davis-Goff wrote that she has 'been craving work that talks about the world around us', that she wanted to 'create a world not unlike our own' that allows her to channel 'all the anger I feel about the dystopia we're living in'.[39] The skrakes act as reminders of the failing signifiers. As new communities and collective identities emerge, the old does not simply disappear, and, like the ghost estates, the skrakes still occupy the landscape during this transitional and unsettled period. The zombie figure matches the pace of Celtic Tiger development: 'I see a dark shape out of the corner of my eye and a half-turn, a breath, is all I manage before it is on top of me.'[40] Orpen has trained all her young life to face the monstrous skrakes, but when she first encounters one, they fit naturally with the landscape, rather than standout as interlopers: 'They'd been half mythic, half nonsense. But they're just grey and ordinary, kind of, part of the background, human-shaped and unobvious. Till they're going for your throat.'[41] The skrakes, like the cracks that eventually overwhelmed the Celtic Tiger excess, were obscure until it was too late.

The skrake fulfils the role of what Boon calls the 'zombie ghoul'. Again, the influence of Romero is evident in the skrakes' hunger for flesh. Boon explains that the image of the zombie was: 'irrevocably changed with the 1968 release of George Romero's *Night of the Living Dead*, in which Romero fuses the mythology of the zombie and the ghoul into the "zombie ghoul." Romero's Night gave zombies agency, a hunger for human flesh.'[42] Boon also suggests that elements of this 'zombie ghoul' are also present in H. P. Lovecraft's 1922 story 'Herbert West – Reanimator', but that the cannibalistic zombie-ghoul owes more to Romero's movie incarnation.[43] Here the skrakes are purpose-driven, quick-moving undead. All ages and genders, they seek out human flesh, and are strong, fighting back:

> Syrupy black blood is oozing from its injuries but the skrake keeps coming
> ...
> The knife meets soft flesh and gritty flesh, and when I pull it out the blood spurts on me.
> ...
> Ruined eyes roll in decayed sockets and its proboscis, pink smeared with black, throbs in the dark cave of its mouth.[44]

Kuhling explains that the zombie became the 'symbolic representation of several overlapping images relevant to the post-austerity context of contemporary Ireland'.[45] While Davis-Goff's skrake has its roots in Romero's zombie, the global economic collapse reanimated the metaphor of the zombie for cultural anxiety, as concern spread about the contamination possibility of Ireland's banking crisis.

Camilla Fojas suggests that the zombie narrative is the ideal metaphor for the death drive of the global debt economy, while also offering the opportunity to rethink the social order. However, as Fojas indicates, when faced with the societal 'clean slate', many mainstream zombie narratives choose to return to the same system. Using examples from *World War Z* and *The Walking Dead*, Fojas explains that:

> In these postcrisis stories, power and symbolic power reverts to the white heterosexual male patriarch and leader from the global North. The postapocalyptic communal formation is not one beyond capitalism or even a precapitalist form or anything approaching communism but the intensification of the logic of capitalism.[46]

Davis-Goff moves away from the 'reactionary and conservative' response and uses the emergency as an opportunity to reimagine Ireland, after the collapse of the Celtic Tiger:

> In writing a post-apocalyptic world, though, I don't have to convince anyone that this world is unfair. We can literally start on the same page. And in creating monsters, at least some of these problems could be dealt with, physically, by characters who wanted to change the dystopias in which they found themselves.[47]

Using the post-apocalyptic setting allows Davis-Goff to create a space to investigate 'toxic masculinity . . . get to talk about the patriarchy, and issues like addiction and loneliness, and the cost of being a protagonist in your own life'.[48]

The girl

The book centres on Orpen, named after the painter; although it is not specified if it is William or Bea, the painting described by Orpen seems to be William Orpen's dystopian *Zonnebeke*, based on the battle of the Somme.[49] Davis-Goff describes Orpen as not 'a creation of mine so much as a by-product of the world she lives in'.[50] Like so many other post-Celtic Tiger novels, the girl is at the centre. Susan Cahill explains that there was a shift in the wake of the crash from 'shaming and blaming of the girl as too closely tied to the commodity to a more feminist critique of the commodification of girlhood in post-Tiger texts'.[51] According to Cahill, young adult novels like Louise O'Neill's *Only Ever Yours* and *Asking for It* challenge the 'dominant representations of the girl in the Tiger period'.[52] *Last Ones Left Alive* fits with Cahill's thesis where 'girlhood, trauma, language, and resistance' are linked: 'These more overtly feminist representations of the girl in the post-Tiger period insist that we pay attention to her – indeed they situate her at the nexus of their powerful feminist critiques.'[53] Orpen is at the centre of post-apocalypse Ireland, offering the viewpoint of a teenage girl that has never met anyone other than Maeve and her mother, Muireann. Orpen is told that other people are dangerous, and that in particular 'men are dangerous'.[54] Davis-Goff claims that the choices Orpen 'has to make seem obvious and essential', but without the shadow of patriarchy, or experience of the events that led to the 'emergency', Orpen has a unique opportunity to reimagine and recreate Ireland into the future. She becomes the hope for the future, and a new generation:

> No matter how much Orpen is warned or prepared, there are dangers out there that she can't really comprehend. In the end, like most parents, they've to hope that they did their jobs well and prepared their child well enough to cope with life, and to at least be on her guard.[55]

The girl in *Last Ones Left Alive* becomes the site of opportunity, the locus for change. Raised by feminist activists, she has little understanding of the role of men in society, or the neo-liberal regime that existed before the 'emergency'. Orpen is ideally situated to change the rules of the zombie genre and move away from patriarchal capitalism. However, the zombies do fulfil Fojas's definition, acting as a 'remainder and terrifying reminder of that system, an imminent threat'. Given the ending of the novel, ripe for both sequels and prequels, it is hard to know if the skrakes 'cannot be fully neutralized'. As Fojas explains, this not simply the manifestation of 'the collapse of the debt economy and survival of life beyond it', because of Davis-Goff's feminist undertones.[56] The collapse does not just represent the economic collapse, just as the skrake is not solely the reanimation of capitalism that consumes the remaining residents of Ireland. The skrake is also a critique of structures of Irish oppression, and the opportunity re-imagining of Ireland outside the shadow of heteronormativity, patriarchy and Catholicism.

Last Ones Left Alive presents a world where men have been 'dispensed with', and Orpen is told from a young age that men are 'trouble' and 'dangerous'. On her seventh birthday Orpen is told that 'Men can do terrible things . . . don't forget that.' Maeve adds:

> 'Men made the skrake, long ago.'
>
> 'By Accident,' Mam puts in, and Maeve nods again.
>
> 'They did terrible things then and they do terrible things now.'[57]

Her upbringing is designed to ensure survival, and these narratives from Muireann and Maeve are supported by the books she reads that contain stories of 'men making the decisions and women suffering for them'.[58] Her parents explain that being able to 'control ourselves' is the 'essential difference' between women and the skrake, and women and men.[59] Orpen was trained to be self-sufficient and to trust no one, so it comes as no surprise that when she meets other survivors – Cillian, Aodh and Nic – she runs. When Cillian asks her to stop running away, the first time she has really heard a man speak she feels 'a glorious spike of anger'.[60] When they go back to find Maeve's infected corpse, Orpen is uncomfortable hearing him talk: 'He's talking like he's sure I want to listen to the noise of him.' [61]

The group have come from Phoenix City and offer Orpen a glimpse of what this matriarchal society might be like. And while Nic explains that 'In Phoenix City there's a code amongst women. We look out for one another; we take care of one another if we can.'[62] The city has seemingly curtailed the agency of those within its confines. Cillian explains that women have two options – 'breeders and banshees' – while 'men have only the one' and are not educated.[63] Cillian never expands on what this 'one' option is, but it is clear that men are imprisoned and required only for the impregnation of the breeders in a reversal of Atwood's *The Handmaid's Tale*. The Banshee also holds significance in Irish folklore, often heard wailing before the passing of a family member, an omen of death. Muireann and Maeve warn Orpen that Phoenix City 'wasn't a good place . . . Those things you read, what they say isn't true anymore. If it ever was.'[64] This first iteration of a changed society has not worked. The phoenix that rose from the ashes of patriarchal capitalism seems to be flawed, yet for Orpen the Banshees represent the warriors she wants to be, and also offer her the chance to get into Phoenix City. Hope still rests with the girl in this post-Celtic Tiger apocalyptic Ireland.

The importance of community

The arrival of Cillian, Nic and Aodh leads to Orpen killing her dog Danger. While they are not necessarily out of danger at this point, the significance of the clunkily named dog cannot be ignored. The same chapter starts with the line 'Danger was ahead of me'.[65] What was ahead of her at that point was Phoenix City. Behind her are the trio, a hap-hazard nuclear family, with the pregnant Nic reminiscent of her own family's escape to

Slanbeg. Orpen is torn between this family, which she saves, and that of the Banshees, which she ends up leaving with at the end of the novel. Despite her training, she craves and needs community: 'It's a problem all on its own, so it is; we're to be afraid of people, and we need them.'[66]

With either the Banshees, or Cillian, Nic and Aodh, Orpen resists the individuality of neo-liberal capitalism, and self-sufficiency changes to community security, and communal support. Fred Botting suggests that:

> Images of small bands of people struggling against undead masses and more barbaric survivors may be dressed up as a fantasy of natural self-sufficiency to end the degeneration of contemporary existence, but they also hold up a mirror of the anti-social contract of neoliberal competition and individuation that exhausts social ties, human energies, and planetary reserves.[67]

While Orpen leaves the nuclear family behind, she does join with the all-female Banshees collective, choosing companionship and community over individuation. She looks to the matriarchal for opportunity and survival in this new Ireland.

The zombies here, and the response of the young hero, are important in the re-imagining of society and the economic and societal collapse of the emergency. The skrake is still in existence at the end of the novel, but they 'do not mark a breaking point, but the condition of living on after being broken'.[68] And what Kuhling would call the desire to form new 'collective solidarities' after this break, which is personal and ideological, highlights another desire 'for a new, more democratic political imaginary that can replace Ireland's monstrous austerity regime. Whether this desire can be realised remains to be seen.'[69] We can only wait to see if this is the case in Orpen's Ireland.

Notes

1. Daryl M., 'Interview with an Author: Sarah Davis Goff', Los Angeles Public Library, *https://www.lapl.org/collections-resources/blogs/lapl/interview-author-sarah-davis-goff* (accessed 18 January 2021).
2. Sarah Davis-Goff, 'I Have Created the Kind of Novel I Wanted to See in the World', *The Irish Times* (2019), *https://www.irishtimes.com/culture/books/writing-the-novel-you-want-to-see-in-the-world-1.3806951* (accessed 10 April 2021).

3. Gerry Smyth, 'Irish National Identity after the Celtic Tiger', *Estudios Irlandeses*, 7/7 (2012), 133.
4. Smyth, 'Irish National Identity after the Celtic Tiger', 133.
5. Kristine Larsen, '"Nightmare Horrors and Perils of the Night": Zombies and Modern Science', *The Irish Journal of Gothic and Horror Studies*, 12 (2013), 44.
6. Smyth, 'Irish National Identity after the Celtic Tiger', 134.
7. Peadar Kirby, 'Development Theory and the Celtic Tiger', *European Journal of Development Research*, 16/2 (2004), 324.
8. 'Under the Terms of the Banks . . .: Wednesday, 17 November 2010: Dáil Éireann Debates', *KildareStreet.com*, https://www.kildarestreet.com/debate/?id=2010-11-17.500.0 (accessed 5 January 2021).
9. Davis-Goff, 'I Have Created the Kind of Novel I Wanted to See in the World'.
10. Rob Kitchin, Rory Hearne and Cian O'Callaghan, 'Housing in Ireland: From Crisis to Crisis', *SSRN Scholarly Paper*, Rochester, NY: Social Science Research Network (17 February 2015), https://papers.ssrn.com/abstract=2566297 (accessed 10 April 2021).
11. Kitchin, Hearne and O'Callaghan, 'Housing in Ireland'.
12. Kitchin, Hearne and O'Callaghan, 'Housing in Ireland'.
13. Carmen Leah Kuhling, 'Zombie Banks, Zombie Politics and the "Walking Zombie Movement": Liminality and the Post-crisis Irish Imaginary', *European Journal of Cultural Studies*, 20/4 (2017), 397–412, 405.
14. Kuhling, 'Zombie Banks, Zombie Politics', 405.
15. Elaine Loughlin, 'Over 250 Ghost Estates Still Haunting Ireland', *Irish Examiner* (7 March 2018), https://www.irishexaminer.com/news/arid-20467973.html (accessed 19 January 2021).
16. David McWilliams, 'A Warning from Deserted Ghost Estates', http://www.davidmcwilliams.ie/a-warning-from-deserted-ghost-estates/ (accessed 3 November 2020).
17. Anthony Haughey, 'Settlement', http://anthonyhaughey.com/projects/settlement/ (accessed 5 January 2021).
18. Anthony Haughey, 'A Landscape of Crisis', *The Canadian Journal of Irish Studies*, 40 (2017), 60.
19. Haughey, 'A Landscape of Crisis', 60.
20. 'Walking with the Ghosts', *Independent* (22 May 2010), https://www.independent.ie/lifestyle/walking-with-the-ghosts-26657225.html (accessed 3 November 2020).
21. Davis-Goff, 'I Have Created the Kind of Novel I Wanted to See in the World', 41.

22. 'The Emergency' was also a term used for the period of measures the Irish Government took during the Second World War, when they maintained the neutrality stance of the country.
23. Sarah Davis-Goff, *Last Ones Left Alive* (London: Tinder Press, 2019), p. 21.
24. Davis-Goff, *Last Ones Left Alive*, p. 120
25. Davis-Goff, *Last Ones Left Alive*, p. 71.
26. Oona Frawley, *Irish Pastoral: Nostalgia and Twentieth-century Irish Literature* (Dublin: Irish Academic Press, 2005); Pat Brereton, 'Cultural and Visual Responses to Climate Change: Ecological Reading of Irish Zombie Movies', in David Robbins, Diarmiud Torney and Pat Brereton (eds), *Ireland and the Climate Crisis* (New York: Springer International Publishing AG, 2020), p. 189.
27. Brereton, 'Cultural and Visual Responses to Climate Change', p. 189.
28. Brereton, 'Cultural and Visual Responses to Climate Change', p. 190.
29. Daniel W. Drezner, 'Metaphor of the Living Dead: Or, the Effect of the Zombie Apocalypse on Public Policy Discourse', *Social Research*, 81/4 (2014), 826.
30. Davis-Goff, *Last Ones Left Alive*, p. 79.
31. Davis-Goff, *Last Ones Left Alive*, p. 78.
32. Brereton, 'Cultural and Visual Responses to Climate Change', pp. 185–6.
33. Brereton, 'Cultural and Visual Responses to Climate Change', p. 186.
34. Emma Radley, 'Violent Transpositions: The Disturbing "Appearance" of the Irish Horror Film', in Claire Bracken and Emma Radley (eds), *Viewpoints, Theoretical Perspectives on Irish Visual Texts* (Cork: Cork University Press, 2013), p. 123.
35. McWilliams, 'A Warning from Deserted Ghost Estates'.
36. Jeffrey Jerome Cohen, *Monster Theory: Reading Culture* (Minneapolis: University of Minnesota Press, 1996), p. 4.
37. Davis-Goff, *Last Ones Left Alive*, p. 21.
38. Davis-Goff, 'I Have Created the Kind of Novel I Wanted to See in the World'.
39. Davis-Goff, 'I Have Created the Kind of Novel I Wanted to See in the World'.
40. Davis-Goff, *Last Ones Left Alive*, p. 11.
41. Davis-Goff, *Last Ones Left Alive*, p. 15.
42. Kevin Alexander Boon, 'Ontological Anxiety Made Flesh: The Zombie in Literature, Film and Culture', in Niall Scott (ed.), *Monsters and the Monstrous: Myths and Metaphors of Enduring Evil* (Amsterdam: Rodopi, 2007), p. 38.
43. Boon, 'Ontological Anxiety Made Flesh', p. 39.
44. Davis-Goff, *Last Ones Left Alive*, pp. 14–15.
45. Kuhling, 'Zombie Banks, Zombie Politics'.
46. Camilla Fojas, *Zombies, Migrants, and Queers: Race and Crisis Capitalism in Pop Culture* (Urbana, Chicago: University of Illinois Press, 2017), p. 81.

47. Davis-Goff, 'I Have Created the Kind of Novel I Wanted to See in the World'.
48. Davis-Goff, 'I Have Created the Kind of Novel I Wanted to See in the World'.
49. Davis-Goff, *Last Ones Left Alive*, p. 22.
50. Davis-Goff, 'I Have Created the Kind of Novel I Wanted to See in the World'.
51. Susan Cahill, 'A Girl is a Half-Formed Thing? Girlhood, Trauma, and Resistance in Post-Tiger Irish Literature', *Lit: Literature Interpretation Theory: Recessionary Imaginings II: Post-Celtic Tiger Ireland and Contemporary Women's Writing*, 28/2 (2017), 153–71.
52. Cahill, 'A Girl is a Half-Formed Thing?', p. 154.
53. Cahill, 'A Girl is a Half-Formed Thing?', p. 155.
54. Davis-Goff, *Last Ones Left Alive*, p. 108.
55. Davis-Goff, 'I Have Created the Kind of Novel I Wanted to See in the World'.
56. Fojas, *Zombies, Migrants, and Queers*, p. 81.
57. Davis-Goff, *Last Ones Left Alive*, pp. 34–5.
58. Davis-Goff, *Last Ones Left Alive*, p. 78.
59. Davis-Goff, *Last Ones Left Alive*, p. 107.
60. Davis-Goff, *Last Ones Left Alive*, p. 86.
61. Davis-Goff, *Last Ones Left Alive*, p. 128.
62. Davis-Goff, *Last Ones Left Alive*, p. 123.
63. Davis-Goff, *Last Ones Left Alive*, p. 129.
64. Davis-Goff, *Last Ones Left Alive*, p. 162.
65. Davis-Goff, *Last Ones Left Alive*, p. 82.
66. Davis-Goff, *Last Ones Left Alive*, p. 207.
67. Fred Botting, 'Undead-Ends: Zombie Debt/Zombie Theory', *Postmodern Culture*, 23/3 (2013), *doi:10.1353/pmc.2013.0043*.
68. Botting, 'Undead-Ends: Zombie Debt/Zombie Theory'.
69. Kuhling, 'Zombie Banks, Zombie Politics'.

PART THREE

UNDEAD CULTURES

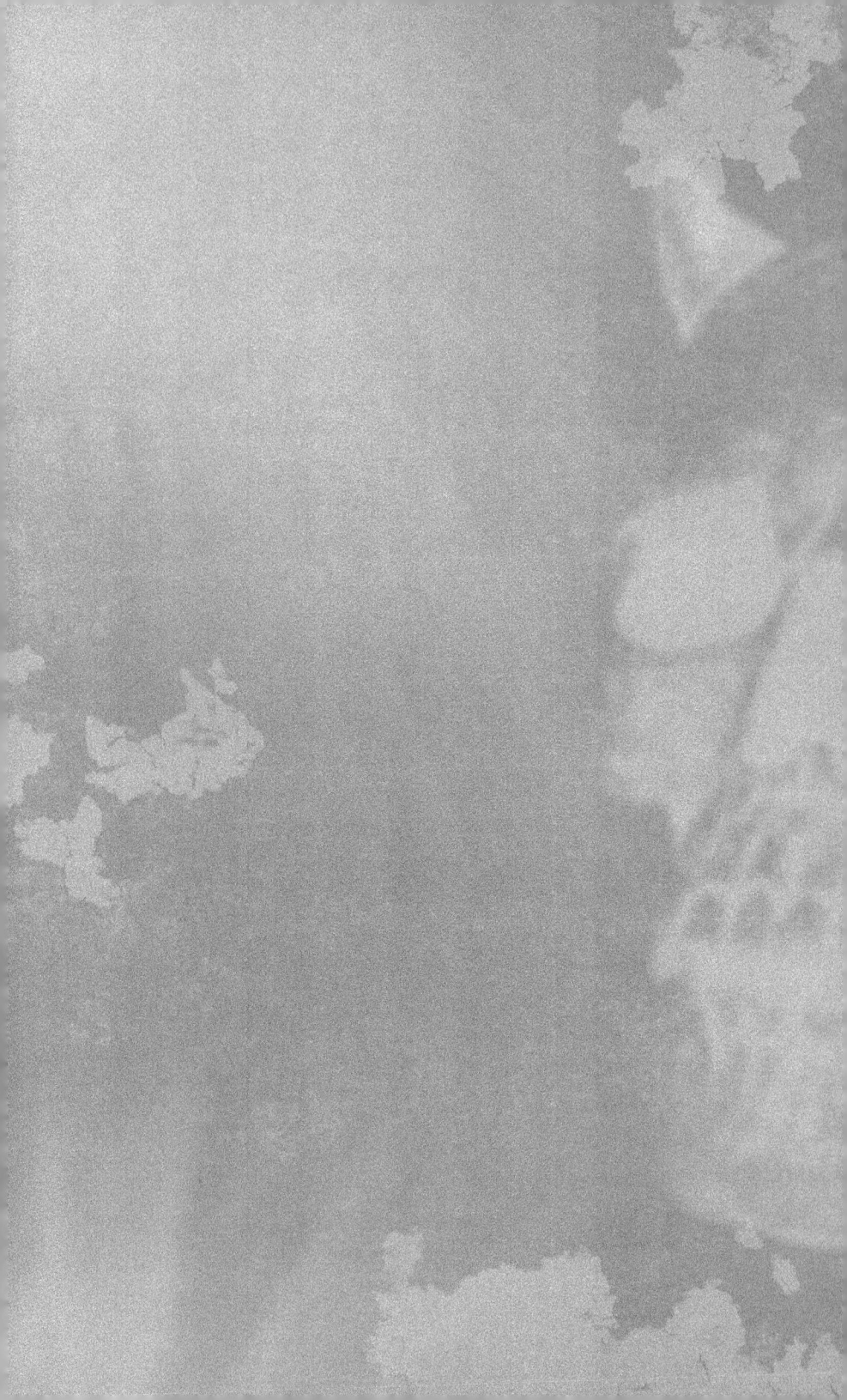

9

Beware the Zuvembies
Comics, Censorship and the Ubiquity of *Not-quite* Zombies

Chera Kee

IMAGINE OPENING an American horror comic in the early 1950s and thumbing through the pages. One story begins with a wife sending her husband off to his night shift at the defence plant. Poor Becky worries about her husband Dave Tibbets's commute because he is 'always in a hurry', and sure enough, Dave takes a curve too fast and his car plummets off a cliff.[1] Luckily for Dave, however, he awakens after the crash relatively unhurt. Except when he tries to hail a passing car, the passengers yell and drive away. When he visits a nearby house to ask for help, the woman inside slams the door in his face with a scream, and when he finally finds a trolley to return home, all of the other passengers flee his presence. Dave cannot figure out what is wrong: he is a zombie who does not know he is a zombie.

Not all of the zombies peopling comics of the early 1950s suffered the kind of identity crisis that Dave does, but his story is emblematic of how the zombie state came to be represented in pre-code comics: zombies were, at once, both clearly zombies but also *not-quite*.[2] Dave, after all, is not the shambling, mindless undead one might expect. He talks, thinks freely and might be mistaken for one of the living if not for his corpse-like appearance. As both living and dead, zombies have nearly always had the peculiar ability to exist as both/and, and one of the most fundamental ways in which zombies inhabit this duality is both by epitomising and defying what it means to be a zombie.

Typical expectations of the zombie picture it as mindless, without a will of its own; but active, intelligent zombies have been a staple of popular American zombie tales from the beginning.[3] While these zombies may seem 'extra-ordinary', often, they are not the exception but the rule. Zombies who talk, zombies who fall in love, zombies who lead rebellions: American media is littered with them. So, it should be no surprise that the undead of comic books follow a similar pattern. Yet, comic-book zombies have rarely featured in academic discussions of zombies in American media. There has been work on Robert Kirkman's *The Walking Dead* (2003–19) and there have been occasional nods to comics in surveys of zombie media, but there has not been sustained attention paid to the history of zombies in comics. That history provides insights into how comic books have shaped wider popular understandings of the zombie.

Surveying the early history of zombies in comics – from their first appearances in action/adventure and superhero titles of the 1930s and 1940s to the implementation of censorship in 1955 – and then examining the influence of these early zombies during their resurrection in comic books of the 1970s, this chapter considers the ways medium and genre played formative roles in shaping the zombie character. From the beginning of their tenure in comics, zombies have often not been 'zombies' in the strictest sense: they have had superhuman strength, they have been able to talk and they have had wills of their own, and much of this is due to the generic uses to which the earliest zombies were put. The history of zombies in comic books thus points to the need for a reappraisal of popular understandings of how zombies evolved in US media. As comic books show, zombies in popular culture have rarely lived up to their zombiness, and expectations of what the 'zombie' is often do not match the actual zombies depicted in media. Examining the early history of zombies in comics thus opens a space to consider what assumptions scholars and fans might hold that undermine contemporary understandings of the zombie.

Zombies and superheroes

Born out of the pulp tradition, the modern American comic book appeared in the 1930s, but it was not until the meteoric rise of the superhero genre in the later parts of the decade that comic books would become a mass hit. While superhero titles were the most popular in the USA throughout the Second World War, by the end of the war, other genres started to gain prominence. One genre that was relatively slow to catch on was horror. While there were horror elements and characters in early comics, it was not until the late 1940s that horror stories started appearing in any sustained sense. During 1947 and 1948, publishers tried standalone horror titles, with mixed results, but it was not until Entertaining Comics (EC) published *The Haunt of Fear*, *The Vault of Horror* and *The Crypt of Terror* (later, *Tales from the Crypt*) in 1950 that the horror genre became popular; when it did, some estimate that there were as many as 'fifty to one hundred horror titles' being released monthly up through 1954.[4]

EC had been publishing well before 1950, but that year, its head, William Gaines, decided to re-brand some of their titles as horror, and his idea worked. The particular EC style of horror, with its twist endings and pointed critiques of 1950s' American life, resonated with readers, soon becoming the blueprint that other publishers rushed to emulate.[5] Jim Trombetta notes that horror comics of the period:

> were genuinely and brazenly subversive in a way that might not even be possible today. In an era that held its values dearly, no dearly held value survived exposure to the horror comic universe: not the 'happy ending', not family, not science, and not the law. This world seems not merely meaningless in an existential sense . . . but also actively malicious.[6]

While EC tended to tell these sorts of stories with a panache that made them memorable even decades later, not every publisher could easily replicate the EC formula, which meant that 'Many 1950s horror comics featured violence, gore and menace for their own sake.'[7] Yet, whether it was subtle and sophisticated or blunt and gory, horror had arrived.

Given this history, it might be logical to assume that zombies did not start appearing in comics until the late 1940s or early 1950s, but as horror elements trickled into other genres during the late 1930s and early 1940s, zombies found their way into comics that were not ostensibly horror. In these non-horror comics, zombies were not necessarily treated as 'horror' characters but as more of a blank slate. In fact, the earliest zombies in comics were in action/adventure and superhero titles, and this shaped their characterisations – as they were moulded to fit crime-fighting and action situations.

Zombies, as they came to be integrated into American popular culture in the late 1920s and early 1930s, were based on stories about Haitian Vodou (popularised as 'voodoo' in the USA). According to the legends, zombie masters controlled zombies who were soulless creatures without wills of their own. As this was translated into US pop culture, masters might use spells, hypnotism or potions to create their zombie slaves, but the result was always the same: the zombies bowed to the will of their master. According to Haitian folklore – and the earliest US short stories and films – zombies were slave workers, and several early comics took up this premise. In a story from *Jackpot Comics* (1941), for instance, the superhero Mr. Justice encounters Zarro, Master of Zombies.[8] Zarro bewitches entire factories of US workers and then steals their bodies to make zombie workers for a factory in Haiti. Mr. Justice finds a way to free the zombie workers from their master's control, promising to get them back to their factory jobs in the USA as soon as possible.

Besides portraying zombies as victims in need of a superhero rescuer, the slave-worker formula could also be tweaked to fit the action/adventure and superhero genres so that zombies might serve as a criminal mastermind's henchmen; when the Second World War intensified, they might become the undead armies that evil doers used against the Allies. In 'The Horror of the Haunted Cathedral', from *Marvel Mystery Comics* (1942), the slave-worker premise was updated to fit current political events and generic considerations: in it, superhero The Angel confronts Nazi General Henchel.[9] Intent on using his zombies to kill Americans, Henchel starts an undead killing spree, sending his zombie army after anyone in his path.

Whether workers, henchmen or armies, most of the earliest comic-book zombies were tools, used by their masters to achieve a goal, and in that sense, they were not inherently evil.[10] They were a threat simply because they could be directed to work for villains or criminals. Yet, as both the Mr. Justice story and 'The Horror of the Haunted Cathedral' illustrate, the zombies' true purpose in these comics was often to showcase the hero's bravery: the hero either rescued the zombies from their master or the zombies were a roadblock for the hero to dispatch on his way to the villain.

Revenge from the grave

In 1948, EC published its first horror story, 'Zombie Terror', in *Moon Girl*.[11] This story not only marked an auspicious moment for EC but for zombies in comics as well. 'Zombie Terror' follows a pattern that would become increasingly common over the next few years: person/group A mistreats person/group B, most likely causing the death of person/group B. Then, person/group B rises from the grave to exact their revenge. In this case, a group of smugglers in the West Indies cause the deaths of a number of native workers. The workers return from the dead as zombies, chasing the smugglers until they die. There are two notable changes from the earlier pattern of zombies as slave workers occurring in this story.

One change is that these zombies are not necessarily controlled by any clear zombie master. They seem to be reanimated by some universal moral code or sense of justice. They come back to life to right a wrong done to them while they were living. These zombies are also no longer background material. They are the point of the story. Readily clear in the title, 'Zombie Terror', this speaks to the shift from seeing zombies as slaves to seeing them as active agents enacting revenge/justice. Even so, the underlying message of this tale was similar to the stories of the early 1940s when zombies were part of action/adventure and superhero tales: evil will be punished. Only now, the zombies were the ones doing the punishing.

Looking back, it is clear that 'Zombie Terror' was revolutionary in its take on the zombie story, but that did not mean that zombie tales changed overnight. There were still many comics where zombies were slaves controlled by a zombie master. Starting in 1951, though, two other trends become obvious: one, stories that focused on the 'Zombie Terror'-style revenge from the grave become more prevalent and, two, evil zombies started appearing. Jim Trombetta argues that in the wake of the Second World War and at the beginning of the Korean War, 'the essence of the zombie nightmare [was] personal guilt'.[12] Thinking about the rise of revenge-from-the-grave-style zombies in this sense, the zombie becomes a metaphor for dealing with survivor's guilt – literally reanimating past guilt and returning it to the present. While the idea of the past haunting the present may be an example of the gothic influence on pre-code horror stories and using monstrous figures as vehicles for revenge was not necessarily new, this was a novel twist on the zombie tale: zombies actively wanting to harm the living.

There was also a strong moral tone to many of these revenge-from-the-grave stories that tied the zombie's resurrection to righting past wrongs: these stories were often about punishing those who had violated the moral code, so zombies might return to catch a murderer or identify an unfaithful spouse. In 'Hating Corpse' (1953), for instance, Nathan Boyd is jealous of Charlie Kennedy for stealing his fiancé, Thyra. Nathan buys Charlie's debt, which includes his house and his car, and then offers Charlie a proposition: divorce Thyra and he will clear Charlie's debt. Charlie refuses and Nathan shoots him but, as the story indicates, 'Although Charlie Kennedy was dead, the hate for Nathan Boyd lived on within his soul! It became the blood in his empty arteries and fired the cells of his brain.'[13] Charlie-the-zombie then lies in wait for Nathan and shoots him. His revenge complete, he writes one final letter to his wife to explain what happened before dying again.

While 'Hating Corpse' tries to explain Charlie's resurrection, most stories did not, and so the revenge-from-the-grave zombie anticipates the Romero-style cannibal zombie texts that became popular after the 1968 film *Night of the Living Dead*, where the cause of regeneration is typically unclear. Furthermore, with *Night of the Living Dead* and much zombie media to follow, zombiism is accompanied by a rather bleak world view: the world has turned upside down and concepts like 'right', 'wrong', 'justice' and 'injustice' do not mean anything anymore. With the pre-code comics, though, while the cause of zombiism might not be locatable, the world view was one where there is still a clear 'right' and 'wrong', and these stories' insistence on a justice-that-must-be-served may have been comforting to those who witnessed the horrors of war, concentration camps and the atomic bomb in the recent past. Therefore, for all the ways in which revenge-from-the-grave zombies are different from their slave-style cousins, they still operate in a world governed by a strict good-versus-evil binary.

Evil zombies also started appearing in the early 1950s. Again, typically, in 1940s' comics, while often used for nefarious purposes, zombies were not malevolent in and of themselves. However, stories with evil zombies often suggested that only bad people (such as criminals) became zombified. In 'The Scourge of the Undead' (1953), for instance, a mysterious visitor to death-row inmate Jules Scholler promises he will survive the electric chair. When Jules does survive, he is at first thrilled and goes on a crime spree, but he soon realises that while he is not dead, his body is decomposing. The mysterious visitor then explains to Jules that this is part of the bargain: 'You will continue to walk the earth among the living because the evil spirit within you lives – but the forces of nature control your flesh!'[14] Here, zombification is directly tied to Jules's 'evil spirit'. In other cases, zombification is a punishment for bad deeds.[15] For instance, in 'Beware the Undead!' (1952), the character Nat Grear is clearly a bad guy, and when he falls off a cliff where he had intended to murder his rich uncle, he becomes a zombie. At that point, another evil-doer, Tamiko, explains 'Ha! Ha! Of course we die! That is our punishment! We die – and live again and rot and die again.'[16] The zombie state thus becomes the nightmare punishment of decomposition and death played on an endless loop.

Throughout their history on film and television screens, zombies have rarely been presented as inherently malicious. Slave zombies might be the tools of an evil master, but that did not make them evil, per se. Similarly, while cannibal-style zombies, like those in *Night of the Living Dead* and most contemporary films, are usually presented as a threat to the living, they are not threatening for any conscious reason. They are simply following the drive to eat. With some 1950s' comics, though, zombies are threatening on their own – something that is hinted at in films such as *Revenge of the Zombies* (1943), where slave zombies revolt against their master – but which is much more pronounced in comics with revenge-from-the-grave stories or evil zombies. In these comics, the zombies mean the living harm. Whether the living deserve it is secondary to the fact that zombies are now imagined as adversaries on their own, without a zombie master as intermediary. These zombies thus defy the very notion of zombiness – that zombies have no will of their own – in that their will towards revenge or towards evil is the main impetus of the plot.

Decomposing corpses

As revenge-from-the-grave stories and evil zombies became more prevalent in comics, more and more zombies were able to talk. Talking zombies were not necessarily new – zombies spoke in 1940s' comics as well[17] – but in the early 1950s, they were numerous. Zombies in comics often explained their motivations to their victims: they expressed their frustration with the living, or in some cases, their desire to simply go back to the grave. In 'Canyon of the Living Dead' (1951), for instance, one of the zombies begs the living protagonist, 'You must release me from this living death trap.'[18] Having zombies speak allowed creators to clearly explain a zombie's motivation. Talking zombies also go hand in hand with a more active zombie character, helping to illustrate that these zombies had independent wills, and desires, of their own.

Part of this may be tied to the EC influence on horror comics. EC titles tended to have twist endings, often poked fun at authority figures and exposed sacred institutions – like the nuclear family and marriage

– as shams. Having clever zombies delivering wicked puns fit the house style, and giving the 'monster' more and more agency – and the ability to explain itself, especially when it was a force for good – undermined traditional notions of good and evil by effectively flipping them. However, this change towards a more agentive zombie was, in part, also the consequence of the constant one-upping of horror publishers trying to secure a readership by outdoing their competitors. Talking, malevolent zombies were a natural step to take in such an environment.

The changes in the zombie's characterisation in the 1950s went hand-in-hand with changes in how the zombie looked. While in films of the 1930s and 1940s, zombies generally resembled the living,[19] albeit with vacant stares and a slow, lumbering gait, in comics, there was a wide variety of physical attributes for zombies from the beginning. Zombies in comics might be blue, green, purple, scarlet or black. A number of zombies at this time were bald; many were muscular and, as they were overwhelmingly male, several either had no shirt or open shirts to show off their strapping chests. This might be related to depictions of zombies in films such as *Ouanga* (1936) or *I Walked with a Zombie* (1943), featuring tall, shirtless male zombies, but it may also be due to the zombie's residence in superhero and action/adventure comics: the zombies in these stories were not necessarily designed to be horrific as much as adversarial. They were basically henchmen, after all. There were even comic-book stories in the early 1940s where characters explicitly remarked on the superhuman strength of zombies, and this makes sense, given that they were the 'muscle' of zombie masters.[20]

Even though there were many of these strong-man zombies, there was still a remarkable hybridity of looks, mainly because as a creature with no concrete mythology dictating behaviour and appearance, creators were free to experiment. This experimentation could naturally go further than it could in film: there were not the same limitations on the medium. Drawing a pink zombie with fangs in a 1940s' comic would have been easier than creating make-up and prosthetics for a similar look on screen. Likewise, there was not the same level of censorship because at the time, in comics, there really was not any formal censorship. However, film-makers were bound by rules that dictated just how gruesome zombies could be – namely, this meant that they could not be very gruesome at all – at least not until Hollywood's Production Code Administration (PCA) died in the 1960s.[21]

Accompanying the transition of zombies from more super-heroic titles to horror and the subsequent rise of malevolent zombies, in the 1950s, the zombie's appearance in comics started to change as well. While bald zombies were still popular, and there were still muscular zombies, more and more zombies were becoming emaciated. By 1952, zombies in comics were generally much bonier;[22] they often dressed in rags – their former clothing hanging off their clearly thinner bodies. By 1953, emaciation was giving way to full-scale decomposition, with stories where a body's decay was the point. In 'Orchids from the Dead' (1953), for example, a prisoner devises a way to escape – to be killed and then revived as a zombie. Only, what he does not anticipate is that once resurrected as a zombie, his body will start decomposing. The people who turned him exploit his gruesome appearance as leverage to force him to work for them. As they explain, they are the only ones who will not flee his presence.[23]

As the zombie became more threatening overall, it became more physically gruesome. Slave zombies in 1940s' superhero titles were typically unwitting henchmen who either needed to blend into the background or provide a quick visual justification for why the superhero's might was necessary in fighting them. However, these zombies often looked human enough to justify a possible rescue. With later, more threatening zombies, this sympathy based on a shared humanity was no longer necessary. These zombies were acting of their own accord and with their own agendas, and this agenda was often placed at odds with the living; therefore, their appearance needed to be at odds with the living as well.

This might have something to do with the comic book's roots in pulp magazines. Paul Douglas Lopes notes that in the early days of comics, publishers borrowed heavily from both 'the industrial logic' of pulp publishing as well as from popular pulp genres and formulas. In particular, he observes that the 'dominant tradition of "realism" in comic book illustration came from illustration found in pulp magazines', adding that 'These artists also eventually incorporated elements of sexuality, violence, and gore found in the more lurid pulp magazines.'[24] In the case of zombies, the more gory and lurid elements of pulps took nearly a decade to take hold, and may have had more to do with the demands of the market than the direct influence of the pulps: with publishers of horror titles vying for readers in the early 1950s, making monsters more and more outrageous-looking – especially on the covers of comic books – was a good way to catch a potential reader's eye.

Yet, Lopes's claims about realism are worth considering. While he is addressing the general style of comic-book illustration in the late 1930s and 1940s, one thing that is striking about the transition from strong-man zombies to decomposing zombies is its timing. For the most part, the decomposing bodies appear after the war. Trombetta suggests that 'the zombies of the fifties are . . . the ones who didn't make it out of Auschwitz'.[25] Given that many comic-book artists served in the war, it is not unreasonable to suggest that their experiences with dead and wounded bodies may have shaped their art. While in discussions of zombies in film, scholars note that with a few notable exceptions,[26] zombies did not become decomposing corpses until 1968's *Night of the Living Dead*, in comics, a change in the zombie's characterisation, coupled with post-war realism and the freedoms offered by the medium, encouraged artists and writers to make their living dead into decomposing corpses much earlier.

The death of the zombie

Even though concerns about the influence of comic books on children date to the early 1940s, it was only after the Second World War that calls for censorship started to threaten the industry.[27] Horror and crime comics became clear targets for groups who wanted to clean up (or in some cases eliminate) comics, and as the 1950s progressed, it started to look more and more likely that the federal government would intervene. So, in 1954, several comic publishers came together to form the Comics Magazine Association of America (CMAA), which quickly moved to form the Comics Code Authority (CCA), a censoring body not unlike Hollywood's PCA, that would oversee the content of comics moving forward. Approved comics would bear a seal on the cover, easily letting concerned parents and guardians know that the comic was safe for children.

The code, which went into effect in January 1955, was particularly harsh towards the horror genre. It stipulated that 'good' had to triumph over 'evil' and that institutions, such as the police and government, had to be respected. The words 'horror' and 'terror' were banned from titles. But, more importantly, 'All scenes of horror, excessive bloodshed, gory or gruesome crimes, depravity, lust, sadism, masochism shall not be permitted.'[28] Vampires, werewolves, ghouls and the walking dead were now banned as well. Horror comics were effectively over, and so was the zombie.[29]

The irony of the code's virtual elimination of horror titles, at least in the case of zombie stories, was that many of these stories were fairly conservative in their politics: the bad were punished, and justice was served. Zombies may have been an unconventional means of delivering that justice, but they delivered it. However, although horror comics were now gone, their influence did not disappear. Horror creators, such as George A. Romero and Stephen King, for instance, claim that pre-code horror comics – especially the EC titles – were formative influences on their later work.[30] There is therefore a direct line that can be drawn between the creepy corpses of pre-1955 horror comics and later horror in other mediums.

Later on, publishers figured out a loophole in the code: it only applied to four-colour standard-sized comic books, and not to black-and-white magazine-sized titles. In the 1960s, some publishers took advantage of this to reprint pre-code horror stories in magazine-sized titles that were, ostensibly, aimed at adult readers.[31] Over the next two decades, these magazines would reprint and redraw numerous pre-code horror stories, both reminding older audiences of earlier stories and introducing new audiences to them. In a sense, then, the decomposing corpses of 1950s' horror comics never really died; they were now simply in black and white. Censorship did not so much kill zombies in comics as it stunted their growth – readers could still find zombie tales throughout the 1960s, but the overwhelming majority were tales that had been told before.[32]

The new undead

The CCA amended the code in 1971. Vampires, werewolves and other monsters were once again acceptable in four-colour comics, which led to a mini-horror boom in the early 1970s. Like the boom of the early 1950s, which inspired dozens and dozens of publishers to try their hands at horror, this mini boom also flooded the market with titles. Mike Howlett observes, 'With over a dozen black-and-white horror titles on the stands in 1973, it was clearly turning into a case of eat or be eaten.'[33] Quickly, the market was over-saturated, and by 1975, the boom was over.

In this brief period, two new zombie characters appeared at Marvel, and while these zombies emerged in a post-*Night of the Living Dead* world, they actually shared more characteristics with their pre-code counterparts than with Romero's cannibalistic undead. But, the remarkable thing about these new zombie characters was that they technically should not have appeared at all: while the 1971 code revisions allowed vampires and werewolves, it remained firm on its ban on zombies. Yet, Marvel found a way around this restriction.

In four-colour comics, Marvel's new zombies were creatures known as 'zuvembies', which Marvel used as stand-ins for zombies.[34] Notably, they appeared in Brother Voodoo's original run in *Strange Tales* in 1973–4 and recurred throughout the 1970s and 1980s in stories linked to the villain Black Talon.[35] Zuvembies were very much like pre-code slave zombies: they were typically background material used to supply henchmen for a villain and easy opponents for a hero to battle.[36] Their look was also very similar to what could be found in pre-code comics: they usually wore rags and had emaciated faces with hollow eyes – but they were not typically decomposing as zuvembies were not necessarily dead and could thus be revived to their former living selves.

Marvel's magazine-sized entry into zombidom was *Tales of the Zombie*, which ran for ten issues from 1973 to 1975. Its titular character was Simon Garth, The Zombie, who was killed by a disgruntled employee and then resurrected by a voodoo priestess. Unlike the zuvembies, Garth was very much dead and very much a decomposing corpse. While he wore rags and was clearly skeletal in composition – notably with hollow eyes and a bony nose and mouth – the rest of his frame was muscular. He was also incredibly strong, so Garth was more akin to the early strong-man zombies than his decomposition might initially suggest. As Mike Howlett notes, Marvel's horror titles in the 1970s tended 'to be more superhero in nature than horror', meaning that, even as a zombie, Garth 'was in pretty damn good shape'.[17]

While Garth is the protagonist of the series, and he is designed to be visually read as super-heroic, like the more malevolent zombies of the 1950s, Garth does some unpleasant things – namely because he is controlled by the Amulet of Damballah, and if it falls into the wrong hands, he is powerless to resist it. This reinforces his status as a slave-style zombie controlled by 'voodoo'. Yet, for all the bad deeds that Garth might do under the amulet's control, his story ultimately revolves around him protecting the living from evil, so like the more agentive zombies from the 1950s, he is also a force for the moral good.

In both cases, with the zuvembies and with Simon Garth, Marvel's zombies seem to harken back to the zombie's roots in the superhero genre rather than to the cannibal-style zombies becoming more popular in the wake of *Night of the Living Dead*. This may be, as Howlett indicates, because Marvel's bread-and-butter has almost always been its superhero titles, and super-heroic sensibilities influence all of their publications regardless of genre,[38] but it also indicates the ways in which zombies remained fairly true to the pre-code templates.

The zombie is dead; long live the zuvembie?

In exploring the early history of zombies in comics, it becomes clear that there is no singular type of zombie. More often than not, zombies in comics from the 1940s and 1950s were creative retellings of the zombie myth: these zombies were sometimes slaves, as in Haitian folklore, but they could also be strong, which bucked both folkloric and popular depictions of zombies in other media. The zombie's appearance in comics also ranged from what one could see in other popular depictions to bodies ravaged by decomposition. Plus, whereas silence had come to be a marker of a zombie's powerlessness in other mediums, in comics, zombies might be silent, but they could also talk, explaining their motivations for acting in the ways that they did. In part, this fluidity of styles is due to the medium itself. With comics, there were not the limitations found in other mediums: if an artist could draw it, it could happen. The original genres in which zombies appeared also encouraged creators to craft zombies who could fight back, which then became zombies who could not only fight but could think and speak.

What happened in comics in the 1940s and early 1950s was similar to what happened in films of the 1960s and 1970s. In both cases, without harsh censorship regulating horror, zombies quickly became more gruesome and more threatening.[39] While comics were ostensibly censored because they were glamorising horror and crime for children, in reality, most zombie stories from this period contained a firm moral compass: evil doers were punished. The underlying message was that justice will prevail. In this sense, the comic-book zombie's roots in the superhero and action/adventure genres seems apparent. In the majority of films of the period, there was a similar message, only the living enacted this justice rather than the undead, and this points to what made early comics truly unique in their approach to zombidom: there was not a preconceived notion within the medium that zombies were powerless, and this led artists towards depictions of zombies that, to modern eyes, look almost out of place in their era. That there were talking, decomposing corpses hunting the living well before *Night of the Living Dead* may take some by surprise.

Even when new zombies appeared in mainstream comic books in the 1970s, the firm moral compass of zombie tales remained. Simon Garth might have been forced to do bad things, but when left to his own means, he was good. In many ways, Garth's characterisation, and the return to slave-style zombies with the zuvembies, points to both the limits of

Marvel's willingness to circumvent the code and the ways in which the earliest depictions of zombies became codified in the medium. Marvel was already pushing the limits of the code with its sidesteps, so introducing cannibal-style zombies might have been seen as going a bit too far. A focus on justice also fit with the overall tone of comic books at the time – while there were underground comix[40] and independent artists who rejected the typical stories being told in the 1970s, a darker, more nihilistic brand of comics was still about a decade away when Simon Garth and the zuvembies first appeared. Plus, the lack of censorship before 1955 had opened the door for experimentation with the zombie character, but for the first decade-and-a-half under censorship, new zombie stories were not being created – old stories were recirculated, and this kept the zombie's characterisation in the medium virtually frozen. It is no wonder that when zombies came back to life in the 1970s, they looked a lot like the zombies of the 1940s and 1950s. In the post-*Night of the Living Dead* world, the zombie's characterisation in comic books was no longer as radical.

In comics, from nearly the beginning, zombies were often not 'zombies' in the strictest sense, and the term 'zuvembie' is useful here because it implies something both familiar and strange: a zombie that is not quite a zombie. Most zombies in comics seem to be as much zuvembie as they are zombie, both embodying and challenging popular expectations of the undead. Acknowledging this encourages a reassessment of collective assumptions of zombiness – what is a zombie if so many of them fall short of some imagined ideal? In pre-code comic books, at least, the zombie was the sum of a host of influences: from a lack of censorship to the lingering spectres of the Second World War. The fact that these varied influences could produce, on one hand, pitiful slaves and, on the other, super-heroic strong men and vehicles of supernatural revenge, speaks to the ways in which the concept of the zombie is far from stable. Furthermore, Simon Garth is a zombie character who seems to encapsulate nearly all modes of the zombie at once: he is the strongman zombie with super-strength, a slave zombie controlled by voodoo, a decomposing corpse, and a free-willed hero. Garth illustrates that whatever preconceived notions one might have about zombies, in practice, they are often not what one might expect.

Assumptions that zombies are simply creatures without wills of their own colour how zombies are theorised. If one comes at texts expecting to find mindless creatures, they might disregard the ways in which creators have been interrogating, altering and deconstructing the zombie, and they might miss the ways in which mediums outside film have influenced depictions of the zombie elsewhere. The zombies of early comic books show the power wielded by genre and medium, and they show how much flexibility there has always been in crafting zombie characters. More than this, the zombies of early comic books show that 'zombie' is not a fixed concept and that scholars of zombie studies need to account for this in their work. Examining comic-book zombies, the one clear challenge for zombie studies moving forward will be to pursue the buried histories that helped craft the contemporary zombie and to take a step back from considering what zombies might represent to the living and to consider what zombies actually are on their own terms.

Notes

1. 'Careless Corpse', *Fantastic Fears*, 8 (July 1953), Four Star Publishing.
2. The era from the late 1930s until 1955, when the Comics Code Authority's rules about comics content went into effect.
3. Chera Kee, *Not Your Average Zombie: Rehumanizing the Undead from Voodoo to Zombie Walks* (Austin: University of Texas Press, 2017).
4. Jim Trombetta, *The Horror! The Horror! Comic Books the Government Didn't Want You to Read!* (New York: Abrams ComicArts, 2010), p. 31.
5. Horror titles at this time followed an anthology format, meaning each issue housed a series of standalone stories. In this way, these titles were not based around a particular character, as superhero comics might be, but were based on a particular guiding theme or genre.
6. Trombetta, *The Horror!*, p. 31.
7. John Benson, 'Ruth Roche and the Iger Studio', in Greg Sadowski, John Benson and Basil Woverton (eds), *Four-Color Fear: Forgotten Horror Comics of the 1950s* (Seattle: Fantagraphics Books, 2017), p. 299.
8. *Jackpot Comics*, 1 (September 1941).
9. 'The Horror of the Haunted Cathedral', *Marvel Mystery Comics*, 28 (February 1942).
10. The DC villain Solomon Grundy's first appearance was in *All-American Comics*, 61, October 1944. He may be the only comic-book zombie before the 1950s who is inherently malevolent on his own. In later versions of his origin story, Grundy is not always a zombie.
11. 'Zombie Terror', *Moon Girl*, 5 (1948), EC.
12. Trombetta, *The Horror!*, p. 168.

13. 'Hating Corpse', *Horrific*, 4 (March 1953), Harwell Publications.
14. 'The Scourge of the Undead', *The Beyond*, 18 (January 1953), Unity Publishing Corp.
15. Using zombification as punishment also supposedly happens in real-world Vodou communities. Wade Davis, in his books *The Serpent and the Rainbow* (New York: Simon & Schuster, 1985) and *Passage of Darkness: The Ethnobiology of the Haitian Zombie* (Chapel Hill: University of North Carolina Press, 1988), argues that certain secret societies of Vodouisants use threats of zombification as a way to keep community members in line.
16. 'Beware the Undead!', *Diary of Horror*, 1 (December 1952), Avon.
17. The zombie Lila Von Altermann speaks in the 1943 film *Revenge of the Zombies*, but talking zombies were otherwise fairly rare until the late 1950s in film.
18. 'Canyon of the Living Dead', *The Hand of Fate*, 8 (December 1951), Humor Publications.
19. There were, of course, exceptions to this rule, but the general trend was for zombies that were not physically deformed or too physically marked by their zombiness.
20. See, for example, the Buck Farrel story in *Crown Comics*, 6 (summer 1946), Golfing Inc.
21. The PCA was established in 1934 by the Motion Picture Producers and Distributors of America (MPPDA) in an effort to prevent government censoring of films. Among other things, the administration issued warnings against 'gruesomeness' in films, which would have impinged on film-makers attempting a decomposing zombie look.
22. The zombies of 'Zombie Terror' straddle these two eras of looks: the zombies are shirtless (although not bald) and have well-defined chests, but their faces are thin and skeletal.
23. 'Orchids from the Dead', *The Hand of Fate*, 17 (April 1953), A. A. Wyn, Inc.
24. Paul Douglas Lopes, *Demanding Respect: The Evolution of the American Comic* (Philadelphia: Temple University Press, 2009), p. 4.
25. Trombetta, *The Horror!*, p. 171.
26. There are a handful of films before 1968 that feature bug-eyed zombies, including *The Ghost Breakers* (1940), *I Walked with a Zombie* (1943) and *I Eat Your Skin* (1964). The 1959 film *Invisible Invaders* includes walking corpses, but they are not decomposing to a great degree. The 1966 British film *Plague of the Zombies* includes decomposing corpses.
27. Lopes, *Demanding Respect*, p. 37.
28. CMAA, Comic Book Code (1954): *https://en.wikisource.org/wiki/Comic_book_code_of_1954* (accessed 13 May 2019).

29. Those horror titles that were able to survive, such as *Adventures into the Unknown*, already met code standards ahead of 1955 and were relatively tame compared to what else was available before the code came into effect.
30. For more on the connection between Romero and pre-code comics, see Chera Kee, 'No Grave Can Hold Them: *Night of the Living Dead* and the Rise and Rebirth of Zombies in Comics', in Bruce Peabody and Gloria Pastorino (eds), *Beyond the Living Dead: Essays on the Romero Legacy* (Jefferson: McFarland, 2021), pp. 32–55.
31. This supposed adult audience was a clever secondary way to side-step the code – if there were any problems with parents upset that their kids were reading these magazines, the publishers could always claim that the titles were intended for adults.
32. Besides these reprints, EC also began re-releasing collections of its horror titles in 1964.
33. Mike Howlett, *The Weird World of Eerie Publications: Comic Gore that Warped Millions of Young Minds!* (Port Townsend: Feral House, 2000), p. 95.
34. The term was borrowed from Robert E. Howard, 'Pigeons from Hell', *Weird Tales* (May 1938), 534–53.
35. *Strange Tales*, 169–73 (1973–4). Brother Voodoo moved over to *Tales of the Zombie* for two issues (no. 6 in July 1974 and no. 10 in March 1975).
36. There were instances where a main character was turned into a zuvembie, such as when Wonder Man was turned into one in *Avengers*, 152 (October 1976), but, more typically, zuvembies were background characters.
37. Howlett, *The Weird World*, p. 95.
38. Howlett, *The Weird World*, p. 95.
39. In terms of Hollywood films, the production code was severely weakening in the 1960s to the point where it was abandoned in favour of the ratings system in 1968.
40. Comic books and comic strips, especially ones written for adults or of an underground or alternative nature.

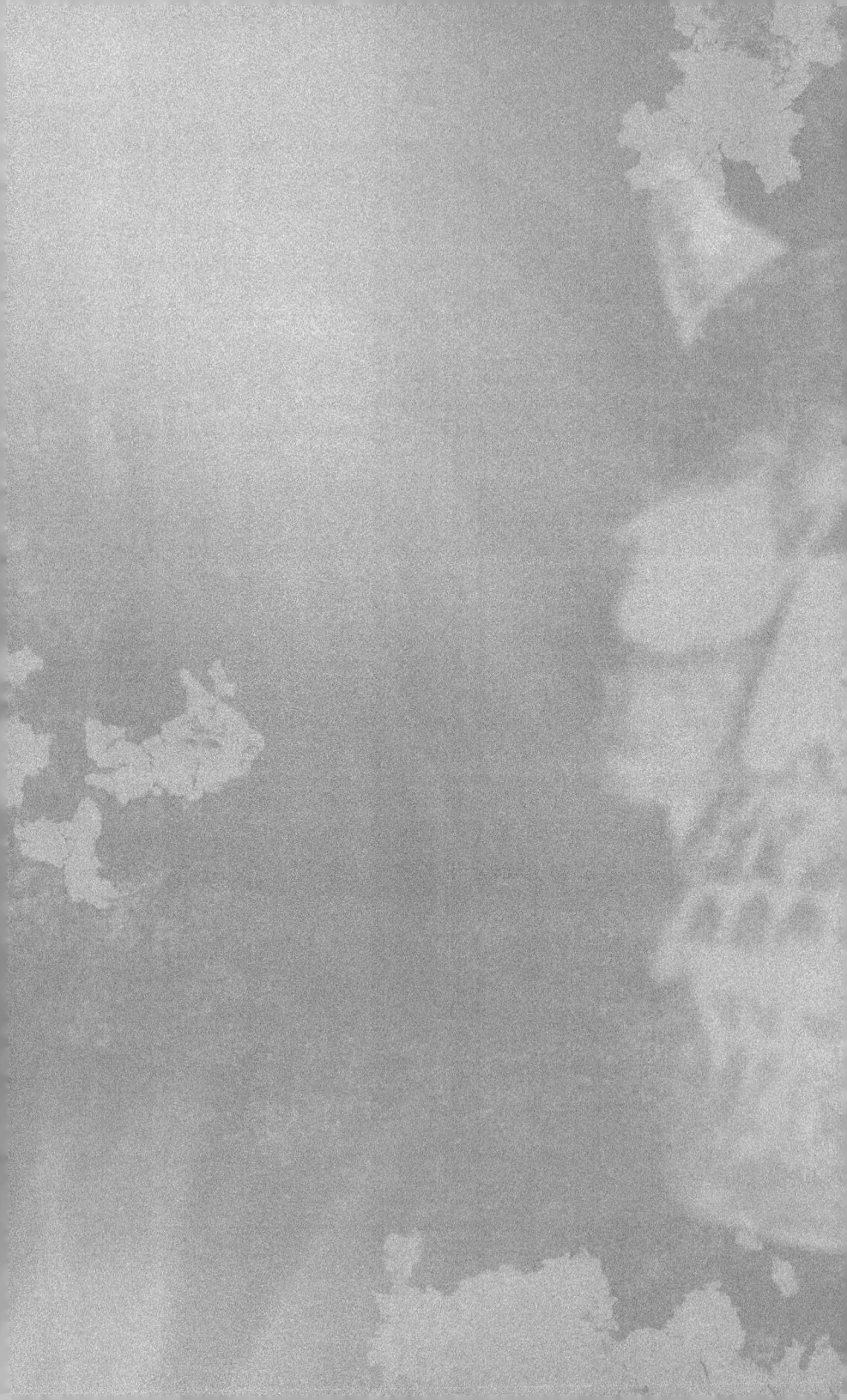

10

Cinematic Voodoo and the Reanimation of Death

Jacques Tourneur's *I Walked with a Zombie*

Peter J. Wright

IN ITS EARLY YEARS, cinema amazed spectators with its ability not only to animate still images but to deceive the eye into believing that motion was actually transpiring on screen. The cinematic illusion of movement is commonly understood to be produced by the mechanical ability of the projector. To create this effect of animated motion, the projector reel rotates frames past a lamp and a lens, while a shutter opens and closes. The frames flicker so rapidly before the eye that the images on screen appear to be springing to life. For early audiences, this trick was so convincing that it aroused an unsettling sensation of the uncanny; a sensation that is, regardless of the contemporary viewer's intellectual awareness, often still associated with the cinematic image.[1] In Freud's work, the 'uncanny' is a positive descriptor for the strange feeling associated with suddenly encountering the familiar in the unfamiliar.[2] But in relation to the history of cinema and sensation, the uncanny might denote something more. For instance, it might not only denote the confusion between animate and inanimate states, which viewers found to be uncanny, but also the realisation that these 'moving' bodies could be suspended in animation long after the subject had 'died' or 'disappeared'. Accordingly, the figure of the zombie, in its resurrected and reanimated form, might not only to resemble the cinematic image but also emblematise its uncanniness.

Established by Caetlin Benson-Allott in *Killer Tapes and Shattered Screens: Video Spectatorship from VHS to File Sharing*, this parallel or association – of the zombie and the reanimated still image – utilises Laura Mulvey's account of the uncanny illusion of cinematic motion.[3] Benson-Allott indicates that film, like the zombie, 'makes uncanny life out of what is known to be dead'. Consequently, she claims that 'the zombie is a metonym for the horror of cinema, a commentary on the medium's illusion and unsettling promise of immortality'.[4] Inspired by Benson-Allott's brief comparison, this chapter further examines the relationship of the zombie and the cinematic image, arguing that the liminal status of the zombie body – between life and death – mirrors the mechanical blending of stillness and motion in cinema. Moreover, adopting Mulvey's exploration of the animation of still images this chapter interrogates the zombie, particularly as it relates to Jacques Tourneur's voodoo zombie classic, *I Walked with a Zombie*.[5] Even though the interdisciplinary flexibility of the zombie metaphor is widely acknowledged, this chapter asserts the figure of the zombie embedded firmly within film and media studies. The zombie is, in effect, the morbid uncanniness of cinematic reanimation rendered incarnate.

In *Death 24x a Second: Stillness and the Moving Image*, Mulvey assesses the inherent uncanniness of the cinematic experience.[6] The capacity of cinema to straddle the tenuous divide between life and death, she writes, provokes an existential contemplation that ultimately renders cinema a form capable of bringing the dead back to life. Similarly, for André Bazin, the photographic process embalms the material image of the human subject, enabling them – or a semblance of them – to return in some animated form, even after death. Indeed, Mulvey argues that the unique capacity of cinema to animate still images actively blurs the threshold between life and death:

> In the cinema organic movement is transformed into its inorganic replica, a series of static, inanimate, images, which, once projected, then become animated to blur the distinctions between the oppositions. The homologies extend: on the one hand, the inanimate, inorganic, still, dead; on the other, organic, animate, moving, alive. It is here, with the blurring of these boundaries, that the uncanny nature

of the cinematic image returns most forcefully and, with it, the conceptual space of uncertainty; that is, the difficulty of understanding time and the presence of death in life.[8]

Although Mulvey's conception of cinema keenly grasps how the form captures and produces an 'in-between' state of stillness and motion, the figure of the zombie – for all its attention to the organic and inorganic, and to the liminal state between life and death – is notably absent from Mulvey's discussion. Characterised by its entrapment within the indeterminate state between the animate and the inanimate, the zombie is a figure whose liminal status corresponds to the uncanniness of cinema's early reception; moreover, the zombie corresponds to Mulvey's conception of the cinematic uncanny – indeed, the terms of her argument recall its undead attributes distinctly.

Adopting the terminology of cultural anthropologist Victor Turner, Roger Luckhurst has identified zombies as 'threshold people'.[9] In elaboration, Luckhurst states that 'the most obvious boundary breach of the zombie is between the seemingly definitive states of life and death'.[10] Following this logic, Mulvey's conception of the cinematic uncanny correlates with the transgressive liminality of the zombie, as both problematise and unsettle the seemingly fixed categories of 'life' and 'death'. This parallel association is allegorised in *IWZ*, thus prompting new readings of the cinematic uncanny. Mirroring certain strands of photography and film theory, *IWZ* depicts the figure of the zombie as analogous to the animating principle of cinema and emphasises an allegiance between the still image and death. Consequently, the zombie, more generally, may not simply be a useful allegory for the liminality of cinema but an emblem par excellence for the inherent uncanniness of the mechanical operations of cinema.

The cinematic uncanny

Mulvey's use of the term 'uncanny' is developed in her discussion of supernatural horror cinema. She writes that 'beyond the physical presence of the inanimate body are those narratives in which the dead return to the world of the living as a ghostly apparition: inorganic but animate'.[11] Mulvey ties the returning dead – a more physicalised version of what Freud called the 'return of the repressed' – to Ernst Jentsch's and Freud's separate conceptions of the uncanny. While Jentsch identifies the uncanny as an encounter with the unfamiliar, Freud conceives of the uncanny, slightly differently, as an experience of the all too familiar.[12] Moreover, Jentsch associates the uncanny with a sudden feeling of 'intellectual uncertainty' about the world, whereas Freud understands the uncanny to signify the resurfacing of one's own repressed beliefs – a feeling that is usually triggered, he suggests, by an encounter with something strangely recognisable.[13] As Freud writes, the 'uncanny is in reality nothing new or alien, but something which is familiar and old-established in the mind and which has become alienated from it only through the process of repression'.[14] Even though Freud's understanding of the uncanny ultimately differs from that of Jentsch, Mulvey links both conceptions of the feeling to compare this peculiar affect with the equally peculiar quality of the cinematic image. Producing equally uncanny effects, the cinematic image, Mulvey suggests, confounds the animate with the inanimate to create a 'phantom-like quality' that transforms 'ghostly images of the now-dead' into 'the appearance of life'.[15]

Still, Mulvey relies on Jentsch's theory of the uncanny to identify what she calls the 'technological uncanny' of cinema. As Mulvey notes, Jentsch describes the uncanny as a momentary feeling of disorientation that is experienced when one is confronted with the strangely unfamiliar.[16] For him, the uncanny is a psychological sensation in which the mind briefly staggers at an occurrence that appears to undermine intellectual certainty. Of course, this sensation is only fleeting, as the mind is generally quick to rationalise the experience once the surprise dissipates.[17] To illustrate the uncanny, Jentsch describes the effect that is produced when one confuses an inanimate object for a living being, and vice versa.[18] He refers to the way in which the inanimate state of automata and wax figures can elicit the uncanny, where the subject is startled upon confusing the inanimate with the animate.[19] For Mulvey, the animation (or reanimation) of still images, which in turn creates the illusion of a motion picture, arguably evokes a similarly uncanny sensation – especially upon considering the accounts of early cinema, when the mechanical processes were still not fully understood. Through such early conceptions, Mulvey compares the mechanical processes of cinema to Jentsch's conception of the uncanny: in its blending of inanimate still images with the optical illusion of motion, she suggests, cinema reproduces the 'phantom-like quality' of the uncanny.[20]

Beyond identifying the way in which cinema operates to deliver uncanny effects, Mulvey also contrasts Jentsh's definition of the uncanny with Freud's reflections on death to explore the way the uncanny attends to the spectatorial reception of cinema. For Freud, the uncanny is not produced by the unfamiliar but involves the return of the long familiar – the return, that is, of that which has been repressed by the psyche. According to Freud:

> Our analysis of instances of the uncanny has led us back to the old, animistic conception of the universe. This was characterised by the idea that the world was peopled with the spirits of human beings . . . It seems as if each one of us has been through a phase of individual development corresponding to this animistic stage in primitive men . . . Everything which now strikes us as 'uncanny' fulfils the condition of touching those residues of animistic mental activity within us and bringing them to expression.[21]

Freud's 'animistic' understanding of the uncanny (and of the universe) suggests that belief in spirits, now long repressed, might resurface when confronted by a situation that initially appears inexplicable. Expanding on Freud, Mulvey suggests that a religious belief in the afterlife may indicate, at least for some, a similar belief in spirits – a belief that the dead may return from beyond the grave in one form or another.[22] Mulvey reads Freud's rejection of Jenstch's claim that 'intellectual uncertainty' leads to uncanny feelings as generative of his more expansive understanding of the uncanny. She notes that although Freud 'accepts that intellectual uncertainty may be a factor', the uncanny is in fact the *combination* of, first, a belief in the afterlife on the part of many 'civilized people' and, secondly, the 'residues of archaic fears and superstitions'.[23] For Freud, this combination leads to what Jentsch identifies as the intellectual uncertainty that precedes the uncanny.[24] In his essay, Freud acknowledges the unconscious fear of the dead that has long been embedded in the human psyche – a fear that returns to 'haunt the present from the past'.[25]

Freud's conception of the uncanny, then, in which a repressed belief (a belief in spirits, say) may return if one is exposed to certain stimuli, may be likened not only to the broader concept of the zombie (who is similarly 'reanimated' under certain conditions) but to the apprehension of still images that 'come alive' – or return from the dead – on the cinematic screen. *IWZ*, whose narrative orbits around an assumption that the dead can return to life, reveals this encapsulation of the uncanny on two levels. First, the film mimics the capacity of cinema to resuscitate images of the dead; secondly, the film reflects and reproduces the uncanny response of the audience entering a darkened theatre to confront the projection of death on screen.

Journey into the unknown

In its narrative and form, *IWZ* is a prefiguration of Mulvey's notion of the cinematic uncanny (or, as she describes it, the 'technological uncanny').[26] Of course, in featuring the zombie – a 'threshold person' – the film presents an entity that blurs the boundary between what is animate and inanimate, alive and dead. However, the film also forces the audience into feeling both doubt and credulity by continuously fluctuating between supernatural and scientific explanations for the narrative events. Indeed, the suggestion that a 'living death' is possible serves to destabilise the structures of logic and rationality that underpin the film, structures that are propped up, for instance, by the film's protagonist, Betsy Connell (Frances Dee), a trained medical nurse. At one point, Betsy travels, despite her training and better judgement, with Jessica Holland (Christine Gordon), one of the implied zombies of the film, to the Hounfour (a voodoo temple and its surroundings) in what is a vain attempt to find a cure for Jessica's apparently cataleptic condition.

On the way to the Hounfour, Betsy guides Jessica through the sugar cane fields where they encounter various emblems of death and decay, such as animal and human skulls as well as the carcass of a dead goat that hangs from a tree. These symbols of death indicate that the pair have crossed a threshold, that they have transmigrated from the realm of the living and into the realm of the dead. But this threshold also connotes the 'crossroads' symbol in voodoo folklore; accompanied by the appearance of another figure – another implied zombie – named 'Carrefour' (Darby Jones) whose French name translates to 'crossroads' and references the Maître Carrefour (Master Crossroads). On the path to the Hounfour, Carrefour stands completely motionless, preventing the women's passage through the fields. Of this scene, J. P. Telotte contends that it 'marks the mid-point in the film' and 'metaphorically summarises our own and Betsy's slow and deliberate journey ever deeper into this dark and menacing world, seeking to narrate its complexities, to find at its centre some explanation for the mysteries it holds'.[27]

With characters frequently approaching the verge of the supernatural, the crossroads appear both at the centre and on the threshold of the film's environment. In a sense, however, the crossroads also represent the cinema screen; indeed, cinema is a window into another world, enabling the opportunity to witness the resurrection of dead bodies on screen. The crossroads, and therefore cinema, are embodied physically by Carrefour, since the zombie body is fixed in a liminal state between life and death. As

Luckhurst describes zombies as 'threshold people', Turner discusses 'liminal entities' – those who subsist in a transitory state, both in a physical and cultural sense:

> The attributes of liminality or of liminal *personae* ['threshold people'] are necessarily ambiguous, since this condition and these persons elude or slip through the network of classifications that normally locate states and positions in cultural space. Liminal entities are neither here nor there; they are betwixt and between the positions assigned and arrayed by law, custom, convention, and ceremonial. As such, their ambiguous and indeterminate attributes are expressed by a variety of symbols in the many societies that ritualise social and cultural transitions. Thus, liminality is frequently likened to death, to being in the womb, to invisibility, to darkness, to bisexuality, to the wilderness, and to an eclipse of the sun or the moon.[28]

As the crossroads symbol suggests a transitory state between physical and metaphysical (or visible and invisible) realms, so the zombie body suggests a site that is located on a threshold between two worlds: and, like the crossroads, the zombie signals a transition into a darkened and obscured space of uncertainty – a space situated outside of and beyond rational thought. This space of uncertainty recalls the darkened space of the cinema, where a portal to otherworldly phenomena is opened by the cinematic illusion of motion and the mechanical transcendence of the life/death distinction. Likewise, for Betsy and Jessica, the path that leads beyond Carrefour symbolises an entry point into the underworld and, with it, the disintegration of natural or customary law. Once they enter the grounds of the Hounfour, all the conventions of logic will dissolve through the process of transition, and all the stable rules of life and death will now appear porous and pliable via the power of voodoo ceremony. Like the transgressive mystique of the zombie itself, the Hounfour is an uncanny space, existing indistinctly between the realms of the known and the unknown, between life and death.

Still death and reanimation

In one sense, any figure who appears on a cinematic screen is, like the zombie, merely a shell of that subject originally photographed by the camera. On screen, the original subject is vacated of their consciousness; they only *resemble* the original subject in outward appearance; they only reproduce the original subject in an image that is the effect of manipulated optical light. *IWZ* reflects this notion of cinema as 'empty projection' through the theme of bodily reanimation – a fundamental characteristic of the zombie. Given that the zombie is a key figure for emptiness and reanimation, it is unsurprising to discover the quality of photographic stillness in the representation of zombies on screen. This is particularly the case in the expressionless and adrift performances of those in *IWZ* who are implied zombies: namely, Jessica and Carrefour. The association of the still image and moving image aligns with the parallel binary of the dead and living subject. After all, although both the zombie and the filmic image are, in an important sense, dead or stultified, they both *appear* to be alive and moving in the context of cinema.

Insofar as *IWZ* calls on an array of metaphors to communicate some reflexive knowledge of the relationship between the still/moving and dead/alive binaries (including the figure of the crossroads, identified above), the film acknowledges the link between the still image and death (as well as the moving image and life). Roland Barthes makes a similar connection between the still image and death in *Camera Lucida*. He claims that the photographic image is the equivalent of death:

> For death must be somewhere in a society; if it is no longer (or less intensely) in religion, it must be elsewhere; perhaps in this image which produces Death while trying to preserve life. Contemporary with the withdrawal of rites, Photography may correspond to the intrusion, in our modern society, of an asymbolic Death, outside of religion, outside of ritual, a kind of abrupt dive into literal Death. *Life / Death*: the paradigm is reduced to a simple click, the one separating the initial pose from the final print.[29]

The ability of the camera to capture an image transforms the subject into an object by effectively encasing the visual likeness of a person within the material confines of the photograph.[30] According to Barthes, this subject-into-object transformation is 'a micro-version of death'.[31] As life is inherently animate (or animated), the process of making life inanimate via the click of the camera parallels the stopping or stultifying operations of death.

This sense of death also emerges at the level of photographic reception. As Eivind Røssaak asserts, even the act of beholding a photograph may conjure an eerie sensation of the spectral.[32] This response, as Barthes suggests, is in some ways equivalent to witnessing the dead return.[33] Extending this point, Barthes states that regardless of 'whether or not the subject is already dead, every photograph has this catastrophe', for there is 'always a defeat of Time in them: *that* is dead and *that* is going to die'.[34] Since the camera is so capable of suspending the perpetual progression of time, it thus produces an enactment of death. Since photographs, according to Bazin, contain the 'disturbing presence of lives halted at a set moment in their duration, freed from their destiny', they also appear to embalm time.[35] But if the inanimate or dead body is represented by the still image, the *reanimation* of the image – its return to motion or life, which can be likened to the resurrection of the corpse – is brought into being through cinema. But cinema does not display 'true motion' but instead offers only an illusion; accordingly, a film must be seen to reanimate the dead only through producing this illusion of life, this illusion of reanimation.

According to Mulvey, this confusion between stillness and motion, death and life, that evokes the uncanny, is where 'the threshold between life and death becomes a space of uncertainty in which boundaries blur between the rational and the supernatural, the animate and the inanimate'.[36] Mulvey proposes that illusions such as these, which are capable of bewildering the mind, serve to cast doubt on the nature of reality, and render the subject susceptible to a belief in any supernatural explanations proposed to explain the uncertainty.[37] In this way, the arrival of the zombie reflects the cinematic illusion of motion and the uncertainty engendered by its appearance. By confusing the spectator with life and death, the zombie, as a figure, conjures and personifies the uncanny sensation already incarnate in the cinematic image itself.

The illusory operations of cinema are further expressed in *IWZ* through several references to the photographic foundation of the cinematic image. *IWZ* emphasises these references to illustrate how the zombie can be an emblem for the ability of cinema to produce an illusion of life. Upon meeting Jessica, for example, Betsy is frightened by her emotionless demeanour. As she slowly approaches Betsy, Jessica's facial expressions remain blank and unchanging. The stony intensity of Jessica's expressionless face is disturbing not only for Betsy but for the viewer too, for they recognise in this deathly look Jessica's status as a 'threshold person', moving between the animate and inanimate orders. Incapable of reacting to the action around her, Jessica embodies the stillness of the photographic image. Indeed, Jessica's zombified state, as well as the sequence in which she drifts across the screen as though she is afloat, allegorises the capacity of cinema to animate or reanimate the still image. Alexander Nemerov in fact describes Jessica as the 'celebratory sign' of cinematic 'motion':

> Jessica glides with such stylised grace, her gown obscuring the actual motion of her legs, that she stands out at first as a celebratory sign of the very motion of motion pictures – the elegance of movement considered for its own sake, and the wonder of the camera's ability to record it. Between her gliding and the unfurling reel there is a symbiotic relation, as if she were the visible expression of cinema's primal power to render action.[38]

As Nemerov suggests, in this scene Jessica allegorises the camera and the uncanny ability of the projector to animate – or to reanimate – a still image through motion. The initial photographic capture effectively interrupts the movement of the subject, rendering a new likeness that, inscribed through chemicals and optical manipulations, assumes a still and deathly form. Once the series of stills is reeled through a projector, however, this inanimate body is charged with the illusion of motion. As such, cinema does not simply animate life but reanimates death; that is, cinema infuses death with the appearance of life. Put another way, cinema can be understood as the 'zombification' of photographed reality.

Standing eerily motionless with a vacant stare, Carrefour also resembles the stillness of the photographic image. When Betsy and Jessica first encounter Carrefour on their passage through the fields, they are startled by his stillness: he does not even blink when they shine a torch directly towards his face. Carrefour's inanimation is further highlighted in a later scene when he enters Fort Holland to abduct Jessica. When confronted, Carrefour sluggishly approaches Paul Holland (Tom Conway), the owner of the plantation, with his arms outstretched threateningly. Before reaching him, however, Carrefour comes to a halt on command of Paul's mother, Mrs Rand (Edith Barrett), who appears from behind him. Upon hearing Mrs Rand's voice, Carrefour not only stops his movement but freezes in his pose, revealing an uncanny resemblance to the photographic properties of the still image. Mrs Rand, whom the audience knows to have participated in a voodoo congregation and to have professed a belief in mystical practices, is now shown to possess the power to control Carrefour's movement on command. Just as the camera can isolate a still image from movement, Mrs Rand's voodooism has the capacity to suspend the motion of a zombie.

Indeed, Mrs Rand, it seems, stultifies the cinematic image to reveal its still photographic components. If death is now represented by the photograph, and the zombie represents its reanimation, then perhaps voodoo – with its hypnotic suggestion – represents the power of cinema to convince us of its continuous motion, to persuade us of cinematic animation.

Even though cinematic animation could be explained in explicitly technological terms, it nevertheless bewildered the mind of early cinemagoers that the illusion of motion could work so seamlessly to deceive the eye. As posited above, the phenomenon of the deceptive animation of cinema can be likened to the use of voodoo in the film, whereby inanimate corpses are made to seem alive and live figures, such as Carrefour, are rendered lifeless – if only momentarily. So, just as the projector animates the deathly cinematic image, the potential for voodoo animates the diegetic world of the film. Indeed, early in the film, Paul describes the diegetic world of *IWZ* as exhibiting 'only death and decay'. Describing Saint Sebastian (the island location of the filmic events), Paul seeks to persuade Betsy of the noxious forces that govern all that happens in the world around them:

> Everything seems beautiful because you don't understand. Those flying fish, they're not leaping for joy, they're jumping in terror. Bigger fish want to eat them. That luminous water, it takes its gleam from millions of tiny dead bodies. The glitter of putrescence. There is no beauty here, only death and decay. Everything good dies here. Even the stars.

Paul's insistence that the island is permeated with an atmosphere of death can be related back to the filmic image, as the filmic image is always haunted by the stillness and decay that lies at its material foundation. Just as voodoo has the power to make it seem as though the dead have risen from the grave, the hypnotic quality of cinema is able to imbue death with the appearance of life, much to the uncanny amazement of its spectator. For Mulvey, the cinematic representation of life is always haunted by the image, and by the deception of this illusion.[39] Indeed, what is perceived as cinematic motion really depends upon this underlying stillness to function. As such, the sensation that is aroused by the reanimated image of life on the cinematic screen reminds the audience that their lives are always bracketed by the inevitability of death. In this way, the emergence of the zombie exposes the inherent uncanniness of life; it reveals that death, although usually hidden from sight, is always lurking just beneath the surface.

Conclusion

In response to an early cinematic screening, Maxim Gorky famously reports that cinema:

> is not life but its shadow, it is not motion but its soundless spectre. It is terrifying to see, but it is the movement of shadows, mere shadows. Curses and ghosts, evil spirits that have cast whole cities into eternal sleep come to mind and you feel as though Merlin's vicious trick had been played out before you.[40]

Gorky's reflection on the disturbing spectre of cinema resonates with Paul Meehan's description of the *mise en scène* of *IWZ* as nightmarish. Meehan remarks that director Jacques Tourneur's 'use of chiaroscuro is breathtaking' and that, with it, Tourneur 'creates a shadow landscape through which the characters move about like somnambulists in a nightmare'.[41] In addition to these shadowy and painterly qualities of the film, the ghost-like figure of Jessica gives sharp expression to Gorky's description of cinema as dark and spectral. Maintaining a constant and complete silence, Jessica floats through each frame, dressed in a white flowing dress that renders her an apparition. Drifting across the haunted scenery, Jessica represents the haunted and spectral quality of cinema, reinforcing the residue of death that lies at the foundation of cinematic experience.

In its thematic and formal depiction of 'living death', *IWZ* illustrates Mulvey's conception of the cinematic uncanny. The film magnifies cinema's peculiar ability to stimulate feelings of unease and uncertainty – feelings that arise out of a confusion between life and death, an uncertainty about the reanimation of still images, and an unease about the preservation and resurrection of the dead on screen. Ultimately, the form and content of the film coalesce in an allegorical dramatisation of the very cinematic processes that induce feelings of the uncanny. Essential to this thematic reanimation of death is the figure of the zombie, a figure Tourneur helped establish as an icon of cinema, embedding the archetype in a dramatic work that itself replicates the feelings of dread induced by all cinematic experiences. The iconicity of the cinematic zombie affirms its position amongst the plethora of zombie metaphors that have been put forth in recent scholarship, thus further demonstrating the elasticity of the zombie as an allegorical tool. However, the cinematic zombie is more than just a metaphor. Quite the contrary, the cinematic zombie physically embodies and represents the uncanny operations of cinematic reanimation. After viewing *IWZ*, for instance, audiences may very well find themselves wondering whether the uncanny experience of cinematic reception is the genuine equivalent of walking with a zombie.

Notes

1. This chapter is indebted to Alan Cholodenko's pioneering theoretical work on animation, in particular how he first proposed and developed the implications for drawing an equivalence between animation and the uncanny. Among his many works on this topic, the crucial work for marking out the new field of animation studies, to which this chapter relates, is his introduction to Alan Cholodenko, *The Illusion of Life: Essays on Animation* (Sydney: Power Publications, 1991).
2. Sigmund Freud, 'The Uncanny', in *The Standard Edition of the Complete Psychological Works of Sigmund Freud, Vol. 17*, ed. and trans. James Strachey et al. (London: The Hogarth Press, 1955), pp. 217–56.
3. Caetlin Benson-Allott, *Killer Tapes and Shattered Screens: Video Spectatorship from VHS to File Sharing* (Berkeley: University of California Press, 2013), p. 36.
4. Benson-Allott, *Killer Tapes and Shattered Screens*, p. 36.
5. *I Walked with a Zombie*, dir. Jacques Tourneur, RKO Radio Pictures, USA (1943). Henceforth referred to as *IWZ*.
6. Laura Mulvey, *Death 24x a Second: Stillness and the Moving Image* (London: Reaktion Books, 2006), pp. 54–66.
7. André Bazin, 'The Ontology of the Photographic Image', in Hugh Gray (ed.), *What is Cinema? Vol. 1* (Berkeley: University of California Press, 1967), p. 10.
8. Mulvey, *Death 24x a Second*, pp. 52–3.
9. Roger Luckhurst, *Zombies: A Cultural History* (London: Reaktion Books, 2015), p. 9.
10. Luckhurst, *Zombies*, p. 9.
11. Mulvey, *Death 24x a Second*, p. 38.
12. Freud, 'The Uncanny', p. 220.
13. Freud, 'The Uncanny', p. 241.
14. Freud, 'The Uncanny', p. 241.
15. Mulvey, *Death 24x a Second*, p. 36.
16. Ernst Jentsch, 'On the Psychology of the Uncanny (1906)', *Angelaki: Journal of the Theoretical Humanities*, 2/1 (1997), 8; originally published 'Zur

Psycholgie der Unheimlichen', *Psychiatrisch-Neurologische Wochenschrift*, 8/22 (1906), 195–8, and 8/23 (1906), 203–5.
17. Jentsch, 'On the Psychology of the Uncanny', 11.
18. Jentsch, 'On the Psychology of the Uncanny', 11.
19. Jentsch, 'On the Psychology of the Uncanny', 12.
20. Mulvey, *Death 24x a Second*, p. 36.
21. Freud, 'The Uncanny', pp. 240–1.
22. Mulvey, *Death 24x a Second*, p. 39.
23. Mulvey, *Death 24x a Second*, p. 39.
24. Mulvey, *Death 24x a Second*, p. 39.
25. Freud, 'The Uncanny', p. 242.
26. Mulvey, *Death 24x a Second*, pp. 27, 36, 42, 43, 44, 50.
27. J. P. Telotte, 'Narration and Incarnation: *I Walked with a Zombie*', *Film Criticism* (ARCHIVE), 6/3 (1982), 25.
28. Victor W. Turner, *The Ritual Process: Structure and Anti-Structure* (London: Routledge & Kegan Paul Ltd, 1969), p. 95.
29. Roland Barthes, *Camera Lucida* [1980] (Sun Prairie: Vintage, 2000), p. 92.
30. Barthes, *Camera Lucida*, p. 13.
31. Barthes, *Camera Lucida*, p. 14.
32. Eivind Røssaak, T*he Still/Moving Image: Cinema and the Arts* (Sunnyvale: LAP Lambert Academic Publishing, 2010), p. 119.
33. Barthes, Camera Lucida, p. 9.
34. Barthes, *Camera Lucida*, p. 96.
35. Bazin, 'The Ontology of the Photographic Image', p. 14.
36. Mulvey, *Death 24x a Second*, p. 37.
37. Mulvey, *Death 24x a Second*, p. 33.
38. Alexander Nemerov, *Icons of Grief: Val Lewton's Home Front Pictures* (Berkeley: University of California Press, 2005), p. 122.
39. Mulvey, *Death 24x a Second*, p. 52.
40. Maxim Gorky [I. M. Pacatus], 'A review of the Lumière program at the Nizhni-Novgorod Fair, as printed in the *Nizhegorodski Listok*' (4 July 1896), in Colin Harding and Simon Popple (eds), *In the Kingdom of Shadows: A Companion to Early Cinema* (London: Cygnus Arts, 1996), p. 5.
41. Paul Meehan, *Horror Noir: Where Cinema's Dark Sisters Meet* (Jefferson: McFarland, 2011), p. 60.

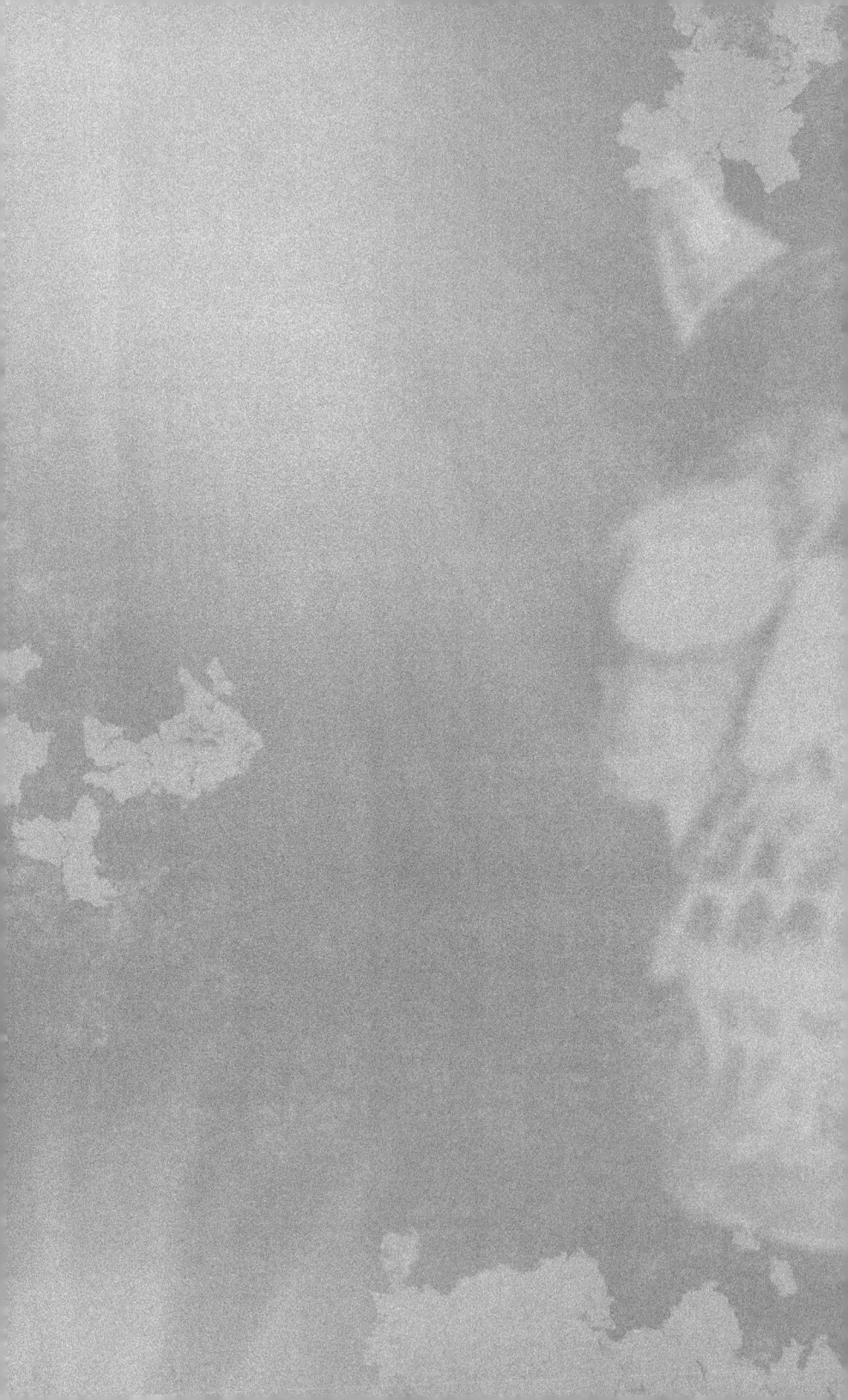

11

'Violence *is* Italian art':
Art and Adaptation in Lucio Fulci's 'Gates of Hell' Trilogy

Miranda Corcoran

IN THE CLOSING MOMENTS of Lucio Fulci's 1981 horror film *The House by the Cemetery*, the camera lingers briefly on the eponymous structure. Before fading to darkness, the screen is filled by a quotation, attributed to novelist Henry James, which acts as a thesis statement for the film: 'No one will ever know whether children are monsters, or monsters are children.'[1] The choice of quotation seems apt, as the film draws heavily from James's 1898 novella 'The Turn of the Screw'. The above line does not, however, appear in 'The Turn of the Screw', nor in any other works by James. The quotation was likely fabricated, either by Fulci himself, or by co-screenwriter Dardano Sacchetti.[2] This falsified quotation is a revealing addition to the denouement of a film permeated by the influence of nineteenth-century American gothic fiction and overflowing with spectacular, excessive violence. Fulci's use of an ersatz quotation, fallaciously ascribed to James, is indicative of the film-maker's playful and appropriative attitude towards American gothic literature, and US horror fiction in general.

While many critics dismissed the Italian director's shift towards American locales and themes as a superficial geographical repositioning, spurred primarily by financial incentives, Fulci's engagement with American gothicism was far more profound and thoughtful than his status as the creator of exploitation cinema suggests. The tropes and themes Fulci borrowed from American gothic literature are part of a complex process of transnational adaptation and appropriation whereby the Rome-born director replicated, and obscured, aspects of American gothic to comment on and critique late twentieth-century Italian culture. In his reimagining of the American gothic, Fulci exploits the blankness of the zombie, employing the figure as an empty vessel whose 'speechless incoherence' provides an appropriate ambiguity through which to conflate US and European cultural anxieties and modes of gothicism.[3] This chapter examines how Fulci constructs the zombie – a creature described by Kyle William Bishop as a quintessentially New World monster[4] – as an embodiment of the American gothic trope of burial and resurrection, or the return of the repressed. Simultaneously, the multivalence inherent to these blank revenants enables the director to make veiled allusions to his own troubled homeland. Comprised of references to American gothicism – and its preoccupation with themes of burial and return – as well as myriad gestures towards the European context in which Fulci was working, these films figure the zombie as the site of multiple anxieties. The multitude of meanings that reside in Fulci's zombies demonstrate his proclivity for adopting and transforming the American gothic essential patterns of internment and re-emergence to reflect not only the horrors of US history but also the traumas of twentieth-century Italy. Consequently, Fulci's 'American' zombie films are heavily intertextual works: they include various influences to create a single cinematic artefact that simultaneously celebrates a preceding literary tradition while also transforming aspects of that tradition into a unique, and distinctly Italian, political commentary.

Fulci's forays into the zombie subgenre have always been controversial. His first dalliance with the undead was the 1979 film *Zombie!* – or *Zombi 2*, as it is sometimes known. Released not long after George A. Romero's successful *Dawn of the Dead* (1978), *Zombie!* was financed by Fabrizio De Angelis and Ugo Tucci, hoping to profit from Romero's film by marketing theirs as a continuation of the franchise.[5] The alternate title *Zombi 2* positions the film as a successor to *Dawn of the Dead*, which was released as *Zombi* in Italy. As Stephen Thrower notes, 'plagiarism, imitation, pastiche and parody of whatever was popular' was an enduring characteristic of Italian popular cinema and, as such, the controversy surrounding Fulci's film stemmed not so much from issues of copyright infringement but more from its disturbing levels of violence.[6] On release in the United Kingdom, where it was titled *Zombie Flesh-Eaters*, *Zombi* was quickly branded with an 'X' rating despite extensive and censorious cuts to its runtime.[7] When the film made the transition to VHS, it was condemned as a 'video nasty' alongside a wider 'group of previously suppressed post-1950s American and European horror films [that] were released on video in Britain. It became the target of a media panic orchestrated, centrally, by a group of moral campaigners and right-wing British newspaper, the *Daily Mail*.'[8]

Despite his reputation as the producer of a shocking string of 1980s' video nasties and his position as the 'Godfather of Gore', a moniker he shared with Herschell Gordon Lewis, Fulci created films that possess a strange and often surreal artistry. The films are saturated in obscene amounts of gore but are also infused with references to art, literature and canonical American and European cinema. In particular, Fulci possessed an affinity for the gothic, as well as for the complexities of high modernism and the absurd sadism of the Theatre of Cruelty. Chas Balun argues that Fulci was an anomaly in the world of exploitation cinema:

> His frequent references and homages to such literary icons as Edgar Allan Poe, Mary Shelley, Henry James, Honore de Balzac, Daphne Du Maurier, Nathaniel Hawthorne, Proust, and Anton [sic] Artaud are rare indeed in a world of sequelized serial killers with masks and big knives.[9]

Although overlooking the richness of 1980s horror cinema, Balun's statement captures the vibrancy of Fulci's intertextual palette. The diversity of literary influences is present throughout Fulci's *oeuvre*. Fulci's intertextualism is most apparent in a series of loosely connected films from the early 1980s known at the 'Gates of Hell' trilogy (hereafter, GOH). Comprising *City of the Living Dead* (*Paura nella città dei morti viventi*) from 1980, *The Beyond* (. . . *E tu vivrai nel terrore! L'aldilà*) and *The House by the Cemetery* (*Quella villa accanto al cimitero*), both from 1981, GOH tells three different stories united by their American setting and narratives which feature zombies unleashed when the gates of hell are opened. Each GOH entry represents a strange admixture of restrained supernatural gothicism and explicit, even sadistic, violence. For Fulci, the more artistic elements of his films are inseparable from their violence, and he famously claimed that 'violence *is* Italian art!'[10]

Although intimately connected to an Italian artistic legacy of aestheticised violence, GOH is also an adaptation, or appropriation, of American gothic conventions. According to Linda Hutcheon, an adaptation is an 'extended, deliberate, announced revisitation of a particular work of art', and, consequently, when developing a definition of adaptation, 'short intertextual allusions to other works or bits of sampled music would not be included'.[11] Hutcheon acknowledges that forms of adaptation may extend beyond a straightforward transposition of materials to encompass even 'a creative *and* an interpretative act of appropriation/salvaging'.[12] The process of adaptation shifts away from direct remediation towards something more akin to appropriation, whereby an adapted text 'effects a more decisive journey away from the informing text into a wholly new cultural product and domain'.[13] Fulci's treatment of American gothic literature resides in such an ambiguous space, appropriating elements of these fictions and transmuting them into distinct textual products. Ben Lanred describes GOH as 'pseudo-adaptations', indefinite texts that are not quite homages, but not quite intertextual pastiches either.[14] Suffused with references, themes and iconography derived from authors such as Henry James, Edgar Allan Poe, H. P. Lovecraft and Clark Ashton Smith, GOH initially appears as a dense intertextual mesh, woven together from diverse strains of nineteenth-century and early twentieth-century American literature. Rather than a collection of references to a variegated group of American gothic texts, GOH actually serves as a sustained effort to adapt the themes and imagery of the American gothic genre to the concerns of an Italian cultural context. According to Bishop, the American gothic mode is defined by a continuous, shifting engagement with evolving cultural anxieties, which ensures that the form never becomes static or fixed but remains dynamic and metamorphic.[15] Moreover, he explains that the zombie 'can be seen as part of this dynamic adaptation', reflecting as it does American gothic's propensity to mould itself to fit new contexts and concerns.[16]

Fulci's rendering of the living dead and their intense connection to the locations in which they are buried, and from which they rise, suggests a preoccupation with the ubiquitous American gothic themes of hidden horror and the return of the repressed. If the European gothic is defined by ancient monuments to terror and corruption, the American gothic, as the product of an infant democracy, is characterised by the horror buried beneath the idyllic national veneer of optimism and opportunity. Teresa A. Goddu claims that, 'Because of America's seeming lack of history and its Puritan heritage, the American gothic . . . takes a turn inward, away from society and toward the psyche and the hidden blackness of the American soul.'[17] This turn inward does not represent a disengagement from America's myriad historical and cultural horrors, but instead, suggests a preoccupation with the hidden, secreted or repressed horrors that are buried beneath the façade of the American ideal. Consequently, while many Italian gothic horror films, like *Black Sunday* (*La maschera del demonio*, 1960) and *The Long Hair of Death* (*I lunghi capelli della morte*, 1964), situate monstrosities amidst the high gothic milieu of forbidding European castles and the sadism of the Inquisition, GOH is firmly enmeshed in a distinctly American mode of gothicism. Central to this revisioning of the American gothic is Fulci's treatment of zombiism, a form of monstrosity intimately connected to the 'New World'. Consequently, while scholars like Steven Zani and Kevin Meaux rightly assert that Fulci's films 'generate anxiety precisely because the very fears they articulate are neither stable nor consistent', the zombies embody a clear historical and intertextual connection to the American soil from which they rise.[18]

The first GOH movie is *City of the Living Dead* (*City* hereafter). Abounding in references to the American gothic, the film repeatedly gestures towards the cosmicism of Lovecraft, the fashionable *fin-de-siècle* spiritualism of James and the ubiquitous premature interments of Poe. *City* opens in the town of Dunwich, a fictional locale familiar to readers of Lovecraft as the abode of eldritch abomination Yog-Sothoth. Lacking the general air of deterioration exhibited by Lovecraft's Dunwich, Fulci's rendering of the town is evocative of a staunchly puritanical New England.[19] Despite being filmed in the Deep South of Savannah, Georgia, this Dunwich, with white-steepled church and austere cemetery, suggests a clear connection to the history of Massachusetts as the origin of American puritanism.[20] The slow pan across aged tombstones, with their grim *momento mori* inscriptions, that constitutes the opening sequence of *City* not only literalises the film's title – providing endless rows of gravestones, a metropolis of death – but also reaches backwards to one of the canonical texts of nineteenth-century American gothic, Nathaniel Hawthorne's *The Scarlet Letter* (1850). Although Hawthorne's novel is cited again later in the film when the characters discuss a local unwed mother who is branded a witch by her community, the opening sequence of *City* recalls Hawthorne's introductory ruminations on the restless, guilt-ridden bones of his ancestors, long since interred in Salem's Charter Street Burial Ground and the belief that their sins are so great as to refuse the finality of this burial. Fulci's interpretation of the American gothic is defined by a preoccupation with 'the culture's dark, repressed, and oppositional elements', and their inevitable return.[21] Yet rather than re-emerging as the diaphanous shades of Victorian ghost stories, Fulci instigates the return of America's historical trauma in the more visceral, potent body of the zombie.

The revenants that emerge from this bleak Puritan cemetery are the echoes of buried historical guilt. Once the gates of hell open, the townspeople go so far as to speculate that the uncanny events plaguing their community may, in the tradition of Hawthorne, be posthumous retribution for their ancestors' roles in the persecution of accused witches. As soon revealed, the town of Dunwich was built on the ruins of the original Salem Village, and so the sins of Dunwich are constructed as the sins of America. *City* constructs the return of the dead as an uncanny re-emergence of the buried historical horror of the Americas. Fulci explained to *Fangoria* magazine in 1980 that in making his controversial film *Zombie!* (1979), he desired to 'recapture the moody atmosphere of witchcraft and paganism, when Europeans first settled in the Caribbean in the 1700s. A time when the concept of zombies – human slaves brought back from the dead – first became popularly known to Western civilization.'[22] Although referencing the Caribbean as opposed to North America, Fulci expresses a clear understanding that zombies are products of the New World, of colonialism and the transatlantic slave trade. They are, in sum, products of the same history that shaped the United States and continue to inform its guilt and nightmares.

City expresses an obsession with American history, and particularly the dark Puritan antecedents of the modern United States. This preoccupation with American darkness is interwoven with sublimated Catholic iconography. The narrative begins with a Catholic priest, Fr Thomas, committing suicide just before All Saints' Day.[23] This act of transgression, a Catholic priest committing a mortal sin, disrupts the boundary between the living and the dead, opening the gates of hell and unleashing reanimated corpses. Fulci's blending of Catholic iconography with the puritanism of New England creates an unsettling fusion whereby *City* appears at once the product of a distinctly Italian sensibility – with weighty sinfulness and quasi-pagan festivals – while simultaneously remaining fundamentally preoccupied with the Massachusetts setting and New World monsters. The film regularly provides uncomfortable conflations of New England puritanism and Italian Catholicism. The locus of the malevolent forces that besiege the town is Fr Thomas, a Catholic priest whose very presence seems incongruous when juxtaposed with the Calvinist style of Dunwich's plain, sparse, white church. Catholicism positioned as a sinister influence is a recurring motif in Fulci's filmography. Here, the melding of oppressive Catholicism with New England's Puritan past and reanimated evil results in a sort of categorical slippage whereby the horrors of European history are conflated with America's foundational sins. Telling, then, is scriptwriter Dardano Sacchetti's original treatment for *City* where Fr Thomas is revealed as one of the 'descendants of the 19 women put on trial for witchcraft in 1692 in Salem'.[24] Issues of historical accuracy aside, a curious imbrication of Italian and American historical horror is woven into this abandoned plot thread. A twentieth-century priest being the descendant of Massachusetts's seventeenth-century Puritan founders seems unlikely; however, in soldering America's history of religious fanaticism to what is undoubtedly an allusion to both the Inquisition and the largely unquestioned power wielded by the Catholic Church in Italy, this abandoned plot thread suggests a congruency of abusive spiritual authority. In a similar instance of historical slippage, a young woman rebuffs the suggestion that her ancestors, the founders of Dunwich, were Salem 'witch-burners'. Here, again, the histories of Europe and the New World overlap: although burning was a common form of execution in Europe throughout the medieval and early modern periods, the American colonies hanged their witches.

The melding of US and European history results in the creation of an ambiguous cinematic space, an interstitial locale that is not quite Europe and not quite America. Instead, *City* subsumes the history of one within the visual and cultural signifiers of the other. The bodies of Fulci's zombies are excessive, overflowing with potential meaning and suffused with various possible interpretations. As Zani and Meaux note, they 'constantly vacillate between biological and theological in origin, spectral and corporeal in substance'.[25] Their ambiguity enables them to embody America's repressed historical guilt while simultaneously manifesting the Italian Catholic context out of which Fulci and Sacchetti were writing. Setting his film in a fictitious New England locale and depicting zombies as American monsters imbued with seemingly incongruous signifiers of Italian culture, Fulci uses the apparatuses of American gothicism to address the crises and conflicts that plagued Italy in the late 1970s and early 1980s.

The years following the student protests and social upheavals of 1968 were a tumultuous era in Italy. The period subsequent to the cultural transformations of the late 1960s became known as the 'Years of Lead' and witnessed an explosion of violent conflict between state and militant terrorist groups which lasted well into the 1980s.[26] In 1980 a bomb detonated at the Bologna train station by the far-right organisation Nuclei Armati Rivoluzionari killed 85 people and wounded more than 200.[27]

Two years earlier, former Italian premier and leader of the Democrazia Cristiana party Aldo Moro was kidnapped by the terrorist group Brigate Rosse.[28] After fifty-five days of captivity, he was executed by his captors. Moro's body was later found riddled with bullets in the trunk of a red Renault parked in the centre of Rome.[29] As Curti observes, the Years of Lead and the brutal murder of the nation's former prime minister marked 'the eruption of death on the political scene'.[30] This eruption of violence onto a comparatively placid public sphere is echoed in GOH, beginning production contemporaneously with the Bologna bombing and released just a few short years after Moro's execution. GOH contains an undeniable preoccupation with eruption, re-emergence and the intrusion of abject violence onto the quotidian space of the everyday. In keeping with the popular critical conception of the American gothic as defined by a horror that is not monumentalised but rather buried and secreted, the monstrosities in GOH are not associated with overt horrors but are instilled with terrors hidden away, only to return as reanimated corpses.

Eric Savoy argues that the American gothic is born out of a tendency in US culture that is 'organized around the imperative to repetition, the return of what is unsuccessfully repressed, and, moreover . . . this return is realized in a syntax, a grammar, a tropic field'.[31] If the grammar or tropic field of the American gothic is predicated on the return of what is unsuccessfully repressed, Fulci translates this very grammar for the Italian context, as the zombies released through the gates of hell enact an explicit return of repressed historical horrors. The zombies bring with them a capacity for violence that destabilises notions of cultural or bodily integrity, dissolving the borders of bodies and effacing the boundary between the world of the living and the realm of the dead. In one of *City*'s most notorious scenes, the reanimated Fr Thomas watches a young couple making out in a parked car. The forbidding gaze of the sinister priest evokes the intrusion of Catholic ecclesiastical authority onto the private lives of ordinary Italians, but his glare also brings an abject dissolution of corporeal boundaries: his very presence causes the girl to vomit up her own internal organs. While such scenes undoubtedly contributed to Fulci's reputation as the 'Godfather of Gore', this explicit expulsion of viscera recalls not only Kristeva's notion of the abject but also Curti's description of the Years of Lead as an 'eruption of death' that disrupts boundaries and corrupts the mundanity of the everyday.

The theme of re-emergence also defines the later entries in GOH and establishes a topos of uncanny disinterment that runs through the series.

Like its predecessor, *The Beyond* (1981) also centres around the opening of the eponymous gates of hell and the revival of the deceased. However, while *City* appropriates and reimagines the trappings of New England puritanism as a means of articulating a surge of repressed political and cultural violence, *The Beyond* takes place in the Deep South of New Orleans and draws explicit inspiration from the South's status as the receptacle of America's banished Otherness. Examining the often-grotesque nature of the southern gothic tradition, Goddu claims that the US south 'serves as the nation's "other," becoming the repository for everything from which the nation wants to disassociate itself'.[32] *The Beyond* explicitly renders the south as a strange, unsettling space – the dark unconscious of the American self. In one of the film's most well-known sequences, the film's protagonist Liza, driving across the Pontchartrain Causeway, experiences a disturbing sensation that the causeway has been unnaturally extended, distorted and stretched across time and space, transforming the road into a bridge to another world. *The Beyond* is saturated by an uncanny atmosphere, the expansive cemeteries of New Orleans and the diaphanous Spanish Moss clinging to its trees adds an intense spectrality. Many of the buildings that appear in the film – including the hotel that Liza inherits from an unknown uncle – are old, crumbling into decay. Fulci's vision of the south is that of a rotting carcass, a stagnant repository of the irrationality, supernaturalism and backwardness from which the rest of America seeks to disassociate itself.

The New Orleans setting is appropriate because the locale appropriates America's tendency to repress the darker, oppositional elements of its culture. Louisiana and the south in general are inextricably bound to America's history of slavery as well as the ingrained desire to banish a legacy of institutionalised racism to the decaying, decadent south. New Orleans is a geographical space with clear links to America's history of colonialism. Located in proximity to the Caribbean, the city has been undeniably influenced by the Caribbean slave trade, the Haitian revolt and the influx of Haitian refugees in the nineteenth century. Consequently, although many have attributed the appearance of the zombie in American culture to the US occupation of Haiti between 1915 and 1934,[33] aspects of the island's culture had already found their way to North America when more than 10,000 Haitians arrived in New Orleans in 1809. Ina J. Fandrich observes that the Haitian migrants 'brought their *Vodou* religion with them, which ultimately merged with the already existing New Orleans or Louisiana *Voodoo* traditions'.[34]

Alongside this spatial connection with the more unsettling and ultimately repressed aspects of American history, *The Beyond* features numerous images evocative of the slave trade. While never explicitly addressing the spectre of slavery – beyond the often-noted parallels between zombies and the enslaved – several subtextual allusions confront the institution and southern racism more broadly. The opening scene features various small boats, lit by torch flames and filled with members of an enraged local mob, drifting towards the hotel that would later be owned by Liza. Storming the hotel, the mob captures a warlock named Schweick whom they whip with chains, crucify and douse in acid. Although Schweick is a white man, the southern setting combined with the enraged mob and the ferocious whipping they inflict on his body clearly conjures the spectre of historical lynchings. In this moment, the lingering horror of slavery and racial violence seems at risk of exploding across the surface of the film; however, by transmuting the object of this violence into a white magician, this historicity is suppressed, veiled with metaphors and ambiguous allusions.

Fulci also borrows heavily from Edgar Allan Poe and echoes the writer's tendency to displace the south's dark history of plantation slavery onto the mystical. The murder of Schweick is a reconstitution of racial violence that banishes race from its representational apparatus in much the same way that Poe's work often addressed race without ever really including characters of colour or explicitly alluding to the subject. Poe's use of contrasting black and white tones, according to scholars, is suggestive of antebellum racial tensions and the numerous illogical violent outbursts throughout his work also bespeak the ubiquitous racialised violence of the period. For instance, Charles L. Crow elucidates how a seemingly de-historicised or displaced story like 'Hop Frog' (1849) engages with antebellum racism. Crow argues that 'Hop-Frog's burning alive of the suspended king and his ministers is a Janus-faced image, recalling both slave rebellions and the lynching of blacks'.[35] The image of the furious mob, the cruciform position of the murdered Schweick's body and the bayou setting all indicate that *The Beyond* in this tradition addresses southern racism indirectly and through the conventions of gothic fiction.

As with *City*, the visual and thematic lexicon of *The Beyond* is grounded in a generic grammar of return and reanimation, the secretion of the horrors of the past deep within the earth and the inevitable return of these repressed nightmares. Drawing on the work of the early twentieth-century American author Clark Ashton Smith, Fulci constructs the basement of the hotel inherited by Liza as the entrance to one of the seven gateways to hell. This narrative conceit not only echoes the American gothic fascination with hidden horror, but also recalls the tendency of weird fiction to view the mundane world as a mere veil obscuring a more disturbing, infinitely terrifying reality. Daniel Quinn describes Smith's 'Zothique cycle', which notably features the deity Thasaidon, 'lord of seven hells', as a clear precursor to Fulci's own seven gateways to hell.[36] Similarly, the opening of Smith's story 'The Door to Saturn' parallels the early scenes of *The Beyond* which also features a furious mob searching for a heretical magician, the wizard Eibon.[37] Both *The Beyond* and 'The Door to Saturn' are preoccupied with the everyday as a thin veil that obscures the much darker supernatural realm that lingers beyond ordinary human perception. Throughout *The Beyond* quotidian reality is repeatedly disrupted by the return of the dead, zombies whose reanimation heralds the disruption of the boundary between the living and the deceased.

The transition point between the world of the living and the dead being located in a basement seems appropriate to Fulci's broader appropriation of the American gothic's grammar of repression and return. The basement, as a receptacle of the repressed, is a motif that runs throughout the America gothic, from Poe's 'The Black Cat' (1843) to Alfred Hitchcock's *Psycho* (1960) and to Stuart Rosenberg's *The Amityville Horror* (1979).[38] According to Bernice Murphy, 'the basement is frequently a place in which unspeakable horrors lurk in the modern horror film'.[39] The basement and the terrors concealed within also exemplify how American gothic fiction pivots on themes of repression, concealment and return. Often constructed beneath an idyllic home, the dream house of suburban fantasy, the basement is emblematic of US gothicism's obsession with the darkness that underpins the nation's conception of itself as the land of freedom and opportunity. Examining the symbolic function of cellars in fiction, Murphy draws attention to Gaston Bachelard's claim that the basement is 'first and foremost the . . . *dark entity* of the house, the one that partakes of subterranean forces. When we dream there, we are in harmony with the irrationality of the depths.'[40] That even the most peaceful, ordered and idyllic home may be positioned atop such a yawning, subterranean chasm suggests a darkness inherent to the American dream and highlights the centrality of repression to the maintenance of that dream. In *The Beyond*, this subterranean darkness is figured as infinite, endless and capable of swallowing the world above. Not only is the basement the dark heart of the home, but it is also the bridge to the land of the dead and, as such, is the ultimate manifestation of repressed horror.

The centrality of basements to the American gothic themes of repression and return is also apparent in the final entry in GOH, *The House by the Cemetery* (*House* hereafter). Drawing inspiration primarily from James's 'The Turn of the Screw', as well as from Stephen King's novel *The Shining* (1977) and its subsequent cinematic adaptation in 1980, *House* continues the series' engagement with hidden horrors and the re-emergence of buried abominations. Perhaps more overtly preoccupied with the American dream than the earlier entries in the trilogy, *House* is centred around a historian, Dr Boyle, who moves from New York to Massachusetts with his family to complete the work of a deceased colleague. Once there, the family's young son is plagued by visions of a spectral girl who warns him to stay away from the Boyles' new home, a rambling Victorian mansion ultimately revealed to hold the reanimated corpse of its original owner, the sinister Dr Freudstein. The film alludes rather explicitly to its various sources, with 'The Turn of the Screw' being the most overt intertextual connection.

Yvonne Griggs notes that, 'There are also a number of films which, though not closely drawing upon "The Turn of the Screw", appropriate certain elements of the tale.'[41] Griggs's lists recent cinematic reworkings of James's text, such as *The Others* (2001), *In a Dark Place* (2006) and *The Orphanage* (2007) which, although not constituting direct remediations of 'The Turn of the Screw', 'appropriate its treatment of female paranoia and its exploration of the over-protective mother figure, forging subtle connections with James's narrative'.[42] *House* derives inspiration from key aspects of James's influential ghost story. For example, the young boy, Bob, regularly encounters a spectral girl-child named May in liminal spaces such as the grounds surrounding his new home. This localisation of the supernatural seems to reflect James's anonymous heroine's tendency to encounter the spirts of Miss Jessel and Quint in intermedial zones, such as stairways and 'on high places, the top of towers, the roof of houses, the outside of windows, the further edges of pools'.[43] Likewise, Dr Boyle's wife, Lucy, complains that she wants to discontinue her medication because they cause hallucinations, a piece of dialogue that raises the possibility that, like the governess in 'The Turn of the Screw', Lucy's maternal paranoia and encounters with the supernatural may be entirely the product of her imagination.

Moving beyond these narrative parallels, *House* mirrors James's novella in its engagement with themes of repression and return. One of the most popular interpretations is that 'The Turn of the Screw' is defined by the uncanny re-emergence of the repressed. Whether the repressed material is read as the horrific corruption of the children by the nefarious Quint and Jessel, or as the suppressed sexuality of the nameless governess, the novella is characterised by the spectral reoccurrence of that which has been buried. *House*, a film that declares its relationship with James's fiction through a fabricated quotation from the author, attempts to bring to the fore this thematic engagement with repression. Reworking aspects of James's narrative, the thematic thread of repression permeates *House* and is centred on the horrors secreted in the subterranean space of the house's basement and the return of the dead from their graves. In this way, *House* echoes the earlier entries in GOH by virtue of emphasising the reimagining and reconfiguring the thematic core of American gothic literature. As an appropriation of 'The Turn of the Screw', Fulci's film reflects Griggs's definition of a revisionary adaption that attempts to 'redefine the source text's dominant discourse' by bringing 'to the fore matters that have lain dormant and present the expectant reader/viewer with alternat ways of engaging with both the originary canonical text and its adaptive offspring'.[44] In reworking the central thematic strands of James's novella, Fulci foregrounds the original text's preoccupation with repression, burial and violent return. In doing so, 'The Turn of the Screw' is situated within the broader thematic framework of American gothic fiction, which is the true focus of Fulci's adaptational intentions. Rather than transmuting individual texts into new cinematic products, Fulci adapts and transforms the central thematic concerns of American gothicism, perpetuating a deeply embedded pattern of repression and return.

In the denouement of *House*, as in *The Beyond*, the epicentre for the undead evil that plagues the film's protagonists is the basement, the dark, secreted thing buried beneath the dream home. However, the basement is not so much an entryway to the realm of the dead that pulsates beneath the terrible house, but the evil machinations of the zombified Dr Freudstein. The deceased doctor, revealed later, had been an army surgeon, discharged for performing illegal experiments, and though he should have died naturally more than a century ago, has kept himself alive by transplanting body parts of the living onto his own rotting flesh, thereby renewing his decaying cells. Freudstein is emblematic of how a dark, repressed past may return to feed upon the living. In the original script, Dr Boyle is described as a historian researching the American Civil War, while Freudstein is connected more explicitly to that conflict, appearing in the final scenes in 'an old and dirty army uniform'.[45] Like *The Beyond*, the spectres of slavery and institutionalised racism dimly haunt *House*. However, *House* also engages in an instance of historical slippage akin to the conflation of European witch hunts and American Puritan persecution that defines *City*. Despite his ostensible Americanness (the involvement with the civil war, the home in Massachusetts) Freudstein is equally evocative of the horrors of European history. The name Freudstein is a portmanteau of Freud – signalling a connection with European psychoanalysis – and Frankenstein – the apotheosis of European gothicism.

That the apparently American monster would possess such a clearly European moniker evokes the kind of categorical obfuscation that occurs earlier in GOH; consequently, viewing the sadistic Freudstein is difficult without connecting his proclivity for human experimentation to that of the Nazis, and by extension to the still recent history of European fascism. In her study of Dario Argento's 1977 film *Suspiria*, Alexandra Heller-Nicholas observes a similarly oblique reference to European fascism, when she highlights the use of Munich's infamous Königsplatz as the locale for one of the film's most violent deaths.[46] Heller-Nicholas emphasises the sub-textual significance of the blind musician Daniel's murder by a coven of a witches, noting not only the historical implications inherent in the use of the Königsplatz as the site of the murder, but also incorporating Julian Horrocks's suggestion that the blind man symbolises Italy, while the guide dog that betrays and devours him is emblematic of Mussolini and Italian fascism.[47] In *House* Fulci's references to the still-recent trauma of fascism are similarly veiled in indirect allusions. Viewed in the context of modern Italian history, Freudstein's status as the living dead and his final, climactic attempt to drag the Boyle family into his subterranean surgery expresses the impossibility of repressing past horrors.

Both *The Beyond* and *The House by the Cemetery* feature dark and ostensibly hidden monstrosities rising from underground depths, indicating that both are defined by the American gothic grammar of repression and return. Rather than simply mimicking the conventions of US gothicism, Fulci frequently adapts and transforms them, rendering them appropriate to the European context in which he was working. Fulci's reworking of American gothic motifs and his transformation of the themes and iconography of New World gothicism for an Italian audience warns against repression on both a personal and national scale. Coming in the decades after the Second World War and the ravages of fascism, GOH is an apt indictment against attempting to banish historical atrocities. In each of these films, what is buried makes a violent return, corrupting the placidity of banal, everyday existence. As Curti observes, the trauma of the Years of Lead and the extensive political violence that had marked much of the 1970s led many Italians to view the dawning 1980s as a new era of comfort and ease.⁴⁸ For Curti, the ubiquitous violence of the preceding decade resulted in a shift away from political and public engagement that transformed the 1980s into an ersatz refugee of consumerist excess, when many ordinary people escaped into television, entertainment and avarice. GOH is the product of an era in which a period of excessive and invasive political violence had ushered in an epoch of repression when both the horrors of history and the conflicts of the present were buried beneath a veneer of placid consumption. By adapting the fictive lexicon of repression and return that defined American gothic fiction to this transitional moment in Italian history, Fulci's films suggests that such attempts to banish the reality of violence and death will always serve as little more than a brief interment whose finality is invariably resisted. The transnational nature of this adaptive work is perhaps one of the earliest attempts to engage with a global zombiism, a paradigm that has become increasingly central to contemporary zombie studies. As an Italian director working at a tumultuous time in his nation's history, Fulci constructs the zombie as a metaphor for the resurgence of repressed violence that recently scarred his country. He does so by employing uniquely American literary conventions. The GOH films thus foreground the zombie as the intersection of numerous diverse histories and cultures, from the American gothic to Italian Catholicism and the legacy of the Caribbean and US slave trades. The blankness of the undead represents an intriguingly ambiguous site, a blank canvas onto which a host of disparate, even contradictory, concerns could be projected and played out.

Notes

1. *The House by the Cemetery* [*Quella villa accanto al cimitero*], dir. Lucio Fulci, Medusa Distribuzione, New York (1981).
2. Roberto Curti, *Italian Gothic Horror Films, 1980–1989* (Jefferson: McFarland, 2019), p. 89.
3. Leo Braudy, *Haunted: On Ghosts, Witches, Vampires, Zombies, and Other Monsters of the Natural and Supernatural Worlds* (New Haven: Yale University Press, 2016), p. 105.
4. Kyle William Bishop, *American Zombie Gothic: The Rise and Fall (and Rise) of the Walking Dead in Popular Culture* (Jefferson: McFarland, 2010), p. 31.
5. Stephen Thrower, *Beyond Terror: The Films of Lucio Fulci* (Godalming: FAB Press, 2002), p. 15.

6. Thrower, *Beyond Terror*, p. 66.
7. British Board of Film Classification: 'Zombie-Flesh-Eaters', https://bbfc.co.uk/releases/zombie-flesh-eaters-film-qxnzzxq6vlgtnjy5ndgy (accessed 11 July 2019).
8. Egan, quoted in Laura Hubner, 'Archiving Gore: Who Owns Zombie Flesh Eaters?', in Laura Hubner, Marcus Leaning and Paul Manning (eds). *The Zombie Renaissance in Popular Culture* (London: Palgrave, 2015), p. 47.
9. Chas Balun, *Lucio Fulci: Beyond the Gates* (Key West: Blackest Heart Books, 1996), pp. 22–3.
10. Thrower, *Beyond Terror*, p. 153.
11. Linda Hutcheon, *A Theory of Adaptation* (London Routledge, 2006), p. 170.
12. Hutcheon, *A Theory of Adaptation*, p. 8.
13. Julie Sanders, *Adaptation and Appropriation* (London: Routledge, 2016), p. 26.
14. Ben Larned, 'Forbidden Tomes: Books to Films – the Literary Influences on Lucio Fulci', *Daily Dead* (2017), https://dailydead.com/forbidden-tomes-book-to-film-the-literary-influences-on-lucio-fulci/ (accessed 12 July 2019).
15. Bishop, *American Zombie Gothic*, p. 32.
16. Bishop, *American Zombie Gothic*, p. 32.
17. Teresa A. Goddu, *Gothic America: Narrative, History, and Nation* (New York: Columbia University Press, 1997), p. 9.
18. Steven Zani and Kevin Meaux, 'Lucio Fulci and the Decaying Definition of Zombie Narratives', in Deborah Christie and Sarah Juliet Lauro (eds), *Better Off Dead: The Evolution of Zombie as Post-human* (New York Fordham: University Press, 2011), p. 108.
19. H. P. Lovecraft, 'The Dunwich Horror', in *The Call of Cthulhu and Other Weird Tales* (New York: Vintage, 2011), p. 100.
20. Julian Petley, 'The Unfilmable? H. P. Lovecraft and the Cinema', in Richard J. Hand and Jay McRoy (eds), *Monstrous Adaptations: Generic and Thematic Mutations in Horror Film* (Manchester: Manchester University Press, 2007), p. 45.
21. Charles L. Crow, 'Preface', in Charles L. Crow (ed.), *A Companion to American Gothic* (West Sussex: Wiley Blackwell, 2014), p. xvii.
22. Quoted in Balun, *Lucio Fulci: Beyond the Gates*, p. 23.
23. Petley, 'The Unfilmable? H. P. Lovecraft and the Cinema', p. 45.
24. Curti, *Italian Gothic Horror Films*, p. 45.
25. Zani and Meaux, 'Lucio Fulci and the Decay Definition of Zombie Narratives', p. 99.
26. Curti, *Italian Gothic Horror Films*, p. 2.
27. Curti, *Italian Gothic Horror Films*, p. 2.
28. Curti, *Italian Gothic Horror Films*, p. 1.
29. Curti, *Italian Gothic Horror Films*, p. 1.

30. Curti, *Italian Gothic Horror Films*, p. 1.
31. Andrew Hock Soon Ng, 'Undead Identities: Asian American Literature and the Gothic', in Charles L. Crow (ed.), *A Companion to American Gothic* (West Sussex: Wiley Blackwell, 2014), p. 249.
32. Goddu, *Gothic America*, p. 3.
33. Braudy, *Haunted*, p. 105.
34. Ina J. Fandrich, 'Yoruba Influences on Haitian Vodou and New Orleans Voodoo', *Journal of Black Studies,* 37 (2007), 786.
35. Charles L. Crow, 'Southern American Gothic', in Jeffrey Andrew Weinstock (ed.), *The Cambridge Companion to America Gothic* (Cambridge: Cambridge University Press, 2017), p. 144.
36. Daniel Quinn, 'She-Devil Otherness and the Last Hieroglyph: Reclaiming the Cosmic in Clark Ashton Smith's "Zothique Cycle"', *Eldritch Dark* (2007), http://www.eldritchdark.com/articles/criticism/72/she-devil-otherness-and-the-last-hieroglyph%3A-reclaiming-the-cosmic-in-clark-ashton-smith%E2%80%99s-%27zothique-cycle%27 (accessed 12 July 2019).
37. Clark Ashton Smith, 'The Door to Saturn', *Eldritch Dark*, http://www.eldritchdark.com/writings/short-stories/50/the-door-to-saturn (accessed 12 July 2019).
38. Edgar Allan Poe, 'The Black Cat', *The United States Saturday Post*, 19 August 1843, 1; Psycho, dir. Alfred Hitchcock, Paramount Pictures, USA (1960), *Amityville Horror*, dir. Stuart Rosenberg, USA (1979).
39. Bernice Murphy, *The Suburban Gothic in American Popular Culture* (London: Palgrave Macmillan, 2009), p. 155.
40. Quoted in Murphy, *The Suburban Gothic*, p. 156.
41. Yvonne Griggs, T*he Bloomsbury Introduction to Adaptation Studies* (London: Bloomsbury, 2016), p. 145.
42. Griggs, *The Bloomsbury Introduction to Adaptation Studies*, p. 145.
43. Henry James, 'The Turn of the Screw', in *The Turn of the Screw and Other Stories* (London: Vintage, 2007), p. 133.
44. Griggs, *The Bloomsbury Introduction to Adaptation Studies*, p. 161.
45. Curti, *Italian Gothic Horror Films*, p. 90.
46. Alexandra Heller-Nicholas, *Suspiria* (Leighton Buzzard: Devil's Advocates, 2015), Kindle edition, n.p.
47. Heller-Nicholas, *Suspiria*, n.p.
48. Curti, *Italian Gothic Horror Films*, p. 2.

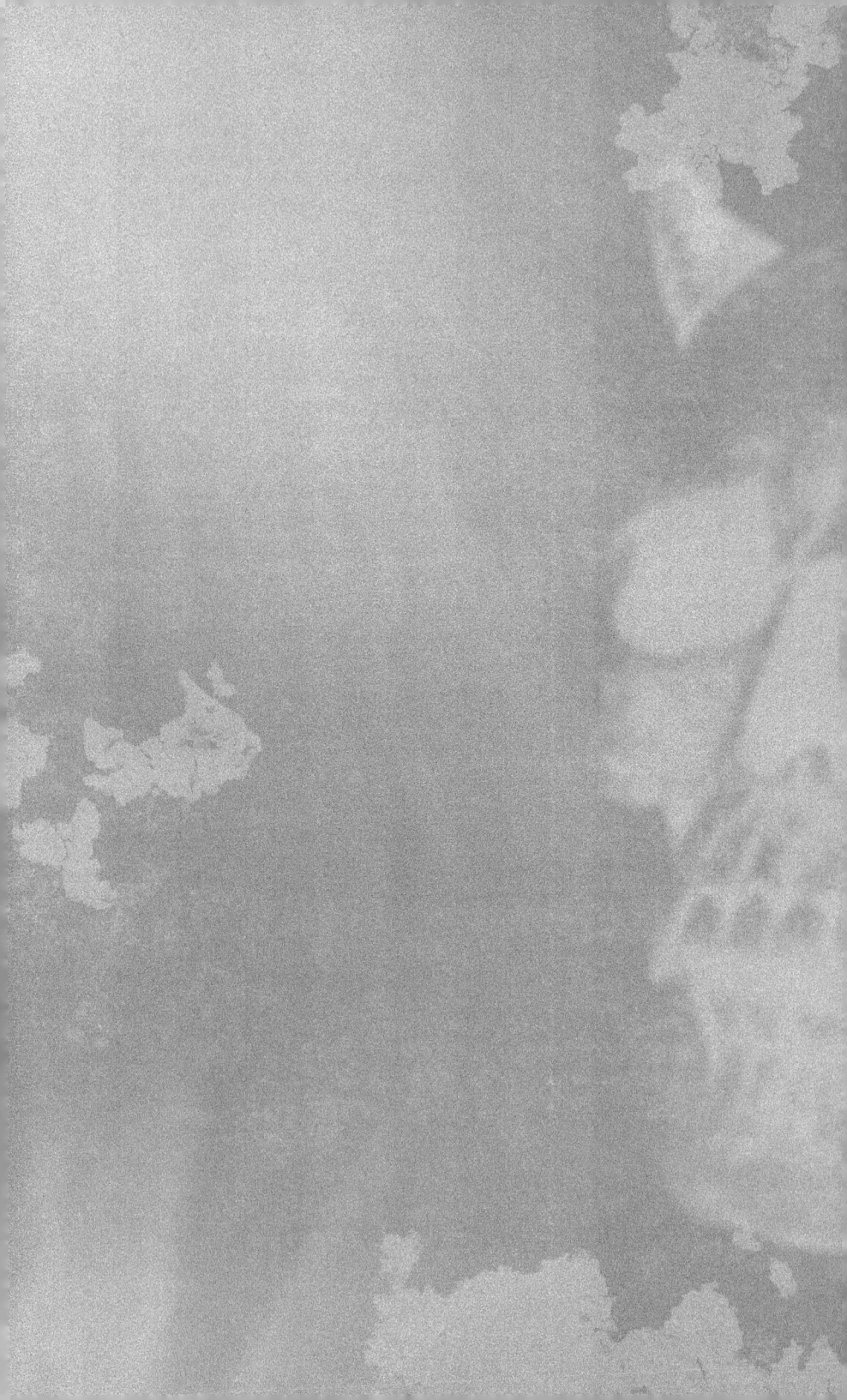

12

Surviving the Shambling Signifieds
Zombies, Language and Chaos

Andrew Ferguson

WHEN *ZONE ONE* was published in 2011, Colson Whitehead seemed an unlikely entrant on the zombie-lit scene. While other Whitehead novels played with genre – detective noir in *The Intuitionist*, small-town folktale in *John Henry Days*, coming-of-age in *Sag Harbor* – all remained within identifiable 'lit-fic' norms. Whitehead monographist Derek C. Maus admits that *Zone One* 'fits into my interpretive framework of postsoul historical metafiction less readily than any of his previous books'.[1] Nonetheless, Maus tries to shoehorn *Zone One* into a 'New York Trilogy', along with the novel *Sag Harbor* and the essay collection *The Colossus of New York*, with little more justification than the three books being written about Whitehead's home city.

Whitehead himself, though, frames his genre play – or what he elsewhere calls his genre 'drag'[2] – as a means of exploring racial erasure, with the cinematic zombie apocalypse providing ample material from the founding of the form:

> I grew up on the first Romero trilogy and various post-apocalyptic films . . . seeing *Night of the Living Dead* when I was in sixth grade, seeing a really strong black protagonist really resonated with me.

I'd seen a lot of blaxploitation films. But seeing just a normal Joe who is on the run from a white mob who wants to destroy him seems to be a part of the American chronicle.[3]

In *Zone One*, race certainly seems consigned to the background: the protagonist is not definitively identified as black until very late in the book, leading one of Whitehead's commentators, Kimberly Fain, to cite the novel as another example of what she calls his 'postracial voice': '*Zone One* is a tribute to how a culture reconstructs hope and rebuilds itself in the wake of an accident or trauma, such as the unfathomable tragedy on 9/11'.[4] But such a reading seems at odds not only with the facts of the book – after all, the Manhattan of *Zone One* is not and will not be rebuilt; it is a PR stunt turned death trap – but also with the deep doubts evinced throughout about what, exactly, is being rebuilt. This chapter argues, instead, that *Zone One* uses the zombie apocalypse as a way of rewriting *Night of the Living Dead* and zombie folklore more generally to give the protagonist an ending in which he no longer falls victim to whiteness re-establishing its own dominance, but rather affirms a Black identity by inscribing his own narrative, on his own terms. Doing so will require the protagonist Mark Spitz to overcome a mediocre education into language (as communicated through conventions of pop culture media, prose fiction and language itself) that purportedly prepares him to battle the cognitive negation that zombies embody, while actually consigning him to the ranks of the dead. Ultimately, zombiism as encountered in *Zone One* is inseparable from the failure of language overwritten by meaningless noise – and the process is not just the preserve of the dead themselves; it also infects the pre-apocalyptic society that spawned them, as well as the post-apocalyptic society attempting to build back the former one with all its mindless hierarchies and prejudices intact.

Zone One emerged into an entertainment landscape already swarming with the undead. After George Romero's re-imagining of the colonialist stereotype of the stupefied labourer as a vengeful revenant and supplanter of humanity – and furthermore, after *28 Days Later* established the speedy viral zombie as the standard model[5] – the zombie horde invaded almost every media channel, moving from film to videogames, TV, comic books, and finally prose fiction. Other genre-straddling authors with lit-fic credibility released zombie projects just the year before: Margaret Atwood, collaborating with Naomi Alderman on 'The Happy Zombie Sunrise Home', and Roberto Bolaño, in the appropriately posthumous short story 'The

Colonel's Son'. And of course, Jane Austen (with help from Seth Grahame-Smith and a remarkable word-of-mouth publicity campaign) had re-entered the bestseller list with *Pride and Prejudice and Zombies*. This latter affront prompted one columnist to declare a state of 'zombie fatigue', admonishing that 'You can't just add "And Zombies" to things', in the face of Grahame-Smith doing exactly that.[6]

Zone One was packaged very differently from *Pride and Prejudice and Zombies*. Doubleday, the publisher of all Whitehead's novels, made sure of that: the book jacket eschewed the overt gore and spatter that was the hallmark of much zombie design, and the paperback copy of the following year bore cover blurbs from *The New York Times Book Review*, the *Los Angeles Times* and *Esquire* rather than any genre authors or outlets. There is no lack of carnage in the book itself – Whitehead's enthusiasm for the genre's conventions cannot be doubted[7] – but his attitude towards that source material is far from Grahame-Smith's hostile takeover of Austen's prose. Instead, the novel is coolly obsessed with the language that the zombies threaten to annihilate; the narrative voice is in a constant battle over whether or not meaning is possible. At the book's beginning, the protagonist is on a routine sweep to eradicate those undead who remain in Manhattan's office buildings. For the first seven pages, he is referred to only by pronoun, as he drifts through memories and impressions from his childhood, flitting between 'monster movies and the city churning below'[8] – even conflating them, in recalling 'the massive central-air units that hunkered and coiled on the striving high rises, glistening like extruded guts'.[9] As a boy, he looked at Manhattan and saw that 'There was a message there, if he could teach himself the language' – but now he can only see 'the city [as] an altar to obscurity . . . the words and names were crevasses to get lost in, looming and meaningless'; even when he tries to recapture that childhood impulse, 'rearranging the architecture into a message . . . a collection of figments and notions of things', all he sees are towers in the midst of a ruined city: 'shapes trudg[ing] like slaves higher and higher into midtown'.[10] This stark metaphor, sufficient to show that there is nothing 'post-racial' in the post-apocalypse, is immediately followed by the naming of the protagonist – not his own name, which is never given, but a nickname that immediately erases any which went before: 'They called him Mark Spitz nowadays. He didn't mind.'[11] The story behind this *nom de guerre* will not be given for more than half the book, and not told in full till nearly the end; in between are only remarks such as 'The name stuck. No harm. Affront was a luxury.'[12] The name is a microaggression that must be borne in the interests of social cohesion, even as it erases and overwrites whatever self-narrative he might otherwise craft. He accepts the language, and in so doing is excluded from it.

This double bind of language is far from new, of course, and the stakes have always been life or death, or perhaps death-in-life. Print, in particular, has never long been separated from death – with Friedrich Kittler emphasising the point by reproducing 'the oldest depiction of a print shop, 1499 – as a dance of death'.[13] The mere act of writing was regarded as a sort of technological despair long before the formation of the Gutenberg Galaxy. In the *Phaedrus*, Socrates refers to written discourses held by his interlocutor as *pharmakia*, which Jacques Derrida glosses as both 'drug' and 'poison'. To write words, for Socrates, was to distort them by fixing them to a certain form and time; mimesis, itself already suspect because twice removed from truth, has the additional and inevitable trouble of introducing flaws into its reproductions. Thus, mimetic poetry is banned from the *Republic*, with Socrates noting that it 'is likely to distort the thought of anyone who hears it, unless he has the knowledge of what it is really like, as a drug to counteract it'.[14] The *pharmakon* of writing must be counteracted by the *pharmakon* of the *logos*. The latter 'comprehends' the former; Derrida writes of how the Socratic *pharmakon* 'alternately and/or all at once petrifies and vivifies, anesthetises and sensitises, appeases and anguishes'.[15] Herein is the 'contradiction' of writing, the clash of the drugs. For Plato, as later for Jean-Jacques Rousseau and Ferdinand de Saussure (both in posthumously released works), writing captures language both as being and as nonbeing – as the hallucinatory compound that allows humankind to reproduce visions and voices not directly present to the sensorium, and also as the zombie powder which deprives them of that sensorium.

So, while logocentric thought had to devalue writing as a sort of 'Death rehearsal', it also had to subject itself to what Kittler would call 'the bottleneck of the signifier':[16] language could not reveal the debasement of alphabetic data encoding without first encoding itself alphabetically. The presence of this 'doubly reinforced absence' leaves the process of signification in crisis, leading Jacques Lacan to picture the signifier jostling and slipping against other signifiers, all of them floating above an incessant stream of signifieds.[17] This slippage places the play of language in the idiom of the zombie film, especially *Night of the Living Dead*, where the few survivors squabble amongst themselves while the hordes of the undead press ever on.[18] There is no escape from them – even Ben, the would-be hero, gets gunned down by a patrol who mistake him for a zombie, in the most tragic of the film's many complex mirror-misrecognition scenes.

Since Lacan, humans have adapted to (or at least incorporated) the floating signifier; bringing it into the context of the digital, N. Katherine Hayles proposed the 'flickering signifier', which exists in the play of pattern and randomness across multiple layers of code. The signifier is suddenly crystallised information, bursting forth from noise; the innate horror of this model is not the present absence of castration, but the random patterning of mutation.[19] In zombie parlance this marks the difference between the 'slow zombie' and the 'fast zombie', but regardless of the model of signification, the signifieds still swarm. Thus, one can add to the picture of signification – to the floating or flickering signifier – the *shambling signified*: the presence of absence in print, the randomised pattern in the digital; 'non-philosophy, bad memory, hypomnesia, writing . . . life going out itself beyond return'.[20] In the context of computers, 'bad memory' is particularly ominous: the zombie is the infected sector on the hard drive, the mutated datum that will eventually, at whatever speed, overwrite all the rest. The shambling signified is the written as the process of unwriting, the effacement at the core of signification. Given the erasure of his former name, Mark Spitz has never truly left the shambling signifieds, even as he places himself in the service of defending human cognition against the embodiment of that process.

This sort of sacrifice is often demanded of a protagonist: from the first inscriptions of narrative logic, literature continually depicts itself and its heroes battling this sort of negation, fighting against the formlessness and amnesia guaranteed to swallow it up in time. From Marduk slaying Tiamat, to Milton's Satan crossing the Abyss, to Borges's Babelian librarians, this recurrent battle – in German, *Chaoskampf* – has been contested time and again, in innumerable forms. But as Hayles shows, it is not sufficient (or even possible) to *defeat* chaos; rather, it must be channelled. This is the foundation of study in complex dynamics, which Hayles examines in *Chaos Bound*.[21] In particular she is interested in how narratives (as a form of new information) develop amid the flux of pattern and randomness, drawing on the 'strange attractor' school of chaos theory to demonstrate the order deeply encoded into even those systems that remain chaotic. The *Chaoskampf* is itself one of these 'strange attractors' for narrative, producing a feedback loop in which a story of 'victory' over chaos reifies that victory by propagating its structure in retellings, thus planting the preconditions for future accumulations of data.

The rise of the zombie, especially in its viral format, marks the final dissolution of the *Chaoskampf*: the failure of language to signify. In almost every zombie narrative, the attack of the dead on humankind corresponds with an attack on human channels of communication – in some cases, such as *Pontypool Changes Everything*, the breakdown of speech is itself what carries the attack; regardless of the platform, the zombie advance represents the destruction of the very means by which humanity might transmit or interpret any data around them.[22] This generalised assault on the intellect, or at least that intellect embodied in humans, is something even Grahame-Smith intuited, his Mr Darcy being introduced not as a man of £10,000 a year, but as the 'slaughter[er of] more than a thousand unmentionables since the fall of Cambridge'.[23] Whatever 'Cambridge' once represented is lost; the education into language and the accompanying privilege once conveyed there no longer hold any value, at least none anywhere near the level of expediency in slaughter.

But in Mark Spitz's world, language has long since ceased to signify all that much; success even before the zombie apocalypse depended on learning to play whatever role would produce the most value for his superiors – a world not actually all that different from the one he occupies post-plague. Mark Spitz emerges from his introductory reverie into a generic 'hypermodern' office space, with desks 'thick and transparent, hacked out of plastic and elevating the curvilinear monitors and keyboards in dioramas of productivity'.[24] Prior to the zombie plague, he had worked in a similar setting, manning a keyboard in the social-media wing of a coffee corporation, a job that 'doesn't require any skills'.[25] Mark Spitz, who relishes his own existence as a mediocre Everyman-type, a 'template' from which others can only deviate, turns out to be 'a natural at ersatz human connection and the postures of counterfeit empathy'.[26] He provides the 'soul' that supposedly separates human from algorithmically generated bot interaction; he is the ghost in this particular machine. Yet that same machine provides him his identity, ready-made: in cultivating an 'individual social-media persona', he is instructed, 'No cussing, no politics, use common sense' – and then that persona, already constrained by corporate imperatives, is further circumscribed by numerous hours on the job, typing pat responses to a variety of keyword prompts, 'spell-checking faux-friendly compositions, hitting Send'.[27] Mark Spitz's job is one that cannot (yet) be automated; his messages require a human touch to protect and advance corporate interests – where once 'typewriter' named 'a profession, a machine, and a sex', now 'persona' names an operator, a function and an exploitable identity.[28] To the coffee company, Mark Spitz's blackness matters only to the extent that it can be leveraged for messages such as 'Why don't you try our seasonal Jamaican blend next time you're in the 'hood?'[29] Any assertion of race beyond this banality would be 'political' and likely not 'common sense' – his racial identity thus exists only in the act of erasure.[30]

In this, Mark Spitz resembles Mavis Beacon, the iconic figure behind the *Mavis Beacon Teaches Typing* games ubiquitous throughout the 1980s and 1990s, and still updated for each successive generation of computing.[31] Mavis Beacon was created during an era when software manufacturers were attempting to find human or at least humanoid characters who could represent the computing logic of the programme, under the theory that consumers would be more likely to forge attachments to such characters rather than faceless subroutines. The project started with *The Chessmaster 2000* depicting the player's opponent, the titular 'Chessmaster', as a wizened greybeard; in seeking a depiction of what a typing instructor might look like, the *Mavis Beacon* developers found their cover model via 'serendipity':

> on a trip to Saks Fifth Avenue . . . there at the perfume counter, while shopping for a gift, [game developers] Abrams and Crane met their typing teacher. Abrams described Renée L'Esperance as a 'stunning Haitian woman', with 'three-inch fingernails' . . . despite the concerns Abrams voiced ('She's never been near a keyboard!'), they soon made a deal. Abrams told us they paid L'Esperance a flat fee [and] bought her a conservative outfit that befitted a typist . . . in order to take the cover photo. As for her long fingernails, Crane said 'Don't worry. We won't show her hands.'[37]

The decision to hire a Black model for the game was a gamble for the time, but one that worked: after initial hesitations from retailers, the branding was embraced, and the character of Mavis Beacon established. Eventually the game would become 'the bestselling program of any kind for the Apple Macintosh'.[33] Already at this early stage, certain aspects of Renée L'Esperance's identity must be suppressed so that she can become Mavis Beacon: most obviously her fingernails, which would hamper typing speed, and presumably also her wardrobe, since a 'conservative outfit' is supplied. But the erasure goes much deeper when L'Esperance's Haitian heritage is considered. She came to the United States after fleeing the Tonton Macoutes – the shock troops of a dictator, François 'Papa Doc' Duvalier, enabled by the United States after the disastrous, bloody occupation of 1915–34 and the decades of CIA interference to follow.[34] L'Esperance's ultimate fate, after being made the face of a computer programme that sold tens of millions of copies, is unknown; at some point she left the US to 'live quietly in the Caribbean'.[35] The programmers did not stay in touch because they did not have to: she was paid only for the individual photo sessions at the time, without any residuals in the years to follow. While L'Esperance fell silent – perhaps still never touching a keyboard, never using the tool her avatar had mastered – the company continued to use and update her image, digitally altering her wardrobe or hairstyle, shifting her from a 'more conservative' to a 'modern professorial type of teacher'.[36] The black body, stripped of its own identity and blocked from access to the technologies of inscription, gets co-opted into endless, unremunerated labour: thus does Renée L'Esperance, the Haitian shop girl, become Mavis Beacon, the American zombie.

L'Esperance's silence is even more striking because Mavis Beacon is quite a vocal presence within the games – although the first few editions limit her to messages delivered on skeuomorphic chalkboards, later versions on CD-ROM provided the sound-file support necessary for the teacher to address her pupils. But even within the first, text-only version, a clear 'voice' is present: engaging, confident, sometimes chiding – if a student's productivity plummeted as attention waned, the programme would tell them to 'knock it off for the day' – but always encouraging. The personality also had a sense of humour, one that was more than a little bizarre. 'Bizarre', in fact, was one of the programme's favourite words: its dictionary, especially in the early editions, seems to favour less-often-used consonants when testing players' typing speed, producing sentences such as 'Sixty-five quizzical sheep kept their jaws dry in a farm bungalow' or 'Squawking gorillas could hex the brave but brazen vixens'.[37] But this surface absurdity concealed perhaps the most important lesson of the programme. *Mavis Beacon Teaches Typing* sought to inculcate touch-typing. Presenting players with nonsense phrases trains them to dissociate words and meanings: neophyte typists are not expected to process the words they are typing, much less to add words of their own; instead, they must concentrate only on reproducing others' words without regard for meaning. In the game, signifiers float often and flicker always, but what is actually being signified is the centrality of a skill deemed necessary to participate in the 'information economy': emptying out one's own mind, the better to reproduce the words of one's hierarchical betters. In a 1989 literature review, Steve Shuller, a New York school computer coordinator, provided a look at historical typing instruction at a time when many districts were debating whether to adopt keyboarding curricula (and if so, whether to invest in *Mavis Beacon* or other programmes).[38] Shuller identifies a shift in inscription that necessitates a shift in pedagogy:

> Industrial Age schools resembled factories, and funds for typewriters were only available to prepare the relatively few students who would become clerks and typists. Information Age schools must prepare the vast majority of students to use computers because they are information management tools.[39]

Mark Spitz, as a competent but by no means exceptional student in a Long Island school, would have come through a keyboarding programme influenced by reports like Shuller's. Spitz would be well trained to use the coffee corporation's information management tools; if that job does not require any skills, it is because keyboarding by that point is thoroughly taken for granted, and the curriculum has prepared him to type meaningless series of words to meet basic goals.

That training has also prepared him for his employment in *Zone One*. The undead he removes from office blocks are now shambling signifieds, severed from whatever identities they once had.[40] All that has shifted is the game he is playing, which is now no longer *Mavis Beacon Teaches Typing*, but rather *The Typing of the Dead*. The latter game is a remake of *The House of the Dead 2*, where players use a gun accessory to shoot a series of increasingly resilient zombies. In *The Typing of the Dead*, however, the player's weapon is not a gun but a keyboard: each zombie appears with a phrase or sentence over its head and can only be dispatched by the player typing those words in correctly.[41] The words themselves are selected at random from an enormous dictionary file, and scale to the skill of the player – slowly increasing throughout, but then becoming easier if the player dies multiple times. However odd the combination initially seems, the game works both as arcade-style horror and as typing instruction; it even maintains statistics on the player's accuracy and words per minute. Kittler, of course, would not be surprised at this close conjunction of inscription technology and gun, although the literalisation of the analogy might prove amusing. But for Spitz, the conjunction of arbitrary language and overwhelming firepower is crucial to survival. What were once parents, siblings or friends can no longer be considered as such once they succumb. As his detail commander says, 'Mustn't humanise them. The whole thing breaks down unless you are fundamentally sure that they are not you.'[42] This sort of distinction does not need to be spelled out to any Black person, or for that matter any person who is indigenous or of colour. The exact same justification has maintained slavery, colonialism, segregation, apartheid, and all the other peculiar institutions through which whiteness has preserved power.

In 'A Zombie Manifesto', Sarah Juliet Lauro and Karen Embry attempt to map the many critical conceptualisations of the zombie, including 'threatening body, brain-dead, brain eater, blindly following its own primal urges; pure necessity, anti-productive, female, avid consumer; cyborg, postcyborg, posthuman, slave, and slave rebellion'.[43] For their own part, they put forward the zombie as 'ontic/hauntic object' that, by virtue of its ambiguous status as 'being', defies the subject-object divide and implies that the only accurate way to speak of the posthuman is in the context of the anti-subjective, swarm-organism 'zombi(i)' yet to come, before suggesting in a B-movie twist ending that, not only are humans likely on their way to zombi(i) status, but they might already be zombi(i)/es, without even knowing it.[44] Lauro and Embry are careful to note that their manifesto is not suggesting the zombie as a symbol of liberation, but rather trying to problematise the nature of embodiment, of what being human means amid the global capitalist order. Other critics are less sanguine still about linguistic forms in the face of zombie direct action, claiming that zombies 'eat through the logic of metaphor ... expos[ing] the arbitrariness of all such forms', or that they are a 'blank text ... a space waiting to be filled ... vulnerable to appropriation'.[45] Why then turn zombies loose on screen or in print? Kyle William Bishop asserts that, beyond serving as 'a reflection of modern society', the zombie can act as a 'preemptive panacea' – a kind of vaccination against the bleakness of experience.[46] This vaccination can skew slightly differently, though: what specifically zombie film and literature allow for is a *simulation*, or a stress test, on portions of the ambient social and cultural network. For Spitz in particular, some form of this stress test has continually been administered since before his birth, and it determines the extent to which he is afforded his humanity.

While it may be true that, in the zombie post-apocalypse, 'the barricade is the only metaphor left', anyone who has grown up Black under modern policing (or policing of any era, for that matter) is familiar with how the distinction between alive and undead must be maintained by words as well as bullets.[47] In the novel, both are manufactured in Buffalo, the fallback position of the survivors after the loss of New York (and presumably the rest of the Atlantic corridor). There what passes for a governmental authority agrees '[e]arly in the reboot . . . on the wisdom of rebranding survival'.[48] The masterstroke of this effort is the United States becoming 'no longer mere survivors, half-mad refugees, a pathetic, shit-flecked, traumatised herd, but the "American Phoenix"', complete with logo and branded merchandise: 'as if the culture was picking up where it left off'.[49] Those sweeping through buildings are ordered to conserve ammunition, not (as in most survival horror games) because they are scarce, but because of the imperative to minimise damage to corporate property, the better to maintain the illusion of imminent rebirth. Spitz wonders if 'the old bigotries [will] be reborn as well', when the Phoenix completes its rise, concluding that, 'If they could bring back paperwork . . . they could certainly reanimate prejudice, parking tickets, and reruns. There were plenty of things in the world that deserved to stay dead, yet they walked.'[50] The culture being 'reanimated' is one that was in the process of zombification long before any literal walking corpses shambled into view.

When the already flimsy physical and metaphorical wall between living and undead falls, it falls quickly, 'as if it had been created for the very instant of its failure'.[51] The American Phoenix differs from the undead in degree, rather than kind. The language they manufacture, lacking in any cognitive content, is useless for (and complicit in) the extinction of consciousness, and yet humans continue shouting blanks into the void, as if like *Typing of the Dead* they will somehow stumble on a combination of words that will kill rather than strengthen the undead. But, as Tatjana Soldat-Jaffe concludes, 'Part of [the zombie's] power . . . is the condition of language itself as a kind of a-human living death.'[52] Mark Spitz discovers this while still on the run, prior to sweeper duty, when he finds a farmhouse occupied by survivors. The farmhouse conjoins three major media flows of the zombie apocalypse: written language, videogames and film. The house holds the entire storehouse of the English language in the form of 'an open volume of the *OED*':[53] the house's previous owner had been a professor who 'taught literary theory . . . making her mark with an evidently groundbreaking collection of essays about "The Body"'.[54] One of the other survivors, meanwhile, formerly 'script[ed] interstitial narrative sequences for a video game company that specialised in first-person shooters. In between levels, Tad's cutscenes . . . allowed players to rest their thumbs. A respite in their quest through the carnage.'[55] Tad even has plans to gamify the post-apocalypse, with levels starting 'in a fortified farmhouse in the middle of the country' and moving on to 'towns, cities, each step more complicated and deadly than the last'. Tad's logic is Buffalo's logic: challenges can be met and overcome; normality can be restored. But as shown by the setting, borrowed from *Night of the Living Dead*, such narrative respites cannot last: the carnage will return, the house will be overrun, not to mention the towns and cities; as Aaron Jaffe writes, the zombie's ultimate victory is guaranteed by demographics.[56] Unlike Romero's film, the black protagonist here survives the military posse – only to find himself swallowed up into their ranks and assigned a new name.

As Mark Spitz tells the story, that cognomen comes from an incident where, faced with an overwhelming number of the undead on a bridge, instead of jumping to the water below, he chooses to shoot his way out in videogame-hero fashion: 'He could not die' kicking around his head; he thinks as he fires that 'This was his world now . . . He was a mediocre man. . . . Now the world was mediocre, rendering him perfect.'[57] When his cohort finds out that he did not make the jump because he could not swim, they fix the name 'Mark Spitz' on him; only later, as he is telling the story to a dying colleague, does he speculate that it might refer more generally to 'the black-people-can't-swim thing'.[58] And with that death in front of him, and the failure of the actual and metaphorical walls separating living from undead, Spitz comes to recognise that 'whatever the next thing was, it would not look like what came before': the Phoenix vision of restoration and rebirth is impossible and undesirable.[59] '[T]he barrier holds until you don't need it anymore', he thinks, and in this thought might be the ultimate solution, if it is such, to the *Chaoskampf* of *Zone One*.[60] Spitz embraces what he as character has a been given – a name, a situation and a reserve of mediocrity – and sets out to inscribe his own narrative upon a mediocre world. Rather than getting gunned down at a farmhouse, or dragged down by the undead, Mark Spitz exits the narrative refusing to bear the burden of narrative closure so often placed on the suffering black body:[61] 'Fuck it, he thought. You have to learn how to swim sometime. He opened the door and walked into the sea of the dead.'[62] Mark Spitz no longer needs the barrier, and so discards it, along with the discourse it was built to protect. That world expires when the words on the page expire – whatever sort of inscription system follows, the world will not look like what came before. Amid the actual ruins of civilisation, separated from the zombi/i swarm now only by linguistic conventions whose uselessness is revealed in the moment, Mark Spitz withdraws his efforts from the continuation of humanity as it was, choosing instead the possibility of survival amid humanity as it might yet be. And in so doing, he leaves open the possibility of writing himself into the new world to come.

Notes

1. Derek C. Maus, *Understanding Colson Whitehead* (Columbia: University of South Carolina Press, 2014), p. 113.
2. Nikesh Shukla, 'Colson Whitehead: Each Book an Antidote', *Guernica*, 24 April 2013, *https://www.guernicamag.com/daily/colson-whitehead-each-book-an-antidote* (accessed 15 February 2022).
3. David Naimon, 'Q + A: Colson Whitehead', *Tin House*, 21 September 2012, *web.archive.org/web/20161023204908/http://www.tinhouse.com/blog/16941/q-and-a-colson-whitehead.html* (accessed 15 February 2022).
4. Kimberly Fain, *Colson Whitehead: The Postracial Voice of Contemporary Literature* (Lanham: Rowman & Littlefield, 2015), p. 137.
5. *28 Days Later*, dir. Danny Boyle, Fox Searchlight (2002).
6. Jonathan McNamara, 'Zombie Fatigue: 4 Signs the Undead Have Jumped the Re-Animated Shark', *The Phoenix New Times*, 29 October 2010, *http://www.phoenixnewtimes.com/arts/zombie-fatigue-4-signs-the-undead-have-jumped-the-re-animated-shark-6572773* (accessed 15 February 2022).
7. On Whitehead's genre commitments in *Zone One* specifically, see Tim Lanzendörfer, 'The Politics of Genre Fiction: Colson Whitehead's *Zone One*', *C21 Literature*, 3/1 (2014).
8. Colson Whitehead, *Zone One* (New York: Doubleday, 2011), p. 5. See further Aaron Jaffe's 'Zombie Demographics', in Edward P. Comentale and Aaron Jaffe (eds), *The Year's Work at the Zombie Research Center* (Bloomington: Indiana University Press, 2014), pp. 106–11.
9. Whitehead, *Zone One*, p. 5.
10. Whitehead, *Zone One*, pp. 7, 9.
11. Whitehead, *Zone One*, p. 9.
12. Whitehead, *Zone One*, p. 26.
13. Friedrich Kittler, *Gramophone, Film, Typewriter* (Stanford: Stanford University Press, 1999), p. 5.
14. Plato, *Republic, Complete Works*, in trans. Alexander Nehemas and Paul Woodruff (Indianapolis: Hackett Publishing, 1997), p. 1200.
15. Jacques Derrida, 'Dissemination', in Vincent B. Leitch (ed.), *The Norton Anthology of Theory & Criticism* (New York: Norton Books, 2010), p. 1729.

16. Derrida, 'Dissemination', p. 1733; Kittler, *Gramophone, Film, Typewriter*, p. 4
17. N. Katherine Hayles, 'Virtual bodies and flickering signifiers', October 66 (1993), 69–91, 73–8.
18. *Night of the Living Dead*, dir. George A. Romero, Continental Distributing, USA (1968).
19. See N. Katherine Hayles, *How We Became Posthuman* (Chicago: University of Chicago Press, 1999), pp. 25–49.
20. Derrida, 'Dissemination', p. 1733.
21. N. Katherine Hayles, *Chaos Bound* (New York: Cornell University Press, 2018).
22. Tony Burgess, *Pontypool Changes Everything* (Toronto: ECW Press, 1998). For an alternate perspective on zombies and linguistic slippage, see Linda Flores Ohlsen's 'The Zombie as a Pronoun', in Joe Trotta, Zlatan Filipovic and Houman Sadri (eds), *Broken Mirrors: Representations of Apocalypses and Dystopias in Popular Culture* (New York: Routledge, 2019).
23. Seth Grahame-Smith and Jane Austen, *Pride and Prejudice and Zombies* (Philadelphia: Quark Books, 2009), p. 12.
24. Whitehead, *Zone One*, p. 14.
25. Whitehead, *Zone One*, p. 184.
26. Whitehead, *Zone One*, pp. 108, 186.
27. Whitehead, *Zone One*, p. 187.
28. Kittler, *Gramophone, Film, Typewriter*, p. 183.
29. Whitehead, *Zone One*, p. 185.
30. This counters the suggestion made in Tim Lanzendörfer's *Books of the Dead: Reading the Zombie in Contemporary Literature* (Jackson: University Press of Mississippi, 2018) that, 'In lieu of race, the novel frames Mark Spitz through a different, and new, identity category: his mediocrity', p. 173.
31. *Mavis Beacon Teaches Typing*, Software Toolworks, 1997.
32. Mike Pearl, 'What's Mavis Beacon Up To These Days? Nothing. She's Fake', *Vice*, 24 August 2015, *http://www.vice.com/read/whats-mavis-beacon-up-to-these-days-nothing-shes-fake-926* (accessed 15 February 2022).
33. William R. Macklin, 'Supertypist Mavis Beacon is a Creation of Marketing', *The Seattle Times*, 19 November 1995, *https://archive.seattletimes.com/archive/?date=19951119&slug=2153259* (accessed 15 February 2022). Macklin's article is possibly the first of a long line in which one tech journalist or another rediscovers the fact that Mavis Beacon was a marketing fabrication; see for instance J. D. Biersdorfer's *New York Times* piece, 'Next Time They'll Say Betty Crocker isn't Real, Either', 31 December 1998, *http://www.nytimes.com/1998/12/31/technology/next-they-ll-say-betty-crocker-*

isn-t-real-either.html (accessed 15 February 2022), which appears to have been carried out independently.

34. See Shannon Rose Riley's *Performing Race and Erasure: Cuba, Haiti, and US Culture 1898–1940* (London: Palgrave, 2016), for searing accounts of how American constructions of Haiti fed both racism at home and Duvalier's *noirisme* abroad.
35. Macklin, 'Supertypist Mavis Beacon is a Creation of Marketing'.
36. Biersdorfer, 'Next They'll Say Betty Crocker isn't Real, Either'.
37. As Yahweasel – the videogame streamer whose video seems to be the only playthrough of the first edition online – remarks: 'Is this what people typed in 1987?!' 'Let's Play *Mavis Beacon Teaches Typing*', *YouTube*, 12 February 2014, https://www.youtube.com/watch?v=DQ3B1PUwr0I (accessed 15 February 2022).
38. Information on the history of typing instruction is sparse, and worthy of future study, particularly as debate about touch-typing has revived of late, when students trained on smartphones tend to be most adept at index-finger 'hunt and peck' or thumb-typed texts. See Anna Maria Feit, Daryl Weir and Antti Oulasvirta, 'How We Type: Movement Strategies and Performance in Everyday Typing', *Proceedings of the ACM Conference on Human Factors in Computing Systems, CHI 2016*, http://userinterfaces.aalto.fi/how-we-type/ (accessed 15 February 2022).
39. Stephen M. Shuller, 'Keyboarding in Elementary Schools: Curricular Issues', August 1989, http://www.stager.org/keyboarding.html (accessed 15 February 2022).
40. Except, that is, for the 'stragglers', who (as opposed to the more traditionally zombified 'skels') cling to some activity or location from before, the mindless repetitions of their lives then carrying over into their afterlives as well. They are perhaps summed up in the mailroom worker that Mark Spitz's team finds gazing perpetually into a copy machine that will never again reproduce language (Whitehead, *Zone One*, p. 100).
41. *The Typing of the Dead*, WOW Entertainment (1999).
42. Whitehead, *Zone One*, p. 195.
43. Sarah Juliet Lauro and Karen Embry, 'A Zombie Manifesto: The Nonhuman Condition in the Era of Advanced Capitalism', *boundary 2*, 35/1 (2008), 105–6.
44. Lauro and Embry, 'A Zombie Manifesto', 88, 108 (see also p. 90).
45. Edward P. Comentale and Aaron Jaffe, 'Introduction', in Edward P. Comentale and Aaron Jaffe (eds), *The Year's Work at the Zombie Research Center* (Bloomington: Indiana University Press, 2014), p. 14; Paul Manning, 'Zombie Fans and Digital Cultures', in Laura Hubner, Marcus Leaning and Paul

Manning (eds), *The Zombie Renaissance in Popular Culture* (London: Routledge, 2015), p. 164.
46. Kyle William Bishop, *American Zombie Gothic: The Rise and Fall (and Rise) of the Walking Dead in Popular Culture* (Jefferson: McFarland, 2010), p. 106.
47. Whitehead, *Zone One*, p. 121.
48. Whitehead, *Zone One*, p. 98.
49. Whitehead, *Zone One*, p. 99.
50. Whitehead, *Zone One*, p. 288.
51. Whitehead, *Zone One*, p. 275.
52. Tatjana Soldat-Jaffe, 'Zombie Linguistics', in Edward P. Comentale and Aaron Jaffe (eds), *The Year's Work at the Zombie Research Center* (Bloomington: Indiana University Press, 2014), p. 387. Harking back again here to *Pontypool*, in this case the Bruce McDonald-directed film (Maple Pictures, 2009), in which the zombie virus is explicitly linguistic in both cause and effect, transmitted not through wounds but through the significations of speech; only the 'meaningless' can be withstood. The auto-generated kill-phrases in *The Typing of the Dead* would, by that standard, suffice; see the 2016 Summer Games Done Quick playthrough by peaches__, including 'goldfish chewing gum', 'Pyramids are amazing' and 'Phonically obscene words' ('*Typing of the Dead* by peaches__ in 31:14 – SGDQ 2016', *YouTube*, 9 July 2016, https://www.youtube.com/watch?v=3KTB5_DRQ9o (accessed 15 February 2022).
53. Whitehead, *Zone One*, p. 211.
54. Whitehead, *Zone One*, p. 213.
55. Whitehead, *Zone One*, p. 217.
56. Jaffe, 'Zombie Demographics', p. 102.
57. Whitehead, *Zone One*, pp. 182–3.
58. Whitehead, *Zone One*, p. 287.
59. Whitehead, *Zone One*, p. 320.
60. Whitehead, *Zone One*, p. 322.
61. An exhaustive list of this cliché and its variations may be found at the TV Tropes page 'Black Dude Dies First', *TVTropes.org.*, http://tvtropes.org/pmwiki/pmwiki.php/Main/BlackDudeDiesFirst (accessed 15 February 2022).
62. Whitehead, Zone One, p. 322.

Bibliography

#Alive, dir. Il Cho, South Korea (2020).
28 Days Later, dir. Danny Boyle, Fox Searchlight, DVD (2002).
Abbott, Stacey, *Undead Apocalypse: Vampires and Zombies in the 21st Century* (Edinburgh: Edinburgh University Press, 2016).
Addison, Heather, *Hollywood and the Rise of Physical Culture* (Abingdon: Routledge, 2003).
Alderman, Naomi, 'There's No Morality in Exercise: I'm a Fat Person and Made a Successful Fitness App', *Medium* (2015), *https://medium.com/matter/i-really-love-my-fat-body-eca64ca3ec78* (accessed 11 April 2019).
Allen, Robert F., Cassandra Jens and Theodore J. Wendt, 'When Zombies Attack, We Can Survive!', *Letters in Biomathematics*, 1/2 (2014), 173–80.
Amityville Horror, dir. Stuart Rosenberg, USA (1979).
An, Jinsoo, *Parameters of Disavowal: Colonial Representation in South Korean Cinema* (Berkeley: University of California Press, 2018).
Asara, Viviana and Emanuele Profumi and Giorgos Kallis, 'Degrowth, Democracy and Autonomy', *Environmental Values*, 22/2 (2013), 217–39.
Ashforth, Blake E. and Glen E. Kreiner, '"How Can You Do It?" Dirty Work and the Challenge of Constructing a Positive Identity', *Academy of Management Review*, 24/3 (1999), 413–34.
Athanassiou, Emilia et al., 'The Modern Gaze of Foreign Architects Travelling to Interwar Greece: Urban Planning, Archaeology, Aegean Culture, and Tourism', *Heritage*, 2/2 (2019), 1117–35.

Atwood, Margaret and Naomi Alderman, 'The Happy Zombie Sunrise Home', 24 October 2012, *https://www.wattpad.com/story/2426517-the-happy-zombie-sunrise-home* (accessed 15 February 2022).

Balun, Chas, *Lucio Fulci: Beyond the Gates* (Key West: Blackest Heart Books, 1996).

Banham, Tom, 'How to Survive the Apocalypse', *Men's Health* (2016), *https://www.menshealth.com/uk/adventure/a749837/how-to-survive-the-apocalypse/* (accessed 22 May 2019).

Barad, Karen, *Meeting the Universe Halfway: Quantum Physics and the Entanglement of Matter and Meaning* (Durham: Duke University Press, 2007).

Barrell, John, 'The Public Prospect and the Private View', in John Barrell (ed.), *The Birth of Pandora: And the Division of Knowledge* (London: Palgrave Macmillan, 1992), pp. 41–61.

Barthes, Roland, *Camera Lucida* [1980] (Sun Prairie: Vintage, 2000).

Bazin, André, 'The Ontology of the Photographic Image', in Hugh Gray (ed.), *What is Cinema? Vol. 1* (Berkeley: University of California Press, 1967), pp. 4–9.

Beckham, Susan G. and Michael Harper, 'Functional Training: Fad or Here to Stay?', *ACSM's Health & Fitness Journal*, 14/6 (2010), 24–30.

Benjamin, Walter, *The Arcades Project* [1999] (Cambridge, MA: Harvard University Press, 2002).

Benson, John, 'Ruth Roche and the Iger Studio', in Greg Sadowski, John Benson and Basil Woverton (eds), *Four-Color Fear: Forgotten Horror Comics of the 1950s* (Seattle: Fantagraphics Books, 2017), p. 299.

Benson-Allott, Caetlin, *Killer Tapes and Shattered Screens: Video Spectatorship from VHS to File Sharing* (Berkeley: University of California Press, 2013).

Berger, Peter L. and Thomas Luckmann, *The Social Construction of Reality: A Treatise in the Sociology of Knowledge* (London: Penguin, 1991).

Beriatos, Elias and Aspa Gospodini, '"Glocalising" Urban Landscapes: Athens and the 2004 Olympics', *Cities*, 21/3 (2004), 187–202.

'Beware the Undead!', *Diary of Horror*, 1 (December 1952), Avon.

The Beyond [*E tu vivrai nel terrore! L'aldilà*], dir. Lucio Fulci, Medusa Distribuzione, Los Angeles (1981).

Biersdorfer, J. D., 'Next They'll Say Betty Crocker Isn't Real, Either', *The New York Times*, 31 December 1998, *http://www.nytimes.com/1998/12/31/technology/next-they-ll-say-betty-crocker-isn-t-real-either.html* (accessed 15 February 2022).

Birth of the Living Dead, dir. Rob Kuhns, Glass Eye Pix/Predestinate Productions, New York (2012).

Bishop, Kyle William, *How Zombies Conquered Popular Culture* (Jefferson: McFarland, 2015).

———, *American Zombie Gothic: The Rise and Fall (and Rise) of the Walking Dead in Popular Culture* (Jefferson: McFarland, 2010).

———, 'The Idle Proletariat: Dawn of the Dead, Consumer Ideology, and the Loss of Productive Labor', *The Journal of Popular Culture*, 43/2 (2010), 234–48.

———, and Angela Tenga (eds), *The Written Dead: Essays on the Literary Zombie* (Jefferson: McFarland, 2017).

'Black Dude Dies First', *TVTropes.org*, http://tvtropes.org/pmwiki/pmwiki.php/Main/BlackDudeDiesFirst (accessed 15 February 2022).

Black, Rebecca W., 'Access and Affiliation: The Literacy and Composition Practices of English-Language Learners in an Online Fanfiction Community', *Journal of Adolescent & Adult Literacy*, 49/2 (2005), 118–28.

Black, Stephen, 'Profit Maximization: Economics "Zombie Concept"', *South African Journal of Economics*, 3/7 (1968), 264–7.

Blackman, Lisa, *The Body* (Albany: Berg, 2008).

———, '"Loving The Alien": A Post–Post-Human Manifesto', *Subjectivity*, 10/1 (2017), 13–25.

Blake, Linnie, *The Wounds of Nations: Horror Cinema, Historical Trauma and National Identity* (Manchester: Manchester University Press, 2008).

Boccia, Michael, 'Versions (Con-, In-, and Per-) in Manuel Puig's and Hector Babenco's *Kiss of the Spider Woman*, Novel and Film', *Modern Fiction Studies*, 32/3 (1986), 417–26.

Boluk, Stephanie and Wylie Lenz (eds), *Generation zombie: Essays on the living dead in modern culture* (Jefferson: McFarland, 2011).

Boon, Kevin Alexander, 'Ontological Anxiety Made Flesh: The Zombie in Literature, Film and Culture', in Niall Scott (ed.), *Monsters and the Monstrous: Myths and Metaphors of Enduring Evil* (Amsterdam: Rodopi, 2007), pp. 33–60.

Borowicz, Jan, 'Holocaust Zombies: Mourning and Memory in Polish Contemporary Culture', in Diana Popescu and Tanja Schult (eds), *Revisiting Holocaust Representation in the Post-Witness Era* (London: Palgrave Macmillan, 2015), pp. 132–48.

Botting, Fred, 'Undead-Ends: Zombie Debt/Zombie Theory', *Postmodern Culture*, 23/3 (2013), *doi:10.1353/pmc.2013.0043*.

Bourdieu, Pierre, 'The Forms of Capital', in Nicole Woolsey Biggart (ed.), *Readings in Economic Sociology* (Malden: Blackwell, 2002), pp. 280–91.

Bowyer, Justin (ed.), *The Cinema of Japan and Korea* (London: Wallflower Press, 2004).

Boy Eats Girl, dir. Stephen Bradley, Element Films, Vancouver (2005).

Brabazon, Tara, 'Don't Fear the Reaper? The Zombie University and Eating Braaaains', *KOME*, 4/2 (2016), 1–16.

Braidotti, Rosi, *The Posthuman* (London: Polity Press, 2013).
—, *Posthuman Knowledge* (London: Polity Press, 2019).
Braudy, Leo, *Haunted: On Ghosts, Witches, Vampires, Zombies, and Other Monsters of the Natural and Supernatural Worlds* (New Haven: Yale University Press, 2016).
Brereton, Pat, 'Cultural and Visual Responses to Climate Change: Ecological Reading of Irish Zombie Movies', in David Robbins, Diarmiud Torney and Pat Brereton (eds), *Ireland and the Climate Crisis* (New York: Springer International Publishing AG, 2020), pp. 185–201.
Bride, Amy, 'Mindless Consumers: Zombies, Subprime Borrowers, and the 2008 Financial Crash', *Theorizing Zombiism Conference*, University College Dublin (2019).
British Board of Film Classification, 'Zombie-Flesh-Eaters', *https://bbfc.co.uk/releases/zombie-flesh-eaters-1970-3* (accessed 11 July 2019).
Brooks, Max, *The Zombie Survival Guide: Complete Protection from the Living Dead* (New York: Broadway Books, 2003).
Brown, Jeffrey A., 'Gender and the Action Heroine: Hardbodies and the Point of No Return', *Cinema Journal* (1996), 52–71.
'Buck Farrel', *Crown Comics*, 6 (summer 1946), Golfing Inc.
Burgess, Tony, *Pontypool Changes Everything* (Toronto: ECW Press, 1998).
Byron, George Gordon, *The Works of Lord Byron; in Verse and Prose. Including his Letters, Journals, etc. with a Sketch of His Life*, ed. Fitz Greene Halleck (New York: George Dearborn, 1836).
Cahill, Susan, 'A Girl Is a Half-Formed Thing? Girlhood, Trauma, and Resistance in Post-Tiger Irish Literature', *Lit: Literature Interpretation Theory: Recessionary Imaginings II: Post-Celtic Tiger Ireland and Contemporary Women's Writing*, 28/2 (2017), 153–71.
Cairns, John, 'Reparations for Environmental Degradation and Species Extinction: A Moral and Ethical Imperative for Human Society', *ESEP* (2003), 25–32.
Campbell, Melissa, 'Survival Rules of Zombieland: Finals Edition', *The Odyssey* (2016), *https://www.theodysseyonline.com/survival-rules-of-zombieland-finals-edition* (accessed 11 May 2019).
Cargo, dir. Ben Howling and Yolanda Ramke, Umbrella Entertainment (2017).
Castoriadis, Cornelius, 'Anthropology, Philosophy, Politics', *Thesis Eleven*, 49/1 (1997), 99–116.
—, 'Democracy as Procedure and Democracy as Regime', *Constellations*, 4/1 (1997), 1–18.
—, 'Power, Politics, Autonomy', in Axel Honneth et al. (eds), *Cultural-political Interventions in the Unfinished Project of Enlightenment* (Cambridge: The MIT Press, 1992), pp. 269–98.

——, The Imaginary Institution of Society, trans. Kathleen Blarney (London: Polity Press, 1987).
—— and Sergio Benvenuto, 'A Conversation between Sergio Benvenuto and Cornelius Castoriadis', in *European Journal of Psychoanalysis*, 6, trans. Joan Tambureno (1998), *http://www.psychomedia.it/jep/number6/castoriadis2.htm* (accessed 19 May 2019).
'Canyon of the Living Dead', *The Hand of Fate*, 8 (December 1951), Humor Publications.
'Careless Corpse', *Fantastic Fears*, 8 (July 1953), Four Star Publishing.
Carey, M. R., The Boy on the Bridge (London: Orbit, 2017).
——, *The Girl with All the Gifts* (London: Orbit, 2014).
Cavaliere, Jeff, '8 Best Exercises for the Zombie Apocalypse (Be Ready!)', *YouTube.com* (2016), *https://www.youtube.com/watch?v=1i3bU5zV8sI* (accessed 14 May 2019).
Cholodenko, Alan, *The Illusion of Life: Essays on Animation* (Sydney: Power Publications, 1991).
Chow, Broderick D. V., 'A Professional Body: Remembering, Repeating and Working out Masculinities in *fin-de-siècle* Physical Culture', *Performance Research*, 20/5 (2015), 30–41.
Christensen, Kyle, 'The Reparative Bite of the Zombie Mouth', *The Velvet Light Trap*, 85 (2020), 4–15.
Christie, Deborah and Sarah Juliet Lauro (eds), *Better off Dead: The Evolution of the Zombie as Post-human* (New York: Fordham University Press, 2011).
Christie, Ian, The Last Machine (London: BBC Education, 1995).
Chung, Hye Jean, 'An Economy of Bodily Violence: Fragmented Bodies and Porous Borders in Korean Cinema', *Journal of Popular Film and Television*, 47/1 (2019), 30–8.
City of the Living Dead [*Paura nella città dei morti viventi*], dir. Lucio Fulci, Medusa Distribuzione, Troy, MI (1980).
'Claire Redfield Workout Routine: Train like the Resident Evil TerraSave Member', *SuperheroJacked.com* (2019), *http://superherojacked.com/2019/04/02/claire-redfield-workout/* (accessed 12 May 2019).
Clark, Andy, 'What Reaching Teaches: Consciousness, Control, and the Inner Zombie', *The British Journal for the Philosophy of Science*, 58/3 (2007), 563–94.
Clarke, Kamari Maxine, 'Beyond Genealogies: Expertise and Religious Knowledge in Legal Cases Involving African Diasporic Publics', *Transforming Anthropology*, 25/2 (2017), 130–55.
CMAA, Comic Book Code (1954), *https://en.wikisource.org/wikiComic_book_code_of_1954*.

Cocarla, Sasha, 'A Love Worth Un-Undying For: Neoliberalism and Queered Sexuality in Warm Bodies', in Shaka McGlotten and Steve Jones (eds), *Zombies and Sexuality: Essays on Desire and the Living Dead* (Jefferson: McFarland, 2014), pp. 52–72.

Cohen, Jeffrey Jerome, *Monster Theory: Reading Culture* (Minneapolis: University of Minnesota Press, 1996).

Cohen, Shlomo, 'The Ethics of De-Extinction', *Nanoethics*, 8 (2014), 165–78.

Colebrook, Claire, *Death of the PostHuman: Essays on Extinction Vol. 1* (Ann Arbor: Open Humanities Press, 2014).

——, 'Extinction Theory', in Jane Elliott and Derek Attridge (eds), *Theory After Theory* (London: Routledge, 2011), pp. 62–72.

Comentale, Edward P., 'Zombie Race', in Sarah Juliet Lauro (ed.), *Zombie Theory: A Reader* (Minneapolis: University of Minnesota Press, 2017), pp. 189–211.

Comentale, Edward P. and Aaron Jaffe (eds), *The Year's Work at the Zombie Research Center* (Bloomington: Indiana University Press, 2014).

Connell, Robert W. and James W. Messerschmidt, 'Hegemonic Masculinity: Rethinking the Concept', *Gender & Society*, 19/6 (2005), 829–59.

Cooper, S. and Joe Blair, 'Mr. Justice', *Jackpot Comics*, 1 (September 1941), M. L. J. Magazines Inc.

Corradino, Anna Chiara, 'Performing Necrophilia', *Whatever. A Transdisciplinary Journal of Queer Theories and Studies*, 3 (2020), 373–400.

Corbett, Stephen et al., 'The Transition to Modernity and Chronic Disease: Mismatch and Natural Selection', *Nature Reviews Genetics*, 19 (2018), 419–30.

Couch, Christina, 'Zombie Workout: Get Fit Enough to Fit the Undead', *Wired.com* (2010), https://www.wired.com/2010/05/st-zombie-workout/ (accessed 29 April 2019).

Courlander, Harold, 'Musical Instruments of Haiti', *The Musical Quarterly*, 27/3 (1941), 371–83.

Craig, Johnny, 'Zombie Terror', *Moon Girl*, 5 (fall 1948), EC.

Crawford, Jamie, 'Pentagon Document Lays Out Battle Plan Against Zombies', *CNN* (2014), https://www.cnn.com/2014/05/16/politics/pentagon-zombie-apocalypse/ (accessed 12 May 2019).

Creed, Barbara, *The Monstrous-Feminine: Film, Feminism, Psychoanalysis* (London: Routledge, 2012).

——, *Phallic Panic: Film, Horror and the Primal Uncanny* (Victoria: Melbourne University Publishing, 2005).

Crow, Charles L., 'Southern American Gothic', in Jeffrey Andrew Weinstock (ed.), *The Cambridge Companion to American Gothic* (Cambridge: Cambridge University Press, 2017), pp. 141–55.

—— (ed.), *A Companion to American Gothic* (West Sussex: Wiley Blackwell, 2014).
Crowley, Martha et al., 'Neo-Taylorism at Work: Occupational Change in the Post-Fordist Era', *Social Problems*, 57/3 (2010), 421–47.
The Cured, dir. David Freyne, Tilted Pictures/Bac Films/Savage Productions, Ireland (2017).
Curti, Roberto, *Italian Gothic Horror Films, 1980–1989* (Jefferson: McFarland, 2019).
Dachis, Adam, 'Zombies, Run! Turns Your Exercise Routine into a Game of Survival', *LifeHacker* (2012), *https://lifehacker.com/zombies-run-turns-your-exercise-routine-into-a-game-o-5892625* (accessed 15 April 2019).
Dalton, Russell, 'Citizenship Norms and the Expansion of Political Participation', *Political Studies*, 56 (2008), 76–98.
Danziger, Kurt, *Naming the Mind: How Psychology Found Its Language* (London: Sage, 1997).
Davis, Wade, *Passage of Darkness: The Ethnobiology of the Haitian Zombie* (Chapel Hill: University of North Carolina Press, 1988).
——, *The Serpent and the Rainbow* (New York: Simon & Schuster, 1985).
——, 'The Ethnobiology of the Haitian Zombi', *Journal of Ethnopharmacology*, 9/1 (1983), 85–104.
Davis-Goff, Sarah, *Last Ones Left Alive* (London: Tinder Press, 2019).
——, 'I Have Created the Kind of Novel I Wanted to See in the World', *The Irish Times* (2019), *https://www.irishtimes.com/culture/books/writing-the-novel-you-want-to-see-in-the-world-1.3806951* (accessed 10 April 2021).
Dawn of the Dead, dir. George A. Romero, Laurel Group Inc., USA (1978).
Dawson, Marcelle C., 'CrossFit: Fitness Cult or Reinventive Institution?', *International Review for the Sociology of Sport*, 52/3 (2017), 361–79.
Day of the Dead, dir. George A. Romero, united Film Distributing Company, USA (1985).
Day of the Dead: Bloodline, dir. Hector Hernandez, Saban Capital Group, USA (2018).
de Mendonça, João Paulo A., Leonardo M. V. Teixeira, Fernando Sato and Lohan R. N. Ferreira, 'Modeling a Hypothetical Zombie Outbreak Can Save Us from Real-World Monsters', *The Mathematical Intelligencer*, 41/3 (2019), 72–9.
Dead Meat, dir. Conor McMahon, Three Way Productions, Ireland (2004).
Dead Murphy, dir. Stephen McCollum, Raw Nerve Productions, Beverly Hills (2006).
Deleuze, Gilles, *Cinema 2: The Time-Image*, trans. Hugh Tomlinson and Robert Galeta, 5th printing [1989] (Minneapolis: University of Minnesota Press, 1997).

Demetriou, Demetrakis Z., 'Connell's Concept of Hegemonic Masculinity: A Critique', *Theory and Society*, 30/3 (2001), 337–61.

Dendle, Peter, 'The Zombie as Barometer of Cultural Anxiety', in Niall Scott (ed.), *Monsters and the Monstrous: Myths and Metaphors of Enduring Evil* (Amsterdam: Rodopi, 2007), pp. 45–57.

Derrida, Jacques, 'Dissemination', in Vincent B. Leitch (ed.), *The Norton Anthology of Theory & Criticism* (New York: Norton Books, 2010), pp. 1697–734.

Descartes, Rene, *Discourse on the Method* [1637] (Peterborough: Cosimo Classics 1924).

Dines, Gail, *Pornland: How Porn Has Hijacked Our Sexuality* (Boston: Beacon Press, 2010).

Drezner, Daniel W., 'Metaphor of the Living Dead: Or, the Effect of the Zombie Apocalypse on Public Policy Discourse', *Social Research*, 81/4 (2014), 825–49.

Duncan, Isadora, *My Life* [1927] (New York: Liveright Publishing, 2013).

Dworkin, Shari L. and Faye Linda Wachs, *Body Panic: Gender, Health, and the Selling of Fitness* (New York: New York University Press, 2009).

Dying Light, Techland, Warner Bros., Interactive Entertainment (2015).

Eaton, George, 'Haitian Magic', *Social Forces*, 19/1 (1940), 95–100.

Erdgasen, Sophus O. S. E. zu et al., 'Ecosystem Service Responses to Rewilding: First-Order Estimates from 27 Years of Rewilding in the Scottish Highlands', *International Journal of Biodiversity Science, Ecosystem, Services & Management*, 14/1 (2018), 165–78.

Fain, Kimberly, *Colson Whitehead: The Postracial Voice of Contemporary Literature* (Lanham: Rowman & Littlefield, 2015).

Fandrich, Ina J., 'Yoruba Influences on Haitian Vodou and New Orleans Voodoo', *Journal of Black Studies*, 37 (2007), 775–91.

'FAQ', *Zombie Experiences UK* (2019), http://zombieexperiences.co.uk/frequently-asked-questions/ (accessed 7 June 2019).

Fear, David, 'Zombie Apocalypse Now: "Night of the Living Dead" at 50', *Rolling Stone* (2018), https://www.rollingstone.com/movies/movie-features/night-of-the-living-dead-50-anniversary-730207/ (accessed 18 May 2019).

Fehrle, Johannes, '"Zombies Don't Recognize Borders": Capitalism, Ecology, and Mobility in the Zombie Outbreak Narrative', *Amerikastudien/American Studies*, 61/4 (2016), 527–44.

Feit, Anna Maria, Daryl Weird and Antti Oulasvirta, 'How We Type: Movement Strategies and Performance in Everyday Typing', *Proceedings of the ACM Conference on Human Factors in Computing Systems, CHI 2016*, http://userinterfaces.aalto.fi/how-we-type/ (accessed 15 February 2022).

Fennell, Jack, *Rough Beasts: The Monstrous in Irish Fiction, 1800–2000* (Oxford: Liverpool University Press, 2019).

Fischer-Hornung, Dorothea and Monika Mueller, *Vampires and Zombies: Transcultural Migrations and Transnational Interpretations* (Jackson: University Press of Mississippi, 2016).

Fojas, Camilla, *Zombies, Migrants, and Queers: Race and Crisis Capitalism in Pop Culture* (Urbana, Chicago: University of Illinois Press, 2017).

Foucault, Michel, *Discipline and Punish* (New York: Penguin, 1991).

Frawley, Oona, *Irish Pastoral: Nostalgia and Twentieth-century Irish Literature* (Dublin: Irish Academic Press, 2005).

Freud, Sigmund, 'A Disturbance of Memory on the Acropolis', in *The Complete Psychological Works of Sigmund Freud*, ed. James Strachey, vol. XXII (London: Hogarth Press, 1964), pp. 237–48.

——, 'The Uncanny', in *The Standard Edition of the Complete Psychological Works of Sigmund Freud, Vol. 17*, ed. and trans. James Strachey et al. (London: The Hogarth Press, 1955), pp. 217–56.

Fromm, Erich, T*he Anatomy of Human Destructiveness* (London: Random House, 1973).

Gallant, Thomas W., *Modern Greece: From the War of Independence to the Present*, 2nd edn (London: Bloomsbury Academic, 2016).

Game of Thrones, dir. David Benioff and Daniel Brett Weiss, HBO (2011–19).

Gandini, Alessandro, 'Digital work: Self Branding and Social Capital in the Freelance Knowledge Economy', *Marketing Theory*, 16/1 (2016), 123–41.

García, Ana Dols, 'New Issues in Refugee Research' (Policy Development and Evaluation Service United Nations High Commissioner for Refugees, October 2013).

Garrett, Greg, *Living with the Living Dead: The Wisdom of the Zombie Apocalypse* (Oxford: Oxford University Press, 2017).

Genz, Stéphanie, 'My Job is Me', *Feminist Media Studies*, 15/4 (2015), 545–61.

Gershon, Ilana, '"I'm not a businessman, I'm a business, man": Typing the neoliberal self into a branded existence', *Hau: Journal of Ethnographic Theory*, 6/3 (2016), 223–46.

Giddens, Anthony, *Beyond Left and Right: The Future of Radical Politics* (London: Polity Press, 1994).

Gill, Rosalind and Andy Pratt, 'In the Social Factory? Immaterial Labour, Precariousness and Cultural Work', *Theory, Culture & Society*, 25/7–8 (2008), 1–30.

The Girl with All the Gifts, dir. Colm McCarty, BFI, London (2016).

Goddu, Teresa A., *Gothic America: Narrative, History, and Nation* (New York: Columbia University Press, 1997).

Godfrey-Smith, Peter, *Other Minds: The Octopus and the Evolution of Intelligent Life* (London: William Collins, 2016).

Goldstein, Bennet, 'I've been Fitbit by a Zombie', *Telegraph Herald* (2018), http://www.telegraphherald.com/news/features/article_17b4dc65-94b6-51b0-a768-c5e56c79e990.html (accessed 2 April 2019).

Gorky, Maxim [I. M. Pacatus], 'A Review of the Lumière Program at the Nizhni-Novgorod Fair, as printed in the *Nizhegorodski Listok*' (4 July 1896), in Colin Harding and Simon Popple (eds), *In the Kingdom of Shadows: A Companion to Early Cinema* (London: Cygnus Arts, 1996), p. 5.

Gould, Deirdre, *After the Cure*, narrated by Miles Taber (Audible, 2016).

Graham, Elaine, *Representations of the Posthuman* (Manchester: Manchester University Press, 2002).

Grahame-Smith, Seth, and Jane Austen, *Pride and Prejudice and Zombies* (Philadelphia: Quark Books, 2009).

Grant, Mira, *Newsflesh* (London: Orbit, 2010–12).

Griggs, Yvonne, *The Bloomsbury Introduction to Adaptation Studies* (London: Bloomsbury, 2016).

Grosrichard, Alain, *The Sultan's Court: European Fantasies of the East* [1979] (London: Verso, 1998).

'Green Lantern', *All-American Comics*, 61 (October 1944), DC.

Gumpert, Matthew, 'The Hollow Men: Towards a Zombie Semiotics', *The Journal of Popular Culture*, 53/2 (2020), 303–26.

Güzeldere, Güven, 'Zombies', in Lynn Nadel et al. (eds), *Encyclopedia of Cognitive Science*, vol. 4 (New York: John Wiley & Sons, 2006), pp. 593–5.

Hamilton, Scott Eric, 'The Girl with All the Gifts: Eco-Zombiism, Critical Lucidity, and the Anthropocalypse', *LIT: Literature, Interpretation, Theory*, 32/4 (2021), 285–304.

Hannabach, Cathy, 'Queering and Cripping the End of the World: Disability, Sex, and Race in *The Walking Dead*', in Shaka McGlotten and Steve Jones (eds), *Zombies and Sexuality: Essays on Desire and the Living Dead* (Jefferson: McFarland, 2014), pp. 106–22.

Haraway, Donna, *The Haraway Reader* (London: Routledge, 2003).

Harding, Colin and Simon Popple (eds), I*n the Kingdom of Shadows: A Companion to Early Cinema* (London: Cygnus Arts, 1996).

Hardt, Michael and Antonio Negri, *Empire* (Cambridge: Harvard University Press, 2000).

Harper, Stephen, 'Zombies, Malls, and the Consumerism Debate: George Romero's *Dawn of the Dead*', *Americana: The Journal of American Popular Culture*, 1/2 (2002), http://www.americanpopularculture.com/journal/articles/fall_2002/harper.htm(accessed 5 October 2017).

Harrison, Rebecca, 'Inside the Cinema Train: Britain, Empire, and Modernity in the Twentieth Century', *Film History*, 26/4 (2014), 32–57.
'Hating Corpse', *Horrific*, 4 (March 1953), Harwell Publications.
Haughey, Anthony, 'Settlement', *http://anthonyhaughey.com/projects/settlement/* (accessed 5 January 2021).
——, 'A Landscape of Crisis', *The Canadian Journal of Irish Studies*, 40 (2017), 53–71.
Hayles, N. Katherine, *Chaos Bound* (New York: Cornell University Press, 2018)
——, *How We Became Posthuman* (Chicago: The University of Chicago Press, 1999).
——, 'Virtual bodies and flickering signifiers', October 66 (1993), 69–91.
Heffernan, Conor, 'The Apocalypse Workout: Health, Identity and Zombies', *Theorizing Zombiism Conference*, University College Dublin (2019).
Heller-Nicholas, Alexandra, *Suspiria* (Leighton Buzzard: Devil's Advocates, 2015), Kindle edition.
Herbrechter, Stefan and Ivan Callus (eds), *Post-Theory, Culture, Criticism* (Amsterdam: Rodopi, 2004).
Herskovits, Melville Jean, *Life in a Haitian Valley* (Princeton: Markus Wiener Publishers, 2007).
Herzfeld, Michael, 'The Absent Presence: Discourses of Crypto-Colonialism', *South Atlantic Quarterly*, 101/4 (2002), 899–926.
——, *Anthropology through the Looking-Glass: Critical Ethnography in the Margins of Europe* (Cambridge: Cambridge University Press, 1987).
Heywood, Leslie, 'We're in This Together: Neoliberalism and the Disruption of the Coach/Athlete Hierarchy in CrossFit', *Sports Coaching Review*, 5/1 (2016), 116–29.
——, *Bodymakers: A Cultural Anatomy of Women's Body Building* (New Brunswick: Rutgers University Press, 1998).
'The Horror of the Haunted Cathedral', *Marvel Mystery Comics*, 28 (February 1942), timely.
The House by the Cemetery [*Quella villa accanto al cimitero*], dir. Lucio Fulci, Medusa Distribuzione, New York (1981).
The House of the Dead 2, WOW Entertainment (1998).
Howard, Robert E., 'Pigeons from Hell', *Weird Tales* (May 1938), 534–53.
Howlett, Mike, *The Weird World of Eerie Publications: Comic Gore that Warped Millions of Young Minds!* (Port Townsend: Feral House, 2000).
Hubner, Laura, 'Archiving Gore: Who Owns Zombie Flesh Eaters?', in Laura Hubner, Marcus Leaning and Paul Manning (eds), *The Zombie Renaissance in Popular Culture* (London: Palgrave, 2015), pp. 41–55.
——, Marcus Leaning and Paul Manning (eds), *The Zombie Renaissance in Popular Culture* (Basingstoke: Palgrave Macmillan, 2014).

Hunt, Lynn, *The Invention of Pornography, 1500–1800: Obscenity and the Origins of Modernity* (New York: Zone Books: 2007).
Hutcheon, Linda, *A Theory of Adaptation* (London Routledge, 2006).
HybridAthlete, 'Fitness for the Zombie Apocalypse', *HybridAthlete.com* (2017), *https://thehybridathlete.com/zombies-eat-fat-people/* (accessed 17 May 2019).
Hyman, Stanley Edgar, 'The War is Simply "a Zombie War of Sleep-walkers", Some Notes on John Steinbeck', *The Antioch Review*, 2/2 (1942), 185–200.
I am Legend, dir. Francis Lawrence, Village Roadshow Pictures (2007).
I Walked with a Zombie, dir. Jacques Tourner, RKO Radio Pictures, USA (1943).
Irish Folklore Commission, *Schools' Folklore Scheme*, 141 (1937–9), 213.
——, *Schools' Folklore Scheme*, 864 (1937–9), pp. 138–9.
——, *Schools' Folklore Scheme*, 668 (1937–9), p. 383.
iZombie, dir. Diane Ruggiero-Wright, Rob Thomas, creators, Warner Bros USA (2015–2019).
Jackpot Comics, 1 (September 1941), MLJ Magazines Inc.
Jacquet, Jennifer et al., 'The Case Against Octopus Farming', *Issues in Science and Technology*, 35/2 (2019), 37–44.
Jakobsen, Annette Svaneklink, 'Experience In-between Architecture and Context: The New Acropolis Museum, Athens', *Journal of Aesthetics & Culture*, 4/1 (2012), *https://doi.org/10.3402/jac.v4i0.18158* (accessed 21 May 2019).
James, Henry, *The Turn of the Screw and Other Stories* (London: Vintage, 2007).
Jensen, Robert, 'Pornography is What the End of the World Looks Like', in Karen Boyle (ed.), *Everyday Pornography* (New York: Routledge, 2010), pp. 105–13.
Jentsch, Ernst, 'On the Psychology of the Uncanny (1906)', *Angelaki: Journal of the Theoretical Humanities*, 2/1 (1997), 7–16.
Jones, Nick, *Hollywood Action Films and Spatial Theory* (Abingdon: Routledge, 2015).
Jones, Steve, 'Porn of the Dead Necrophilia, Feminism, and Gendering the Undead', in Cory Rushton and Christopher Moreman (eds), *Zombies Are Us: Essays on the Humanity of the Walking Dead* (Jefferson: McFarland, 2011), pp. 40–60.
Joseph, Celucien L., 'The Problem and Impossibility of Vodou Religion in the Writings of Dantès Bellegarde', *The Journal of Pan African Studies*, 6/8 (2014), 204–28.
Jowett, Lorna, '"I got a new kill poncho": *Santa Clarita Diet* and the Pleasures of Zombie Embodiment', *Theorizing Zombiism Conference*, University College Dublin (2019).
Kabat-Zinn, Jon, 'Mindfulness-based Interventions in Context: Past, Present, and Future', *Clinical Psychology: Science and Practice*, 10/2 (2006), 144–56.

Kee, Chera, 'No Grave Can Hold Them: *Night of the Living Dead* and the Rise and Rebirth of Zombies in Comics', in Bruce Peabody and Gloria Pastorino (eds), *Beyond the Living Dead: Zombies and the Romero Legacy* (Jefferson: McFarland, 2021), pp. 32–55.

———, *Not Your Average Zombie: Rehumanizing the Undead from Voodoo to Zombie Walks* (Austin: University of Texas Press, 2017).

Kelly, Daniel, *Yuck! The Nature and Moral Significance of Disgust* (Cambridge, MA: The MIT Press, 2011).

Kendall, Erike Nicole, 'How to Survive a Zombie Invasion', *A Black Girl's Guide to Weight Loss* (2011), *https://blackgirlsguidetoweightloss.com/exercise-101/how-to-survive-a-zombie-invasion/* (accessed 12 May 2019).

Kendrick, Walter, T*he Secret Museum: Pornography in Modern Culture* (Berkeley: University of California Press, 1987).

Kenemore, Scott, *Zombie-in-Chief* (New York: Talos, 2017).

Khan, Ali S., 'Run For Your Lives', *CDC.com* (2012), *https://blogs.cdc.gov/publichealthmatters/2012/03/run-for-your-lives/* (accessed 13 May 2019).

Kim, Jaecheol, 'Biocalyptic imaginations in Japanese and Korean films: undead nation-states in *I Am a Hero* and *Train to Busan*', *Inter-Asia Cultural Studies*, 20/3 (2019), 437–51.

Kirby, Peadar, 'When Banks Cannibalize the State: Responses to Ireland's Economic Collapse', *Socialist Register*, 48/48 (2011), 249–68.

———, 'Development Theory and the Celtic Tiger', *European Journal of Development Research*, 16/2 (2004), 301–28.

Kirk, Robert, 'Reply to Don Locke on Zombies and Materialism', *Mind*, 86/342 (1977), 262–4.

———, 'Sentience and Behaviour', *Mind*, 83 (1974), 43–60.

Kirkman, Robert et al., *The Walking Dead* (Image, 2003–19).

Kirsh, Steven J., *Parenting in the Zombie Apocalypse* (Jefferson: McFarland, 2019).

Kitchin, Rob, Rory Hearne and Cian O'Callaghan, 'Housing in Ireland: From Crisis to Crisis', *SSRN Scholarly Paper*, Rochester, NY: Social Science Research Network (17 February 2015), *https://papers.ssrn.com/abstract=2566297* (accessed 10 April 2021).

Kittler, Friedrich, *Gramophone, Film, Typewriter* (Stanford: Stanford University Press, 1999).

Kligler-Vilenchik, Neta, 'Alternative citizenship models: Contextualizing new media and the new "good citizen"', *New Media & Society*, 19/11 (2017), 1887–903.

Knickerbocker, Daniel, 'Why Zombies Matter: The Undead as Critical Posthumanist', *bohemica litteraria*, 18 (2015), 59–82.

Kovacs, Judith and Christopher Rowland, *Revelation: The Apocalypse of Jesus Christ* (Oxford: Blackwell Publishing, 2004).

Kristeva, Julia, *Powers of Horror: An Essay on Abjection* (New York: Columbia University Press, 1982).

Kuhling, Carmen Leah, 'Zombie Banks, Zombie Politics and the "Walking Zombie Movement": Liminality and the Post-crisis Irish Imaginary', *European Journal of Cultural Studies*, 20/4 (2017), 397–412.

Kyrölä, Katariina, *The Weight of Images: Affect, Body Image and Fat in the Media* (London: Routledge, 2014).

Lamb, Matthew D. and Hillman, Cory, 'Whiners Go Home: Tough Mudder, Conspicuous Consumption, and the Rhetorical Proof of Fitness', *Communication & Sport*, 3/1 (2015), 81–99.

Lanzendörfer, Tim, 'The Politics of Genre Fiction: Colson Whitehead's *Zone One*', *C21 Literature*, 3/1 (2014).

Land of the Dead, dir. George A. Romero, Universal Pictures, USA (2005).

Lanzendörfer, Tim, *Books of the Dead: Reading the Zombie in Contemporary Literature* (Jackson: University Press of Mississippi, 2018).

Larned, Ben, 'Forbidden Tomes: Books to Films – the Literary Influences on Lucio Fulci', *Daily Dead* (2017), *https://dailydead.com/forbidden-tomes-book-to-film-the-literary-influences-on-lucio-fulci/* (accessed 12 July 2019).

Larsen, Kristine, '"Nightmare Horrors and Perils of the Night": Zombies and Modern Science', *The Irish Journal of Gothic and Horror Studies*, 12 (2013), 44–62.

Larsen, Lars Bang, 'Zombies of Immaterial Labor: The Modern Monster and the Death of Death', in Sarah Juliet Lauro (ed.), *Zombie Theory: A Reader* (Minneapolis: University of Minnesota Press, 2017), pp. 157–70.

Lauro, Sarah Juliet, 'Ron Honthaner's *House on Skull Mountain*: Zombie Gothic', in Simon Bacon (ed.), *The Gothic: A Reader* (Oxford: Peter Lang, 2018), pp. 69–76.

—— (ed.), *Zombie Theory: A Reader* (Minneapolis: University of Minnesota Press, 2017).

——, *The Transatlantic Zombie: Slavery, Rebellion, and Living Death* (New Jersey: Rutgers University Press, 2015).

—— and Karen Embry, 'A Zombie Manifesto: The Nonhuman Condition in the Era of Advanced Capitalism', *boundary 2*, 35/1 (2008), 85–108.

Lavin, Mary, 'The Dead Soldier', in David Marcus (ed.), *The Poolbeg Book of Irish Ghost Stories* (Dublin: Poolbeg, 1993), pp. 61–79.

——, 'The Green Grave and the Black Grave', in Peter Haining (ed.), *Great Irish Stories of the Supernatural* (New York: Pan Books, 1993), pp. 362–78.

Lawson, Roger, 'The Zombie Apocalypse: Friends Don't Let Friends Get Eaten', *Rog Law Fitness* (2012), *http://roglawfitness.com/zombie-apocalypse-survival-workout/* (accessed 2 April 2019).

Le Corbusier, *Towards a New Architecture* (New York: Dover Publications, 1986).

Le Fanu, Sheridan, *Ghost Stories of Chapelizod* (Dublin: Good Press, 2020).

LeCapois, Teejay, *Vampire's Guide to the Zombie Apocalypse* (New York: Lulu, 2019).

Lee, Hyangjin, *Contemporary Korean Cinema: Culture, Identity, and Politics* (Manchester: Manchester University Press, 2013).

Lee, Sangjoon (ed.), *Rediscovering Korean Cinema* (Ann Arbor: University of Michigan Press, 2019).

Lefebvre, Henri, *Writings on Cities*, ed. Eleonore Kofman and Elizabeth Lebas (New York: Blackwell Publishers, 1996).

Legauldt, J., 'Zombie bacteria', *Recherche*, 4/38 (1972), 898–900.

Lelwica, Michelle Mary, *Shameful Bodies: Religion and the Culture of Physical Improvement* (New York: Bloomsbury Publishing, 2017).

Lending, Mari, 'Negotiating Absence: Bernard Tschumi's New Acropolis Museum in Athens', *The Journal of Architecture*, 23/5 (2018), 797–819.

Lever, Charles, 'The Mountain Pass', in *Weird Tales: Irish* [1843] (Edinburgh: William Paterson, 1886), pp. 144–5 (also listed as *Irish Weird Tales*).

Lewis, C. S., *The Problem of Pain* (New York: Harper Collins, 2009).

Liu, Dong, Sarah Ainsworth and Roy Baumeister, 'A meta-analysis of social networking online and social capital', *Review of General Psychology*, 20/4 (2016), 369–91.

Lobell, Jarrett A., 'A New Home for the Treasures of the Acropolis', *Archaeology* (2009), 32–7.

Long, Christian B., 'Infrastructure after the Zombie Apocalypse', *Journal of Asia-Pacific Pop Culture*, 1/26 (2016), 181–203.

Longridge, Chris, 'Why Zombies Have Taken Over Pop Culture', *DigitalSpy* (2017), *https://www.digitalspy.com/tv/a827385/why-zombies-have-taken-over-pop-culture/* (accessed 26 May 2019).

Lopes, Paul Douglas, *Demanding Respect: The Evolution of the American Comic* (Philadelphia: Temple University Press, 2009).

Loughlin, Elaine, 'Over 250 Ghost Estates Still Haunting Ireland', *Irish Examiner* (7 March 2018), *https://www.irishexaminer.com/news/arid-20467973.html* (accessed 19 January 2021).

Loukaki, Argyro, 'Whose Genius Loci? Contrasting Interpretations of the "Sacred Rock of the Athenian Acropolis"', *Annals of the Association of American Geographers*, 87/2 (1997), 306–29.

Lovecraft, H. P., 'The Dunwich Horror', in T*he Call of Cthulhu and Other Weird Tales* (New York: Vintage, 2011), pp. 99–153.
Luckhurst, Roger, *Zombie: A Cultural History* (London: Reaktion Books, 2018).
Lynch, Colum, 'Rebranding Haiti: The Voodoo Tours', *Foreign Policy* (26 September 2011), *https://foreignpolicy.com/2011/09/26/rebranding-haiti-the-voodoo-tours/* (accessed 15 May 2018).
Lynch, Rachael, 'Gina and the Kryptonite: Mortgage Shagging in Anne Enright's *The Forgotten Waltz*', *Lit: Literature, Interpretation, Theory*, 28/2 (2017), 115–33.
Lyons, Joseph, '"The Pawnbroker": A Study of the Flashback in Novel and Film', *Western Humanities Review*, 20/3 (1966), 243–8.
Lyons, Mary E., *Sorrow's Kitchen: The Life and Folklore of Zora Neale Hurston* (New York: Simon & Schuster, 1993).
M., Daryl, 'Interview with an Author: Sarah Davis Goff', Los Angeles Public Library, *https://www.lapl.org/collections-resources/blogs/lapl/interview-author-sarah-davis-goff* (accessed 18 January 2021).
MacCormack, Patricia, 'Zombies without Organs: Gender, Flesh and Fissure', in Shawn McIntosh and Marc Leverette (eds), *Zombie Culture: Autopsies of the Living Dead* (Lanham: The Scarecrow Press, 2008), pp. 87–102.
Macdonald, Charlotte, *Strong, Beautiful and Modern: National Fitness in Britain, New Zealand, Australia and Canada, 1935–1960* (Vancouver: UBC Press, 2013).
McCall, Pete, 'How Can I Physically Prepare for a Zombie Apocalypse', *Ace Fitness* (2012), *https://www.acefitness.org/education-and-resources/lifestyle/blog/2940/how-can-i-physically-prepare-for-a-zombie-apocalypse* (accessed 15 April 2019).
McCullick, Bryan et al., 'Butches, Bullies and Buffoons: Images of Physical Education Teachers in the Movies', *Sport, Education and Society*, 8/1 (2003), 3–16.
McDermott, Andy, 'The Zombie Apocalypse Survival Workout', *Muscle and Fitness* (2015), *https://www.muscleandfitness.com/workouts/workout-routines/zombie-apocalypse-survival-workout* (accessed 15 April 2019).
McGlotten, Shaka and Steve Jones (eds), *Zombies and Sexuality: Essays on Desire and the Living Dead* (Jefferson: McFarland, 2014).
McGlotten, Shaka and Sarah Vangundy, 'Zombie Porn 1.0: Or, Some Queer Things Zombie Sex Can Teach Us', *Qui Parle: Critical Humanities and Social Sciences*, 21/2 (2013), 101–25.
McIntosh, Shawn and Marc Leverette (eds), *Zombie Culture: Autopsies of the Living Dead* (Lanham: Scarecrow Press, 2008).
McKenzie, Shelly, *Getting Physical: The Rise of Fitness Culture in America* (Kansas: University Press of Kansas, 2013).

Macklin, William R., 'Supertypist Mavis Beacon is a Creation of Marketing', *The Seattle Times*, 19 November 1995, https://archive.seattletimes.com/archive/?-date=19951119&slug=2153259 (accessed 15 February 2022).

McLuhan, Marshall, *Understanding Media: The Extensions of Man* (Cambridge, MA: The MIT Press, 1994).

McNally, David, 'Ugly Beauty: Monstrous Dreams of Utopia', in Sarah Juliet Lauro (ed.), *Zombie Theory: A Reader* (Minneapolis: University of Minnesota Press, 2017), pp. 124–36.

McNamara, Jonathan, 'Zombie Fatigue: 4 Signs the Undead Have Jumped the Re-Animated Shark', *The Phoenix New Times*, 29 October 2010, http://www.phoenixnewtimes.com/arts/zombie-fatigue-4-signs-the-undead-have-jumped-the-re-animated-shark-6572773 (accessed 15 February 2022).

McNeal, Richard A., 'Archaeology and the Destruction of the Later Athenian Acropolis', *Antiquity*, 65/246 (1991), 49–63.

McWilliams, David, 'A Warning from Deserted Ghost Estates', http://www.davidmcwilliams.ie/a-warning-from-deserted-ghost-estates/ (accessed 3 November 2020).

Manning, Paul, 'Zombie Fans and Digital Cultures', in Laura Hubner, Marcus Leaning and Paul Manning (eds), *The Zombie Renaissance in Popular Culture* (London: Routledge, 2015), pp. 160–73.

Maus, Derek C., *Understanding Colson Whitehead* (Columbia: University of South Carolina Press, 2014).

Marion, Isaac, *Warm Bodies* (New York: Atria Books, 2010).

Marks, Laura Helen, '"I Eat Brains . . . or Dick": Sexual Subjectivity and the Hierarchy of the Undead in Hardcore Film', in Shaka McGlotten and Steve Jones (eds), *Zombies and Sexuality: Essays on Desire and the Living Dead* (Jefferson: McFarland, 2014), pp. 159–79.

Markula, Pirkko, 'The Technologies of the Self: Sport, Feminism, and Foucault', *Sociology of Sport Journal*, 20/2 (2003), 87–107.

Marx, Karl, *Grundrisse: Foundations of the Critique of Political Economy* (Rough Draft), trans. Martin Nicolaus, 23rd edn [1973] (New York: Penguin Books, 1993).

——, *Early Writings*, trans. Rodney Livingstone and Gregor Benton [1975] (New York: Penguin Books, 1992).

Mavis Beacon Teaches Typing, Software Toolworks, 1987.

Meehan, Paul, *Horror Noir: Where Cinema's Dark Sisters Meet* (Jefferson: McFarland, 2011).

Mendoza, Kerry-Anne, *Austerity: The Demolition of the Welfare State and the Rise of the Zombie Economy* (Oxford: New Internationalist, 2014).

Métraux, Alfred, *Voodoo*, trans. Hugo Charteris, 2nd edn (London: Sphere Books, 1974).
Miéville, China, 'M. R. James and the Quantum Vampire: Weird; Hauntological; Versus and/or and and/or or?', *Collapse: Journal of Philosophical Research and Development*, IV (2008), 105–28.
'Milla Jovovich Workout Routine and Diet Plan: Train like Leeloo, Alice, The Blood Queen and Artemis', *SuperheroJacked.com* (2019), http://superhero-jacked.com/2019/04/11/milla-jovovich-workout/ (accessed 14 April 2019).
Miller, Susan, *Disgust: The Gatekeeper Emotion* (New York: Routledge, 2013).
Miller, Thaddeus R. et al., 'The New Conservation Debate: The View from Practical Ethics', *Biological Conservation*, 144 (2011), 948–57.
Miller, William Ian, *The Anatomy of Disgust* (Cambridge, MA: Harvard University Press, 1997).
Mintz, Sidney and Michel-Rolph Trouillot, 'The Social History of Haitian Vodou', in Donald J. Cosentino (ed.), *Sacred Arts of Haitian Vodou* (California: University of California Museum, 1995), pp. 123–47.
Mitchell, Audra, 'Beyond Biodiversity and Species: Problematizing Extinction', *Theory, Culture & Society*, 33/5 (2015), 23–42.
Moon, Jerred, 'Are You Fit Enough to Survive a Zombie Apocalypse?', *End of Three Fitness* (2012), http://www.endofthreefitness.com/are-you-fit-enough-to-survive-a-zombie-apocalypse/ (accessed 11 May 2019).
Moulier Boutang, Yann, *Cognitive Capitalism* (London: Polity Press, 2011).
Muchembled, Robert, *Orgasm and the West: A History of Pleasure from the 16th Century to the Present* (New York: Polity, 2008)
Mulligan, Rikk, 'Zombie Apocalypse: Plague and the End of the World in Popular Culture', in Karolyn Kinane and Michael A. Ryan (eds), *End of Days: Essays on the Apocalypse from Antiquity to Modernity* (Jefferson: McFarland, 2009), pp. 349–68.
Mulvey, Laura, *Death 24x a Second: Stillness and the Moving Image* (London: Reaktion Books, 2006).
Muno, Wolfgang, 'Winter Is Coming? *Game of Thrones* and Realist Thinking', in Ulrich Hamenstädt (ed.), *The Interplay between Political Theory and Movies* (Cham: Springer, 2019), pp. 135–49.
Munz, Philip, Ioan Hudea, Joe Imad and Robert J. Smith, 'When Zombies Attack! Mathematical Modelling of an Outbreak of Zombie Infection', in Jean Michel Tchuenche and Christinah Chiyaka (eds), *Infectious Disease Modelling Research Progress* (Hauppauge, NY: Nova Science Publishers, Inc., 2009), pp. 133–50.
Murphy, Bernice, *The Suburban Gothic in American Popular Culture* (London: Palgrave, 2009).

Murray, Padmini Ray, 'Gender, Nation and Embodiment in Byron's Poetry' (unpublished PhD thesis, University of Edinburgh, 2008).

Naimon, David, 'Q + A: Colson Whitehead', *Tin House*, 21 September 2012, *web.archive.org/web/20161023204908/http://www.tinhouse.com/blog/16941/q-and-a-colson-whitehead.html* (accessed 15 February 2022).

Nemerov, Alexander, *Icons of Grief: Val Lewton's Home Front Pictures* (Berkeley: University of California Press, 2005).

NerdFitness, 'How to Survive a Zombie Apocalypse', *NerdFitness* (2011), *https://www.nerdfitness.com/blog/how-to-survive-a-zombie-apocalypse/* (accessed 2 May 2019).

Newbury, Michael, 'Fast Zombie/Slow Zombie: Food Writing, Horror Movies, and Agribusiness Apocalypse', *American Literary History*, 24/1 (2012), 87–114.

Ng, Andrew Hock Soon, 'Undead Identities: Asian American Literature and the Gothic', in Charles L. Crow (ed.), *A Companion to American Gothic* (West Sussex: Wiley Blackwell, 2014), pp. 249–63.

Night of the Living Dead, dir. George A. Romero, Continental Distributing, USA (1968).

'Nuggets for Travellers' series, vol. 7 (Edinburgh and London: William Paterson, 1886), pp. 136–52.

Nussbaum, Martha, *Hiding from Humanity: Disgust, Shame, and the Law* (New Jersey: Princeton University Press, 2009).

Nye, Robert A., 'Western Masculinities in War and Peace', *The American Historical Review*, 112/2 (2007), 417–38.

Ó Cadhain, Máirtín, *Graveyard Clay*, trans. Liam Mac Con Iomaire and Tim Robison (New Haven: Yale University Press, 2016).

——, *The Dirty Dust/Cré na Cille* (New Haven: Yale University Press, 2015).

O'Connell, Frederick [as 'Conall Cearnach'], 'The Homing Bone', in David Marcus (ed.), *The Poolbeg Book of Irish Ghost Stories* [1924] (Dublin: Poolbeg Press Ltd, 1993), pp. 14–25.

O'Hearn, Michael, *Zombies vs. Mummies: Clash of the Living Dead* (Mankato: Capstone Press, 2011).

Ohlsen, Linda Flores, 'The Zombie as a Pronoun', in Joe Trotta, Zlatan Filipovic and Houman Sadri (eds), *Broken Mirrors: Representations of Apocalypses and Dystopias in Popular Culture* (New York: Routledge, 2019)

'Orchids from the Dead', *The Hand of Fate*, 17 (April 1953), A. A. Wyn, Inc.

Orpana, Simon, 'Spooks of Biopower: The Uncanny Carnivalesque of Zombie Walks', *TOPIA: Canadian Journal of Cultural Studies*, 25 (2011), 153–76.

The Otago Witness, 'Horrible Superstition of the Vandoux Heretics, or Snakeworshippers of Haiti', in *Otago Witness* (29 October 1864).

Ouanga, dir. Terwilliger, George Terwilliger Productions, California (1936).

Overlord, dir. J. J. Abrams, Warner Bros., USA (2018).

Papastathis, Charalambos K., 'The Hellenic Republic and the Prevailing Religion', *BYU Law Review*, 4 (1996), 815–52.

Paquet, Darcy, *New Korean Cinema: Breaking the Waves* (London: Wallflower Press, 2009).

Parker, Joe, 'How Prostitution Works', in Christine Stark and Rebecca Whisnant (eds), *Not For Sale* (Melbourne: Spinifex, 2004).

Peaches__, '*Typing of the Dead* by peaches__ in 31:14 – SGDQ 2016', *YouTube*, 9 July 2016, *https://www.youtube.com/watch?v=3KTB5_DRQ9o* (accessed 15 July 2016).

Pearl, Mike, 'What's Mavis Beacon Up To These Days? Nothing. She's Fake', *Vice*, 24 August 2015, *http://www.vice.com/read/whats-mavis-beacon-up-to-these-days-nothing-shes-fake-926* (accessed 15 February 2022).

Peck, Jamie, 'Zombie Neoliberalism and the Ambidextrous State', *Theoretical Criminology*, 14/1 (2010), 104–10.

Peterson, Christopher, *Monkey Trouble: The Scandal of Posthumanism* (New York: Fordham University Press, 2018).

Petley, Julian, 'The Unfilmable? H. P. Lovecraft and the Cinema', in Richard J. Hand and Jay McRoy (eds), *Monstrous Adaptations: Generic and Thematic Mutations in Horror Film* (Manchester: Manchester University Press, 2007), pp. 35–47.

Petmezas, Socrates, 'History of Modern Greece', in *About Greece* (Athens: Hellenic Ministry of Press and Mass Media-Secretariat General of Information, 2001), pp. 17–43.

Philippides, Dimitris, 'The Phantom of Classicism in Greek Architecture', in *A Singular Antiquity – 3rd Supplement* (Athens: Benaki Museum, 2008), pp. 375–82.

Plantzos, Dimitris, 'Behold the Raking Geison: The New Acropolis Museum and its Context-Free Archaeologies', *Antiquity*, 85/328 (2011), 613–25.

Plato, *Republic, Complete Works*, trans. Alexander Nehemas and Paul Woodruff (Indianapolis: Hackett Publishing, 1997).

Poe, Edgar Allen, 'The Black Cat', *The United States Saturday Post*, 19 August 1843, 1.

Pontypool, dir. Bruce McDonald. Maple Pictures, DVD (2009).

Potter, Amy E., 'Voodoo, Zombies, and Mermaids: U.S. Newspaper Coverage of Haiti', *Geographical Review*, 99/2 (2010).

Psycho, dir. Alfred Hitchcock, Paramount Pictures, USA (1960).

Queen, Carol, *Real Live Nude Girl: Chronicles of Sex-Positive Culture* (New Jersey: Cleis Press, 2002).

Quiggin, John, *Zombie Economics: How Dead Ideas Still Walk Among Us* (Princeton: Princeton University Press, 2010).

Quinn, Daniel, 'She-Devil Otherness and the Last Hieroglyph: Reclaiming the Cosmic in Clark Ashton Smith's "Zothique Cycle"', *Eldritch Dark* (2007), http://www.eldritchdark.com/articles/criticism/72/she-devil-otherness-and-the-last-hieroglyph%3A-reclaiming-the-cosmic-in-clark-ashton-smith%E2%80%99s-%27zothique-cycle%27 (accessed 12 July 2019).

Radley, Emma, 'Violent Transpositions: The Disturbing "Appearance" of the Irish Horror Film', in Claire Bracken and Emma Radley (eds), *Viewpoints, Theoretical Perspectives on Irish Visual Texts* (Cork: Cork University Press, 2013).

Raun, Tobias, 'Capitalizing Intimacy: New Subcultural Forms of Microcelebrity Strategies and Affective Labour on YouTube', *Convergence: The International Journal of Research into New Media Technologies*, 24/1 (2018), 99–113.

Return of the Living Dead, dir. Dan O'Bannon, Orion Pictures, USA (1985).

Revenge of the Zombies, dir. Steve Sekely, Monogram Pictures, USA (1943).

Riley, Rose, *Performing Race and Erasure: Cuba, Haiti, and US Culture 1898–1940* (London: Palgrave, 2016),

Robbins, David, Diarmuid Torney and Pat Brereton, *Ireland and the Climate Crisis* (New York: Springer International Publishing AG, 2020).

Roden, David, *Posthuman Life* (London: Routledge, 2015).

Roberts, Steven V., 'Greece Striving to Protect Acropolis from Pollution and Tourists', *The New York Times* (19 February 1975), 6.

Romaniello, John, 'The End is About to Begin', *Roman Fitness Systems* (2012), http://romanfitnesssystems.com/articles/zombie-apocalypse/ (accessed 2 May 2019).

Rose, Nikolas, *Inventing our Selves: Psychology, Power, and Personhood* (Cambridge: Cambridge University Press, 1998).

Røssaak, Eivind, *The Still/Moving Image: Cinema and the Arts* (Sunnyvale: LAP Lambert Academic Publishing, 2010).

Rozin, Paul et al., 'Individual differences in disgust sensitivity: Comparisons and evaluations of paper-and-pencil versus behavioral measures', *Journal of Research in Personality*, 33/3 (1999), 330–51.

Rubin, Gayle, *Deviations: A Gayle Rubin Reader* (Durham: Duke University Press, 2011).

Ruthven, Andrea, 'Pride and Prejudice and Post-Feminist Zombies', in Maria Alonso Alonso, Jeannette Bello Mota, Alba de Béjar Muíños and Laura Torrado Mariñas (eds), *Weaving New Perspectives Together: Some Reflections on Literary Studies* (Newcastle upon Tyne: Cambridge Scholars Publishing, 2012), pp. 155–70.

Ryan, Courtney, 'At Zombie Races, It's Survival of the Undeadest', *The New York Times* (2013), https://www.nytimes.com/2013/08/01/fashion/at-zombie-races-its-survival-of-the-undeadest.html (accessed 23 May 2019).

Said, Edward W., *Orientalism* [1978] (London: Penguin Books, 2003).

Sanders, Julie, *Adaptation and Appropriation* (London: Routledge, 2016).

Sandler, Roland, 'The Ethics of Reviving Long Extinct Species', *Conservation Biology*, 28/2 (2013), 354–60.

Santa Clarita Diet, dir. Victor Fresco, Kapital Entertainment, Netflix, USA (2017–19).

Sarrazin, François and Jane Lecomte, 'Evolution in the Anthropocene', *Science*, 351/6276 (2016), 922–3.

Schneider, Lambert, 'A Journey through Times and Cultures? Ancient Greek Forms in American Nineteenth-Century Architecture: An Archaeological View', *Economic History Working Papers*, 28/08 (London School of Economics and Political Science Department of Economic History, April 2008), pp. 1–59.

Schudson, Michael, *The Good Citizen: A History of American Civic Life* (Cambridge, MA: Harvard University Press, 1998).

Scottish Government, 'Scottish Biodiversity Strategy', https://www.gov.scot/policies/biodiversity/scottish-biodiversity-strategy/ (accessed 21 September 2019).

'The Scourge of the Undead', *The Beyond*, 18 (January 1953), Unity Publishing Corp.

Seabrook, William, *The Magic Island* (Mineola: Courier Dover Publications, 2016).

Shaun of the Dead, dir. Edgar Wright, WT2, UK (2004).

Shaviro, Steven, 'Contagious Allegories: George Romero', in Sarah Juliet Lauro (ed.), *Zombie Theory: A Reader* (Minneapolis: University of Minneapolis Press, 2017), pp. 7–19.

Shildrick, Margrit, *Leaky Bodies and Boundaries: Feminism, Postmodernism and (Bio)ethics* (London: Routledge: 1997).

Shuen Chan, Rain, 'The Family Trouble in Post-Millennial Zombie Cinema: The Father-Hero in *I Am Legend* (2007) and *World War Z* (2013)', *Theorizing Zombiism Conference*, University College Dublin (2019).

Shukla, Nikesh, 'Colson Whitehead: Each Book an Antidote', *Guernica*, 24 April 2013, https://www.guernicamag.com/daily/colson-whitehead-each-book-an-antidote (accessed 15 February 2022).

Shuller, Stephen M., 'Keyboarding in Elementary Schools: Curricular Issues', August 1989, http://www.stager.org/keyboarding.html (accessed 15 February 2022).

Simpson, George Eaton, 'The Belief System of Haitian Vodun', *American Anthropologist*, 47/1 (1945), 35–59.

Singer, Peter (ed.), *A Companion to Ethics* (London: Blackwell, 1993).

Smith, Clarissa and Feona Attwood, 'Emotional Truths and Thrilling Slide Shows: the Resurgence of Antiporn Feminism', in Tristan Taormino, Constance Penley, Celine Parrenas Shimizu and Mireille Miller-Young (eds), *The Feminist Porn Book: The Politics of Producing Pleasure* (New York: CUNY Press, 2013), pp. 41–57.

Smith, Clark Ashton, 'The Door to Saturn', *Eldritch Dark*, http://www.eldritchdark.com/writings/short-stories/50/the-door-to-saturn (accessed 12 July 2019).

Smyth, Gerry, 'Irish National Identity after the Celtic Tiger', *Estudios Irlandeses*, 7/7 (2012), 132–7.

Sodikoff, Genese Marie, 'The Time of Living Dead Species: Extinction Debt and Futurity in Madagascar', in Paik PY and M. Wiesner-Hanks M. (eds), *Debt: Ethics, the Environment and the Economy* (Bloomington: Indiana University Press, 2013), pp. 140–63.

Soldat-Jaffe, Tatjana, 'Zombie Linguistics', in Edward P. Comentale and Aaron Jaffe (eds), *The Year's Work at the Zombie Research Center* (Bloomington: Indiana University Press, 2014), pp. 361–88.

Spellmeyer, Kurt, 'After Theory: From Textuality to Attunement with the World', *College English*, 58/8 (1996), 893–913.

Spitznagel, Eric, 'George A. Romero: Who Says Zombies Eat Brains?', *Vanity Fair*, https://www.vanityfair.com/hollywood/2010/05/george-romero (accessed 12 January 2021).

Stone, William J., 'Physical Activity and Health: Becoming Mainstream', *Complementary Health Practice Review*, 9/2 (2004), 118–28.

Strange Tales, 169–73 (September 1973–April 1974), Marvel Comics.

Stratton, Jon, 'Zombie Trouble: Zombie Texts, Bare Life and Displaced People', *European Journal of Cultural Studies*, 14/3 (2011), 265–81.

Summers, Montague, *Witchcraft and Black Magic* [1946] (London: Arrow Books Ltd, 1974).

Supervert, *Necrophilia Variations* (New York: Supervert 32C Inc., 2005).

Tales of the Zombie, 1–10 (July 1973–March 1975), Marvel Comics.

Tasker, Yvonne, *Spectacular Bodies: Gender, Genre and the Action Cinema* (Abingdon: Routledge, 2012).

Telotte, J. P., 'Narration and Incarnation: *I Walked with a Zombie*', *Film Criticism (ARCHIVE)*, 6/3 (1982), 18–31.

Thacker, Eugene, I*n the Dust of this Planet: Horror of Philosophy Volume 1* (Winchester: Zero Books, 2011).

Thibaudeau, Christian, 'Refined Physique Transformation: What if I Had to Do It All Over Again', *T-Nation* (2007), https://www.t-nation.com/workouts/refined-physique-transformation (accessed 23 May 2019).

—— and Chris Shugart, 'The Zombie Apocalypse Workout: Train to be Prepared for Anything', *T-Nation* (2015), *https://www.t-nation.com/workouts/zombie-apocalypse-workout* (accessed 29 April 2019).

Thomas, Kette, 'Haitian Zombie, Myth, and Modern Identity', *Comparative Literature and Culture*, 12/2 (2010), 1–9.

Thrower, Stephen, *Beyond Terror: The Films of Lucio Fulci* (Godalming: FAB Press, 2002).

Todorov, Tzvetan, *Imperfect Garden: The Legacy of Humanism* (Princeton: Princeton University Press, 2002).

Totaro, Donald, 'Seom/The Isle', in Justin Bowyer (ed.), *The Cinema of Japan and Korea* (London: Wallflower Press, 2004), pp. 207–16.

Toulalan, Sarah, 'Pornography, Procreation and Pleasure in Early Modern England', in Bradford K. Mudge (ed.), *The Cambridge Companion to Erotic Literature* (Cambridge: Cambridge University Press, 2017), pp. 105–22.

Tournikiotis, Panayotis (ed.), *The Parthenon and its Impact in Modern Times* (Athens: Melissa, 1996).

Train to Busan/Busanhaeng, dir. Yeon Sang-ho, Next Entertainment World, South Korea (2016).

Trombetta, Jim, *The Horror! The Horror! Comic Books the Government Didn't Want You to Read!* (New York: Abrams ComicArts, 2010).

Tudor, Andrew, 'Unruly Bodies, Unquiet Minds', *Body & Society*, 1/1 (1995) 25–41.

Tufano, Fani Mallouhou, 'Ē Anastúlōsē tōn Mnēmeíōn tēs Akrópolēs: 1975–2000 [Restoration of the Acropolis Monuments: 1975–2000]' (Athens: Greek Ministry of Culture, 1999), *https://www.culture.gr/DocLib/appendix8-gr.pdf* (accessed 10 May 2021).

Tumblety, Joan, 'Rethinking the Fascist Aesthetic: Mass Gymnastics, Political Spectacle and the Stadium in 1930s France', *European History Quarterly*, 43/4 (2013), 707–30.

Turner, Victor W., *The Ritual Process: Structure and Anti-Structure* (London: Routledge & Kegan Paul Ltd, 1969).

The Typing of the Dead, WOW Entertainment (1999).

'Under the Terms of the Banks . . .: Wednesday, 17 November 2010: Dáil Éireann Debates', *KildareStreet.com*, *https://www.kildarestreet.com/debate/?id=2010-11-17.500.0.* (accessed 5 January 2021).

Vance, Norman, 'Decadence from Belfast to Byzantium', *New Literary History*, 35/4 (2004), 563–72.

Wacquant, Loïc, *Body & Soul* (Oxford: Oxford University Press, 2004).

'Walking with the Ghosts', *Independent* (22 May 2010), *https://www.independent.ie/lifestyle/walking-with-the-ghosts-26657225.html* (accessed 3 November 2020).

Waller, Gregory A., *The Living and the Undead: Slaying Vampires, Exterminating Zombies* (Illinois: University of Illinois Press, 2010).
Warm Bodies, dir. Jonathan Levine, Mandeville Films, California (2013).
Weeks, Jeffery, *Invented Moralities: Sexual Values in an Age of Uncertainty* (New York: Columbia University Press, 1991).
Wei, M. L., 'If More People Cut Out Gluten, the Zombies Would Wake Up: The Construction of Health-related Concerns by Gluten-free Food Consumers', *British Food Journal* (2021), 1–12.
We're Alive, Wayland Productions (2009–14).
West, Caroline, 'Hashtags and Hand Wringings: Conversations on Porn in Ireland', *Porn Studies*, 6/2 (2018), 258–61.
Whelan, Andrew, Ruth Walker and Christopher Moore (eds), *Zombies in the Academy: Living Death in Higher Education* (Bristol: Intellect, 2013).
White Zombie, dir. Tod Browning, United Artists Corporation, USA (1932).
Whitehead, Colson, *Zone One* (New York: Anchor, 2012).
——, *Zone One* (New York: Doubleday, 2011).
——, *Sag Harbor* (New York: Doubleday, 2009).
——, *The Colossus of New York: A City in Thirteen Parts* (New York: Doubleday, 2003).
——, *John Henry Days* (New York: Doubleday, 2001).
——, *The Intuitionist* (New York: Doubleday, 1999).
Whitehead, Erin, 'Workout I Did: The Zombie Apocalypse Workout', *Fit Bottomed Girls* (2014), https://fitbottomedgirls.com/author/erin-whitehead/ (accessed 5 May 2019).
Wilde, Poppy, 'Zombies, Deviance, and the Right to Posthuman Life', *Theorizing Zombiism Conference*, University College Dublin (2019).
Williams, Linda, *Hardcore: Power, Pleasure, and the 'Frenzy of the Visible'* (Berkeley: University of California Press, 1989).
Winter, Katy, 'Obese Mother Lost Nearly SEVEN STONE after She Became a Fan of TV Show *The Walking Dead* and Wanted to be Fit Enough to Survive a Zombie Apocalypse', *MailOnline* (2014), https://www.dailymail.co.uk/femail/article-2821666/Obese-mother-lost-nearly-SEVEN-STONE-fan-TV-Walking-Dead-wanted-fit-survive-zombie-apocalypse.html (accessed 11 April 2019).
World War Z, dir. Marc Forster, Skydance Productions (2013).
Wylie, Turrell, 'Ro-Langs: The Tibetan Zombie', *The History of Religions*, 4/1 (1964), 69–80.
Yahweasel, 'Let's Play *Mavis Beacon Teaches Typing*', *YouTube*, 12 February 2014. https://www.youtube.com/watch?v=DQ3B1PUwr0I (accessed 15 February 2022).

Žižek, Slavoj, *The Puppet and the Dwarf: The Perverse Core of Christianity* (Cambridge, MA: The MIT Press, 2003).
Zombie! [*Zombi 2*; *Zombie Flesh Eaters*], dir. Lucio Fulci, Variety Film, Italy, US, UK (1979).
'Zombie Escape at Panic Point 5k Run to Attract 1,850 Participants', *NCHeadlines* (2012), *https://www.ncheadlines.com/releases/zombie-escape-at-panic-point-5k-mud-run-to-attract-1850-participants* (accessed 15 April 2019).
'Zombie Nutritionist Recommends All-Brain Diet', *The Onion* (2002), *https://www.theonion.com/zombie-nutritionist-recommends-all-brain-diet-1819566596* (accessed 2 May 2019).
Zombie Strippers, dir. Jay Lee, Sony Pictures Entertainment, USA (2008).
'Zombie Terror', *Moon Girl*, 5 (1948), EC.
'The Zombie WODS', *ZombieWODS.com* (2019), *http://thezombiewods.com* (accessed 25 May 2019).
Zombieland, dir. Ruben Fleischer, Columbia Pictures, USA (2009).

Index

#Alive 3, 98
9/11 106, 232
28 Days Later 40, 142, 232
50 Shades of Grey 66

Abject (abjection) 47, 59, 60, 62, 64–70, 74, 75, 97, 98, 121, 220
Abrams, J. J. (*Overlord*) 43
Acropolis 139–40, 145–8, 155, 156
adaptation 213–16, 219, 221, 224–5
Addison, Heather 47, 54
Ainsworth, Sarah 22, 33
Alderman, Naomi (*Zombies, Run!*) 44, 46, 51, 52, 53, 232
Allen, Robert F. 14
Aloha 'Oe (song) 79, 80, 88, 95
AMC (*The Walking Dead*) 49
American comics 11, 179–95
American Horror Comics 7, 11, 179–95
Angel, Joanna 9, 60
anthropocene 10, 120, 123, 129, 131, 134, 136
anthropocalypse 131, 134

anthropocentrism 27
apocalypse (survival of) 40, 45, 48, 49, 51, 125, 132, 133
Architecture (buildings, museum) 147–8, 151–3, 155, 156
Argento, Dario (*Suspiria*) 226, 229, 257
Ashforth, Blake E. and Glen E. Kreiner 74, 76
Attwood, Feona 69, 76
Atwood, Margaret 170, 232
Austen, Jane 223, 244, 256, 267; *see also* Grahame-Smith, Seth; *Pride and Prejudice and Zombies*
autonomy (the state, state apparatus) 22, 23, 148–9, 156, 157
Avengers (comic) 195
Avengers (film) 47

Bakhtin, Mikhail 28
Balun, Chas 215, 228
Barad, Karen 27, 34
Barthes, Roland 204–5, 210, 248
Baumeister, Roy 22, 33

Bazin, André 198, 205, 209, 210
Beckham, Susan 42, 53
Bellegarde, Dantès 140, 153
Benson, John 193, 248
Benson-Allott, Caetlin 198, 209
Berger, Peter L. 71, 76
The Beyond 12, 215, 221–3, 225, 226
BDSM 60
binary 30, 32, 71, 73, 94, 184, 204
biodiversity 120, 123, 125, 130, 131, 132, 134, 135
biological conservation 131, 136
Birth of the Living Dead 107, 116
Bishop, Kyle William 13, 14, 106, 114, 115, 116, 154, 214, 216, 227, 228, 240, 246
Black, Rebecca 15, 41
Black, Stephen 2, 13
Black Sunday 217
Blake, Linnie 87, 97
Blackman, Lisa 24, 34
blackness 216, 237
Boccia, Michael 13
bodies (corpses, black bodies)
Bokor 141–2, 151, 152
Bolaño, Roberto 232
borders (boundaries of) 9, 14, 59, 60, 62, 64, 65, 69, 70, 72, 74, 96, 97, 220
The Boy on the Bridge 10, 119
Bradley, Stephen 112, 116
Braidotti, Rosi 2 6, 31, 45, 35
Braudy, Leo 227, 229
Bride, Amy 250
British Board of Film Classification 228, 250
Brooks, Max (*World War Z*) 28, 29, 34, 35, 41, 80, 96, 167
  The Zombie Survival Guide 41, 52

Boutang, Yann Moulier 33
Burgess, Tony (*Pontypool Changes Everything*) 244
Byron, Lord George Gordon (*Childe Harold's Pilgrimage*) 143–4, 155, 154, 155
Byzantine Empire 144

Cairns, John 132, 136
Callus, Ivan 120, 134
camera (photography, cinematic gaze) 79, 81, 89, 203–6, 213
capitalism 3, 8, 11, 14, 21, 25, 32, 33, 35, 53, 70, 72, 86, 89, 97, 134, 154, 160, 162, 165–6, 169–71, 173, 245
  consumption 3, 32, 42, 44, 53, 70, 80, 94, 140, 142–3, 148, 152, 162–3, 227
  material production 9, 32, 42, 60, 72, 83, 124, 142, 150, 147
  use-value 125, 127
Carey, M. R. (*The Boy on the Bridge*, *The Girl with All the Gifts*) 10, 119–22, 129, 130, 132, 133, 135, 136, 137
Cargo 28, 35
Caribbean slave trade (slavery) 105, 140, 141, 143, 148, 182–5, 187, 190–2, 218, 221–2, 225, 227, 233, 240
Castoriadis, Cornelius 10, 149–52, 156, 157
Cavaliere, Jeff 48, 55
Chan, Rain Shuen 34
Christie, Ian 14, 86, 97
censorship 11, 179, 180, 186, 188, 189, 191, 192, 235, 236

chaos (chaos theory, *Chaoskampf*) 61, 83, 231
The Chessmaster 2000 237
Cholodenko, Alan 209
Chong, Annabel 65
Chow, Broderick 50, 56
Christensen, Kyle 63–4, 75
Chung, Hye Jean 84, 86, 96, 97
Chung-Hee, Park (President, Korea) 83
citizen 8, 9, 20, 22–6, 32, 33, 43, 83, 90, 152, 162
City of the Living Dead 12, 217, 217–19, 221, 222, 226
colonialism 139, 153, 166, 218, 221, 240
Cocarla, Sasha 31, 32, 36
Cohen, Jerome 166, 173
Cohen, Shlomo 122–4, 135
Colebrook, Claire 127–9, 132–3, 136, 137
Comentale, Edward 96
comics
   Adventures into the Unknown 195
   Avengers 195
   'The Scourge of the Undead' (*The Beyond*) 194
   Crown Comics 194
Comics Code Authority (CCA) 188–9, 193
Comics Magazine Association of America (CMAA) 188, 194, 251
Connell, R. W. 47, 54
corpse 3, 10 , 21, 32, 67–8, 194, 108–9, 111, 113, 114, 126, 170, 183–4, 188, 189, 190, 191, 192, 193, 194, 205, 207, 218, 220, 224, 241
Corcoran, Miranda 12, 213

Corradino, Anna Chiara 70, 76
Courlander, Harold 2, 13
Covid-19 4
Creed, Barbara 62, 64, 65, 75
crossfit 46, 53, 54
Crow, Charles L. ('Hop Frog') 222, 228, 229
Crypto-colony 139, 151;
   see also zombie colony
crypto-colonialism 139, 153
cultural capital 139, 147
cultural zombie 152;
   see also zombie colony
The Cured 113–16
Curti, Roberto 220, 226–7, 228, 229

Dachis, Adam (*LifeHacker*) 45, 53
Dalton, Russell 33
Danziger, Kurt 34
Dead Meat 112–13, 116
Descartes, Rene 27, 34
Dendle, Peter 52, 153, 154
Dines, Gail 68, 75
Daily Mail 55, 215
Datura 139, 141, 151
Davis, Wade (*The Serpent and the Rainbow, Passage of Darkness: The Ethnobiology of the Haitian Zombie*) 194, 253
Davis-Goff, Sarah 5–6, 10–11, 113, 116, 159–61, 162, 163, 165, 166, 167, 168–71, 172, 173, 174; *see also Last Ones Left Alive*; 'skrakes'
Dawn of the Dead 12, 19, 20, 33, 40, 42, 50, 70, 98, 107, 143, 154, 214, 249; *see also* Romero
Day of the Dead 107; *see also* Romero
Day of the Dead: Bloodline 32, 36

de-extinction 121–5, 132, 133, 134, 135
Dekker, Fred (*Night of the Creeps*) 46
de Saussure, Ferdinand 234
disgust 30, 59–62, 64–5, 70–4, 76, 77, 93
Dionysus 146
Dezner, Daniel W. 165, 173
Doyle, Arthur Conan 115
Duncan, Isadora 146, 155
Dworkin, Shari 54
Dying Light 19
Dystopia 20, 25, 26, 39, 159, 162, 166, 168

eco-horror 3
elitism 119–22, 125, 128, 129, 131, 132, 133, 134, 134, 135
Embry, Karen 29, 30–1, 32, 35, 36, 45, 53, 88, 97, 120, 134, 154, 240
erasure (racial, identity, name) 86, 89, 94, 231, 235, 237, 245
Esquire 233
Estimé, Dumarsais 141
european gothic
Evil Dead 60, 62
Evil Head 60, 62–3, 65

Fain, Kimberly 232
Fandrich, Ina J. 221, 229
Fathers 9, 28, 34, 79–81, 85, 88, 89, 90, 95, 110
Fehrle, Johannes 14, 85, 97
Femininity 5, 6, 8
feminism (feminist posthuman theory) 26, 35, 56, 75, 76
Fennell, Jack 9, 10, 103
Ferguson, Andrew 12, 231

Fit Bottomed Girls 49, 55
Fitness 8, 22, 28, 39–51, 52, 53, 54, 55
Fleischer, Ruben 35, 39, 40
    Zombieland 28, 35, 40, 42, 43, 51
Fleshlight 64
Flynn, Deirdre 10, 11, 158
Fordism 142, 143
Foucault, Michel 23, 34
Freud, Sigmund 63, 70, 145, 155, 197, 199–201, 209, 210, 226
    castration 63–4, 66, 73
    uncanny 65, 75, 90, 104, 111, 154, 166, 197–203, 205–9, 210, 218, 220–1, 224
Freyne, David 113, 116
Fromm, Erich 67, 70, 75
Fulci, Lucio *see Zombie!*; *Zombi 2*; *Zombie Flesh-Eaters*; *City of the Living Dead*; *The Beyond*; *The House by the Cemetery*

Gallant, Thomas W. 143, 154
Game of Thrones (HBO) 29, 35, 43, 53
Garrett, Greg 125, 135
Gaze 79, 85, 90, 147, 156, 220
Gershon, Ilana 21, 33
gender 3, 4, 7, 9, 23, 30, 35, 47, 50, 54, 55, 59, 63, 64, 70, 74, 85, 90, 121, 133, 155, 160, 167
ghosts (ghost stories) 10, 84, 95, 104, 108–9, 111, 114, 116, 199–200, 208, 217, 224, 227
The Ghost Breakers 194
ghost estates (Ireland) 163, 164, 166, 172, 173
Gibbon, Edward 43
Gill, Rosalind 23, 33, 34

The Girl with All the Gifts (novel and film) 10, 31, 35, 80, 96, 120–1, 125, 127, 129, 130, 134
globalisation 86, 106, 161
Goddu, Teresa A. 216, 221
Godfrey-Smith, Peter 134, 135
Goldstein, Bennet 48, 55
Gould, Deirdre (*After the Cure*) 19, 33
Graham, Elaine 26, 34
Graham-Smith, Seth 233, 236, 244; see also Jane Austen; *Pride and Prejudice and Zombies*
Grant, Mira (*Newsflesh* Series) 19, 33
Greece 7, 139–40, 143–5, 147–8, 151, 152, 154, 155, 156
Griggs, Yvonne 224–5, 229
Gumpert, Matthew 71, 76
Güzeldere, Güven 106, 115

Hamilton, Scott Eric 1, 10, 19, 134, 136
Halloween 49
Haraway, Donna 32, 36
Harper, Michael 42, 53
Harper, Stephen 154
Harper's New Monthly Magazine 1
Harrison, Rebecca 97
haunted house 108, 164
Hawai'i 80, 83
 Lili'uokalani 80
Hawthorne, Nathaniel (*The Scarlet Letter*) 215, 218, 218
Hayles, N. Katherine 12, 33, 235, 244
Heffernan, Conor 1, 8, 9, 28, 35
Heller-Nicholas, Alexandra 226, 229
Herbrechter, Stefan 120, 134
Hern, Lafcadio 1

Herzfeld, Michael 139, 151, 153, 155, 157
heteronormativity 31, 72, 85
heterosexuality 25, 28, 168
Heywood, Leslie 42, 46, 48, 50, 52, 54, 55
Hillman, Cory 45, 53
Hitchcock, Alfred (*Psycho*) 223, 229
homosexuality 73
hope 28, 30, 31, 49, 85, 90, 95, 121, 131, 169, 170, 232
horde 1, 10, 31, 42–3, 45, 46, 85, 89, 90, 93, 95, 97, 107, 114, 143, 232, 234
horror 3, 7, 9–11, 19, 32, 41, 42, 46, 52, 62, 63, 65, 66, 67, 69, 70, 74, 75, 84, 87, 88, 97, 105, 110, 122, 127, 133, 135, 165, 172, 173, 179, 181–91, 193, 195, 198, 199, 210, 213–20, 222–9, 235, 239, 241
The House by the Cemetery 12, 213, 215, 224–6
House of the Dead 12
The House of the Dead 2 239
Howard, Robert E. ('Pigeons from Hell', *Weird Tales*) 195
Howlett, Mike 189, 190, 195
Human-minus concept 111–12, 114
human nature 26, 142
humanism 21, 24, 25, 29, 30, 32, 34
Hurston, Zora Neale 141, 153
Hybridathlete 47, 54
Hyman, Stanley Edgar 13

I Am Legend 28, 34, 40, 47
I Eat Your Skin 194
I Walked with a Zombie 2, 186, 197, 199, 201–2, 204, 205, 207–9

Imad, Joe 115, 116
information economy 238
International Monetary Fund (IMF) 83, 161
Instagram 25
Irish Folklore Commission 108, 116
Invisible Invaders 194
iZombie 3

Jacobs, W. W. ('The Monkey's Paw') 110
Jacquet, Jennifer 136
James, Henry ('The Turn of the Screw', *The Others*, *In a Dark Place*, *The Orphanage*) 213, 215–17, 224, 225, 229
Jens, Cassandra 14
Jensen, Robert 69, 75
Jentsch, Ernst 199–201, 209, 210
Jinsoo, An 84, 95, 97
Jones, Nick 47, 54
Jones, Steve 28, 29, 30, 34, 35, 36, 73, 74, 75, 77
Joon-ho, Bong (*Snowpiercer/bande-dessinée*) 86
Jowett, Lorna 31, 36

Kee, Chera 9, 11, 12, 179, 193, 195
Kendall, Erike Nicole (*A Black Girl's Guide to Weight Loss*, 'How to Survive a Zombie Invasion') 49, 55
Kendrick, Walter 74
Kenemore, Scott (*Zombie-in-Chief: Eater of the Free World*) 5, 6, 14
Kenny, Enda (Irish Taoiseach) 69
Kerasovitis, Konstantinos 10, 139
K-Horror (Korean Horror Cinema) 84, 87

Kim, Jaecheol 88, 90, 93–4, 95, 97, 98
Kim, Ki-duk (*The Isle*) 84, 96
King, Stephen (*The Shining*) 189, 224
Kingdom (Netflix) 3
Kirk, Robert 2, 13
Kirkland, Robert (*The Walking Dead*) 180
Kirsh, Steven 88, 98
Kligler-Vilenchik, Neta 23, 33
Knickerbocker, Daniel 121, 134
Korea
   South 3, 9, 83, 85, 87, 88, 90
   North 85, 86
Korean Cinema 83, 84, 85, 86, 96, 97
Kristeva, Julia 65–7, 75, 220
Kyrölä, Katariina 33

L.A. Zombie 59
LaBruce, Bruce 59
Lacan, Jacques 234–5
Lamb, Matthew 45, 53
Land of the Dead 3, 80, 96, 107
Landy, Derek (*Boy Eats Girl*) 112
Larned, Ben 228
Larsen, Kristine 161, 172
Larsen, Lars Bang 35
Last Ones Left Alive 5, 10, 14, 113, 116, 159–60, 168–9 173, 174
Lauro, Sarah Juliet 6, 13, 14, 19, 29, 30–1, 32, 33, 34, 35, 36, 45, 53, 75, 88, 96, 97, 108, 115, 116, 120, 134, 154, 228, 240, 245
Lavin, Mary ('The Green Grave and the Black Grave', 'The Dead Soldier') 110–11, 116
Lawson, Roger 42, 52
LeCapois, Teejay (*Vampire's Guide to The Zombie Apocalypse*) 41, 52

L'Esperance, Renée 237–8
Le Fanu, Joseph Sheridan ('The
    Village Bully') 109, 116
Lecomte, Jane 131, 136
Lee, Hyangjin 83–5, 96, 197
Lefebvre, Henri 147, 156
Legauldt, J. 13
Lelwica, Mary Michelle 50, 56
Lever, Charles (*Jack Hinton, the
    Guardsman*, 'The Mountain Pass')
    103, 108, 115
Lewis, C. S. 151, 157
Lewis, Herschell Gordon 215
LGBTQIA+ 30
liberal humanism 25, 27, 29
LifeHacker 45, 53
Linnea Quigley's Horror Workout 41,
    52
Liu, Dong 22, 33
living dead (liminal state) 188, 199,
    202, 216, 226
London Protocol 143
Long, Christian 87, 97
The Long Hair of Death 217
Longridge, Chris 50, 56
Lopes, Paul Douglas 187, 194
Los Angeles Times 233
Lovecraft, H. P. ('Herbert West –
    Reanimator', Dunwich) 167,
    216, 217, 228
Luckhurst, Roger 134, 199, 203, 209
Luckmann, Thomas 71, 76
Lyons, Joseph 13
Lyons, Mary E. 153

MacCormack, Patricia 30, 35
Macklin, William R. 244, 245
Marcus, David 116
Marks, Laura Helen 60, 74

Marion, Isaac (*Warm Bodies*) 31, 32,
    36
Martelly, Michel 141
Martin, G. R. R. (*Game of Thrones*)
    43
Maxim, Gorky 208, 210
Marx, Karl, 154
marxism (wage labour) 125, 142
Matheson, Richard 40
mathematics 4
Mavis Beacon (Renee L'Esperance)
    237–9, 244, 245
Mavis Beacon Teaches Typing 237–9,
    244, 245
McCollum, Stephen (*Dead Murphy*)
    112, 116
McGlotten, Shaka 28–30, 35, 36, 72,
    74, 76
McMahon, Conor (*Dead Meat*) 116
McNally, David 28, 32, 34, 35, 36,
    62, 75
McNamara, Jonathan 243
Meaux, Kevin 217, 219, 228
mediocrity 242, 244
Medium 44, 51
Meehan, Paul 208, 210
Men's Health 39, 51
Miéville, China 104, 115
Miller, Susan 71, 72, 76
Miller, Thaddeaus 131, 132, 136
Miller, William Ian 73, 77
Miller-Young, Mireille 76
Mitchell, Audra 121, 134
Monad 149
monsters 14, 20, 25, 30–2, 35, 52,
    63–5, 68, 105, 106, 108, 112,
    114, 145, 153, 157, 166, 168,
    173, 187, 189, 213, 218, 219
monstrosity 63, 217

monstrous 9, 23, 50, 52, 59, 63–5, 68, 71, 75, 124–5, 153, 157, 166, 171, 173, 183
Moon, Jarred (*End of Three Fitness*) 45–6, 54
Moreman, Christopher 75
Motion Picture Producers and Distributors of America (MPPDA) 194
mothers 31, 79, 88, 89, 93, 110, 113, 160, 169, 206, 217, 214
Mulvey, Laura 198–202, 205, 207, 208, 209, 210
Mulligan, Rikk 51
Munz, Philip Ioan Hudea 115, 116
Murphy, Bernice 223, 229
Muscle and Fitness 39, 51

necrophilia 9, 59, 66, 67, 70, 73, 75, 76, 77
Nemerov, Alexander 206, 210
neoliberalism 21–2, 24, 31–2, 34, 36, 52, 83, 85, 97, 162
NerdFitness 37, 54, 55
Netflix 3, 25, 36
New York (Manhattan) 224, 231, 239, 241
New York Times 45, 52, 147, 156, 233, 239
The New York Times Book Review 233
Night of the Giving Head 59
Night of the Living Dead (Romero) 3, 40, 51, 107, 142, 154, 166, 167, 184, 185, 188, 189, 190, 191–2, 195, 231, 232, 234, 242
Nihilism 90
Ng, Andrew Hock Soon 229
nonhuman 10, 24, 27, 35, 53, 62, 97, 119–25, 127, 129, 131, 132, 133, 134, 149, 154

North Korea 9, 85, 86
North Korean Cinema 85
Nuclei Armati Rivoluzionari 219
Nussbaum, Martha 73, 76, 77

O'Bannon, Dan (*Return of the Living Dead*) 40
O'Brien, Harvey 9, 79
Ó Cadhain, Máirtín (*Cré na Cille*) 111, 116
O'Connell, Frederick, aka Conall Cearnach ('The Homing Bone') 22, 23, 109, 111, 116
O'Hearn, Michael (*Zombies vs. Mummies*) 41
Ophiocordyceps unilateralis (*Zombie-Ant Fungus*) 119, 126
The Onion 41, 52
The Orient (Orientalism) 144, 155
the other (otherness) 4, 27, 30, 32, 90, 96, 121, 125, 141, 144, 149, 150, 151, 219, 221
Otto; or Up with Dead People 59
Ottoman Empire (King Otto) 143
Ouanga 186

Parker, Joe 68, 75
Paquet, Darcy 83, 96
Parrenas Shimizu, Celine 76
patriarchy 168, 169
Pearl, Mike 244
Penley, Constance 76
Peterson, Christopher 133, 137
Petley, Julian 228
Petmezas, Socrates 154
photograph/photography 111, 163, 164, 198, 199, 203–7, 209, 210; *see also* camera
Plague of the Zombies 194

pulp magazines 180, 187
Pratt, Andy 23, 33, 34
privilege 26, 27, 46–8, 50, 89, 129, 133, 236
p-zombie 2, 106
parents 66, 126–8, 160, 164, 170, 188, 195, 239
Poe, Edgar Allen ('Thou Art the Man!', 'The Black Cat') 104, 215–17, 222–3, 229, 234
Pontypool Changes Everything 236, 244
Pre-code comics/horror 179, 183–4, 189–90, 192, 195
Presley, Elvis 80
Pride and Prejudice and Zombies 233, 244
Plato 234, 243
Production Code Administration (PCA) 186, 188, 194
Protected Areas (PAs) 131–2
pornography (porn, zombie porn, inspiration porn) 9, 28, 59–75
Porn of the Dead 59, 60–4, 66, 73, 75, 77
postcolonialism 2
posthumanism 3, 19, 21, 26–7, 29–30, 97, 98, 137
puritanism 217, 218, 221

Queen, Carol 72, 76
Quiggin, John 14
Quinn, Daniel 223, 229

race 4, 23, 35, 45, 96, 126, 130, 173, 222–32, 237, 244, 245
racism 221–2, 225, 245
Radley, Emma 165, 173
Raimi, Sam 60

Raun, Tobias 24, 34
reanimation 105, 169, 197, 198, 200, 203, 204–5, 207–9, 222, 223
rebirth 195, 241–2, 259
Resident Evil 40, 47–50, 55
Return of the Living Dead 40, 107
Revenge of the Zombies 185
revenant 103–4, 108, 109–11, 214, 218, 232
Rocky (film) 47
Roden, David 34
Rollin, Jean (*Zombie Lake*) 43
Roman Empire (Alexander) 43, 144
Romaniello, John (*Roman Fitness Systems*, 'Zombie Survival Guide') 43, 44, 53
Romero, George A. 3, 7, 12, 14, 29, 33, 34, 40, 70, 96, 98, 106–7, 113, 120, 142–3, 154, 166, 167, 184, 189, 195, 214, 231–2, 242, 244; *see also Night of the Living Dead*; *Dawn of the Dead*; *Day of the Dead*; *Land of the Dead*; *Birth of the Living Dead*
Rosenberg, Stuart (*The Amityville Horror*) 223, 229
Røssaak, Eivind 204, 210
Rousseau, Jean-Jacques 234
Rozin, Paul 76
Rubin, Gayle 60, 61, 66, 69, 73, 74, 75, 76
Rushton, Cory 75
Ruthven, Andrea 72, 76

Sacchetti, Dardano 213, 219
Sadowski, Greg 193
Said, Edward W. 144, 145
Sandler, Roland 123, 128, 135, 136
Sanders, Julie 228

Sang-ho, Yeon 9, 96, 98; *see also Train to Busan*
Santa Clarita Diet 3, 4, 31, 36
Sarrazin, François 131, 136
Savoy, Eric 220
scientific positivism 105
Schudson, Michael 23, 33
Scottish Government 135
Seabrook, William Buchler (*The Magic Island*) 1, 105, 142, 154
Second World War (Nazis, Auschwitz) 173, 181–3, 188, 192, 226
self 20–4, 26–30, 33, 44, 47, 56, 64, 68, 71–2, 74, 83, 84, 87, 89, 90, 93, 109, 113, 120–1, 123, 131–2, 140, 145, 151, 152, 162, 163, 170–1, 221, 234
sexism 84
shambling signified 231, 235, 239
Shaun of the Dead 19, 33, 47, 107
Shildrick, Margrit 30, 35, 63
Shugart, Chris 46, 52, 54, 55
signifier 150, 162, 166, 219, 234–5, 238, 244
signified 93, 234–5, 238–9
simulation 5, 240
Singer, Peter 121, 134
Simpson, George Eaton 1, 153
skrakes 113, 159–61, 163, 166–7, 169
Smith, Clarissa 69, 76
Smith, Clark Ashton ('The Door to Saturn') 216, 222–3, 229
Smith, Robert J. 115, 116
Snyder, Zack (*Dawn of the Dead*) 40
Socrates (*Phaedrus, pharmakon, pharmakia, Republic*) 154, 234
Sodikoff, Genese 130, 136
Soldat-Jaffe, Tatjana 241, 246

Spellmeyer, Kurt 133, 136
Spielberg, Stephen (*War of the Worlds*) 97
Spitznagel, Eric 14
Star Trek 115
State of Emergency 41
Su-chang, Kong (*The Guard Post*) 87
Summers, Montague 105, 115
supernaturalism 221
Supervert 67, 75
survival 10, 11, 27–9, 39–43, 47, 51, 52, 53, 54, 67, 89, 93, 95, 98, 112, 120–1, 123, 125, 127, 129–30, 132, 134, 143, 160, 169–70, 239, 241, 243

Taino population 140
Tasker, Yvonne 54
Taormino, Tristan 76
Taylorism 142
Teeth 63
Telegraph Herald 48, 55
Telotte, J. P. 202, 210
Terminator 47, 48, 49
Terminator 2 48
Terminator: Dark Fate 49
Testosterone Nation 46
Thacker, Eugene 122, 134, 135
Theorizing Zombiism Conference 5–7, 35, 36, 96
theory 4–6, 13, 14, 29, 33, 34, 47, 53, 54, 60–1, 66–7, 75, 90, 96, 97, 120, 122, 133, 134, 136, 137, 172, 173, 174, 199, 200, 228, 235, 237, 241, 243
Thibaudeau, Christian 46, 52, 54, 55
T-Nation 39, 48, 51, 52
Todorov, Tzvetan 34
Totaro, Donato 84, 96

Tonton Macoutes 238
Toulalan, Sarah 75
Tournikiotis, Panayotis 155
Train to Busan 3, 9, 79
Trombetta, Jim 181, 183, 188, 193, 194
Tudor, Andrew 13
Tufano, Fani Mallouhou 156
Turner, Victor W. 199, 203, 210
The Typing of the Dead 239, 241, 245, 246

uncanny 65, 75, 90, 104, 111, 154, 166, 197–203, 205–9, 210, 218, 220–1, 224
undead 3–4, 7–8, 10–11, 13, 14, 32, 39, 40, 48, 50, 51, 52, 53, 65, 74, 75, 80, 95, 97, 107–9, 111–14, 115, 116, 122, 132, 134, 148, 166, 167, 171, 174, 177, 179–80, 182, 184, 189, 191–2, 193, 194, 199, 214, 225, 227, 229, 232, 233, 234, 239, 240–2, 243
US Center for Disease Control 45
US Department of Defense 45

vampire(s) 14, 41, 52, 64, 105, 107, 115, 188, 189, 227
Vampire's Guide to the Zombie Apocalypse 41
Vanity Fair 5
Vangundy, Sarah 72, 76
video games 106, 232, 241–2, 245
Vint, Sherryl 85, 89, 97, 98
voodoo 105, 113, 140–1, 145, 147, 148, 154, 182, 190, 192, 193, 194, 197, 198, 202–3, 206–7, 221

Wachs, Faye Linda 54
Wacquant, Loïc 50, 56
Wagner, Keith 63, 87, 90, 93, 96, 97, 98
Wagner, Peter 62
Waller, Gregory A. 14
The Walking Head 60
The Walking Dead (AMC) 49, 55, 75, 167, 180, 227, 246
Warm Bodies (novel, film) 31, 32, 36
Weeks, Jeffery 74, 77
Wendt, Theodore J. 14
We're Alive (podcast) 19, 33
werewolves 188, 189
West, Caroline 9, 69, 76
witches 182, 218–19, 226, 227
White Walkers (*Game of Thrones*) 29, 43
White Zombie 1, 2, 142, 154, 166
whiteness 25, 26, 90, 168, 222, 232, 240
Wilde, Poppy 8, 19, 96
Williams, Linda 77
Winter, Katy 55
Wired.com 39, 41, 51
The World's Biggest Gang Bang (Annabel Chong) 65
World War Z 28, 29, 34, 35, 41, 80, 96, 167
Wright, Edgar (Shaun of the Dead) 33, 47
Wright, Peter 11, 12, 197
Wylie, Turrell 2, 13

Yeon, Sang-ho 79, 96, 98
 Train to Busan 3, 9, 79–98
 Seoul Station 96, 98

Zani, Steven 217, 219, 228

Žižek, Slavoj 85
zombi 141, 153, 240, 242
Zombie! (*Zombi 2, Zombie Flesh-Eaters*) 194
Zombification 25, 65, 69, 141–3, 151–2, 184, 194, 206, 241
zombiism 1–2, 4, 5, 6–7, 11, 12–13, 34, 35, 36, 40, 48, 50, 59, 62, 69, 71, 74, 70, 96, 106, 113, 120, 122, 125, 132–3, 134, 184, 217, 227, 232, 250
eco-zombiism 134
zombie colony 10, 139–40, 151–2; *see also* crypto-colony; cultural zombie

Zombie Experiences UK 42
Zombieland 28, 35, 39, 40, 42, 43
zombie mouth (bite, monstrous orality) 63, 64, 73, 75, 79, 85, 113, 126, 142, 148, 151, 164
zombie porn 9, 59
Zombies, Run! 39, 42, 44, 53
Zombie Strippers 143, 154
Zombie Survival Guide 41
Zombie Studies Network 6
Zombies vs. Mummies 41
Zone One 41; *see also* Whitehead, Colson
zu Erdgasen, Sophus 135
Zuvembies 11, 179, 190, 191, 195

also in series

Lindsey Decker, *Transnationalism and Genre Hybridity in New British Horror Cinema* (2021)

Stacey Abbott and Lorna Jowett (eds), *Global TV Horror* (2021)

Michael J. Blouin, *Stephen King and American Politics* (2021)

Eddie Falvey, Joe Hickinbottom and Jonathan Wroot (eds), *New Blood: Critical Approaches to Contemporary Horror* (2020)

Darren Elliott-Smith and John Edgar Browning (eds), *New Queer Horror Film and Television* (2020)

Jonathan Newell, *A Century of Weird Fiction, 1832–1937* (2020)

Alexandra Heller-Nicholas, *Masks in Horror Cinema: Eyes Without Faces* (2019)

Eleanor Beal and Jonathan Greenaway (eds), *Horror and Religion: New literary approaches to Theology, Race and Sexuality* (2019)

Dawn Stobbart, *Videogames and Horror: From Amnesia to Zombies, Run!* (2019)

David Annwn Jones, *Re-envisaging the First Age of Cinematic Horror, 1896–1934: Quanta of Fear* (2018)